Resource Economics, Second Edition

Resource Economics is a text for students with a background in calculus and intermediate microeconomics and a familiarity with the spreadsheet program Excel. The book covers basic concepts (Chapter 1); shows how to set up spreadsheets to solve simple dynamic allocation problems (Chapter 2); and presents economic models for fisheries, forestry, nonrenewable resources, and stock pollutants (Chapters 3–6). Chapter 7 examines the maximin utility criterion when the utility of a generation depends on consumption of a manufactured good, harvest from a renewable resource, or extraction from a nonrenewable resource. Within the text, numerical examples are posed and solved using Excel's Solver. Exercises are included at the end of each chapter. These problems help to make concepts operational, develop economic intuition, and serve as a bridge to the study of real-world problems in resource management.

Jon M. Conrad is Professor of Resource Economics in the Department of Applied Economics and Management at Cornell University. He taught at the University of Massachusetts, Amherst, from 1973 to 1977, joining the Cornell faculty in 1978. His research interests focus on the use of dynamic optimization techniques to manage natural resources and environmental quality. He has published articles in the *Journal of Political Economy*, the *Quarterly Journal of Economics*, the *American Journal of Agricultural Economics*, the *Canadian Journal of Economics, Land Economics, Marine Resource Economics, Biomathematics, Ecological Economics, Natural Resource Modeling*, and the *Journal of Environmental Economics and Management*, where he served as an Associate Editor. He is coauthor, with Colin Clark, of the text *Natural Resource Economics: Notes and Problems* (Cambridge University Press, 1987) and is past President of the Resource Modeling Association. Cambridge published the first edition of *Resource Economics* in 1999.

Resource Economics

Second Edition

JON M. CONRAD

Cornell University

CAMBRIDGE UNIVERSITY PRESS
Cambridge, New York, Melbourne, Madrid, Cape Town, Singapore,
São Paulo, Delhi, Dubai, Tokyo, Mexico City

Cambridge University Press
32 Avenue of the Americas, New York, NY 10013-2473, USA

www.cambridge.org
Information on this title: www.cambridge.org/9780521697675

First published 1999
Second edition 2010

Printed in the United States of America

A catalog record for this publication is available from the British Library.

Library of Congress Cataloging in Publication data
Conrad, Jon M.
Resource economics / Jon M. Conrad. – 2nd ed.
p.   cm.
Includes bibliographical references and index.
ISBN 978-0-521-87495-3 – ISBN 978-0-521-69767-5 (pbk.)
1. Natural resources–Management–Mathematical models.
2. Resource allocation–Mathematical models.   I. Title.
HC59.15.C656 2010
333.7–dc22   2010014626

ISBN 978-0-521-87495-3 Hardback
ISBN 978-0-521-69767-5 Paperback

The first edition of this text was dedicated to my wife, Janice, and our sons, Andrew and Benjamin (a.k.a. Benj). This second edition is dedicated to our grandchildren, Grady and McKenna.

Contents

Preface to the Second Edition:
What Stayed, What Went, What's New?

The second edition of *Resource Economics* has expanded the first six chapters of the first edition, added an entirely new Chapter 7 ("Maximin Utility with Renewable and Nonrenewable Resources"), and deleted Chapter 7 ("Option Value and Risky Development") and Chapter 8 ("Sustainable Development") from the first edition. Most of the exercises at the end of each chapter are new. In Chapter 1, "Basic Concepts," separate sections have been added on simulation, steady state, and local stability (1.1); extraction of a nonrenewable resource (1.2); asymptotic depletion of a nonrenewable resource (1.5); the maximum principle and dynamic programming in discrete time (1.6); dynamic programming in a two-period, two-state model (1.7); and the Markov decision model and stochastic dynamic programming (1.8). The last three sections in Chapter 1 were designed to introduce students to more advanced methods of dynamic optimization that would be encountered in a graduate program.

Chapter 2, "Solving Numerical Allocation Problems Using Excel's Solver," has been significantly expanded and now presents 11 problems to show how Excel's Solver can be used to find the optimal rotation for an even-aged stand of trees (2.1); the steady-state optimal fish stock (2.2); the optimal date of exhaustion for a nonrenewable resource (2.3); the optimal first-period harvest in a two-period, two-state fishery (2.4); the optimal linear harvest policy in a finite-horizon fishery (2.5); the optimal escapement in a finite-horizon fishery (2.6); the optimal escapement for one "realization" in a stochastic fishery (2.7); the mine-manager's problem (2.8); approximating the asymptotic approach to a steady-state optimum (2.9); the most rapid approach to an optimal pollution stock (2.10); and optimal escapement with stochastic growth (2.11).

Chapter 3, "The Economics of Fisheries," now has a section on regulated open access (3.6) and an expanded discussion of bioeconomic-based policies, including the first of two articles by John Tierney, "A Tale of Two Fisheries" (3.10). Section 3.11 discusses marine reserves and rotational management in a fishery with an application to the Atlantic sea scallops (and culinary advice from the Sea Grant Program at the University of Delaware).

Chapter 4, "The Economics of Forestry," is essentially unchanged from the first edition, although some pesky typos have been corrected. (Hopefully no new ones have been introduced!)

Chapter 5, "The Economics of Nonrenewable Resources," has had improvements in exposition and includes the second of John Tierney's articles, a classic entitled "Betting the Planet." There is also a postscript to "Betting the Planet" (5.9).

Chapter 6, "Stock Pollutants," swaps out Section 6.6 from the first edition, which dealt with recycling and now presents a two-period, two-state model of climate change. Other than that switch, things are much the same.

The new Chapter 7, "Maximin Utility with Renewable and Nonrenewable Resources," introduces the maximin criterion to a macroeconomic growth model with both renewable and nonrenewable resources. The maximin criterion is applied in models with nonoverlapping and overlapping generations.

One thing hasn't changed, and that's the underlying philosophy of the text: *Simple numerical problems make theoretical concepts operational and provide a bridge to serious empirical research.* Have fun!

Jon M. Conrad
Ithaca, New York
August 2009

Acknowledgments

I would like to thank Cornell University and the College of Agriculture and Life Sciences, which has been my academic home for the past 30 years. I thank the countless Cornell undergraduate and graduate students who listened, questioned, and discussed the concepts and models contained in this text. They had to put up with the relentless problem sets and take-home exams that I claimed would give them a deeper understanding of the economics of dynamic allocation. Chris Castorena proofread the manuscript and compiled the index. Norm Van Vactor graciously allowed me to include his photo, which graphically shows the effects of capital stuffing in a vessel-length-restricted fishery. I appreciate the University of Delaware Sea Grant Program's willingness to allow me to include its description of the sea and bay scallops along with culinary advice for their proper preparation. Finally, I especially want to thank John Tierney for allowing the inclusion of his two articles, "A Tale of Two Fisheries" and "Betting the Planet." These articles always stimulate classroom discussion and provide an articulate respite to the math and models in *Resource Economics*.

1

Basic Concepts

1.0 RENEWABLE, NONRENEWABLE, AND ENVIRONMENTAL RESOURCES

Economics might be defined as the study of how society allocates scarce resources. The field of *resource economics*, would then be the study of how society allocates scarce natural resources, such as stocks of fish, stands of trees, fresh water, oil, and other naturally occurring resources. A distinction is sometimes made between *resource* and *environmental economics*, where the latter field is concerned with the way wastes are disposed and the resulting quality of air, water, and soil serving as waste receptors. In addition, environmental economics is concerned with the conservation of natural environments and biodiversity.

Natural resources are often categorized as being renewable or nonrenewable. A renewable resource must display a significant rate of growth or renewal on a relevant economic time scale. An economic time scale is a time interval for which planning and management are meaningful. The notion of an economic time scale can make the classification of natural resources a bit tricky. For example, how should we classify a stand of old-growth coast redwood or an aquifer with an insignificant rate of recharge? While the redwood tree is a plant and can be grown commercially, old-growth redwoods may be 800 to 1,000 years old, and the remaining stands may be more appropriately viewed as a nonrenewable resource. While the water cycle provides precipitation that will replenish lakes and streams, the water contained in an aquifer with little or no recharge may be economically more similar to a pool of oil (a nonrenewable resource) than

1

to a lake or reservoir that receives significant recharge from rain or melting snow.

A critical question in the allocation of natural resources is, "How much of the resource should be harvested (extracted) today?" Finding the "best" allocation of natural resources over time can be regarded as a dynamic optimization problem. What makes a problem a dynamic optimization problem? The critical variable in a dynamic optimization problem is a stock or *state variable* that requires a difference or differential equation to describe its evolution over time. The other key feature of a dynamic optimization problem is that a decision taken today, in period t, will change the amount or level of the state variable that is available in the next period, $t + 1$.

In a dynamic optimization problem, it is common to try to maximize some measure of net economic value, over some future horizon, subject to the dynamics of the harvested resource and any other relevant constraints. The solution to a natural resource dynamic optimization problem would be a schedule or "time path" indicating the optimal amount to be harvested (extracted) in each period or a "policy" indicating how harvest depends on the size of the resource stock. The optimal rate of harvest or extraction in a particular time period may be zero. For example, if a fish stock has been historically mismanaged, and the current stock is below what is deemed optimal, then zero harvest (a moratorium on fishing) may be best until the stock recovers to a size where a positive level of harvest is optimal.

Aspects of natural resource allocation are illustrated in Figure 1.1. On the right-hand side (RHS) of this figure I depict a trawler harvesting tuna. The tuna stock at the beginning of period t is denoted by the variable X_t, measured in metric tons. In each period, the level of net growth is assumed to depend on the size of the fish stock and is given by the function $F(X_t)$. I will postpone a detailed discussion of the properties of $F(X_t)$ until Chapter 3. For now, simply assume that if the tuna stock is bounded by some *environmental carrying capacity*, denoted K, so that $K \geq X_t \geq 0$, then $F(X_t)$ might be increasing as X_t goes from a low but positive level to where $F(X_t)$ reaches a maximum, at $X_t = X_{\mathrm{MSY}}$, and then $F(X_t)$ declines as X_t goes from X_{MSY} to K.

Let Y_t denote the harvest of tuna in period t, also measured in metric tons, and assume that net growth occurs before harvest. Then the change in the tuna stock, going from period t to period $t + 1$, is the

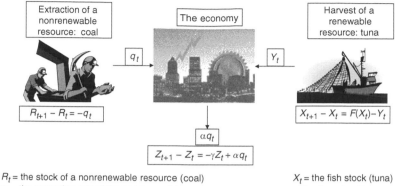

R_t = the stock of a nonrenewable resource (coal) X_t = the fish stock (tuna)
q_t = the extraction rate of the nonrenewable resource Y_t = the rate of harvest
αq_t = the flow of waste when q_t is consumed, $1 > \alpha > 0$ $F(X_t)$ = the net growth function

Z_t = a stock pollutant (CO_2)
γz_t = amount of pollutant removed via degradation

Figure 1.1. Renewable, nonrenewable, and environmental resources.

difference $X_{t+1} - X_t$ and is given by the difference equation

$$X_{t+1} - X_t = F(X_t) - Y_t \qquad (1.1)$$

If harvest exceeds net growth, $Y_t > F(X_t)$, the tuna stock declines, and $X_{t+1} - X_t < 0$. If harvest is less than net growth, $Y_t < F(X_t)$, the tuna stock increases, and $X_{t+1} - X_t > 0$.

We might rewrite Equation (1.1) in *iterative form* as $X_{t+1} = X_t - Y_t + F(X_t)$. As we will see, the iterative form is often used in spreadsheets and computer programs. During period t, harvest Y_t flows to the economy, where it yields a net benefit to various firms and individuals. The portion of the stock that is not harvested, $X_t - Y_t \geq 0$, is sometimes referred to as *escapement*. Escapement plus net growth $F(X_t)$ determine the inventory of tuna at the start of period $t + 1$. The stock X_t also conveys a benefit to the economy because it provides the basis for growth, and it is often the case that larger stocks will lower the cost of harvest in period t. Thus, implicit in the harvest decision is a balancing of current net benefit from Y_t and future benefit from a slightly larger stock X_{t+1}.

In some fishery models, growth depends on escapement, where escapement is calculated as $S_t = X_t - Y_t \geq 0$. The fish stock available for harvest in period $t + 1$ is determined according to the equation $X_{t+1} = S_t + F(S_t)$. Given an initial stock level X_0 and a harvest schedule or harvest policy (where Y_t depends on X_t), it is relatively simple to use a spreadsheet to *simulate* the dynamics of our tuna stock.

On the left-hand side (LHS) of Figure 1.1 I depict miners extracting a nonrenewable resource, say, coal. The remaining reserves of coal in period t are denoted by R_t, and the current rate of extraction is denoted by q_t. With no growth or renewal, the change in the stock is the negative of the amount extracted in period t, so

$$R_{t+1} - R_t = -q_t \qquad (1.2)$$

In iterative form, we might write $R_{t+1} = R_t - q_t$.

The amount of coal extracted also flows into the economy, where it generates net benefits, but in contrast to harvest from the tuna stock, consumption of the nonrenewable resource generates a residual waste flow αq_t, say, CO_2, assumed to be proportional to the rate of extraction $(1 > \alpha > 0)$.

This residual waste can accumulate as a *stock pollutant*, denoted Z_t. The change in the stock pollutant might depend on the relative magnitudes of the waste flow and the rate at which the stock pollutant is assimilated into the environment, say, carbon sequestration by plants. Let the stock pollutant be reduced by an amount given by the term $-\gamma Z_t$, where the parameter γ is called the *assimilation* or *degradation coefficient*, and it is usually assumed that $1 > \gamma > 0$. The change in the stock pollutant then would be given by the difference equation

$$Z_{t+1} - Z_t = -\gamma Z_t + \alpha q_t \qquad (1.3)$$

If the waste flow exceeds the amount degraded, $Z_{t+1} - Z_t > 0$. If the amount degraded exceeds the waste flow, $Z_{t+1} - Z_t < 0$. In iterative form, this equation might be written as $Z_{t+1} = (1 - \gamma)Z_t + \alpha q_t$.

Not shown in Figure 1.1 are the consequences of different levels of Z_t. Presumably, there would be some *social* or *external cost* imposed on the economy (society). This is sometimes represented through a damage function $D(Z_t)$. Damage functions will be discussed in greater detail in Chapter 6.

If the economy is represented by the cityscape in Figure 1.1, then the natural environment, surrounding the economy, can be thought of as providing a flow of renewable and nonrenewable resources, as well as various media for the disposal of unwanted (negatively valued) wastes. Missing from Figure 1.1, however, is one additional service, usually referred to as *amenity value*. A wilderness, a pristine stretch of beach, or a lake with "swimmable" water quality provides individuals in the economy with places for observing flora and fauna, relaxation, and recreation that are fundamentally different from comparable services provided at a city zoo, an exclusive beach hotel, or a backyard swimming pool. The amenity value provided by various natural environments may depend on the location of economic activities (including the harvest and extraction of resources) and the disposal of wastes. Thus the optimal rates of harvest, extraction, and disposal should take into account any reduction in amenity values. In general, current net benefit from, say, Y_t or q_t must be balanced with the discounted future costs from reduced resource stocks X_{t+1} and R_{t+1} *and* any reduction in amenity values caused by harvest, extraction, or disposal of associated wastes.

1.1 POPULATION DYNAMICS: SIMULATION, STEADY STATE, AND LOCAL STABILITY

In this section I will illustrate the use of the iterative form of Equation (1.1) to simulate the dynamics of a fish stock. I will use a spreadsheet to perform the simulation, and in the process, I will define what is meant by a *steady-state equilibrium* and the *local stability* for such equilibria for a single, first-order difference equation. A steady state is said to be locally stable if neighboring states are attracted to it and unstable if the converse is true.

In iterative form, Equation (1.1) was written as $X_{t+1} = X_t + F(X_t) - Y_t$. To make things more concrete, suppose that the net-growth function takes the form $F(X_t) = rX_t(1 - X_t/K)$, where I will call $r > 0$ the *intrinsic growth rate* and $K > 0$ the *environmental carrying capacity*. This net-growth function is drawn as the concave (from below) symmetric curve in Figure 1.2.

We will assume that fishery managers have a simple rule for determining *total allowable catch* Y_t, where the harvest rule takes the form

$$Y_t = \alpha X_t \tag{1.4}$$

We will assume that $r > \alpha > 0$ for reasons that will become apparent in a moment. Equations that express harvest or total allowable catch

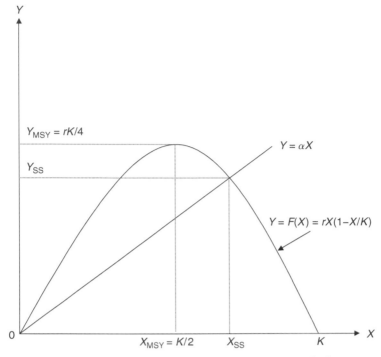

Figure 1.2. Steady-state equilibrium for Equation (1.6).

as a function of stock size are also called *feedback harvest policies*. This particular harvest policy is simply a line through the origin and is also drawn in Figure 1.2. Substituting the specific forms for our net-growth function and the feedback harvest policy into the iterative form of Equation (1.1) yields

$$X_{t+1} = X_t + rX_t(1 - X_t/K) - \alpha X_t = (1 + r - \alpha - rX_t/K)X_t \quad (1.5)$$

We can see that Equation (1.5) is almost begging for a spreadsheet. If we had *parameter values* for r, α, and K and an *initial condition* X_0, we could program Equation (1.5) and have the spreadsheet calculate X_1. With the same parameters and X_1, we could then calculate X_2, and so on. The fill-down feature on a spreadsheet means that we need only type Equation (1.5) once.

Before constructing our spreadsheet and doing some simulations, we might ask the following question: "Would it ever be the case that the feedback harvest policy would lead to a steady-state equilibrium where $X_{t+1} = X_t = X_{SS}$ and $Y_{t+1} = Y_t = Y_{SS}$?" The unknowns X_{SS} and Y_{SS} are *constant* levels for the fish stock and harvest rate, respectively, that are sustainable *ad infinitum*. The short answer to our question is, "Maybe." If the steady-state equilibrium is locally stable, and if X_0 is in what is called the *basin of attraction*, then, over time, $X_t \rightarrow X_{SS}$.

We might rewrite Equation (1.5) one last time as

$$X_{t+1} = (1 + r - \alpha - rX_t/K)X_t = G(X_t)$$

For equations such as $X_{t+1} = G(X_t)$, steady-state equilibria, also called *fixed points*, must satisfy $X = G(X)$. For our net-growth function and harvest policy, there will be a single (unique) steady-state equilibrium at

$$X_{SS} = \frac{K(r - \alpha)}{r} \tag{1.6}$$

For $X_{SS} > 0$, we need $r > \alpha > 0$. Graphically, X_{SS} occurs at the intersection of $Y = \alpha X$ and $Y = rX(1 - X/K)$ in Figure 1.2. It can be shown that X_{SS} will be locally stable *if and only if* $|G'(X_{SS})| < 1$. We refer to Equation (1.6) as an *analytic expression* for X_{SS} because our algebra allowed us to obtain an expression where X_{SS} is isolated on the LHS, whereas on the RHS we have nothing but parameters (K, r, and α).

In Figure 1.2 I also have included the reference values $X_{MSY} = K/2$ and $Y_{MSY} = rX_{MSY}(1 - X_{MSY}/K) = rK/4$. $X_{MSY} = K/2$ is called the stock level that supports *maximum sustainable yield*. When $X_{MSY} = K/2$ is substituted into the net-growth function and the expression is simplified, it will imply that the maximum sustainable yield is $Y_{MSY} = rK/4$.

We are almost ready to build our spreadsheet to simulate a fish population whose dynamics are described by Equation (1.5). Knowing Equation (1.6) and the necessary and sufficient condition for local stability will allow us to calculate X_{SS} and know whether $X_t \rightarrow X_{SS}$ if X_0 is in the basin of attraction. With $G(X_t) = (1 + r - \alpha - rX_t/K)X_t$, we can take a derivative and show that $G'(X_t) = 1 + r - \alpha - 2rX_t/K$. With $X_{SS} = K(r - \alpha)/r$, we then can show that $G'(X_{SS}) = 1 - r + \alpha$. Recall that the local stability of X_{SS} required that $|G'(X_{SS})| < 1$, so if $|1 - r + \alpha| < 1$, we would expect that $X_t \rightarrow X_{SS}$.

	A	B	C	D	E	F	G	H
1	Spreadsheet S1.1							
2								
3	$r =$	1						
4	$K =$	1						
5	$\alpha =$	0.5						
6	$X_{ss} =$	0.5						
7	$Y_{ss} =$	0.25						
8	$\lvert G'(X_{ss})\rvert =$	0.5						
9	$X_0 =$	0.1						
10								
11								
12	t	X_t	Y_t					
13	0	0.1	0.05					
14	1	0.14	0.07					
15	2	0.1904	0.0952					
16	3	0.24934784	0.12467392					
17	4	0.311847415	0.155923707					
18	5	0.370522312	0.185261156					
19	6	0.418496684	0.209248342					
20	7	0.452605552	0.226302776					
21	8	0.474056542	0.237028271					
22	9	0.486355208	0.243177604					
23	10	0.492991424	0.246495712					
24	11	0.496446592	0.248223296					
25	12	0.498210669	0.249105335					
26	13	0.499102133	0.249551066					
27	14	0.49955026	0.24977513					
28	15	0.499774928	0.249887464					
29	16	0.499887413	0.249943707					
30	17	0.499943694	0.249971847					
31	18	0.499971844	0.249985922					
32	19	0.499985921	0.249992961					
33								
34								
35								
36								
37			Time Paths for X_t and Y_t					
38	0.6							
39	0.5							
40	0.4							
41								
42	0.3							
43	0.2							
44								
45	0.1							
46	0							
47								
48	0		5	10		15	20	
49				t				
50								
51								

Spreadsheet S1.1

In Spreadsheet S1.1, I have set $r = 1$, $K = 1$, and $\alpha = 0.5$. For consistency throughout this text, I will put parameter labels in column A of the spreadsheets and their specific values in the same row but in column B. In cells A6, A7, A8, and A9, I also enter labels for X_{SS}, Y_{SS}, $\lvert G'(X_{SS})\rvert$, and the initial condition X_0. In cell B6, I program $=$ \$B\$4 * (\$B\$3 − \$B\$5)/\$B\$3. In cell B7, I program $=$ \$B\$3 * \$B\$6 *

(1 − $B$6/$B$4). In cell B8, I program = ABS(1 − $B$3 + $B$5). In cell B9, I simply enter the number 0.1. With the carrying capacity normalized so that $K = 1$, an $X_0 = 0.1$ might be symptomatic of a bad case of *overfishing* that has resulted in a stock level that is only 1/10 its carrying capacity, which would be the stock level in the unexploited fishery.

In row 12, columns A, B, and C, I type the labels for t, X_t, and Y_t. In cell A13, I enter 0 and do a series fill-downs ending in 19 in cell A32. In cell B13, I type = $B$9. In cell C13, I type = $B$5 ∗ B13. *Note:* I omit the dollar sign ($) when I want a variable to iterate when using a fill-down or a fill-across. This allows me to program an iterative equation only once. In cell B14, I program = (1 + $B$3 − $B$5 − $B$3 ∗ B13/$B$4) ∗ B13. I then do a one-cell fill-down from cell C13 to cell C14, and then I do a fill-down from B14:C14 to B32:C32. If you do this correctly, you should get = (1 + $B$3 − $B$5 − $B$3 ∗ B31/$B$4) ∗ B31 in cell B32 and = $B$5 ∗ B32 in cell C32. I finally select cells A13:C13 through A32:C32, click on the "Chart Wizard," and select the scatter diagram with lines. After entering the chart title and placing t on the x axis, we end up with the chart in the lower right-hand corner of Spreadsheet S1.1. We see from our previous calculations for X_{SS}, Y_{SS}, and $|G'(X_{SS})|$ that when we simulate the fish population from $X_0 = 0.1$, X_t in fact converges to $X_{SS} = 0.5$, whereas Y_t converges to $Y_{SS} = 0.25$.

One of the great things about setting up the spreadsheet in this manner is that we can change a parameter, and the spreadsheet instantly recomputes and replots variables and charts. What happens if we change r to $r = 2.6$? In this case, the spreadsheet computes $X_{SS} = 0.80769231$ and $Y_{SS} = 0.40384615$, but the local stability condition is *not* satisfied because $|G'(X_{SS})| = 1.1 > 1$. From the plot of X_t and Y_t we see that we will never converge to the steady-state equilibrium. Looking at the numerical values for X_t and Y_t, we see that they have locked into what is called a *two-point cycle*. We will see that a single nonlinear difference equation or two or more nonlinear difference equations (called a *dynamical system*) are capable of complex dynamic behavior, including *deterministic chaos*, where the steady-state equilibrium, calculated in advance of simulation, is never reached.

I.2 EXTRACTION OF A NONRENEWABLE RESOURCE

In Section 1.5 I will present a nonrenewable-resource model where the optimal extraction policy, in feedback form, is given by the equation

$$q_t^* = [\delta/(1+\delta)]R_t \tag{1.7}$$

	A	B	C	D	E	F	G	H
1	Spreadsheet S1.2							
2								
3	$\delta =$	0.02						
4	$R_0 =$	1						
5								
6	t	R_t	q_t					
7	0	1	0.019607843					
8	1	0.980392157	0.019223376					
9	2	0.961168781	0.018846447					
10	3	0.942322335	0.018476909					
11	4	0.923845426	0.018114616					
12	5	0.90573081	0.017759428					
13	6	0.887971382	0.017411204					
14	7	0.870560179	0.017069807					
15	8	0.853490371	0.016735105					
16	9	0.836755266	0.016406966					
17	10	0.8203483	0.016085261					
18	11	0.804263039	0.015769864					
19	12	0.788493176	0.015460651					
20	13	0.773032525	0.0151575					
21	14	0.757875025	0.014860295					
22	15	0.74301473	0.014568916					
23	16	0.728445814	0.014283251					
24	17	0.714162562	0.014003187					
25	18	0.700159375	0.013728615					
26	19	0.68643076	0.013459427					
27	20	0.672971333	0.013195516					
28	21	0.659775817	0.012936781					
29	22	0.646839036	0.012683118					
30	23	0.634155918	0.01243443					
31	24	0.621721488	0.012190617					
32	25	0.609530871	0.011951586					
33	26	0.597579285	0.011717241					
34	27	0.585862044	0.011487491					
35	28	0.574374553	0.011262246					
36	29	0.563112307	0.011041418					
37	30	0.552070889	0.010824919					
38	31	0.54124597	0.010612666					
39	32	0.530633304	0.010404575					
40	33	0.520228729	0.010200563					
41	34	0.510028166	0.010000552					
42	35	0.500027613	0.009804463					
43	36	0.49022315	0.009612219					
44	37	0.480610932	0.009423744					
45	38	0.471187188	0.009238964					
46	39	0.461948223	0.009057808					
47	40	0.452890415	0.008880204					
48	41	0.444010211	0.008706083					
49	42	0.435304128	0.008535375					
50	43	0.426768753	0.008368015					
51	44	0.418400739	0.008203936					
52	45	0.410196803	0.008043075					

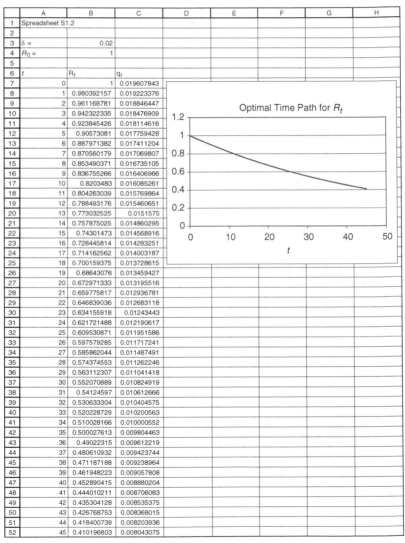

Optimal Time Path for R_t

Spreadsheet S1.2

where q_t^* is the optimal rate of extraction in period t, $1 > \delta > 0$ is a per-period discount rate, and $R_t > 0$ are remaining reserves in period t. I will discuss the rate of discount in greater detail in the next section. At this point, I will simply note that the discount rate reflects society's *rate of time preference* and that a positive rate of discount indicates that an additional dollar of net benefit in period t would be viewed as equivalent to having an additional $(1 + \delta)$ dollars of net benefit in period $t+1$. In this section I simply wish to show how the feedback extraction policy and remaining reserves can be simulated on a spreadsheet.

Substituting Equation (1.7) into Equation (1.2) and writing it in iterative form yields

$$R_{t+1} = R_t - [\delta/(1 + \delta)]R_t = \rho R_t \tag{1.8}$$

where $\rho = 1/(1 + \delta)$ is called the *discount factor*, and with $1 > \delta > 0$, $1 > \rho > 0$. Equation (1.8) implies that remaining reserves decline exponentially to zero as $t \to \infty$ and, by extension to Equation (1.7), that the optimal rate of extraction declines exponentially to zero as well.

In Spreadsheet S1.2, I calculate the time paths for R_t and q_t^* when $\delta = 0.02$ and $R_0 = 1$. The spreadsheet shows the values of R_t and q_t^* for $t = 0, 1, \ldots, 45$. In cell B7, I have typed = \$B\$4, and in cell C7, I have typed = (\$B\$3/(1 + \$B\$3)) * B7. In cell B8, I have typed = B7 − C7. I then did a one-cell fill-down from cell C7 to cell C8 and then a fill-down from B8:C8 to B52:C52 to get the values for R_t and q_t^* for $t = 0, 1, \ldots, 45$.

1.3 DISCOUNTING

When attempting to determine the optimal allocation of natural resources over time, one immediately confronts the issue of time preference. Most individuals exhibit a preference for receiving benefits now, as opposed to receiving the same level of benefits at a later date. Such individuals are said to have a *positive time preference*. In order to induce these individuals to save (thus providing funds for investment), an interest payment or premium, over and above the amount borrowed, must be offered. A society composed of individuals with positive time preferences typically will develop "markets for loanable funds" (capital markets), where the interest rates that emerge are like prices and reflect, in part, society's underlying time preference.

An individual with a positive time preference will discount the value of a note or contract that promises to pay a fixed amount of money at some future date. For example, a bond that promises to pay $10,000 ten years from now is not worth $10,000 today in a society of individuals with positive time preferences. Suppose that you own such a bond. What could you get for it if you wished to sell it today? The answer will depend on the credit rating (trustworthiness) of the government or corporation promising to make the payment, the expectation of inflation, and the taxes that would be paid on the interest income. Suppose that the payment will be made with certainty, there is no expectation of inflation, and no tax will be levied on the earned interest. Then the bond payment would be discounted by a rate that would approximate society's "pure" rate of time preference. I will denote this rate by the symbol δ and refer to it as the *discount rate*. The risk of default (nonpayment), the expectation of inflation, or the presence of taxes on earned interest would raise private market rates of interest above the discount rate. (Why?)

If the discount rate were 3%, so $\delta = 0.03$, then the *discount factor* is defined as $\rho = 1/(1 + \delta) \approx 0.97$. The present value of a $10,000 payment made 10 years from now would be $\$10,000/(1 + \delta)^{10} = \rho^{10}\$10,000 \approx \$7,441$. This should be the amount of money you would get for your bond if you wished to sell it today. Note that the amount $7,441 is also the amount you would need to invest at a rate of 3%, compounded annually, to have $10,000 in 10 years.

The present-value calculation for a single payment can be generalized to a future *stream of payments* in a straightforward fashion. Let N_t denote a payment made in year t. Suppose that these payments are made over the horizon $t = 0, 1, \ldots, T$, where $t = 0$ is the current year (period) and $t = T$ is the last year (or terminal period). The present value of this stream of payments can be calculated by adding up the present value of each individual payment. We can represent this calculation mathematically as

$$N = \sum_{t=0}^{t=T} \rho^t N_t \qquad (1.9)$$

Suppose that $N_0 = 0$ and $N_t = A$ for $t = 1, 2, \ldots, \infty$. In this case, we have a bond that promises to pay A dollars every year from next year until the end of time. Such a bond is called a *perpetuity*, and with $1 > \rho > 0$ when $\delta > 0$, Equation (1.9), with $T \to \infty$, becomes an infinite geometric progression that converges to $N = A/\delta$. This special result might be used to approximate the value of certain long-lived projects or the decision to preserve a natural environment for all future generations. For example, if a proposed park were estimated to provide $A = \$10$ million in annual net benefits into the indefinite future, it would have a present value of $500 million when $\delta = 0.02$.

Another bit of finite math that I will make use of in subsequent chapters is the present value of the constant payment A over the horizon $t = 0, 1, \ldots, \infty$. We now receive A in period $t = 0$ and for the rest of time thereafter. You would be correct to conclude that the present value is now $N = A + A/\delta = A[(1 + \delta)/\delta]$. This is also the conclusion when you evaluate the infinite series

$$N = \sum_{t=0}^{\infty} \rho^t A = A \sum_{t=0}^{\infty} \rho^t = A \left[\frac{1}{(1-\rho)} \right] = A \left[\frac{1}{\delta/(1+\delta)} \right]$$
$$= A[(1+\delta)/\delta] \tag{1.10}$$

One last bit of finite math that also will be used in future chapters involves calculation of the present value of a constant payout, say, A dollars, for the finite horizon $t = 0, 1, \ldots, T$. In this case,

$$N = \sum_{t=0}^{T} \rho^t A = A \left[\sum_{t=0}^{\infty} \rho^t - \sum_{t=T+1}^{\infty} \rho^t \right] = A \left[\frac{1}{(1-\rho)} - \frac{\rho^{T+1}}{(1-\rho)} \right]$$
$$= \frac{A}{(1-\rho)}(1 - \rho^{T+1}) = [(1+\delta)/\delta]A(1 - \rho^{T+1}) \tag{1.11}$$

The preceding examples presume that time can be partitioned into discrete periods (e.g., years). In some resource-allocation problems, it is useful to treat time as a continuous variable, where the future horizon becomes the interval $T \geq t \geq 0$. Recall the formula for compound interest. It says that if A dollars are put in the bank at interest rate δ and compounded m times over a horizon of length T, then the value at the end of the horizon will be given by

$$V(T) = A(1 + \delta/m)^{mT} = A[(1 + \delta/m)^{m/\delta}]^{\delta T} = A[(1 + 1/n)^n]^{\delta T} \tag{1.12}$$

where $n = m/\delta$. If interest is compounded continuously, both m and n tend to infinity; then $[1 + 1/n]^n = e$, the base of the system of natural logarithms. This implies that $V(T) = Ae^{\delta T}$. Note that $A = V(T)e^{-\delta T}$ becomes the present value of a promise to pay $V(T)$ at $t = T$ (from the perspective of $t = 0$). Thus the continuous-time discount factor for a payment at instant t is $e^{-\delta t}$, and the present value of a continuous stream of payments $N(t)$ is calculated as

$$N = \int_0^T N(t)e^{-\delta t}dt \tag{1.13}$$

Equation (1.13) is the continuous-time analogue of Equation (1.9). If $N(t) = A$ (a constant) and if $T \to \infty$, Equation (1.13) can be integrated directly to yield $N = A/\delta$, which is interpreted as the present value of an asset that pays A dollars in each and every instant into the indefinite future.

Our discussion of discounting and present value has focused on the mathematics of making present-value calculations. The practice of discounting has an important ethical dimension, particularly with regard to the way resources are harvested over time, the evaluation of investments or policies to protect the environment, and more generally, how the current generation weights the welfare and options of future generations.

In financial markets, the practice of discounting might be justified by society's positive time preference and by the economy's need to allocate scarce investment funds to firms that have expected returns that equal or exceed the appropriate rate of discount. To ignore the time preferences of individuals and to replace competitive capital markets with the decisions of some savings/investment czar likely would lead to inefficiencies, a reduction in the output and wealth generated by the economy, and the oppression of what many individuals regard as a fundamental economic right. The commodity prices and interest rates that emerge from competitive markets are highly efficient in allocating resources toward economic activities that are demanded by the individuals with purchasing power.

While the efficiency of competitive markets in determining the allocation of labor and capital is widely accepted, there remain questions about discounting and the appropriate rate of discount when allocating natural resources over time or investing in environmental quality. Basically, the interest rates that emerge from capital markets reflect society's underlying rate of discount (time preference), the riskiness of a particular asset or portfolio, and the prospect of general inflation. These factors, as already noted, tend to raise market rates of interest above the discount rate.

Estimates of the discount rate in the United States have ranged between 2% and 5%. This rate will vary across cultures at a point in time and within a culture over time. A society's discount rate would, in theory, reflect its collective "sense of immediacy," which, in turn, may reflect a society's level of development. A society where time is of the essence or where a large fraction of the populace is on the brink of starvation presumably would have a higher rate of discount.

As we will see in subsequent chapters, higher discount rates tend to favor more rapid depletion of nonrenewable resources and lower stock levels for renewable resources. High discount rates can make investments to improve or protect environmental quality unattractive when compared with alternative investments in the private sector. High rates of discount will greatly reduce the value of harvesting decisions or investments that have a preponderance of their benefits in the distant future. Recall that a single payment of $10,000 in 10 years had a present value of $7,441 at $\delta = 0.03$. If the discount rate increases to $\delta = 0.10$, its present value drops to $3,855. If the payment of $10,000 would not be made until 100 years into the future, it would have a present value of only $520 at $\delta = 0.03$ and the minuscule value of $0.72 (72 cents) if $\delta = 0.10$.

The exponential nature of discounting has the effect of weighting near-term benefits much more heavily than benefits in the distant future. If 75 years were the life span of a single generation, and if that generation had absolute discretion over resource use and adopted a discount rate of $\delta = 0.10$, then the weight attached to the welfare of the next generation would be similarly minuscule. Such a situation could lead to the current generation throwing one long, extravagant, resource-depleting party that left subsequent generations with an impoverished inventory of natural resources, a polluted environment, and very few options to change their economic destiny.

There are some who would view the current mélange of resource and environmental problems as being precisely the result of tyrannical and selfish decisions by recent generations. Such a characterization would not be fair or accurate. While many renewable resources have been mismanaged (such as marine fisheries and tropical rain forests) and various nonrenewable resources may have been depleted too rapidly (oil reserves in the United States), the process, though nonoptimal, has generated both physical and human capital in the form of buildings, a housing stock, highways, public infrastructure, modern agriculture, and the advancement of science and technology. These also benefit and have expanded the choices open to future generations. Further, any single generation is usually closely "linked" to the two generations that preceded it and the two generations that will follow. The current generation historically has made sacrifices in their immediate well-being to provide for parents, children, and grandchildren. While intergenerational altruism may not be obvious in the functioning of financial markets, it is more obvious in the way we have collectively tried to regulate the use of natural resources and the quality of the environment. Our policies have not always been effective, but their motivation seems to derive from a sincere concern for future generations.

Determining the "best" endowment of human and natural capital to leave future generations is made difficult because we do not know what they will need or want. Some recommend that if we err, we should err on the side of leaving more natural resources and undisturbed natural environments. By saving them now, we derive certain amenity benefits and preserve the options to harvest or develop in the future.

The process of discounting, to the extent that it reflects a stable time preference across a succession of generations, is probably appropriate when managing natural resources and environmental quality for the maximum benefit of an ongoing society. Improving the well-being of the current generation is a part of an ongoing process seeking to improve the human condition. And when measured in terms of infant mortality, caloric intake, and life expectancy, successive generations have been made better off.

Nothing in the preceding discussion helps us in determining the precise rate of discount that should be used for a particular natural resource or environmental project. In the analysis in future chapters, I will explore the sensitivity of harvest and extraction rates, forest rotations, and rates of waste disposal to different rates of discount. This will enable you to get a numerical feel for the significance of discounting.

1.4 A DISCRETE-TIME EXTENSION OF THE METHOD OF LAGRANGE MULTIPLIERS

In subsequent chapters you will encounter many problems where the object is to maximize some measure of economic value subject to resource dynamics. Such problems often can be viewed as special cases of a more general dynamic optimization problem. The method of Lagrange multipliers is a technique for solving constrained optimization problems. It is used regularly to solve static allocation problems, but it can be extended to solve dynamic problems as well. We will work through the mathematics of a relatively general renewable-resource problem in this section.

Let X_t again denote the biomass measure of a renewable resource in period t. In a fishery, X_t might represent the number of metric tons of some (commercially valued) species. In a forest, it may represent the volume of standing (merchantable) timber.

Let Y_t denote the level of harvest, measured in the same units as X_t. For renewable resources, I will frequently assume that resource dynamics can be described by a first-order difference equation such as Equation (1.1). In that equation $X_{t+1} - X_t = F(X_t) - Y_t$, where $F(X_t)$ was the net-growth function for the resource. It assumed that the net growth going from period t to period $t + 1$ was a function of resource abundance in period t. I will assume that the net-growth function has continuous first- and second-order derivatives. The current resource stock is represented by the initial condition X_0, denoting the stock at $t = 0$.

The net benefits from resource abundance and harvest in period t are denoted by π_t and given by the function $\pi_t = \pi(X_t, Y_t)$, which is also assumed to have continuous first- and second-order derivatives. Higher levels of harvest normally will yield higher net benefits. The resource stock, X_t, may enter the net-benefit function because a larger stock conveys cost savings during search and harvest or because an intrinsic value is placed on the resource itself. We will assume that there is an upper bound on $\pi(X_t, Y_t)$ such that $\overline{\pi} \geq \pi(X_t, Y_t) \geq 0$.

In Section 1.1, we simply assumed that the linear harvest policy $Y_t = \alpha X_t$ was intrinsically appealing when $\alpha < r$, perhaps because it would lead to a stable steady state at $X_{SS} = K(r - \alpha)/r$ when $|1 - r + \alpha| < 1$. In reality, there are an infinite number of potential harvest policies that might be acceptable. What we would like to do in this section is find the "best" harvest policy that maximizes the present value of net benefits. The optimization problem of interest seeks to

$$\text{Maximize}_{\{Y_t\}} \ \pi = \sum_{t=0}^{\infty} \rho^t \pi(X_t, Y_t)$$

$$\text{Subject to } X_{t+1} - X_t = F(X_t) - Y_t$$

$$X_0 > 0 \text{ given}$$

Thus the objective is to maximize π, the present value of net benefits, subject to the equation describing resource dynamics and the initial condition $X_0 > 0$.

How can we find the optimal Y_t? Will it be unique? Will optimal harvest guide the stock to a steady-state optimum where $X_{t+1} = X_t = X^*$? These are difficult but important questions. Let's take them one at a time.

Recall from calculus that when seeking the extremum (i.e., maximum, minimum, or inflection point) of a single-variable function, a necessary condition is that the first derivative of the function, when evaluated at a candidate extremum, must equal zero. Our optimization problem is more complex because we have to determine the values for Y_t that maximize π, and we have constraints in the form of our first-order difference equation and the initial condition X_0. We can, however, follow a similar procedure after forming the appropriate Lagrangian expression for our problem. This is done by introducing a set of new variables, denoted λ_t, called *Lagrange multipliers*. In general, every *state variable*, whose change is defined by a difference equation, will have an associated Lagrange multiplier. This means that X_t will be associated with λ_t, X_{t+1} will be associated with λ_{t+1}, and so on. It will turn out that the new variables λ_t will have an important economic interpretation. They are also called *shadow prices* because their value indicates the marginal value of an incremental increase in X_t.

We form the *Lagrangian expression* by writing the difference equation in *implicit form*, $X_t + F(X_t) - Y_t - X_{t+1}$, premultiplying it by $\rho^{t+1}\lambda_{t+1}$, and then adding all such products to the objective function. The Lagrangian expression for our problem takes the form

$$L = \sum_{t=0}^{\infty} \rho^t \{\pi(X_t, Y_t) + \rho\lambda_{t+1}[X_t + F(X_t) - Y_t - X_{t+1}]\} \quad (1.14)$$

The rationale behind writing the Lagrangian this way is as follows: Since the Lagrange multipliers are interpreted as shadow prices that measure the value of an additional unit of the resource, we can think of the difference equation, written implicitly, as defining the level of X_{t+1} that will be available in period $t+1$. The value of an additional (marginal) unit of X_{t+1} in period $t+1$ is λ_{t+1}. This value is discounted one period, by ρ, to put it on the same present-value basis as the net benefits in period t. Thus the expression in the braces $\{\bullet\}$ is the sum of net benefits in period t and the discounted value of the resource stock (biomass) in period $t+1$. This sum then is discounted back to the present by ρ^t, and similar expressions are summed over all periods.

After forming the Lagrangian expression, we proceed to take a series of *first-order partial derivatives* and set them equal to zero. Collectively, they define the first-order necessary conditions, analogous to the first-order condition for a single-variable function. They will be used in solving for the optimal levels of Y_t, X_t, and λ_t along an *approach path* and at the steady-state *bioeconomic optimum* $[X^*, Y^*, \lambda^*]$, if one exists. For our problem, the necessary conditions require

$$\frac{\partial L}{\partial Y_t} = \rho^t[\partial\pi(\bullet)/\partial Y_t - \rho\lambda_{t+1}] = 0 \quad (1.15)$$

$$\frac{\partial L}{\partial X_t} = \rho^t\{\partial\pi(\bullet)/\partial X_t + \rho\lambda_{t+1}[1 + F'(\bullet)]\}$$

$$- \rho^t\lambda_t = 0 \quad (1.16)$$

$$\frac{\partial L}{\partial(\rho\lambda_{t+1})} = \rho^t[X_t + F(X_t) - Y_t - X_{t+1}] = 0 \quad (1.17)$$

The partial of the Lagrangian with respect to X_t may seem a bit puzzling. When we examine the Lagrangian and the representative term in period t, we observe X_t as an argument of the net-benefit function $\pi(X_t, Y_t)$ by itself and as the sole argument in the net-growth function $F(X_t)$. These partials appear in the braces $\{\bullet\}$ in Equation (1.16). Where did the last term, $-\rho^t \lambda_t$, come from? If we think of the Lagrangian as a long sum of expressions, and if we wish to take the partial with respect to X_t, we need to find all the terms involving X_t. When we back up one period, from t to $t - 1$, most of the terms are subscripted $t - 1$, with the notable exception of the last term, which becomes $-\rho^t \lambda_t X_t$, with partial derivative $-\rho^t \lambda_t$.

In addition to Equations (1.15) through (1.17), there are two boundary conditions. The first is simply the initial condition that $X_0 > 0$ is known and given. The second boundary condition for this infinite-horizon problem requires $\lim_{t \to \infty} \rho^t \lambda_t X_t = 0$. This last condition is called the *transversality condition*. It requires that the discounted value of the resource stock go to zero as time goes to infinity. Mathematically, this condition is required for the present-value measure π to converge to a finite value when maximized. If the transversality condition did not hold, and if the present value of net benefits were infinite, it would be impossible to determine, from the feasible harvest schedules, which one is best.

For infinite-horizon problems, we typically are interested in whether a unique steady-state optimum X^*, exits and, if $X_0 \neq X^*$, what the optimal approach will be from X_0 to X^*. There are only two types of approach paths to X^*. When the Lagrangian is nonlinear in the control variable, in our case Y_t, the approach to a unique, stable X^* will be *asymptotic*, meaning that $X_t \to X^*$ as $t \to \infty$. The other alternative approach path is called the *most rapid approach path* (MRAP). Along this approach path, it is optimal to drive X_t to X^* as rapidly as possible, and X^* is reached in finite time.

Spence and Starrett (1975) identify sufficient conditions for the MRAP to be optimal. They first solve the state equation describing the change in the resource stock for Y_t. This yields $Y_t = X_t - X_{t+1} + F(X_t)$. They then substitute this expression into the net-benefit function, yielding $\pi[X_t, X_t - X_{t+1} + F(X_t)]$. If $\pi[X_t, X_t - X_{t+1} + F(X_t)] = M(X_t) + N(X_{t+1})$, then the net-benefit function is said to be *additively separable* in X_t and X_{t+1}. If the net-benefit function is additively separable in X_t and X_{t+1}, one can write the present value of net benefits as

$$\pi = \sum_{t=0}^{\infty} \rho^t \pi(X_t, Y_t) = \sum_{t=0}^{\infty} \rho^t [M(X_t) + N(X_{t+1})]$$

$$= M(X_0) + \sum_{t=1}^{\infty} \rho^t [M(X_t) + (1+\delta)N(X_t)]$$

$$= M(X_0) + \sum_{t=1}^{\infty} \rho^t V(X_t)$$

where $V(X) = M(X) + (1+\delta)N(X)$. Thus, if the original net-benefit function is additively separable in X_t and X_{t+1}, the present value of net benefits depends *only* on X_t.

The function $V(X)$ is said to be *quasi-concave* if for any X_1 and X_2 where $V(X_1) = c$ and $V(X_2) \geq c$, $V[\alpha X_1 + (1-\alpha)X_2] \geq c$ for all $\alpha \in [0, 1]$. Proposition 4 from Spence and Starrett (1975, p. 396) states that *if $V(X)$ is quasi-concave and is maximized at X^*, and if the most rapid approach path from X_0 to X^* is well defined and feasible, then it is an optimal path.*

By a "most rapid approach path," Spence and Starrett mean that the control variable Y_t is chosen from its feasible set so as to move X_t from X_0 to X^* as rapidly as possible. In a renewable-resource optimization problem, the MRAP involves setting the control at its upper bound $Y_{\max}$ or at its lower bound, say, zero, if $Y_{\max} \geq Y_t \geq 0$. Which bound is optimal is usually obvious from the nature of the problem and a comparison of X_0 to X^*. In Chapter 2, we will work through an example, for a stock pollutant, where the MRAP from Z_0 to Z^* is optimal.

Let's return to Equations (1.15) through (1.17) and see if we can give them an economic interpretation. We can rewrite these equations as

$$\frac{\partial \pi(\bullet)}{\partial Y_t} = \rho \lambda_{t+1} \tag{1.18}$$

$$\lambda_t = \frac{\partial \pi(\bullet)}{\partial X_t} + \rho \lambda_{t+1}[1 + F'(\bullet)] \tag{1.19}$$

$$X_{t+1} = X_t + F(X_t) - Y_t \tag{1.20}$$

The LHS of Equation (1.18) is the marginal net benefit of an additional unit of the resource harvested in period t. For a harvest strategy to be optimal, this marginal net benefit must equal the discounted shadow price of the stock in period $t + 1$. The term $\rho \lambda_{t+1}$ is also called *user cost*. Thus Equation (1.18) requires that we account for two types of costs, the standard marginal cost of harvest in the current period [which has already been accounted for in $\partial\pi(\bullet)/\partial Y_t$] and the future cost that results from the decision to harvest an additional unit of the resource today, that is, $\rho\lambda_{t+1}$. In some problems we may see this condition written $\partial\pi(\bullet)/\partial Y_t = p - \partial C(X_t, Y_t)/\partial Y_t = \rho\lambda_{t+1}$, where $p > 0$ is the unit price of the harvested resource (say, a pound of fish on the dock) and $\partial C(X_t, Y_t)/\partial Y_t$ is the marginal cost of harvest when the stock is at the level X_t. Then $p - \partial C(X_t, Y_t)/\partial Y_t = \rho\lambda_{t+1}$ says that the optimal level of harvest today equates price less marginal cost to user cost.

On the LHS of Equation (1.19) we have λ_t, the value of an additional unit of the resource, in situ, in period t. When optimally managed, the marginal value of an additional unit of the resource in period t equals the current-period marginal net benefit $\partial\pi(\bullet)/\partial X_t$ plus the marginal benefit that an unharvested unit will convey in the next period $\rho\lambda_{t+1}[1+F'(X_t)]$. Note that this last term is the discounted value of the marginal unit itself plus its marginal growth.

Equation (1.20) is simply a rewrite of Equation (1.1), but now obtained from the partial of the Lagrangian with respect to $\rho\lambda_{t+1}$. This should occur in general; that is, the partial of the Lagrangian with respect to a discounted multiplier should yield the difference equation for the associated state variable, in this case the resource stock.

Under the Spence-Starrett conditions for optimality of the MRAP, there typically will be a transitional period, say, for $\tau > t \geq 0$, where X_t and λ_t are changing, followed by a period $\infty > t \geq \tau$, where X_t and λ_t are unchanging. In this latter, infinitely long interval, the variables, or "system," is said to have reached a steady state because $X_{t+1} = X_t = X^*$, $Y_{t+1} = Y_t = Y^*$, and $\lambda_{t+1} = \lambda_t = \lambda^*$. This triple, $[X^*, Y^*, \lambda^*]$, is called the *steady-state bioeconomic optimum*.

It is often possible to solve for the steady-state optimum by evaluating the first-order necessary conditions in steady state. In steady state, we can dispense with all the time subscripts in Equations (1.18) through (1.20), which simply become three equations in three unknowns $[X^*, Y^*, \lambda^*]$ and may be written as

$$\rho\lambda = \frac{\partial\pi(\bullet)}{\partial Y} \qquad (1.21)$$

$$\rho\lambda[1 + F'(X) - (1+\delta)] = \frac{-\partial\pi(\bullet)}{\partial X} \qquad (1.22)$$

$$Y = F(X) \qquad (1.23)$$

Equation (1.22) required a little bit of algebra and use of the definition $\rho = 1/(1 + \delta)$. It can be further manipulated to yield

$$-\rho\lambda[\delta - F'(X)] = \frac{-\partial\pi(\bullet)}{\partial X} \qquad (1.24)$$

Multiplying both sides by –1, substituting Equation (1.21) into Equation (1.24), and isolating δ yields

$$F'(X) + \frac{\partial\pi(\bullet)/\partial X}{\partial\pi(\bullet)/\partial Y} = \delta \qquad (1.25)$$

Equation (1.25) has been called the *fundamental equation of renewable resources*. Equations (1.23) and (1.25), requiring $Y = F(X)$, can be solved simultaneously for X^* and Y^*.

Equation (1.25) has an interesting economic interpretation. On the LHS, the term $F'(X)$ may be interpreted as the *marginal net growth rate*. The second term is called the *marginal stock effect* and measures the marginal value of the stock relative to the marginal value of harvest. The two terms on the LHS sum to what might be interpreted as the *resource's rate of return*. It is a stationary rate of return from maintaining the stock at X^*. Equation (1.25) thus requires that the optimal steady-state values X^* and Y^* cause the resource's rate of return to equal the rate of discount δ, which presumably equals the rate of return on investments elsewhere in the economy. From this *capital-theoretic point of view*, the renewable resource is seen as an asset that under optimal management will yield a rate of return comparable with that of other capital assets. Are all renewable resources capable of yielding a stationary rate of return equal to the rate of discount? We will return to this question in Chapter 3.

Equation (1.23) results when Equation (1.1) is evaluated at steady state. It has an obvious and compelling logic. At the bioeconomic optimum, and in fact at any sustainable equilibrium, harvest must equal net growth. If this were not the case, if net growth exceeded harvest or if harvest exceeded net growth, the resource stock would be changing, and we could not, by definition, be at a steady-state equilibrium. Thus $Y = F(X)$ at any sustainable equilibrium, including the steady-state bioeconomic optimum.

Equation (1.25), by the implicit function theorem, will imply a curve in $X - Y$ space. Its exact shape and placement will depend on the functional forms for $F(X)$ and $\pi(X, Y)$, their parameters, and

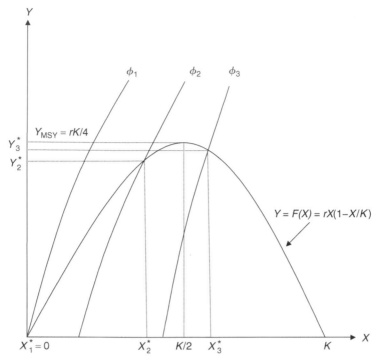

Figure 1.3. Maximum sustainable yield (MSY) and three bioeconomic optima.

the discount rate δ. Several possible curves (for different underlying parameters) are labeled ϕ_1, ϕ_2, and ϕ_3 in Figure 1.3. The net-growth function is again assumed to take the *logistic form*, namely, $Y = F(X) = rX(1 - X/K)$. The intersection of $Y = F(X)$ and a particular $Y = \phi(X)$ would graphically represent the solution of Equations (1.23) and (1.25) and therefore depict the steady-state optimal values for X^* and Y^*.

Figure 1.3 shows four equilibria: three bioeconomic optima and *maximum sustainable yield* (MSY). The bioeconomic optimum at the intersection of ϕ_1 and $F(X)$ would imply that extinction is optimal! Such an equilibrium might result if a slowly growing resource were confronted by a high rate of discount and if harvesting costs for the last members of the species were less than their market price.

The intersection of $F(X)$ and ϕ_2 implies an optimal resource stock of X_2^* positive but less than $K/2$ that supports MSY $= rK/4$. This would be the case if the marginal stock effect is less than the discount rate. [Study Equation (1.25) to figure out why this is true.]

The curve ϕ_3 implies a large marginal stock effect, greater in magnitude than the discount rate δ. The optimal stock in this case is $X_3^* > K/2$. This would occur if smaller fishable stocks significantly increased cost. In such a case, it may be optimal to maintain a stock greater than the maximum sustainable yield stock. The conclusion to be drawn from Figure 1.3 is that the optimal stock, from a bioeconomic perspective, may be less than or greater than the stock level supporting maximum sustainable yield.

1.5 ASYMPTOTIC DEPLETION OF A NONRENEWABLE RESOURCE

In Section 1.2, I simply stated that there was a simple nonrenewable-resource model where the optimal extraction policy took the form $q_t^* = [\delta/(1+\delta)]R_t$. In this section I will detail the model, verify the optimal extraction policy, and note that $R^* = 0$ is the steady-state optimum (optimal remaining reserves are zero) but that the optimal approach is asymptotic with $R_t \to 0$ as $t \to \infty$. If we can derive $q_t^* = [\delta/(1+\delta)]R_t$, then we can simply refer to back to Spreadsheet S1.2 as a numerical example when $\delta = 0.02$ and $R_0 = 1$.

The model assumes that the extraction rate $q_t > 0$ provides net benefits to society according to the function $\pi(q_t) = \ln[q_t]$, where $\ln[\bullet]$ is the natural-log operator. Recall that $\ln[q_t]$ is strictly concave in q_t and that $d(\ln[q_t])/dq_t = 1/q_t$. Remaining reserves are assumed to evolve according to $R_{t+1} - R_t = -q_t$. This state equation assumes that all initial reserves are known and represented by $R_0 > 0$ and that no additional reserves will be discovered. The Lagrangian for the problem seeking to maximize the discounted value of net benefits subject to the depletion of remaining reserves may be written as

$$L = \sum_{t=0}^{\infty} \rho^t \{\ln[q_t] + \rho\lambda_{t+1}(R_t - q_t - R_{t+1})\} \qquad (1.26)$$

$\partial L/\partial q_t = 0$ implies that $1/q_t = \rho\lambda_{t+1}$, which says that an optimal extraction rate balances the marginal net benefit from extraction in period t to the discounted shadow price (or user cost) of remaining reserves in period $t+1$. $\partial L/\partial R_t = 0$ implies that $\rho\lambda_{t+1} - \lambda_t = 0$, which, in turn, implies that $\lambda_{t+1} = (1+\delta)\lambda_t$ and, more generally, that $\lambda_t = (1+\delta)^t\lambda_0$. This equation says that the shadow price on remaining reserves is rising at the rate of discount. The two partial derivatives together imply that $q_t = 1/\lambda_t = 1/[(1+\delta)^t\lambda_0] = \rho^t/\lambda_0$. Because marginal net benefit goes to infinity as $q_t \to 0$, it will always be optimal to have some positive level of extraction, although it becomes infinitesimal as $t \to \infty$. Thus

$$R_0 = \sum_{t=0}^{\infty} q_t = (1/\lambda_0) \sum_{t=0}^{\infty} \rho^t = \frac{(1+\delta)}{\delta\lambda_0} \tag{1.27}$$

Solving for λ_0 yields $\lambda_0 = (1+\delta)/(\delta R_0)$. On substitution into our expression for q_t, we obtain $q_t = \rho^{t+1}\delta R_0$. Substituting this last expression for q_t into our iterative form $R_{t+1} = R_t - q_t$, which is also implied by $\partial L/\partial[\rho\lambda_{t+1}] = 0$, and doing some sample iterations, we should be able to convince ourselves that $R_t = \rho^t R_0$ or $R_0 = R_t/\rho^t$. Substituting this expression for R_0 into $q_t = \rho^{t+1}\delta R_0$ yields $q_t^* = [\delta/(1+\delta)]R_t$ as posited in Section 1.2.

1.6 THE MAXIMUM PRINCIPLE AND DYNAMIC PROGRAMMING IN DISCRETE TIME

There are two other methods that might be used to solve discrete-time dynamic optimization problems. They are the *maximum principle* and *dynamic programming*. Because the same problem might be solved by the method of Lagrange multipliers, the maximum principle, or dynamic programming, one should suspect that there are some fundamental relationships between the three methods. This is in fact the case, and in economic models, these relationships reflect more generally on the economic concepts of wealth and income. These relationships are plumbed more deeply and more elegantly in Weitzman (2003).

The key operational concept in the maximum principle is the *current-value Hamiltonian*. For the general renewable-resource problem, used to introduce the method of Lagrange multipliers, I will define the current-value Hamiltonian as

$$H_t \equiv \pi(X_t, Y_t) + \rho\lambda_{t+1}[F(X_t) - Y_t] \tag{1.28}$$

The Lagrangian expression, defined in Equation (1.14), contains the current-value Hamiltonian and may be rewritten as

$$L = \sum_{t=0}^{\infty} \rho^t [H_t + \rho\lambda_{t+1}(X_t - X_{t+1})] \tag{1.29}$$

The first-order necessary conditions for the optimal harvest of the renewable resource can be expressed in terms of partial derivatives of the current-value Hamiltonian. Specifically, Equations (1.18) through (1.20) are implied by the following equations:

$$\frac{\partial H_t}{\partial Y_t} = 0 \Rightarrow \frac{\partial \pi(\bullet)}{\partial Y_t} = \rho\lambda_{t+1} \tag{1.30}$$

$$\rho\lambda_{t+1} - \lambda_t = -\frac{\partial H_t}{\partial X_t} \Rightarrow \lambda_t = \frac{\partial \pi(\bullet)}{\partial X_t} + \rho\lambda_{t+1}[1 + F'(\bullet)] \tag{1.31}$$

$$X_{t+1} - X_t = \frac{\partial H_t}{\partial(\rho\lambda_{t+1})} \Rightarrow X_{t+1} = X_t + F(X_t) - Y_t \tag{1.32}$$

In addition to Equations (1.30) through (1.32), we also assume that the transversality condition, $\lim_{t\to\infty}\rho^t\lambda_t X_t = 0$, and our initial condition, $X_0 > 0$, are given.

The current-value Hamiltonian is a useful concept not only because it provides a simplified and more direct route to the first-order conditions but also because it has an important interpretation. Weitzman (2003) refers to the optimized current-value Hamiltonian as *properly accounted income*. Why? We will write the optimized current-value Hamiltonian as

$$H_t^* = \pi(X_t^*, Y_t^*) + \rho\lambda_{t+1}[F(X_t^*) - Y_t^*] \tag{1.33}$$

The term $\pi(X_t^*, Y_t^*)$ represents the flow of net benefits from the optimal harvest of the optimal stock in period t. You may think of this as a *dividend* from the optimal management of the fish stock. The second term on the RHS of Equation (1.33) is the discounted shadow price in period $t+1$ times the optimal change in the fish stock because $X_{t+1}^* - X_t^* = F(X_t^*) - Y_t^*$. This second term may be regarded as the *capital gain* from optimal management of the fish stock. *Properly accounted income is the sum of the optimized dividend plus the optimized capital gain.* These two income components are critical to the optimal management of *any* asset.

The key concept in dynamic programming is the *value function*, which is defined as the optimized present value when the resource stock is currently X_t. The value function assumes optimal harvest or, more generally, optimal management of an asset. Optimized present value depends *only* on X_t, because it presumes optimal behavior in period t and in the future. If you do your best (via optimal management), your present value will depend only on your endowment in period t, that is, X_t. We will define the value function as

$$V(X_t) \equiv \underset{\{Y_\tau\}}{\text{maximum}} \left[\sum_{\tau=t}^{\infty} \rho^{(\tau-t)} \pi(X_\tau, Y_\tau) \right] \equiv \sum_{\tau=t}^{\infty} \rho^{(\tau-t)} \pi(X_\tau^*, Y_\tau^*)$$

$$(1.34)$$

The optimality condition in dynamic programming is often called the *Bellman equation*, after the mathematician Richard Bellman. For our current problem, it requires

$$V(X_t) \equiv \underset{\{Y_t\}}{\text{maximum}} \left[\pi(X_t, Y_t) + \rho V(X_{t+1}) \right]$$

$$\equiv \underset{\{Y_t\}}{\text{maximum}} \left[\pi(X_t, Y_t) + \rho V(X_t + F(X_t) - Y_t) \right]$$

$$(1.35)$$

Note, in the second line in Equation (1.35), that the discounted value function in $t + 1$ depends on $X_{t+1} = X_t + F(X_t) - Y_t$, and thus we influence the optimized present value in $t + 1$ by our decision on the level of Y_t. For $Y_{\max} > Y_t > 0$, the Bellman equation requires that the partial derivative of the bracketed expression on the RHS of Equation (1.35) equal zero.

$$\frac{\partial[\bullet]}{\partial Y_t} = \frac{\partial \pi(\bullet)}{\partial Y_t} + \rho V'(X_{t+1})(-1) = \frac{\partial \pi(\bullet)}{\partial Y_t} - \rho V'(X_{t+1}) = 0 \quad (1.36)$$

Now for a critical observation. $V'(X_{t+1})$ is the marginal value of an incremental increase in X_{t+1}, assuming that the resource is optimally managed in $t+1$ and in all future periods. However, this is precisely the interpretation of λ_{t+1} along the optimal trajectories $[X_t^*, Y_t^*]$. Thus we conclude that $\rho V'(X_{t+1}) = \rho \lambda_{t+1}$. Equation (1.36) from the Bellman equation has the same requirement as Equation (1.30) from the maximum principle or Equation (1.18) from the method of Lagrange multipliers. They all imply that $\partial \pi(\bullet)/\partial Y_t = \rho \lambda_{t+1} = \rho V'(X_{t+1})$.

Let's suppose that $\partial \pi(\bullet)/\partial Y_t = \rho V'[X_t + F(X_t) - Y_t]$, which is an equation in X_t and Y_t, can be solved for the *optimal feedback harvest* *policy* $Y_t^* = \phi(X_t)$. Weitzman (2003) notes that dynamic programming and the maximum principle imply the following relationship between wealth and properly accounted income:

$$\delta V(X_t) = H_t^* = \pi\lfloor X_t, \phi(X_t)\rfloor + \rho\lambda_{t+1}[F(X_t) - \phi(X_t)] \qquad (1.37)$$

$V(X_t)$ is the optimized present value or wealth obtainable from the optimal management of the resource. What if you were the sole owner of this resource? (Perhaps you have exclusive harvest rights, in perpetuity, over the fish stock in the lake.) If you decided to sell the harvest rights, what would they be worth to another harvester also adept at optimal management? Presumably, they also would be worth $V(X_t)$. If you sold your rights for $V(X_t)$, you could put the proceeds in a risk-free account, where they would earn interest income equal to $\delta V(X_t)$. Thus $\delta V(X_t)$ is the opportunity cost (interest income foregone) of the continued ownership of your exclusive harvest rights. In a competitive economy with many potential, competent managers, the interest income from the sale of your harvest rights should precisely equal the properly accounted income from continued ownership and optimal management. However, this properly accounted income is simply the maximized current-value Hamiltonian. Thus, in a competitive, arbitrage-free economy, $\delta V(X_t) = H_t^*$.

It is also possible to derive the fundamental equation of renewable resources, Equation (1.25), from the maximum principle or the Bellman equation. For our renewable resource, the optimized Bellman equation implies that

$$V(X_t) = \pi(X_t, Y_t^*) + \rho V[X_t + F(X_t) - Y_t^*] \qquad (1.38)$$

The envelope theorem implies that

$$V'(X_t) = \frac{\partial \pi(\bullet)}{\partial X_t} + \rho V'(X_{t+1})[1 + F'(X_t)] \qquad (1.39)$$

At the steady-state bioeconomic optimum, $X_{t+1} = X_t = X^*$, and Equation (1.39) becomes

$$V'(X^*) = \frac{\partial \pi(\bullet)}{\partial X} + \rho V'(X^*)[1 + F'(X^*)] \qquad (1.40)$$

Equation (1.40) implies that $\rho V'(X^*)[\delta - F'(X^*)] = \partial\pi(\bullet)/\partial X$. But $\rho V'(X^*) = \partial\pi(\bullet)/\partial Y$, and isolating δ on the RHS yields

$$F'(X^*) + \frac{\partial\pi(\bullet)/\partial X}{\partial\pi(\bullet)/\partial Y} = \delta \qquad (1.41)$$

which is identical to Equation (1.25). Both equations presume that $X = X^*$ and $Y = Y^* = F(X^*)$.

1.7 DYNAMIC PROGRAMMING IN A TWO-PERIOD, TWO-STATE MODEL

Dynamic programming is the principal method for solving dynamic optimization problems when the evolution of a resource stock is influenced by a random variable. Depending on the resource, the random variable might reflect a random occurrence in the environment or random human error. For example, the size of a fish stock next year may be partially influenced by prevailing wind, sea temperature, and the presence or absence of El Niño or La Niña. The amount of water in a reservoir might depend on the amount and timing of precipitation. The volume of timber next year may depend on whether lightning causes a forest fire. The population of a marine mammal or sea bird might depend on whether an oil spill occurs.

In this section we will consider a simple two-period, two-state model where $t = 0$ denotes the present period and $t = 1$ denotes the future. The future is uncertain because there are two possible states, $s = 1$ and $s = 2$. We will be dealing with a simple model where the fish stock in the future depends on the outcome of a random variable not known in $t = 0$, when a decision must be made regarding current-period harvest. In a two-state model, the random variable can assume only one of two possible values. Dynamic programming will require that you optimize your harvest decision *in each future state* and then make your current harvest decision so as to maximize discounted expected value, presuming that you optimize in whichever future state actually occurs. Consider the following example.

The fish stock in the present, $t = 0$, is known to be $X_0 > 0$. If you harvest $X_0 > Y_0 \geq 0$ in $t = 0$, the stock in the future will be a stochastic function of escapement $X_0 - Y_0 > 0$. In future state 1, the stock will be $X_{1,1} = z_1 G(X_0 - Y_0)$, whereas in future state 2, the stock will be

$X_{1,2} = z_2 G(X_0 - Y_0)$, where $G(X_0 - Y_0)$ is a concave growth function and z_1 and z_2 are the two possible outcomes of the random variable z. We will assume that $z_1 > 1 > z_2 > 0$ with probabilities $\Pr(z = z_1) = \varepsilon_1$ and $\Pr(z = z_2) = \varepsilon_2$, where $1 > \varepsilon_s > 0$ for $s = 1$, 2 and $\varepsilon_1 + \varepsilon_2 = 1$.

We begin by seeking the optimal harvest decisions in each of the two future states. Suppose that the net revenue from harvest in either future state depends, in part, on the fishable stock. A larger stock reduces search costs and increases net revenues. Suppose that the net revenue in future state s is given by

$$\pi_{1,s} = p_1 Y_{1,s} - (c/2) Y_{1,s}^2 / [z_s G(X_0 - Y_0)] \qquad (1.42)$$

where $p_1 > 0$ is the known (previously contracted) unit price for fish on the dock in $t = 1$, $Y_{1,s} \geq 0$ is the amount harvested in future state s, and $c > 0$ is a cost parameter.

Net revenue in each future state is a concave quadratic function of $Y_{1,s}$. The simple first-order condition $d\pi_{1,s}/dY_{1,s} = 0$ implies that $Y_{1,s}^* = p_1 z_s G(X_0 - Y_0)/c$. Note that $Y_{1,1}^* > Y_{1,2}^*$ because $z_1 > 1 > z_2 > 0$. We can substitute the optimal harvest rates back into their respective expressions for net revenue to get expressions for *state-dependent optimized net revenue*. This substitution and some algebraic simplification yield $\pi_{1,s}^* = [p_1^2 z_s G(X_0 - Y_0)]/(2c)$. Note that with $X_0 > 0$ given, state-dependent optimized net revenue depends only on Y_0.

We are now ready to determine optimal harvest in $t = 0$. Our objective is to maximize *discounted expected net revenue*, assuming that we harvest optimally in whatever future state is realized. This objective is accomplished by defining the *value function* $V(X_0)$ as

$$V(X_0) = \max_{Y_0} \{ p_0 Y_0 - (c/2) Y_0^2 / X_0 + \rho [p_1^2/(2c)]$$

$$\times G(X_0 - Y_0)(\varepsilon_1 z_1 + \varepsilon_2 z_2) \} \qquad (1.43)$$

We can again accomplish maximization of the expression in braces on the RHS of Equation (1.43) by setting $d\{\bullet\}/dY_0 = 0$. This first-order condition implies that

$$p_0 = \frac{cY_0}{X_0} + \rho \frac{p_1^2}{2c} (\varepsilon_1 z_1 + \varepsilon_2 z_2) G'(X_0 - Y_0) \qquad (1.44)$$

which is a single equation in Y_0 and X_0. If you were given a tractable form for $G(X_0 - Y_0)$, you would be able to solve for the optimal level of harvest in $t = 0$ as a function of X_0. This would be the *optimal feedback policy* $Y_0^* = \phi(X_0)$. Equation (1.44) has a nice interpretation. On the LHS, p_0 is the marginal revenue of an incremental increase in Y_0. On the RHS, cY_0/X_0 is the marginal cost, in $t = 0$, of that incremental increase in Y_0. The term $\rho[p_1^2/(2c)](\varepsilon_1 z_1 + \varepsilon_2 z_2)G'(X_0 - Y_0)$ is the user cost of an incremental increase in Y_0. User cost in this model is the marginal loss in discounted expected future net revenues resulting from an incremental increase in Y_0.

If we had an analytical expression for $Y_0^* = \phi(X_0)$, we could substitute it into the RHS of Equation (1.43), and we would have accomplished the maximization that defines the value function. We also would have an expression that now only depends on X_0. The value function $V(X_0)$ is a subtle and powerful concept. It says that if you faithfully optimize, the best you can expect to do depends *only* on the current value of your state variable, in our case X_0.

1.8 A MARKOV DECISION MODEL AND STOCHASTIC DYNAMIC PROGRAMMING

Let's consider a generalization of our two-period, two-state model that falls into a class of models called *Markov decision models*. The qualifier *Markov* refers to the fact that the net-benefit (or reward) function and the probability distributions generating future random variables depend only on the current state (resource stock) X_t and the current action (harvest or extraction decision) Y_t. We consider problems where the optimization horizon is $t = 0, 1, \ldots, T$. If $T < \infty$, we have a finite-horizon problem. If $T \to \infty$, we have an infinite-horizon problem. Now z_{t+1} is a random variable whose realized value is *not* known from the perspective of period t. It may be the case that the probability distribution generating z_{t+1} will depend on the current resource stock and harvest rate X_t and Y_t. If so, we will denote the conditional probability distribution that will generate z_{t+1} by $f(z_{t+1}|X_t, Y_t)$. In many problems, it is assumed that all future random variables $z_{t+1}, z_{t+2}, z_{t+3}, \cdots$ are *independently and identically distributed* (i.i.d.) by the distribution $f(z)$. In this case, the random variables are generated by a stationary process that does not depend on X_t and Y_t.

The resource stock in period $t+1$ is unknown from the perspective of period t because the decision on the level for Y_t only partially influences the future value of the resource stock, which is determined according to the equation $X_{t+1} = G(X_t, Y_t; z_{t+1})$. Our net-benefit function (sometimes called the *reward function*) is again denoted by $\pi(X_t, Y_t)$. For an infinite-horizon problem ($T \to \infty$), the Bellman equation, representing the value of X_t if you optimally harvest (manage) the resource forever, is given by

$$V(X_t) = \max_{Y_t}\{\pi(X_t, Y_t) + \rho \underset{z}{E}[V(X_{t+1})]\} \tag{1.45}$$

where $E_z[V(X_{t+1})]$ is the *expectation operator*, taken over all possible values (the support) of z_{t+1}. The maximization might be achieved when X_t and Y_t are continuous by taking a partial derivative of the braced expression on the RHS of Equation (1.45) and setting it equal to zero. This yields

$$\frac{\partial \pi(\bullet)}{\partial Y_t} + \rho \underset{z}{E}\{V'(X_{t+1})\partial G(X_t, Y_t; z_{t+1})/\partial Y_t\} = 0 \tag{1.46}$$

Note that I have substituted $X_{t+1} = G(X_t, Y_t; z_{t+1})$ into the value function $V(X_{t+1})$. For renewable and nonrenewable resources, it is usually the case that $\partial G(X_t, Y_t; z_{t+1})/\partial Y_t < 0$.

Note that Equation (1.46) is a single equation in X_t and Y_t. If we can solve it for Y_t as a function of X_t, we will have obtained an analytical expression for our optimal feedback policy $Y_t^* = \phi(X_t)$. This feedback policy may depend on the discount factor ρ, the bioeconomic parameters in the functions $\pi(\bullet)$ and $G(\bullet)$, and parameters in the probability distribution $f(\bullet)$. Recall in our simple two-period, two-state model of the preceding section that Y_0^* depended on the discrete probabilities ε_1 and ε_2.

In most discrete-time Markov problems, we will need to resort to numerical methods to approximate the unknown value function $V(X_t)$ and the optimal feedback policy. Because X_t is itself a random variable, induced by z_{t+1}, we should expect that it will have a probability distribution. *Note:* If we substitute the optimal feedback policy into the state equation, we obtain

$$X_{t+1} = G[X_t, \phi(X_t); z_{t+1}] \tag{1.47}$$

With a known initial condition $X_0 > 0$, functional forms for $G(\bullet)$ and $\phi(\bullet)$, and a distribution $f(\bullet)$ generating realizations for z_{t+1}, you could stochastically iterate (simulate) Equation (1.47) forward in time. After a transition period, reflecting the influence of $X_0 > 0$, we should expect the resource stock to fluctuate according to a stationary distribution. There may be conditions where the intrinsic growth rate for the resource is small relative to the variance for z_{t+1} with the result that $X_t \to 0$ (extinction) with probability 1 as $t \to \infty$.

1.9 EXERCISES

E1.1 I now add an economic dimension to Spreadsheet S1.1, which was a simulation of the linear harvest policy $Y_t = \alpha X_t$, $r > \alpha > 0$. Suppose that net revenue from the fishery is given by $\pi_t = pY_t - (c/2)(Y_t^2/X_t)$, where $p > 0$ is the per-unit (or sometimes called the *exvessel*) price for fish on the dock and $c > 0$ is a cost parameter. With the simulated values for X_t and Y_t, we then calculate $\pi = \sum_{t=0}^{19} \rho^t \pi_t$, the present value of net revenues, where $\rho = 1/(1 + \delta)$ is the discount factor and $\delta > 0$ is the discount rate. We are adding three economic parameters (p, c, δ) to the three biological parameters (r, K, α) and the initial condition X_0. I modify Spreadsheet S1.1 to become Spreadsheet E1.1 here, where $r = 1$, $K = 1$, $\alpha = 0.5$, $X_0 = 0.1$, $p = 5$, $c = 1$, and $\delta = 0.05$. In cell D17, I have programmed = ($B$14^A17) * ($B$11 * C17 − ($B$12/2) * ((C17^2)/B17)), and I fill-down from D17 through cell D36. In cell D13, I put the label π, and in cell E13, I type = SUM($D$17:$D$36), which sums the discounted net revenue for $t = 0, 1, 2, \ldots, 19$. The present value for net revenue for this exercise is $\pi = 11.6780729$. Reproduce Spreadsheet E1.1 on your computer. In Chapter 2 we will return to this problem and ask the question, "What is the value of α that maximizes π?" (If you are not already aware of their obsession, economists always want to optimize something!)

E1.2 Fisheries are often managed by trying to ensure that some number of fish escape harvest. Recall that we defined *escapement* as $S_t \equiv X_t - Y_t$. We will call a target escapement policy an *S^* policy*. Under the (heroic) assumptions that the fish stock and harvest can be measured precisely, the level of harvest and actual escapement in period t are calculated according to the expressions $Y_t = \max[0, X_t - S^*]$ and $S_t = \min[X_t, S^*]$, where

	A	B	C	D	E	F
1	E1.1 Present Value of Net Revenue under the Linear Harvest Policy					
2						
3	$r =$	1				
4	$K =$	1				
5	$\alpha =$	0.5				
6	$X_{SS} =$	0.5				
7	$Y_{SS} =$	0.25				
8	$|G'(X_{SS})| =$	0.5				
9	$X_O =$	0.1				
10						
11	$p =$	5				
12	$c =$	1				
13	$\delta =$	0.05		$\pi =$	11.67807295	
14	$\rho =$	0.952380952				
15						
16	t	X_t	Y_t	$(\rho\char94 t)^*\pi\,(t)$		
17	0	0.1	0.05	0.2375		
18	1	0.14	0.07	0.316666667		
19	2	0.1904	0.0952	0.41015873		
20	3	0.24934784	0.12467392	0.511565593		
21	4	0.311847415	0.155923707	0.609324395		
22	5	0.370522312	0.185261156	0.689495576		
23	6	0.418496684	0.209248342	0.74168559		
24	7	0.452605552	0.226302776	0.763938499		
25	8	0.474056542	0.237028271	0.762042803		
26	9	0.486355208	0.243177604	0.744583646		
27	10	0.492991424	0.246495712	0.718803176		
28	11	0.496446592	0.248223296	0.689372346		
29	12	0.498210669	0.249105335	0.658878064		
30	13	0.499102133	0.249551066	0.628625728		
31	14	0.49955026	0.24977513	0.599228715		
32	15	0.499774928	0.249887464	0.570950678		
33	16	0.499887413	0.249943707	0.543884936		
34	17	0.499943694	0.249971847	0.518043972		
35	18	0.499971844	0.249985922	0.493402901		
36	19	0.499985921	0.249992961	0.469920842		
37						
38						
39						
40						
41						
42						
43						
44						
45						
46						
47						
48						
49						
50						
51						
52						

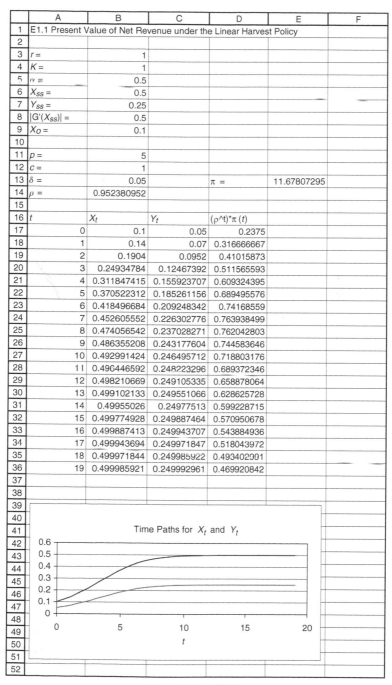

Time Paths for X_t and Y_t

Spreadsheet E1.1

max[•] means "select the largest element in [•]" and min[•] means "select the smallest element in [•]." These functions can be used in Excel spreadsheets. Take a moment to convince yourself that these rules for harvest and actual escapement make sense. The fish stock is assumed to evolve according to the equation $X_{t+1} = (1 - m)S_t + rS_t(1 - S_t/K)$, where $1 > m > 0$ is the per-period mortality rate for fish that escape harvest, $r > 0$ is the intrinsic growth rate, and $K > 0$ is the environmental carrying capacity. As in Exercise E1.1, you will again assume that net revenue is given by $\pi_t = pY_t - (c/2)(Y_t^2/X_t)$. The horizon is $t = 0, 1, 2, \ldots, 19$ and $\pi = \sum_{t=0}^{19} \rho^t \pi_t$. For parameter values, set $m = 0.1$, $r = 0.5$, $K = 300$ million (pounds), $p = 5$, $c = 20$, $\delta = 0.05$, $X_0 = 100$ million (pounds), and $S^* = 150$ million (pounds). In Spreadsheet E1.2, in cells C15, D15, and E15, I program $= \max(0, B15 - \$B\$11)$, $= \min(B15, \$B\$11)$, and $= (\$B\$9^\wedge A15) * (\$B\$6 * C15 - (\$B\$7/2) * ((C15^\wedge 2)/B15))$, respectively. In cell B16, I program $= (1 - \$B\$3) * D15 + \$B\$4 * D15 * (1 - D15/\$B\$5)$. I do a one-cell fill-down from C15:E15 to C16:E16 and then do a fill-down from B16:E16 through B34:E34. In cell D11, I put the label π, and in cell E11, I type $= \text{sum}(\$E\$15:\$E\$34)$, which returns the present value for $t = 0, 1, 2, \ldots, 19$. Construct your own version of Spreadsheet E1.2 to verify the calculation for π. In Chapter 2 we will seek the value of S^* that maximizes π.

E1.3 In this exercise you will modify Spreadsheet E1.2 to allow for the stochastic evolution of the fish stock. This will be an exercise in stochastic simulation. Let z_{t+1} be an *independent and identically distributed* random variable. Specifically, we will assume that the z_{t+1} values are generated by a uniform random variable. Values of a uniform random variable are generated within the interval (support) (a, b) so that $b > z_{t+1} > a$. It can be shown that the expected value of z_{t+1} is $E(z) = (a + b)/2$, and the variance is $\text{var}(z) = (b - a)^2/12$. In this exercise we will assume that $b = 1.4$ and $a = 0.6$, so $E(z) = 1$. The fish stock evolves stochastically because $X_{t+1} = z_{t+1}[(1 - m)S_t + rS_t(1 - S_t/K)]$. Spreadsheet E1.3 is a modification of Spreadsheet E1.2. In cell F14, I put the label $z(t + 1)$, and I then highlight cells F16:F34. These will be the cells where Excel will place the 19 random draws from

	A	B	C	D	E
1	E1.2 Simulation of an Escapement Policy				
2					
3	$m =$	0.1			
4	$r =$	0.5			
5	$K -$	300,000,000			
6	$p =$	5			
7	$c =$	20			
8	$\delta =$	0.05			
9	$\rho =$	0.952380952			
10	$X(0) =$	100,000,000			
11	$S^* =$	150,000,000		$\pi =$	$844,706,277
12					
13					
14	t	X_t	Y_t	S_t	$(\rho^\wedge t)^*\pi\,(t)$
15	0	100,000,000	0	100,000,000	$0
16	1	123,333,333	0	123,333,333	$0
17	2	147,314,815	0	147,314,815	$0
18	3	170,071,316	20,071,316	150,000,000	$66,229,569
19	4	172,500,000	22,500,000	150,000,000	$68,409,499
20	5	172,500,000	22,500,000	150,000,000	$65,151,904
21	6	172,500,000	22,500,000	150,000,000	$62,049,432
22	7	172,500,000	22,500,000	150,000,000	$59,094,698
23	8	172,500,000	22,500,000	150,000,000	$56,280,664
24	9	172,500,000	22,500,000	150,000,000	$53,600,633
25	10	172,500,000	22,500,000	150,000,000	$51,048,222
26	11	172,500,000	22,500,000	150,000,000	$48,617,354
27	12	172,500,000	22,500,000	150,000,000	$46,302,242
28	13	172,500,000	22,500,000	150,000,000	$44,097,373
29	14	172,500,000	22,500,000	150,000,000	$41,997,498
30	15	172,500,000	22,500,000	150,000,000	$39,997,617
31	16	172,500,000	22,500,000	150,000,000	$38,092,969
32	17	172,500,000	22,500,000	150,000,000	$36,279,018
33	18	172,500,000	22,500,000	150,000,000	$34,551,446
34	19	172,500,000	22,500,000	150,000,000	$32,906,139

Spreadsheet E1.2

the uniform distribution. Now go to the Tools Menu and select "Data Analysis." From the "Data Analysis" submenu, select "Random Number Generation." From the "Random Number Generation" submenu select the "Uniform Distribution." There is just one random variable, z_{t+1}, but there will be 19 random numbers (draws). Specify that the random numbers will lie between $a = 0.6$ and $b = 1.4$. Set the "Random Seed" to 1. Select the "Output Range" to be F16:F34, and click "OK." A warning will come up that Excel is about to overwrite existing

	A	B	C	D	E	F
1	E1.3 Simulation of an Escapement Policy in a Stochastic Environment					
2						
3	$m =$	0.1				
4	$r =$	0.5				
5	$K =$	300,000,000				
6	$p =$	5				
7	$c =$	20				
8	$\delta =$	0.05				
9	$\rho =$	0.952380952				
10	$X(0) =$	100,000,000				
11	$S^* =$	150,000,000		$\pi =$	$444,681,909	
12						
13						
14	t	X_t	Y_t	S_t	$(\rho^\wedge t)^*\pi(t)$	$z(t+1)$
15	0	100,000,000	0	100,000,000	$0	
16	1	124,701,905	0	124,701,905	$0	1.01109653
17	2	110,098,438	0	110,098,438	$0	0.740580462
18	3	113,430,513	0	113,430,513	$0	0.846906949
19	4	141,153,162	0	141,153,162	$0	1.027625355
20	5	223,282,381	73,282,381	150,000,000	$98,642,425	1.35810419
21	6	127,198,416	0	127,198,416	$0	0.737382122
22	7	175,559,676	25,559,676	150,000,000	$64,377,872	1.161784722
23	8	134,745,521	0	134,745,521	$0	0.781133457
24	9	157,719,965	7,719,965	150,000,000	$22,445,999	0.99581286
25	10	120,708,411	0	120,708,411	$0	0.699758904
26	11	96,536,783	0	96,536,783	$0	0.667116306
27	12	109,057,326	0	109,057,326	$0	0.911703848
28	13	109,180,393	0	109,180,393	$0	0.821784112
29	14	118,947,703	0	118,947,703	$0	0.894442579
30	15	198,232,622	48,232,622	150,000,000	$59,553,165	1.386767174
31	16	177,383,297	27,383,297	150,000,000	$43,357,464	1.028308969
32	17	209,163,686	59,163,686	150,000,000	$56,050,612	1.212543107
33	18	192,713,355	42,713,355	150,000,000	$49,403,778	1.117178869
34	19	209,365,841	59,365,841	150,000,000	$50,850,594	1.213715018

X_t Under an S* Policy in a Stochastic Environment

Spreadsheet E1.3

data in cells F16:F34. Click "OK," and Excel should generate the same random numbers on your spreadsheet as were generated in Spreadsheet E1.3 because they are associated with the random seed number 1. We now modify the equation in cell B16 to become $= F16 * ((1 - \$B\$3) * D15 + \$B\$4 * D15 * (1 - D15/\$B\$5))$ and fill down from B16:B34. Because the stock is evolving stochastically, we see X_t fluctuating. If the stock falls below $S^* = 150$ million, then harvest is zero (no fishing!). Present value has fallen to \$444,681,909 compared with the nonstochastic (deterministic) model in Spreadsheet E1.2, where $\pi = \$844,706,277$. At the bottom of Spreadsheet E1.3, we do a bar diagram plot of X_t that fluctuates from a low of 96,536,783 in $t = 11$ to a high of 223,282,381 in $t = 5$. We will return to this spreadsheet in Chapter 2 to find out the value of S^* that maximizes present value for this particular realization for z_{t+1}.

E1.4 There are no spreadsheets in this exercise. You will need to use some calculus, algebra, and some of the present-value formulas from Section 1.3. Consider the nonrenewable resource where remaining reserves evolve according to the iterative equation $R_{t+1} = R_t - q_t$, with $R_0 > 0$ given. The net revenue from extraction q_t is given by $\pi_t = pq_t - (c/2)q_t^2$. The current-value Hamiltonian may be written as $H_t \equiv pq_t - (c/2)q_t^2 - \rho\lambda_{t+1}q_t$. Show that the first-order necessary conditions imply that $p - cq_t = \rho\lambda_{t+1}$ and $\rho\lambda_{t+1} = \lambda_t$ and therefore that $\lambda_t = \lambda_0(1 + \delta)^t$. Now suppose that remaining reserves will be completely exhausted at some unknown future date $t = T$, implying $R_T = q_T = 0$. Evaluating the first-order conditions at $t = T$ implies that $p = \rho\lambda_{T+1} = \lambda_T = \lambda_0(1 + \delta)^T$ and that $\lambda_0 = p(1 + \delta)^{-T}$. Show that this implies that $q_t = (p/c)(1 - \rho^{T-t})$. This last equation is the equation for optimal extraction. The only problem is that T is unknown. However, with complete exhaustion in $t = T$, we also know that $\sum_{t=0}^{t=T-1} q_t = \sum_{t=0}^{t=T-1} (p/c)(1 - \rho^{T-t}) = R_0$. Here is where you need to use some of the finite math and converging series used in the present-value formulas in Section 1.3. Show that this last equation will imply an *implicit equation* $G(T) = T - (1/\delta)(1 - \rho^T) - cR_0/p$ and that $G(T) = 0$ at $T = T^*$, the optimal date of exhaustion. In Chapter 2, I will show how Excel's Solver can be used to find the roots (zeros) of implicit equations such as $G(T)$. In discrete-time models, we might have to round $T = T^*$ to the nearest integer.

E1.5 The optimal value for unknown variables in economic allocation problems also might require finding the root or zero of an implicit equation. Let us return to the two-period, two-state model of Section 1.7 and see how an implicit equation might arise when trying to determine the optimal level of harvest Y_0^* in $t = 0$. Suppose that the fish stock in future state s depends on escapement in $t = 0$ according to $X_{1,s} = z_s\alpha(X_0 - Y_0)^\beta$, where $s = 1$, 2, $\alpha > 0$, and $1 > \beta > 0$. We will assume that $z_1 > 1 > z_2 > 0$, $\Pr(z = z_1) = \varepsilon_1$, $\Pr(z = z_2) = \varepsilon_2$, $1 > \varepsilon_s > 0$, and $\varepsilon_1 + \varepsilon_2 = 1$. Suppose further that the net revenue in future state s takes the form $\pi_{1,s} = p_1 Y_{1,s} - (c/2)[Y_{1,s}^2/z_s\alpha(X_0 - Y_0)^\beta]$. Show that optimal state-dependent harvest is given by $Y_{1,s}^* = p_1[z_s\alpha(X_0 - Y_0)^\beta]/c$ and that optimized state-dependent net revenue is given by $\pi_{1,s}^* = p_1^2[z_s\alpha(X_0 - Y_0)^\beta]/2c$. The value function for the initial fish stock $X_0 > 0$ becomes $V(X_0) = \max_{Y_0}[p_0 Y_0 - (c/2)(Y_0^2/X_0) + \rho(\varepsilon_1\pi_{1,1}^* + \varepsilon_2\pi_{1,2}^*)]$. Show that the optimal level of harvest in $t = 0$ must satisfy $G(Y_0) = p_0 - cY_0/X_0 - \rho p_1^2\alpha\beta(X_0 - Y_0)^{\beta-1}(\varepsilon_1 z_1 + \varepsilon_2 z_2)/(2c) = 0$. As with the other exercises in this chapter, we will return to E2.5 in Chapter 2 and show how Solver can be used to numerically find Y_0^*.

2

Solving Numerical Allocation Problems Using Excel's Solver

2.0 INTRODUCTION AND OVERVIEW

Numerical allocation problems can serve at least two functions. First, they can make theory and methods less abstract and more meaningful. Second, they can serve as a useful bridge from theory and general models to the actual analysis of "real world" resource-allocation problems. By a *numerical problem*, I mean a problem where functional forms have been specified, and all relevant parameters and initial conditions have been estimated or assigned values. For example, in Section 1.4, the general net-benefit function took the form $\pi_t = \pi(X_t, Y_t)$. A *specific functional form*, used in Exercises E1.1 through E1.3, was $\pi_t = pY_t - (c/2)(Y_t^2/X_t)$, where $p > 0$ was a parameter denoting the per-unit price for fish on the dock, Y_t was the level of harvest in period t, $c > 0$ was a cost parameter, and X_t was the fish stock in period t. In a numerical problem, we would need values for $p > 0$ and $c > 0$, which might be estimated econometrically or simply assigned values based on a knowledge of current market prices and the cost of operating a fishing vessel.

Numerical analysis might involve solving an implicit equation for the steady-state value of a resource stock, the deterministic or stochastic simulation of a harvest or extraction policy, or the selection of escapement, harvest, or extraction rates to maximize some measure of present value. By *simulation*, I will usually mean the forward iteration of one or more difference equations. For example, in Spreadsheet S1.1, you were told that a fish stock evolved according to $X_{t+1} = (1 + r - \alpha - rX_t/K)X_t = G(X_t)$. With numerical values for r, α, K,

41

and X_0, it was relatively simple to use spreadsheet software to determine the evolution of X_t and $Y_t = \alpha X_t$ over some future horizon $t = 0, 1, 2, \ldots, T$. Simulation analysis is frequently referred to as a "what if" analysis. *If* we follow this harvest policy over the next 20 years, *what* will happen to the fish stock? In Exercise E1.3, you performed a stochastic simulation where a stochastic process, in the form of a random variable, influenced the evolution of a fish stock.

Optimization asks the question, "What's best?" Economists are always wondering what's best. What is the best mix of inputs for a firm seeking to produce a particular level of output? What is the best allocation of a consumer's limited budget? What conditions describe an optimal allocation of resources and distribution of output for an economy? What is the optimal level for a public good? What is the optimal harvest policy for a fish stock? In this chapter we will construct numerical problems where we seek to maximize a measure of present value by the selection of a single variable or a set (vector) of variables. As mentioned in the exercises at the end of Chapter 1, we will return to some of the spreadsheets you have already constructed and seek the value of α for the linear harvest policy and S^*, for the escapement policy that maximize present value. We also will set up spreadsheets where there are columns containing harvest or extraction rates over some future horizon and seek the vector of those values that maximizes present value. We will start with the problem of finding the value of a single variable that maximizes a function and thus drives its first derivative to zero.

2.1 OPTIMAL ROTATION FOR AN EVEN-AGED FOREST

In Chapter 4 we will develop a model that seeks to determine the optimal length of time to allow an even-aged stand of trees to grow before cutting them down and replanting. In forestry, this is called the *Faustmann rotation problem*. I won't go into the details here, but the present value of net revenues, from a recently replanted acre of land, where the current and future stands are cut when they reach age T, is given by the function

$$\pi(T) = \frac{pQ(T) - c}{e^{\delta T} - 1} \tag{2.1}$$

where $p > 0$ is the net price per board foot of timber, $Q(T)$ is the volume (board feet) of timber harvested at the end of each rotation when current and future stands are all cut at age T, $c > 0$ is the cost of replanting the parcel, and $\delta > 0$ is the discount rate. Rotation age T is assumed to be a continuous variable. A specification for $Q(T)$ that gives a good fit to timber volume for many commercially grown trees takes the form $Q(T) = e^{a-b/T}$, for $T > 0$, and where $a > 0$ and $b > 0$ are parameters that will depend on the species-specific growth rate and maximum timber volume per acre. With this specification for $Q(T)$, Equation (2.1) becomes

$$\pi(T) = \frac{pe^{a-b/T} - c}{e^{\delta T} - 1} \tag{2.2}$$

This is a single-variable function, and with parameter values for a, b, δ, p, and c, we can use Excel's Solver to find the value of T that maximizes $\pi(T)$. Alternatively, we could take the derivative $\pi'(T)$, set it to zero, and see if we can solve that equation for an analytic expression where T is isolated on the left-hand side (LHS), and only parameters and functional operators appear on the right-hand side (RHS). To verify that we have found the value of T that maximizes $\pi(T)$, we need to check that the value of the second derivative, $\pi''(T)$, evaluated at the candidate T, is negative. Alternatively, we could plot $\pi(T)$ and check, visually, that our candidate T occurs at a global maximum for $\pi(T)$. For many problems, including the Faustmann rotation problem, it may not be possible to get an analytic expression for the optimal T, and you would need to use an algorithm to numerically find the value of T that drives $\pi'(T)$ to zero. Let's illustrate Solver's ability to find the value of T that maximizes $\pi(T)$ or drives $\pi'(T)$ to zero.

In Spreadsheet S2.1, cells B3:B7 contain the parameter values for a, b, c, p, and δ. The net present value of our recently replanted acre is $\pi(T) = (pe^{a-b/T} - c)/(e^{\delta T} - 1)$ when trees are cut and the acre is replanted every T years. This equation is programmed as $= (\$B\$6 * \text{EXP}(\$B\$3 - \$B\$4/\$B\$9) - \$B\$5)/(\text{EXP}(\$B\$7 * \$B\$9) - 1)$ in cell B11, where T^*, in cell B9, was originally set at 50 but was subsequently changed by Excel's Solver when it was asked to maximize $\pi(T)$. Some calculus and careful algebra will reveal that

$$\pi'(T) = \frac{(b/T^2)(e^{\delta T} - 1)pe^{a-b/T} - \delta(pe^{a-b/T} - c)e^{\delta T}}{(e^{\delta T} - 1)^2} \tag{2.3}$$

	A	B	C	D	E	F	G	H
1	S2.1 The Value of *T* that Maximizes π(*T*) and Drives π'(*T*) to Zero							
2								
3	a =	10						
4	b =	53.27						
5	c =	300			A Plot of π(*T*)			
6	p =	1		$2,000.00				
7	δ =	0.05		$1,000.00				
8				$0.00				
9	*T* =	30.00						
10	Q(*T*) =	3730.87		−$1,000.00				
11	π(*T*) =	$985.34						
12	π'(*T*) =	1.70733E-06		−$2,000.00				
13				−$3,000.00				
14	*T*	π(*T*)						
15	1	-$5,851.25		−$4,000.00				
16	2	-$2,852.50						
17	3	-$1,853.75		−$5,000.00				
18	4	-$1,354.83						
19	5	-$1,054.41		−$6,000.00				
20	6	-$848.71						
21	7	-$689.83		−$7,000.00				
22	8	-$552.53				*T*		
23	9	-$423.69						
24	10	-$297.48						
25	11	-$172.26						
26	12	-$48.61						
27	13	$71.96						
28	14	$187.71						
29	15	$297.10						
30	16	$398.92						
31	17	$492.34						
32	18	$576.88						
33	19	$652.39						
34	20	$718.93						
35	21	$776.76						
36	22	$826.26						
37	23	$867.91						
38	24	$902.23						
39	25	$929.78						
40	26	$951.13						
41	27	$966.83						
42	28	$977.43						
43	29	$983.43						
44	30	$985.34						
45	31	$983.59						
46	32	$978.62						
47	33	$970.81						
48	34	$960.53						
49	35	$948.10						
50	36	$933.82						
51	37	$917.96						
52	38	$900.77						

The plot x-axis shows 0, 10, 20, 30, 40.

Spreadsheet S2.1

This equation is programmed in cell B12. In cell B10 we programmed $Q(T) = e^{a-b/T}$, so we would know the timber volume at the optimal rotation. Clicking on cell B11 and going to the Tools menu, slide down the menu items and release on "Solver." Solver assumes that you want cell B11 to be the "Set Target Cell," which you could maximize, minimize, or drive to zero by changing another cell or cells in the spreadsheet that influence (appear in the formula in) cell B11. Remember, we initially entered the number 50 in cell B9 as a guess for T^*. When $T^* = 50$, $\pi(T) = 651.92$, and $\pi'(T) = -21.0481827$. Tell Solver you want to maximize the value in cell $B$11 by allowing it to change the value in cell $B$9. Click the "Solve" button, and Solver iterates the value in cell B9, trying to produce the largest value it can in cell B11. It stops when $T = 30.0010693338813$, which we round to 30.00. When Solver stopped, it returned the message, "Solver has converged to the current" (solution). Click the "OK" button in the Solver dialogue box, and then, using the current solution for T^*, run Solver again. This time Solver returns the message "Solver found a solution. All constraints" (are satisfied). The value of T^* was not changed from the previous, current solution, but running Solver a second time is advisable when there are constraints on the choice or state variables. *Note:* The value of $\pi'(T)$ is now 1.70733E−06, which we probably can regard as "close enough" to zero. In Spreadsheet S2.1, we evaluate and plot $\pi(T)$ as a visual check that $T^* = 30.00$ corresponds to an approximate maximum. In this problem, taking the second derivative, $\pi''(T)$, is a real grunt.

2.2 SOLVING AN IMPLICIT EQUATION FOR THE OPTIMAL STEADY-STATE FISH STOCK

In Section 1.4, I referred to Equation (1.25) as the "fundamental equation of renewable resources." I rewrite that equation here as

$$F'(X) + \frac{\partial\pi(\bullet)/\partial X}{\partial\pi(\bullet)/\partial Y} = \delta \tag{2.4}$$

for easier reference. This equation, along with the steady-state requirement that harvest equals net growth, $Y = F(X)$, will lead to a single equation in X. Depending on the functional forms for $F(X)$ and $\pi(X, Y)$, that equation might allow for an explicit solution for X^*, but more often than not, it will result in an implicit equation that must be solved numerically for X^*.

Consider the case where $F(X) = rX \ln(K/X)$ and $\pi(X, Y) = pY - (c/2)Y^2/X$, where $\ln(\bullet)$ is the natural log operator. Some careful calculus will reveal $F'(X) = r[\ln(K/X) - 1]$, $\partial\pi(\bullet)/\partial X = (c/2)(Y/X)^2$, and $\partial\pi(\bullet)/\partial Y = p - c(Y/X)$. On substituting $Y = rX \ln(K/X)$ into the partial derivatives of the net revenue function, Equation (2.4) implies

$$r[\ln(K/X) - 1] + \frac{(c/2)[r \ \ln(K/X)]^2}{p - cr \ \ln(K/X)} = \delta \qquad (2.5)$$

and after transposing δ and multiplying all terms by $p - cr \ \ln(K/X)$, we define the implicit equation

$$G(X) \equiv [r \ln(K/X) - (r + \delta)][p - cr \ln(K/X)] + (c/2)[r \ln(K/X)]^2 \qquad (2.6)$$

where $X = X^*$ makes $G(X) = 0$. Since $G(X)$ is nonlinear, it may have more than one value of X where $G(X) = 0$. If this is the case, you will need to determine which value of X produces the highest value for $\pi[X, \ F(X)]/\delta$, the present value of net revenues when X is maintained in perpetuity.

In Spreadsheet S2.2, we use Solver to find the roots (zeros) of Equation (2.6) when $r = 1$, $K = 1$, $p = 5$, $c = 11$, and $\delta = 0.02$. For these parameter values, there are two values of X that drive $G(X)$ to zero. Solver reveals these to be $X = 0.07493$ and $X = 0.69918$. For the first root, $\pi[X, \ F(X)]/\delta = -89.8139$, whereas for the second root, the optimal steady-state fish stock, $\pi[X, \ F(X)]/\delta = 37.92826$.

	A	B	C
	A	B	C
1	S2.2 Optimal	Steady-State	Fish Stock
2			
3	$r =$	1	
4	$K =$	1	
5	$p =$	5	
6	$c =$	11	
7	$\delta =$	0.02	
8			
9	$X =$	0.699178808	
10	$Y =$	0.250200272	
11	$F'(X) =$	−0.642151236	
12	$\partial\pi(\bullet)\partial X =$	0.70430656	
13	$\partial\pi(\bullet)\partial Y =$	1.063663591	
14	$G(X) =$	3.98676E-07	
15	$\pi(X) / \delta$	37.92825707	

Spreadsheet S2.2

In cell B11, I have programmed $= \$B\$3*(LN(\$B\$4/\$B\$9)-1)$, whereas in cells B12 and B13, I have programmed $= (\$B\$6/2)*(\$B\$3*LN(\$B\$4/\$B\$9))^\wedge 2$ and $= \$B\$5 - \$B\$6*\$B\$3*LN(\$B\$4/\$B\$9)$, respectively. In cell B14, I programmed $= (\$B\$3*LN(\$B\$4/\$B\$9) - (\$B\$3 + \$B\$7))*(\$B\$5 - \$B\$6*\$B\$3*LN(\$B\$4/\$B\$9)) + (\$B\$6/2)*(\$B\$3*LN(\$B\$4/\$B\$9))^\wedge 2$. The initial guess for X was 0.75 in cell B9. I then called up Solver, asking it to change cell B9 so as to drive cell B14 to zero. Solver quickly converges to $X = 0.69918$. If your initial guess is $X = 0.07$, Solver converges to $X = 0.07493$, the smaller root for $G(X)$.

2.3 SOLVING AN IMPLICIT EQUATION FOR THE OPTIMAL DATE OF EXHAUSTION

In Exercise E1.4 you hopefully confirmed that the optimal extraction rate was given by the equation $q_t^* = (p/c)(1 - \rho^{T-t})$, where the optimal date of exhaustion (depletion) satisfying $\sum_{t=0}^{t=T-1} q_t^* = R_0$ also satisfied $G(T) = T - (1/\delta)(1 - \rho^T) - cR_0/p = 0$. With parameter values for p, c, δ, and R_0 we can find the optimal date of exhaustion and then plot $q_t^* = (p/c)(1 - \rho^{T-t})$. We do this in Spreadsheet S2.3, where $p = 65$, $c = 15$, $\delta = 0.10$, and $R_0 = 109.8757$. (The value of R_0 was strategically adopted after trial and error with Solver in order to get a value for T that would be close to an integer, in this case $T \approx 35$.) As an initial guess, we might start with a value of $T = 50$. This would result in the value $G(T) = 14.72925474$, not close to zero. Calling up Solver and asking it to drive the expression for $G(T)$ in cell B10 to zero by changing the guess for T in cell B9 yields the numerical values for T and $G(T)$ in Spreadsheet S2.3. In that spreadsheet we also plot $q_t^* = (p/c)(1 - \rho^{T-t})$.

2.4 OPTIMAL FIRST-PERIOD HARVEST IN A TWO-PERIOD, TWO-STATE MODEL

In Exercise E1.5, you were asked to show that the optimal first-period harvest in a two-period, two-state model was the level of Y_0 that maximized the expected discounted value of net revenue, assuming that the

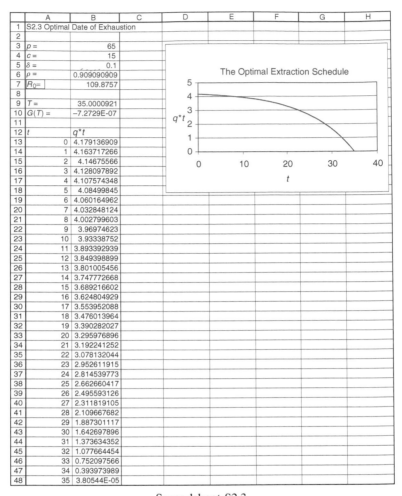

	A	B	C	D	E	F	G	H
1	S2.3 Optimal Date of Exhaustion							
2								
3	$p =$	65						
4	$c =$	15						
5	$\delta =$	0.1						
6	$\rho =$	0.909090909			The Optimal Extraction Schedule			
7	$R_0 =$	109.8757						
8								
9	$T =$	35.0000921						
10	$G(T) =$	–7.2729E-07						
11								
12	t	$q*t$						
13	0	4.179136909						
14	1	4.163717266						
15	2	4.14675566						
16	3	4.128097892						
17	4	4.107574348						
18	5	4.08499845						
19	6	4.060164962						
20	7	4.032848124						
21	8	4.002799603						
22	9	3.96974623						
23	10	3.93338752						
24	11	3.893392939						
25	12	3.849398899						
26	13	3.801005456						
27	14	3.747772668						
28	15	3.689216602						
29	16	3.624804929						
30	17	3.553952088						
31	18	3.476013964						
32	19	3.390282027						
33	20	3.295976896						
34	21	3.192241252						
35	22	3.078132044						
36	23	2.952611915						
37	24	2.814539773						
38	25	2.662660417						
39	26	2.495593126						
40	27	2.311819105						
41	28	2.109667682						
42	29	1.887301117						
43	30	1.642697896						
44	31	1.373634352						
45	32	1.077664454						
46	33	0.752097566						
47	34	0.393973989						
48	35	3.80544E-05						

Spreadsheet S2.3

resource was optimally harvested in each of the two future states. The value function, telling us the expected discounted value of the initial fish stock, was defined in that problem as

$$V(X_0) \equiv \max_{Y_0}[p_0 Y_0 - (c/2)(Y_0^2/X_0) + \rho(\varepsilon_1 \pi_{1,1}^* + \varepsilon_2 \pi_{1,2}^*)] \quad (2.7)$$

where the optimized harvest rate in each future state was given by $Y_{1,s}^* = p_1 z_s \alpha (X_0 - Y_0)^\beta / c$, and the optimized net revenue, based on that harvest policy, was $\pi_{1,s}^* = p_1^2 z_s \alpha (X_0 - Y_0)^\beta / (2c)$.

Taking a derivative with respect to Y_0 of the bracketed expression on the RHS of Equation (2.7) and setting it to zero does not permit an analytic expression for Y_0^* but does lead to an implicit expression that can be numerically solved for Y_0^*. In Exercise E1.5, you were asked to show that this implicit expression could be written as

$$G(Y_0) = p_0 - \frac{cY_0}{X_0} - \rho p_1^2 \alpha \beta (X_0 - Y_0)^{\beta-1} \frac{\varepsilon_1 z_1 + \varepsilon_2 z_2}{2c} \qquad (2.8)$$

In Spreadsheet S2.4, we set $p_0 = 1$, $p_1 = 1.124$, $c = 2$, $z_1 = 1.5$, $z_2 = 0.5$, $\varepsilon_1 = 0.5$, $\varepsilon_2 = 0.5$, $\delta = 0.02$, $X_0 = 1$, $\alpha = 1$, and

	A	B	C
1	S2.4 Optimal First-Period		Harvest
2			
3	$p_0 =$	1	
4	$p_1 =$	1.124	
5	$c =$	2	
6	$z_1 =$	1.5	
7	$z_2 =$	0.5	
8	$\varepsilon_1 =$	0.5	
9	$\varepsilon_2 =$	0.5	
10	$\delta =$	0.02	
11	$\rho =$	0.980392157	
12	$X_0 =$	1	
13	$\alpha =$	1	
14	$\beta =$	0.5	
15			
16	$Y_0 =$	0.400055918	
17	$V(X_0) =$	0.479854621	
18	$G(Y_0) =$	1.01466E-10	
19	$Y^*_{1,1} =$	0.652954563	
20	$Y^*_{1,2} =$	0.217651521	
21			
22	$\pi^*_{1,1} =$	0.366960465	
23	$\pi^*_{1,2} =$	0.122320155	
24	$\pi^*_0 =$	0.240011181	
25	$V(X_0) =$	0.479854621	

Spreadsheet S2.4

$\beta = 0.5$. We can find the optimal level for first-period harvest by either asking Solver to maximize the bracketed expression on the RHS of Equation (2.7) or by driving the expression for $G(Y_0)$ in Equation (2.8) to zero. In Spreadsheet S2.4, we specified an initial guess of $Y_0 = 0.5$ and asked Solver to maximize the RHS of Equation (2.7), which was programmed in cell B17. As a check, we also programmed $G(Y_0)$ in cell B18. Solver changed the initial guess to the optimal first-period harvest of $Y_0^* = 0.400055918$, which maximizes the expected discounted value of the initial stock $V(X_0 = 1) = 0.479854621$. *Note:* $V(X_0 = 1) = 0.479854621 = \pi_0^* + \rho(\varepsilon_1 \pi_{1,1}^* + \varepsilon_2 \pi_{1,2}^*)$, as shown at the bottom of Spreadsheet S2.4.

2.5 THE OPTIMAL LINEAR HARVEST POLICY

In Exercise E1.1, we added an economic dimension to our linear harvest policy, $Y_t = \alpha X_t$, by specifying an expression for net revenue that took the form $\pi_t = pY_t - (c/2)(Y_t^2/X_t)$. Recall that when coupled with logistic growth, the linear harvest policy resulted in the iterative equation $X_{t+1} = (1 + r - \alpha - rX_t/K)X_t$, as given in Equation (1.5). When $\alpha = 0.5$ and $X_0 = 0.1$ we simulated the fish stock, harvest, and discounted net revenue for $t = 0, 1, 2, \ldots, 19$ in Spreadsheet E1.1. We now ask Solver to maximize $\pi = \sum_{t=0}^{19} \rho^t \pi_t$ by changing the value of α.

In Spreadsheet E1.1, the sum of discounted net revenue was calculated in cell E13 as $\pi = 11.6780729$. This was the result of perhaps an arbitrary decision on the part of managers to set $\alpha = 0.5$. Is there another value of α that might produce a higher value for π? Select "Solver" from under the Tools menu, and when the Solver dialogue box comes up, specify $E$13 as the set cell that you wish to maximize by changing the value of α in cell $B$5. Click the "Solve" button, and Solver changes α to 0.47511437, raising π to 11.706665. The fish stock now converges to $X_{SS} = 0.52487871$, so we can maximize discounted net revenue by a slight reduction in α, which increases the fish stock and lowers the cost of harvest. The optimized spreadsheet is shown in Spreadsheet S2.5.

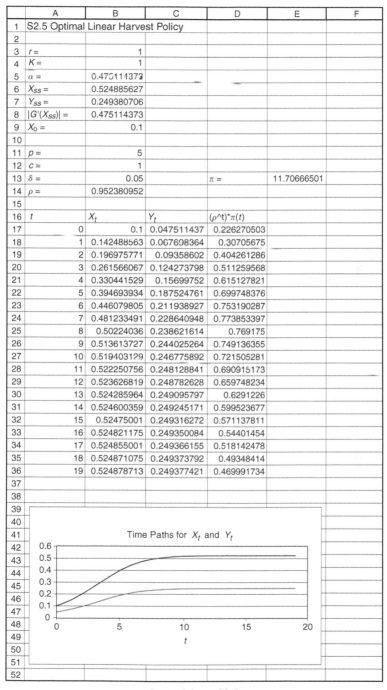

	A	B	C	D	E	F
1	S2.5 Optimal Linear Harvest Policy					
2						
3	$r =$	1				
4	$K =$	1				
5	$\alpha =$	0.475111373				
6	$X_{SS} =$	0.524885627				
7	$Y_{SS} =$	0.249380706				
8	$|G'(X_{SS})| =$	0.475114373				
9	$X_0 =$	0.1				
10						
11	$p =$	5				
12	$c =$	1				
13	$\delta =$	0.05		$\pi =$	11.70666501	
14	$\rho =$	0.952380952				
15						
16	t	X_t	Y_t	$(\rho^\wedge t)^*\pi(t)$		
17	0	0.1	0.047511437	0.226270503		
18	1	0.142488563	0.067698364	0.30705675		
19	2	0.196975771	0.09358602	0.404261286		
20	3	0.261566067	0.124273798	0.511259568		
21	4	0.330441529	0.15699752	0.615127821		
22	5	0.394693934	0.187524761	0.699748376		
23	6	0.446079805	0.211938927	0.753190287		
24	7	0.481233491	0.228640948	0.773853397		
25	8	0.50224036	0.238621614	0.769175		
26	9	0.513613727	0.244025264	0.749136355		
27	10	0.519403129	0.246775892	0.721505281		
28	11	0.522250756	0.248128841	0.690915173		
29	12	0.523626819	0.248782628	0.659748234		
30	13	0.524285964	0.249095797	0.6291226		
31	14	0.524600359	0.249245171	0.599523677		
32	15	0.52475001	0.249316272	0.571137811		
33	16	0.524821175	0.249350084	0.54401454		
34	17	0.524855001	0.249366155	0.518142478		
35	18	0.524871075	0.249373792	0.49348414		
36	19	0.524878713	0.249377421	0.469991734		
37						
38						
39						
40						
41						
42						
43						
44						
45						
46						
47						
48						
49						
50						
51						
52						

Spreadsheet S2.5

2.6 OPTIMAL ESCAPEMENT IN A FINITE-HORIZON
DETERMINISTIC MODEL

In Exercise E1.2, you set up a spreadsheet to simulate the fish stock, harvest, and discounted net revenue under a target escapement policy. Recall that *escapement* was defined as $S_t \equiv X_t - Y_t$, and under an S^* policy, $Y_t = \max[0, \ X_t - S^*]$, and $S_t = \min[X_t, \ S^*]$. The fish stock evolved according to the iterative equation $X_{t+1} = (1 - m)S_t + rS_t(1 - S_t/K)$, and as in Exercise E1.1, net revenue was given

	A	B	C	D	E
1	S2.6 The Optimal Level of Escapement				
2					
3	$m =$	0.1			
4	$r =$	0.5			
5	$K =$	300,000,000			
6	$p =$	5			
7	$c =$	20			
8	$\delta =$	0.05			
9	$\rho =$	0.952380952			
10	$X(0) =$	100,000,000			
11	$S^* =$	115,673,319		$\pi =$	$908,139,691
12					
13					
14	t	X_t	Y_t	S_t	$(\rho^{\wedge}t)^*\pi(t)$
15	0	100,000,000	0	100,000,000	$0
16	1	123,333,333	7,660,014	115,673,319	$31,945,306
17	2	139,642,119	23,968,800	115,673,319	$71,385,828
18	3	139,642,119	23,968,800	115,673,319	$67,986,503
19	4	139,642,119	23,968,800	115,673,319	$64,749,051
20	5	139,642,119	23,968,800	115,673,319	$61,665,762
21	6	139,642,119	23,968,800	115,673,319	$58,729,298
22	7	139,642,119	23,968,800	115,673,319	$55,932,664
23	8	139,642,119	23,968,800	115,673,319	$53,269,204
24	9	139,642,119	23,968,800	115,673,319	$50,732,575
25	10	139,642,119	23,968,800	115,673,319	$48,316,738
26	11	139,642,119	23,968,800	115,673,319	$46,015,941
27	12	139,642,119	23,968,800	115,673,319	$43,824,706
28	13	139,642,119	23,968,800	115,673,319	$41,737,815
29	14	139,642,119	23,968,800	115,673,319	$39,750,300
30	15	139,642,119	23,968,800	115,673,319	$37,857,429
31	16	139,642,119	23,968,800	115,673,319	$36,054,694
32	17	139,642,119	23,968,800	115,673,319	$34,337,804
33	18	139,642,119	23,968,800	115,673,319	$32,702,670
34	19	139,642,119	23,968,800	115,673,319	$31,145,400

Spreadsheet S2.6

by the equation $\pi_t = pY_t - (c/2)(Y_t^2/X_t)$. In Exercise E1.2, you simulated the fish stock, harvest, and discounted net revenue for an arbitrary target escapement policy where $S^* = 150$ million (metric tons). We can now ask Solver if there is a better target escapement policy, one that maximizes $\pi = \sum_{t=0}^{19} \rho^t \pi_t$. In Spreadsheet E1.2, when $S^* = 150$ million, $\pi = \$844,706,277$. In Spreadsheet S2.6, we have asked Solver to maximize the value of discounted net revenue in cell E11 by changing the value of S^* in cell B11. The optimal level for escapement in this problem is $S^* = 115,673,319$, yielding a discounted net revenue of $\pi = \$908,139,691$.

2.7 OPTIMAL ESCAPEMENT FOR ONE REALIZATION (SEED 1) OF Z_{t+1}

In Exercise E1.3, the iterative equation describing the evolution in the fish stock was made stochastic with $X_{t+1} = z_{t+1}[(1 - m)S_t + rS_t(1 - S_t/K)]$, where the z_{t+1} were *i.i.d.* random variables drawn from a uniform distribution with $b > z_{t+1} > a$. A column with 19 random draws for z_{t+1} was added to Spreadsheet E1.2 using Excel's random number generator when $b = 1.4$ and $a = 0.6$. The specific values of z_{t+1} are also called a *realization*, and each realization is associated with a random seed number, in this case random seed 1. The target escapement level was set at $S^* = 150$ million, and for the realization with random seed 1, the discounted net revenue was $\pi = \$444,681,909$. We now ask Solver to find the best escapement level for this realization. The results are shown in Spreadsheet S2.7, *where we started from an initial guess of $S^* = 70$ million.* After selecting "Solver" from the Tools menu, we specify cell $\$E\$11$ as the "Set Target Cell" to be maximized by changing the value of escapement in cell $\$B\$11$. After clicking the "Solve" button, Solver quickly finds the escapement level that maximizes discounted net revenue to be $S^* = 111,798,693$, resulting in $\pi = \$468,365,302$. *Note:* $\pi(X_t, S_t) = p(X_t - S_t) - (c/2)(X_t - S_t)^2/X_t$ is nonlinear in S_t, and depending on the realization, π may have one or more *local maxima*. For random seed 1, if you start with an initial guess of $S^* = 150$ million, Solver converges to a local maximum at $S^* = 157,594,871$, with $\pi^* = \$448,995,321$. Starting from $S^* = 70$ million, Solver will converge to the global maximum $S^* = 111,798,693$, with

	A	B	C	D	E	F
1	S2.7 Optimal Escapement for One Realization (Seed #1) of $z(t+1)$					
2						
3	$m =$	0.1				
4	$r =$	0.5				
5	$K =$	300,000,000				
6	$p =$	5				
7	$c =$	20				
8	$\delta =$	0.05				
9	$\rho =$	0.952380952				
10	$X(0) =$	100,000,000				
11	$S^* =$	111,798,693		$\pi =$	$468,365,302	
12						
13						
14	t	X_t		Y_t	S_t	$(\rho^t)^*\pi(t)$	$z(t+1)$
15	0	100,000,000	0	100,000,000	$0	
16	1	124,701,905	12,903,212	111,798,693	$48,728,373	1.01109653
17	2	100,486,838	0	100,486,838	$0	0.740580462
18	3	104,891,316	0	104,891,316	$0	0.846906949
19	4	132,061,020	20,262,327	111,798,693	$57,772,499	1.027625355
20	5	184,276,527	72,477,834	111,798,693	$60,587,313	1.35810419
21	6	100,052,866	0	100,052,866	$0	0.737382122
22	7	143,352,291	31,553,598	111,798,693	$62,763,572	1.161784722
23	8	105,989,336	0	105,989,336	$0	0.781133457
24	9	129,119,258	17,320,565	111,798,693	$40,847,795	0.99581286
25	10	94,947,900	0	94,947,900	$0	0.699758904
26	11	78,654,271	0	78,654,271	$0	0.667116306
27	12	90,992,745	0	90,992,745	$0	0.911703848
28	13	93,346,767	0	93,346,767	$0	0.821784112
29	14	103,900,932	0	103,900,932	$0	0.894442579
30	15	176,769,778	64,971,085	111,798,693	$41,394,686	1.386767174
31	16	139,527,738	27,729,045	111,798,693	$38,269,678	1.028308969
32	17	164,525,840	52,727,147	111,798,693	$41,298,132	1.212543107
33	18	151,586,192	39,787,499	111,798,693	$39,268,981	1.117178869
34	19	164,684,853	52,886,160	111,798,693	$37,434,272	1.213715018
35						
36						
37						
38		X_t Under an S^* Policy in a Stochastic Environment				
39	200,000,000					
40						
41	150,000,000					
42						
43	100,000,000					
44						
45	50,000,000					
46						
47	0					
48		1 2 3 4 5 6 7 8 9 10 11 12 13 14 15 16 17 18 19 20				
49		t				
50						
51						
52						

Spreadsheet S2.7

π = \$468,365,302. As a rule of thumb, if you are unsure about the existence of local maxima, it is wise to run Solver from a wide range of initial guesses to make sure that it converges to the same maximum. You also can plot $\pi(S)$ to see if it has a single peak.

2.8 AN OPTIMAL DEPLETION PROBLEM: THE MINE MANAGER'S PROBLEM

In the preceding three sections we asked Solver to maximize discounted net revenue by changing a single policy parameter α or S^*. It is also possible to ask Solver to optimize a cell by changing a column or vector of variables. The vector of variables might correspond to a harvest or extraction schedule. We will start with an optimal depletion problem known as the *mine manager's problem*.

This problem assumes that you are extracting a nonrenewable resource in foreign country under a concession that will expire in $T = 10$. The probability of an extension or renewal of the concession is viewed as zero. The current period is $t = 0$, and you are trying to maximize discounted net revenue over the interval $t = 0, 1, 2, \ldots, 9$, where net revenue in period t is given by $\pi_t = pq_t - (c/2)(q_t^2/R_t)$, where $q_t \geq 0$ is the rate of extraction and $R_t \geq 0$ are remaining reserves in period t, $p > 0$ is the fixed unit price for q_t over the life of the concession, and $c > 0$ is a cost parameter. Remaining reserves in $t = 0$ have been normalized so that $R_0 = 1$, and they evolve according to the iterative equation $R_{t+1} = R_t - q_t$. This allows us to interpret $q_t \geq 0$ as the fraction of initial reserves extracted in period t. A mathematical statement of the mine manager's problem would look as follows:

$$\text{Maximize}_{\{q_t\}_{t=0}^{t=9}} \pi = \sum_{t=0}^{t=9} \rho^t [pq_t - (c/2)(q_t^2/R_t)]$$

$$\text{Subject to } R_{t+1} = R_t - q_t, R_t \geq q_t, R_0 = 1, R_{10} \geq 0$$

We will use Solver to find the optimal extraction schedule $\{q_t\}_{t=0}^{t=9}$ when $p = 1$, $c = 4$, and $\delta = 0.05$. In Spreadsheet S2.8a, we provide an arbitrary guess of $q_t = 0.1$ for $t = 0, 1, 2, \ldots, 9$. Note that in $t = 9$ you actually incur a negative present value of $\rho^9 \pi_9 = -0.0644609$, so we might guess that Solver should be able to increase the sum of discounted net revenues above the level $\pi = 0.38220163$ that results

	A	B	C	D	E
1	S2.8a The Initial Spreadsheet for the Mine Manager's Problem				
2					
3	$p =$	1			
4	$c =$	4			
5	$\delta =$	0.05			
6	$\rho =$	0.952380952			
7	$R_o =$	1			
8					
9	t	q_t	R_t	$(\rho{\wedge}t)^*\pi t$	
10	0	0.1	1	0.08	
11	1	0.1	0.9	0.074074074	
12	2	0.1	0.8	0.068027211	
13	3	0.1	0.7	0.061702686	
14	4	0.1	0.6	0.054846832	
15	5	0.1	0.5	0.04701157	
16	6	0.1	0.4	0.03731077	
17	7	0.1	0.3	0.023689378	
18	8	0.1	0.2	3.75721E-17	
19	9	0.1	0.1	−0.06446089	
20	10		0.00000000		
21					
22			$\pi =$	0.382201628	
23					
24					
25					
26			A Plot of q^*t and R^*t		
27	1.5				
28					
29	1				
30					
31	0.5				
32					
33	0				
34	0 2 4 6 8 10 12				
35	t				
36					
37					
38					

Spreadsheet S2.8a

	A	B	C	D	E
1	S2.8b The Optimized Spreadsheet for the Mine Manager's Problem				
2					
3	$p =$	1			
4	$c =$	4			
5	$\delta =$	0.05			
6	$\rho =$	0.952380952			
7	$R_o =$	1			
8					
9	t	q_t	R_t	$(\rho^{\wedge}t)^*\pi t$	
10	0	0.13628961	1	0.099139894	
11	1	0.121325353	0.86371039	0.083085925	
12	2	0.108085219	0.742385038	0.069489853	
13	3	0.096356429	0.634299818	0.057947466	
14	4	0.085946282	0.537943389	0.04811436	
15	5	0.076679823	0.451997108	0.039695679	
16	6	0.068395363	0.375317285	0.032436131	
17	7	0.060941731	0.306921922	0.026111017	
18	8	0.054174171	0.245980191	0.020516189	
19	9	0.047951519	0.19180602	0.015454984	
20	10		0.14385450		
21					
22			$\pi =$	0.491991498	
23					
24					
25					
26			A Plot of q^*t and R^*t		
27		1.5			
28					
29		1			
30					
31		0.5			
32					
33		0			
34		0 2 4 6 8 10 12			
35		t			
36					
37					
38					

Spreadsheet S2.8b

$$\frac{p}{(c - \delta^* q_t)}$$

from our initial guess for $\{q_t\}_{t=0}^{t=9}$. We then call up Solver and ask it to maximize the value in cell $D$22 by changing the values in the cells $B$10:$B$19. We also specify a single constraint that $C$20 \geq 0$. This says that $R_{10} \geq 0$. Click the "Solve" button, and Solver converges to a "current solution" on its first run. Run Solver again using the current solution as the new initial guess, and Solver comes up with the optimal solution shown in Spreadsheet S2.8*b*.

Now the extraction rate starts at $q_0 = 0.13628961$ and declines to $q_9 = 0.04795152$. Because the cost of extraction goes to infinity as remaining reserves go to zero (and price is assumed constant at $p = 1$), it is optimal to abandon $R_{10} = 0.14385450$ because the marginal extraction cost equals the marginal value on extraction. The Lagrangian for the mine manager's problem may be written

$$L = \sum_{t=0}^{t=9} \rho^t[pq_t - (c/2)(q_t^2/R_t) + \rho\lambda_{t+1}(R_t - q_t - R_{t+1})] \qquad (2.9)$$

and the $\partial L/\partial q_t = 0$ in $t = 9$ implies $p - c(q_9/R_9) = \rho\lambda_{10}$. From the mine manager's point of view, however, remaining reserves *after* period $t = 9$ have a shadow value of zero, so $\lambda_{10} = 0$, and $q_9/R_9 = p/c = 0.25$, which is the ratio that Solver adopts in its optimal extraction schedule.

2.9 APPROXIMATING THE ASYMPTOTIC APPROACH TO A BIOECONOMIC OPTIMUM

It is sometimes possible to approximate the asymptotic approach to a bioeconomic optimum in an *infinite-horizon problem* by specifying the "correct" *final function* in a *finite-horizon problem*. I will illustrate such a final function for a simple fishery model that allows analytic expressions for optimal steady-state biomass X^* and optimal steady-state harvest Y^*.

Consider a country where some residents enjoy eating whales and some residents enjoy observing whales. The net-benefit function for this country might take the form $\pi(X_t, Y_t) = \ln(Y_t) + \beta \ln(X_t)$, where $\ln(\bullet)$ is the natural log operator. The net benefit to consumers of whale meat is given by $\ln(Y_t)$, whereas the net benefit of whale watchers is given by $\ln(X_t)$ and $\beta \geq 0$ is a parameter weighting the welfare of whale watchers relative to consumers of whale meat.

Suppose that the evolution of the whale stock is given by the difference equation $X_{t+1} - X_t = rX_t(1 - X_t/K) - Y_t$, implying that $F(X_t) = rX_t(1 - X_t/K)$. Recall that the fundamental equation of renewable resources required $F'(X) + [\partial\pi(\bullet)/\partial X]/[\partial\pi(\bullet)/\partial Y] = \delta$, and with $Y = F(X)$, we had a two-equation system whose solution was the steady-state bioeconomic optimum $[X^*, Y^*]$. With these functional forms for $\pi(X, Y)$ and $F(X)$, we have $F'(X) = r(1 - 2X/K)$, $\partial\pi(\bullet)/\partial X = \beta/X$, and $\partial\pi(\bullet)/\partial Y = 1/Y$. With $Y = rX(1 - X/K)$, the fundamental equation requires $r(1 - 2X/K) + \beta r(1 - X/K) = \delta$, which can be solved for X^* yielding

$$X^* = \frac{K[r(1+\beta) - \delta]}{r(\beta + 2)} \tag{2.10}$$

When $r = 1$, $K = 1$, $\beta = 4$, and $\delta = 0.02$, Equation (2.10) implies that $X^* = 0.83$ and then $Y^* = 0.1411$. These are the steady-state values for stock and harvest at the bioeconomic optimum. In an infinite-horizon problem where $X_0 \neq X^*$, the approach would be asymptotic because the necessary conditions for a most rapid approach path (MRAP) are *not* met. Can we construct a finite-horizon problem that Solver can solve that would approximate the approach from X_0 to X^*?

Consider the finite-horizon problem

$$\underset{\{Y_t\}_{t=0}^{t=19}}{\text{Maximize}} \ \pi = \sum_{t=0}^{t=19} \rho^t[\ln(Y_t) + \beta \ln(X_t)]$$

$$+ \rho^{19}\{\ln[rX_{20}(1 - X_{20}/K)] + \beta \ln(X_{20})\}/\delta$$

Subject to $X_{t+1} = (1 + r - rX_t/K)X_t - Y_t, X_0 = 0.1$

The objective function is the sum of the discounted net benefits over the interval $t = 0, 1, 2, \ldots, 19$ and a final function $\psi(X_{20}) = \rho^{19}\{\ln[rX_{20}(1 - X_{20}/K)] + \beta \ln(X_{20})\}/\delta$. We want the final function to represent the discounted value of maintaining X_{20} forever by harvesting $Y = rX_{20}(1 - X_{20}/K)$ forever, beginning in $t = 20$. The net benefit in each period $t = 20, 21, \ldots, \infty$ is $\pi(X_{20}) = \ln[rX_{20}(1 - X_{20}/K)] + \beta \ln(X_{20})$. What is the present value of maintaining X_{20} by harvesting $Y = rX_{20}(1 - X_{20}/K)$ forever? Mathematically, it would be calculated as $\psi(X_{20}) = \sum_{t=20}^{\infty} \rho^t \pi(X_{20})$. Now for a critical observation. For a given choice (fixed value for) X_{20}, $\pi(X_{20})$ is a constant and can be moved outside the summation operator so that

$$\psi(X_{20}) = \pi(X_{20}) \sum_{t=20}^{\infty} \rho^t = \pi(X_{20})\rho^{20} \sum_{t=0}^{\infty} \rho^t = \pi(X_{20})\rho^{20} \left[\frac{1}{(1-\rho)}\right]$$

$$= \pi(X_{20})\rho^{20} \left[\frac{(1+\delta)}{\delta}\right] = \rho^{19}\pi(X_{20})/\delta$$

(2.11)

Note that the last expression for $\psi(X_{20})$ in Equation (2.11) is the same as the expression for the final function in the mathematical statement of our finite-horizon optimization problem. Larger values of X_{20} may allow for larger values for $\pi(X_{20})$, which, in turn, may increase $\psi(X_{20})$, thus giving Solver an incentive to carefully consider the levels it chooses for Y_t over the interval $t = 0, 1, 2, \ldots, 19$ because they will influence X_{20}. Let's see if Solver behaves optimally.

In Spreadsheet S2.9, we enter the parameter values, the expression for ρ, and the initial condition in cells \$B\$3:\$B\$8. In cells \$B\$10:\$B\$11, we program

$$X^* = \frac{K[r(1+\beta) - \delta]}{r(\beta + 2)} \quad \text{and} \quad Y^* = rX^*(1 - X^*/K)$$

We then set up columns for t, Y_t, X_t, and $\rho^t\pi_t$. Under the label Y_t, we place a guess for the optimal harvest and for simplicity set $Y_t = 0.05$ for $t = 0, 1, 2, \ldots, 19$. In cell D14, we program $= (\$B\$7^\wedge A14) * (LN(B14) + \$B\$5 * LN(C14))$. In cell C15, we program $= (1 + \$B\$3 - \$B\$3 * C14/\$B\$4) * C14 - B14$. We can fill down from cell C15 through cell C34 and from cell D14 through cell D33. In cell D34, we program the final function $= (\$B\$7^\wedge\$A\$33) * (LN(\$B\$3 * \$C\$34 * (1 - \$C\$34/\$B\$4)) + \$B\$5 * LN(\$C\$34))/\$B\$6$. In cell D36, the set target cell, we program $= SUM(\$D\$14:\$D\$34)$. We then highlight the values for t, Y_t, and X_t, do a line-scatter plot, and place it at the bottom of the spreadsheet. This initial version is shown as Spreadsheet S2.9a. As an exercise, program your own version of Spreadsheet S2.9.

We now call up Solver, specifying \$D\$36 as the set target cell to be maximized by changing cells \$B\$14:\$B\$33. The natural log operators in the objective function will cause Solver to crash if Y_t or X_t become negative, so we need to bound Y_t away from zero. We do this by adding the constraint \$B\$14:\$B\$33 $> = 0.0001$.

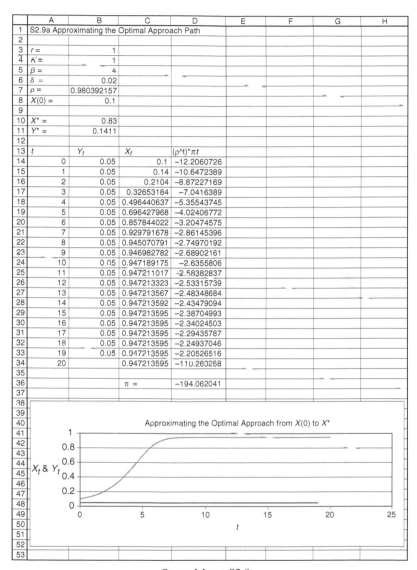

	A	B	C	D	E	F	G	H
1	S2.9a Approximating the Optimal Approach Path							
2								
3	$r =$	1						
4	$K =$	1						
5	$\beta =$	4						
6	$\delta =$	0.02						
7	$\rho =$	0.980392157						
8	$X(0) =$	0.1						
9								
10	$X^* =$	0.83						
11	$Y^* =$	0.1411						
12								
13	t	Y_t	X_t	$(\rho^t)^*\pi t$				
14	0	0.05	0.1	−12.2060726				
15	1	0.05	0.14	−10.6472389				
16	2	0.05	0.2104	−8.87227169				
17	3	0.05	0.32653184	−7.0416389				
18	4	0.05	0.496440637	−5.35543745				
19	5	0.05	0.696427968	−4.02406772				
20	6	0.05	0.857844022	−3.20474575				
21	7	0.05	0.929791678	−2.86145396				
22	8	0.05	0.945070791	−2.74970192				
23	9	0.05	0.946982782	−2.68902161				
24	10	0.05	0.947189175	−2.6355806				
25	11	0.05	0.947211017	−2.58382837				
26	12	0.05	0.947213323	−2.53315739				
27	13	0.05	0.947213567	−2.48348684				
28	14	0.05	0.947213592	−2.43479094				
29	15	0.05	0.947213595	−2.38704993				
30	16	0.05	0.947213595	−2.34024503				
31	17	0.05	0.947213595	−2.29435787				
32	18	0.05	0.947213595	−2.24937046				
33	19	0.05	0.947213595	−2.20526516				
34	20		0.947213595	−110.263258				
35								
36			$\pi =$	−194.062041				
37								
38								
39								
40								
41								
42								
43								
44								
45								
46								
47								
48								
49								
50								
51								
52								
53								

Spreadsheet S2.9a

It will turn out that this constraint will not be binding at Solver's solution, but it is needed during Solver's search. Run Solver three times. After the third time, Solver reports that it has converged to a solution and all constraints are satisfied. The optimized version is Spreadsheet S2.9*b*.

	A	B	C	D	E	F	G	H
1	S2.9b Approximating the Optimal Approach Path							
2								
3	r =	1						
4	K =	1						
5	β =	4						
6	δ=	0.02						
7	ρ =	0.980392157						
8	X(0) =	0.1						
9								
10	X* =	0.83						
11	Y* =	0.1411						
12								
13	t	Y_t	X_t	$(\rho\wedge t)^*\pi t$				
14	0	0.011094679	0.1	−13.71163				
15	1	0.02360223	0.178905321	−10.4215767				
16	2	0.04655084	0.302201297	−7.5488831				
17	3	0.079996014	0.46652613	−5.25395912				
18	4	0.112955192	0.635409616	−3.69049065				
19	5	0.13198444	0.75411866	−2.85657846				
20	6	0.138697943	0.807557927	−2.51333085				
21	7	0.140511295	0.824268106	−2.38142183				
22	8	0.140958539	0.828607007	−2.31409119			.	
23	9	0.141066045	0.829665902	−2.26380442				
24	10	0.141091873	0.82992025	−2.2182601				
25	11	0.141098025	0.829981006	−2.17449424				
26	12	0.141099575	0.829995516	−2.13179329				
27	13	0.141099965	0.8299989	−2.08997868				
28	14	0.141099943	0.829999661	−2.04899605				
29	15	0.141099967	0.829999942	−2.00881852				
30	16	0.141099861	0.830000013	−1.96943022				
31	17	0.141100044	0.830000143	−1.93081257				
32	18	0.141100291	0.830000005	−1.89295274				
33	19	0.141099841	0.829999711	−1.85583918				
34	20		0.83000006	−92.7918723				
35								
36			π =	−166.069014				
37								
38								
39								
40			Approximating the Optimal Approach from X(0) to X*					

Approximating the Optimal Approach from X(0) to X*

Spreadsheet S2.9b

In comparing the initial spreadsheet with the optimized spreadsheet, Solver starts with very low harvest rates ($Y_0 = 0.01109468$) because the initial stock ($X_0 = 0.1$) is so low compared with the steady-state optimal stock ($X^* = 0.83$). In the optimized spreadsheet, we see that Solver, though ignorant of our analytic solution for X^*, selects harvest rates that approximate the optimal asymptotic approach from $X_0 = 0.1$ to $X^* = 0.83$. Because the values for Y_t and X_t are positive but less than one, the values for π in both the initial and optimized spreadsheets are negative. This is the result of the natural log operators in the objective function. Note in comparing the initial spreadsheet to the optimized spreadsheet that $-166.06901 > -194.06204$. We could have added a constant to the objective function, say, 200. The optimal solution would not change, but the optimized objective function would have the value $\pi = 200 - 166.06901 = 33.93099$.

2.10 THE MOST RAPID APPROACH PATH TO
AN OPTIMAL POLLUTION STOCK

To illustrate the most rapid approach path, consider an economy seeking to manage a stock pollutant. The stock pollutant Z_t changes according to the first-order difference equation $Z_{t+1} - Z_t = -\gamma Z_t + \alpha Q_t$, where Q_t is the output of the economy in period t that also results in a waste flow of $\alpha Q_t, 1 > \alpha > 0$. In each period, a portion of the stock pollutant degrades into harmless components at a rate given by $-\gamma Z_t$. Let's suppose that the economy exports Q_t at a per-unit price of $p > 0$ but must endure the damage caused by the stock pollutant. Suppose that the damage in period t is given by the function $D(Z_t) = (c/2)Z_t^2$, where $c > 0$. These assumptions lead to a net-benefit function given by $\pi(Q_t, Z_t) = pQ_t - (c/2)Z_t^2$.

Solving the state equation for Q_t yields $Q_t = [Z_{t+1} - (1 - \gamma)Z_t]/\alpha$. Substituting this expression into the net-benefit function and doing a bit of algebra yields $\pi(Z_t, Z_{t+1}) = -[(p/\alpha)(1 - \gamma)Z_t + (c/2)Z_t^2] + (p/\alpha)Z_{t+1}$. We see that our original net-benefit function is additively separable in Z_t and Z_{t+1}. The relevant component functions are $M(Z) = -[(p/\alpha)(1 - \gamma)Z + (c/2)Z^2]$ and $N(Z) = (p/\alpha)Z$. The stationary value function is given by $V(Z) = M(Z) + (1 + \delta)N(Z) = (p/\alpha)(\delta + \gamma)Z - (c/2)Z^2$. We also see that $V(Z)$ is a strictly concave quadratic in Z. (A strictly concave function is quasi-concave but *not* vice versa.) Thus, for our simple economy, there is an optimal pollution stock Z^*, and if $Z_0 \neq Z^*$, it is optimal to go from Z_0 to Z^* as rapidly as possible. As noted in Chapter 1, the MRAP will involve setting Q_t at either an upper or lower bound until Z_t reaches Z^*. Suppose that $Q_{\max} \geq Q_t \geq 0$, so that $Q_{\max}$ is the upper bound on Q_t, whereas zero is the lower bound. In this example, the optimal setting for Q_t along the MRAP requires

$$Q_t^* = \begin{cases} Q_{\max} & \text{if } Z_t < Z^* \\ (\gamma/\alpha)Z^* & \text{if } Z_t = Z^* \\ 0 & \text{if } Z_t > Z^* \end{cases} \qquad (2.12)$$

Note that to maintain $Z_t = Z^*, \alpha Q^* = \gamma Z^*$ or $Q^* = (\gamma/\alpha)Z^*$.

What is the optimal pollution stock? Given that we have derived the expression for $V(Z)$, we can solve for Z^* by finding the value of Z that satisfies $V'(Z) = 0$. In this case, $V'(Z) = (p/\alpha)(\delta + \gamma) - cZ = 0$, implying that $Z^* = [p(\delta + \gamma)]/(\alpha c)$.

Let's suppose that in its desire to generate export earnings, our economy allowed the stock pollutant to accumulate to an excessive level so that at $t = 0, Z_0 > Z^*$. With $Z_0 > Z^*$, it is optimal for the economy to discontinue production, $Q_t^* = 0$, until the stock pollutant decays down to Z^*. In numerical examples, in the last period before reaching Z^*, say, in period $\tau - 1$, $Q_{\tau-1}^*$ might assume a value *between* $Q_{\max}$ and zero if to do otherwise would result in *overshooting* Z^* in period τ.

In Spreadsheet S2.10, we solve a numerical example where $\alpha = 0.5$, $c = 0.48$, $\delta = 0.02$, $\gamma = 0.1$, $p = 2$, $Q_{\max} = 10$, and $Q_{\min} = 0$. In cell B11, we program $= \$B\$8 * (\$B\$5 + \$B\$7)/(\$B\$3 * \$B\$4)$, which returns $Z^* = 1$. In cell B12, we program $= (\$B\$7/\$B\$3) * \$B\$11$, which is the steady-state relationship $Q^* = (\gamma/\alpha)Z^* = 0.2$. In cell B13, we do a bit of rigging. To give you a neat, clean numerical example, we want to specify a value for $Z_0 > Z^*$ that will decay to Z^* in, say, $t = 7$. If this is what we want, for sake of exposition, then $Z_0 = Z^*/[(1 - \gamma)^7]$, and in cell B13, we program $= \$B\$11/((1 - \$B\$7)^{\wedge}7$.

We now want to see if Solver will agree with Spence and Starrett that this is a MRAP problem with $Z_0 = 2.09075158$ and that it is optimal to set $Q_t^* = 0$ for $t = 0, 1, \ldots, 6$, at which point $Z_7 = Z^* = 1$ and $Q_t^* = (\gamma/\alpha)Z^* = 0.2$ for $t \geq 7$. In cells A17, B17, C17, and D17, place the labels t, Q_t, Z_t, and $\rho^t \pi_t$, respectively. Below the label t we use a series fill-down to create a 21-period finite horizon. In cells B18:B37, we entered a column of zeros as our initial guess for the optimal values Q_t^*. In cell C18, we program $= \$B\$13$. In cell D18, we program $= (\$B\$6^{\wedge}A18) * (\$B\$8 * B18 - (\$B\$4/2) * (C18^{\wedge}2))$, and in cell C19, we program the Excel version of $Z_1, = (1 - \$B\$7) * C18 + \$B\$3 * B18$. We do a one-cell fill-down from cell D18 to cell D19, then a fill-down from

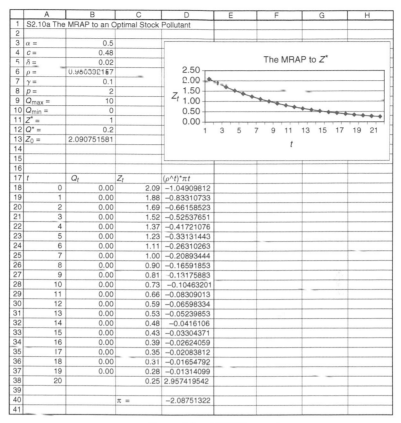

The table within the spreadsheet image:

	A	B	C	D	E	F	G	H
1	S2.10a The MRAP to an Optimal Stock Pollutant							
2								
3	$\alpha =$	0.5						
4	$c =$	0.48						
5	$\delta =$	0.02						
6	$\rho =$	0.980392157						
7	$\gamma =$	0.1						
8	$p =$	2						
9	$Q_{max} =$	10						
10	$Q_{min} =$	0						
11	$Z^* =$	1						
12	$Q^* =$	0.2						
13	$Z_0 =$	2.090751581						
14								
15								
16								
17	t	Q_t	Z_t	$(\rho^\wedge t)^*\pi t$				
18	0	0.00	2.09	−1.04909812				
19	1	0.00	1.88	−0.83310733				
20	2	0.00	1.69	−0.66158523				
21	3	0.00	1.52	−0.52537651				
22	4	0.00	1.37	−0.41721076				
23	5	0.00	1.23	−0.33131443				
24	6	0.00	1.11	−0.26310263				
25	7	0.00	1.00	−0.20893444				
26	8	0.00	0.90	−0.16591853				
27	9	0.00	0.81	−0.13175883				
28	10	0.00	0.73	−0.10463201				
29	11	0.00	0.66	−0.08309013				
30	12	0.00	0.59	−0.06598334				
31	13	0.00	0.53	−0.05239853				
32	14	0.00	0.48	−0.0416106				
33	15	0.00	0.43	−0.03304371				
34	16	0.00	0.39	−0.02624059				
35	17	0.00	0.35	−0.02083812				
36	18	0.00	0.31	−0.01654792				
37	19	0.00	0.28	−0.01314099				
38	20		0.25	2.957419542				
39								
40			$\pi =$	−2.08751322				
41								

Spreadsheet S2.10a

cells C19:D19 through cells C37:D37, and then a one-cell fill-down from cell C37 to cell C38.

Finally, we need to approximate the solution to an infinite-horizon problem on a finite-horizon spreadsheet. As in Section 2.9, when approximating the asymptotic approach from X_0 to X^*, we program the appropriate final function, which for this problem, in cell D38, is

= ((B6$^\wedge$A37)/$B$5) * ($B$8 * ($B$7/$B$3) * C38 − ($B$4/2) * (C38$^\wedge$2)). This final function is based on the following algebra:

$$\pi(Z_{20}) = \sum_{t=20}^{\infty} \rho^t [p(\gamma/\alpha)Z_{20} - (c/2)Z_{20}^2]$$

$$= \rho^{20}[p(\gamma/\alpha)Z_{20} - (c/2)Z_{20}^2]\sum_{t=0}^{\infty} \rho^t \qquad (2.13)$$

	A	B	C	D	E	F	G	H
1	S2.10b The MRAP to an Optimal Stock Pollutant							
2								
3	$\alpha =$	0.5						
4	$c =$	0.48						
5	$\delta =$	0.02						
6	$\rho =$	0.980392157						
7	$\gamma =$	0.1						
8	$p =$	2						
9	$Q_{max} =$	10						
10	$Q_{min} =$	0						
11	$Z^* =$	1						
12	$Q^* =$	0.2						
13	$Z_0 =$	2.090751581						
14								
15								
16								
17	t	Q_t	Z_t	$(\rho\wedge t)^*\pi t$				
18	0	0.00	2.09	-1.04909812				
19	1	0.00	1.88	-0.83310733				
20	2	0.00	1.69	-0.66158523				
21	3	0.00	1.52	-0.52537651				
22	4	0.00	1.37	-0.41721076				
23	5	0.00	1.23	-0.33131443				
24	6	0.00	1.11	-0.2607039				
25	7	0.20	1.00	0.139007329				
26	8	0.20	1.00	0.13630938				
27	9	0.20	1.00	0.130916504				
28	10	0.20	1.00	0.126110334				
29	11	0.20	1.00	0.129069957				
30	12	0.20	1.00	0.129939589				
31	13	0.20	1.00	0.126501059				
32	14	0.20	1.00	0.121120313				
33	15	0.20	1.00	0.116770017				
34	16	0.20	1.00	0.114758429				
35	17	0.20	1.00	0.114060169				
36	18	0.20	1.00	0.112504892				
37	19	0.20	1.00	0.11197823				
38	20		1.00	5.492322892				
39								
40			$\pi =$	3.022972818				

Spreadsheet S2.10b

$$= \rho^{20}[p(\gamma/\alpha)Z_{20} - (c/2)Z_{20}^2][(1+\delta)/\delta]$$
$$= \rho^{19}[p(\gamma/\alpha)Z_{20} - (c/2)Z_{20}^2]/\delta$$

The final function tells Solver that whatever it ultimately selects for Z_{20}, via its choices for Q_t^* for $t = 0, 1, \ldots, 19$, it must maintain Z_{20} forever by setting $Q_t = (\gamma/\alpha)Z_{20}$ for $t \geq 20$. This gives Solver a strong incentive to select the Q_t^*, for $19 \geq t \geq 0$, so as to have $Z_{20} \approx Z^*$. In cell D40, we program = SUM(\$D\$18:\$D\$38).

We now call up Solver. In the "Parameter" box, we tell Solver that we want to maximize \$D\$40 by changing \$B\$18:\$B\$37 subject to the constraints \$B\$18:\$B\$37<=\$B\$9 and \$B\$18:\$B\$37>=\$B\$10. When we click "OK" in the Solver "Parameter" box, Solver searches for the optimal Q_t. Remember, initially we entered a guess that $Q_t^* = 0$ for $t = 0, 1, \ldots, 19$. Also, Solver knows nothing about Spence and Starrett's Proposition 4, MRAP problems, and the fact that we previously calculated $Z^* = 1$ and $Q^* = 0.2$. Nonetheless, Solver converges to the solution shown in the optimized version in Spreadsheet S2.10a, which is the MRAP to the values for Z^* and Q^* that we expected, based on our analytic expressions.

2.11 OPTIMAL ESCAPEMENT WITH STOCHASTIC GROWTH

I conclude this chapter by returning to Spreadsheet S2.7, where the fish stock in period $t + 1$ was a stochastic function of escapement. Recall in this example that $X_{t+1} = z_{t+1}[(1 - m)S_t + rS_t(1 - S_t/K)]$, $Y_t = \max[0, \ X_t - S^*], S_t = \min[X_t, \ S^*]$, and $\pi_t = pY_t - (c/2)(Y_t^2/X_t)$. In Spreadsheet S2.7 we sought the value of S^* that maximized $\pi = \sum_{t=0}^{t=19} \rho^t \pi_t$ for the first realization of z_{t+1} associated with random seed 1. The global maximum $\pi^* = \$468,365,302$ was obtained when $S^* = 111,798,693$. But this was but one realization of z_{t+1} from the uniform distribution $z_{t+1} \approx U(0.6, \ 1.4)$. What would be the optimal escapement level S^* for other realizations (random seeds)?

In Spreadsheet S2.11, I show the optimal S^* and the resulting π^* for random seeds 1 through 20. Basic descriptive statistics for S^* and π^* are also provided. We see that the optimal S^* ranges from a minimum of $S^* = 80,199,242$ to a maximum of $S^* = 177,326,739$ with a sample mean of $S^* = 122,175,505$ and median of $S^* = 118,249,798$. Optimized net revenue π^* ranges from $\pi^* = \$353,869,805$ to $\pi^* = \$958,865,391$ with an mean and median of $\pi^* = \$592,561,209$ and $\pi^* = \$551,963,021$, respectively.

Without advance knowledge of the realization for z_{t+1}, what is the optimal escapement level S^* for an infinite-horizon problem? Based on Spreadsheet S2.11, we might opt for a constant escapement policy using the sample mean $S^* = 122,175,505$ or the median $S^* = 118,249,798$ as the best constant escapement policy, assuming that we know that $z_{t+1} \approx U(0.6, \ 1.4)$. While perhaps intuitively appealing, this would not be the correct approach for the infinite-horizon problem with stochastic growth. The correct way to answer this question is with dynamic programming. This would require the development of numerical algorithms that would allow one to solve for the value function $V(X_t)$ and

	A	B	C	D	E	F
1	S2.11 Optimal Escapement for Random Seeds 1–20.					
2						
3	Seed #	S^*	π^*		S^* Descriptive Statistics	
4	1	111,798,693	$468,365,302		Mean	122,175,505
5	2	165,385,776	$767,963,955		Median	118,249,798
6	3	88,324,517	$539,786,995		$s =$	28,429,549
7	4	80,199,242	$353,869,805		$s^2 =$	8.08239E+14
8	5	177,326,739	$958,865,391		Range	97,127,497
9	6	91,683,648	$538,225,260		Minimum	80,199,242
10	7	160,237,735	$579,968,817		Maximum	177,326,739
11	8	109,673,998	$510,733,568			
12	9	113,461,901	$638,145,668		π^* Descriptive Statistics	
13	10	87,602,235	$465,229,028		Mean	$592,561,209
14	11	118,083,550	$564,139,047		Median	$551,963,021
15	12	118,416,047	$523,799,022		$s =$	$150,233,022
16	13	116,586,596	$479,303,222		$s^2 =$	2.26E+16
17	14	133,497,845	$698,582,339		Range	$604,995,586
18	15	122,163,209	$682,898,136		Minimum	$353,869,805
19	16	135,347,732	$739,762,452		Maximum	$958,865,391
20	17	87,128,311	$500,393,659			
21	18	132,958,371	$367,236,008			
22	19	128,063,622	$746,754,628			
23	20	165,570,331	$727,201,884			
24						

Optimal Escapement, S^*, for Random Seeds 1–20

Optimized π^* for Random Seeds 1–20

Spreadsheet S2.11

the optimal escapement policy $S_t = S(X_t)$, where optimal escapement may *not* be constant but rather may depend on the current stock size X_t.

This dynamic programming problem is beyond the scope of this text and the built-in features of Excel and Solver. We can, at least, write the Bellman equation corresponding to Equation (1.45) in Chapter 1 as

$$V(X_t) = \max_{S_t}\{p(X_t - S_t) - (c/2)[(X_t - S_t)^2/X_t] + \rho \underset{z_{t+1}}{E}[\, V(X_{t+1})]\}$$

(2.14)

where $X_{t+1} = z_{t+1}[(1 - m)S_t + rS_t(1 - S_t/K)]$, $Y_t = X_t - S_t \geq 0$. For a discussion of the numerical methods and a tool box of MATLAB utilities that might be used to solve such infinite-horizon dynamic programming problems, see Miranda and Fackler (2002).

2.12 EXERCISES

E2.1 We will see (in Chapter 4) that another possible specification of the volume function in even-aged plantation forestry is the cubic $Q(T) = aT + bT^2 - dT^3$, where T is the age at which the current stand is cut and the parcel is replanted. The present value of the recently replanted parcel, when it is cut and replanted every T years, is given by the expression $\pi = [p(aT + bT^2 - dT^3) - c]/(e^{\delta T} - 1)$, where a, b, and d are positive parameters of the volume function that are specific to the tree species being cultivated and where $p > 0$ is the net unit price for timber, $c > 0$ is the cost of replanting the parcel, and $\delta > 0$ is the discount rate. Verify that

$$\pi'(T) = \frac{p(a + 2bT - 3dT^2)(e^{\delta T} - 1)}{-\delta e^{\delta T}[p(aT + bT^2 - dT^3) - c]}{(e^{\delta T} - 1)^2}$$

For $a = 10$, $b = 1$, $d = 0.0025$, $p = 1$, $c = 150$, and $\delta = 0.05$, set up a spreadsheet and use Solver to maximize π by changing your initial guess for T. Numerically verify that the value of T that maximizes π also drives $\pi'(T)$ to zero.

E2.2 You will see in Chapter 3 that a fishery production function that might be appropriate when searching for schools of fish takes the form $Y = qX^\beta E$, where Y is harvest, X is the fish stock,

E is the level of fishing effort, $q > 0$ is the catchability coefficient, and $1 > \beta > 0$ is called the *catchability exponent.* Suppose
that total cost is proportional to effort and given by the cost
equation $C = cE$, where $c > 0$ is the unit cost of effort. Show
that $Y = qX^\beta E$ and $C = cE$ imply that the *fishery cost function* is
$C = (c/q)X^{-\beta}Y$. This allows us to write the net revenue function
as $\pi = [p - (c/q)X^{-\beta}]Y$. Suppose further that the net growth
function is given by the logistic form $F(X) = rX(1-X/K)$. Show
that the fundamental equation of renewable resources [Equation
(1.25)] leads to the implicit expression

$$G(X) = [r(1 - 2X/K) - \delta][pX^\beta - (c/q)] + \beta(c/q)r(1 - X/K)$$

It will be shown in Chapter 3 that when $\beta = 1$, $G(X) = 0$ will
imply an analytic solution for the optimal steady-state fish stock
given by the equation

$$X^*_{\beta=1} = \left(\frac{K}{4}\right)\left[\left(\frac{c}{pqK} + 1 - \frac{\delta}{r}\right) + \sqrt{\left(\frac{c}{pqK} + 1 - \frac{\delta}{r}\right)^2 + \frac{8c\delta}{pqKr}}\right]$$

When $\beta = 0$, the optimal steady-state fish stock also has an
analytic solution given by the equation

$$X^*_{\beta=0} = \frac{K(r - \delta)}{2r}$$

When $1 > \beta > 0$, $G(X) = 0$ at $X = X^*$ and $X^*_{\beta=1} > X^* > X^*_{\beta=0}$.
For $r = 1$, $K = 1$, $\delta = 0.02$, $p = 2$, $c = 0.42581$, $q = 1$, and
$\beta = 0.5$, set up a spreadsheet and use Solver to drive $G(X)$ to
zero. Also calculate $X^*_{\beta=1}$ and $X^*_{\beta=0}$.

E2.3 Consider the nonrenewable resource infinite-horizon problem

$$\underset{\{q_t\}_{t=0}^\infty}{\text{Maximize}} \sum_{t=0}^{\infty} \rho^t 2\sqrt{q_t}$$

$$\text{Subject to } R_{t+1} = R_t - q_t, R_0 = 1$$

This problem has the associated Lagrangian

$$L = \sum_{t=0}^{\infty} \rho^t[2\sqrt{q_t} + \rho\lambda_{t+1}(R_t - q_t - R_{t+1})]$$

I will show in Chapter 5 that this problem has an analytic solution
$q_t^* = [(\delta^2 + 2\delta)R_0]/(1+\delta)^{2(t+1)}$. Set up a spreadsheet with $\delta = 0.1$

and $R_0 = 1$, and calculate the values for q_t^* for $t = 0, 1, 2, \ldots, 49$. You should observe that when $\delta = 0.1$, the initial reserves $R_0 = 1$ are essentially depleted by $T = 50$. Now, on the same spreadsheet, set up new columns for q_t, R_t, and $\rho^t 2\sqrt{q_t}$. Use the values, to two decimals, from the analytic solution as an initial guess for Solver when it seeks to solve the finite-horizon problem

$$\underset{\{q_t\}_{t=0}^{49}}{\text{Maximize}} \sum_{t=0}^{49} \rho^t 2\sqrt{q_t}$$

$$\text{Subject to } R_{t+1} = R_t - q_t, R_0 = 1$$

Because Solver stops if $q_t < 0$, you may need to add the constraints that $R_t \geq q_t \geq 0$. Can Solver improve on the analytic solution to this problem?

E2.4 Consider the optimal escapement problem for salmon on a particular stream in Alaska. Suppose that $X_{t+1} = S_t e^{r(1-S_t/K)}$, where $S_t = \min[X_t, S^*]$ is escapement in period t, $Y_t = \max[0, X_t - S^*]$ is the level of allowed harvest in period t, $r > 0$ is the intrinsic growth rate, and $K > 0$ is the carrying capacity of the stream. The net revenue in period t is given by $\pi_t = pY_t - (c/2)(Y_t^2/X_t)$, where $p > 0$ is the unit price for fish on the dock and $c > 0$ is a cost parameter. Consider the problem

$$\underset{S^*}{\text{Maximize}} \sum_{t=0}^{19} \rho^t [pY_t - (c/2)(Y_t^2/X_t)]$$

$$\text{Subject to } X_{t+1} = S_t e^{r(1-S_t/K)}$$

$$S_t = \min[X_t, S^*]$$

$$Y_t = \max[0, X_t - S^*]$$

when $K = 300,000$ (salmon), $r = 1$, $p = 5$, $c = 1$, $\delta = 0.02$, $\rho = 1/(1+\delta)$, and $X_0 = 100,000$ (salmon). Suppose that the initial policy was $S^* = 150,000$. Programming this in Excel leads to Spreadsheet E2.4. Reproduce this spreadsheet on your computer to verify all the calculations. What is the value for S^* that maximizes the present value of net revenue for this problem?

E2.5 A fish stock has been overfished, and managers have imposed a moratorium on fishing and, after the moratorium, will limit the number of vessels to no more than $E_{max} = 100$. Denoting E_t as

Resource Economics

	A	B	C	D	E
1	E2.4 Optimal Escapement with $X(t+1) = S(t)*EXP(r*(1-S(t)/K))$				
2					
3	$r =$	1			
4	$K =$	300,000			
5	$c =$	1			
6	$p =$	5			
7	$\delta =$	0.02			
8	$\rho =$	0.980392157			
9	$X_o =$	100,000			
10					
11	$S^* =$	150,000		$\pi^* =$	$ 7,084,266.86
12					
13	t	X_t	Y_t	S_t	$(\rho{\wedge}t)*\pi t$
14	0	100,000	0	100,000	$0
15	1	194,773	44,773	150,000	$214,432
16	2	247,308	97,308	150,000	$449,247
17	3	247,308	97,308	150,000	$440,439
18	4	247,308	97,308	150,000	$431,803
19	5	247,308	97,308	150,000	$423,336
20	6	247,308	97,308	150,000	$415,035
21	7	247,308	97,308	150,000	$406,897
22	8	247,308	97,308	150,000	$398,919
23	9	247,308	97,308	150,000	$391,097
24	10	247,308	97,308	150,000	$383,428
25	11	247,308	97,308	150,000	$375,910
26	12	247,308	97,308	150,000	$368,539
27	13	247,308	97,308	150,000	$361,313
28	14	247,308	97,308	150,000	$354,229
29	15	247,308	97,308	150,000	$347,283
30	16	247,308	97,308	150,000	$340,473
31	17	247,308	97,308	150,000	$333,797
32	18	247,308	97,308	150,000	$327,252
33	19	247,308	97,308	150,000	$320,836
34	20	247,308			

Spreadsheet E2.4

the number of vessels allowed to fish in period t, if and when the moratorium is lifted, the limited-entry program implies that $E_{max} = 100 \geq E_t \geq E_{min} = 0$. Suppose that the net revenue in period t is given by $\pi_t = (pqX_t - c)E_t$, where $p > 0$ is the dockside per-unit price for fish, $q > 0$ is the catchability coefficient, X_t is

	A	B	C	D	E
1	E2.5 How Long the Moratorium?				
2					
3	$r =$	1			
4	$K =$	1,500,000			
5	$p =$	$5			
6	$q =$	0.001			
7	$c =$	$2,000			
8	$\delta =$	0.02			
9	$\rho =$	0.980392157			
10	$X_o =$	100,000			
11	$E_{max} =$	100			
12	$E_{min} =$	0	$\pi^* =$		$0
13					
14	t	E_t	X_t	Y_t	$(\rho\wedge t)^*\pi t$
15	0	0	100,000	0	$0.00
16	1	0	193,333	0	$0.00
17	2	0	361,748	0	$0.00
18	3	0	636,255	0	$0.00
19	4	0	1,002,630	0	$0.00
20	5	0	1,335,082	0	$0.00
21	6	0	1,481,868	0	$0.00
22	7	0	1,499,781	0	$0.00
23	8	0	1,500,000	0	$0.00
24	9	0	1,500,000	0	$0.00
25	10	0	1,500,000	0	$0.00
26	11	0	1,500,000	0	$0.00
27	12	0	1,500,000	0	$0.00
28	13	0	1,500,000	0	$0.00
29	14	0	1,500,000	0	$0.00
30	15	0	1,500,000	0	$0.00
31	16	0	1,500,000	0	$0.00
32	17	0	1,500,000	0	$0.00
33	18	0	1,500,000	0	$0.00
34	19	0	1,500,000	0	$0.00
35	20		1,500,000		

Spreadsheet E2.5

the fish stock in period t, and $c > 0$ is the unit cost of effort. In this problem, harvest is given by the production function $Y_t = qX_tE_t$. The fish stock evolves according to $X_{t+1} = [1 + r(1 - X_t/K) - qE_t]X_t$, where $r > 0$ is once again the intrinsic growth rate, and $K > 0$ is ecosystem carrying capacity. Consider the problem

$$\underset{E_{\max} \geq E_t \geq 0}{\text{Maximize}} \quad \sum_{t=0}^{19} \rho^t (pqX_t - c)E_t$$

$$\text{Subject to} \quad X_{t+1} = [1 + r(1 - X_t/K) - qE_t]X_t$$

$$X_0 > 0 \quad \text{given}$$

With $r = 1$, $K = 1{,}500{,}000$, $p = \$5$, $q = 0.001$, $c = \$2{,}000$, $\delta = 0.02$, and $X_0 = 100{,}000$, we program the initial spreadsheet E2.5, where the moratorium has been extended for the 20-year interval $t = 0, 1, 2, \ldots, 19$. Use Solver to maximize $\pi^* = \sum_{t=0}^{t=19} \rho^t \pi_t$ by changing E_t subject to $E_{\max} \geq E_t \geq E_{\min}$. What is the optimal present value for the limited-entry fishery with $E_{\max} = 100$? How long is the optimal moratorium with the current value of $E_{\max}$? Did the managers select the best value for $E_{\max}$? Why or why not?

3

The Economics of Fisheries

3.0 INTRODUCTION AND OVERVIEW

In this chapter we will explore, in greater detail, the general renewable-resource model used to introduce the method of Lagrange multipliers in Chapter 1. This model will serve as a vehicle to compare managed and unmanaged fisheries and to analyze policies that have been employed in an attempt to correct for *overfishing* and *stock depletion*. Overfishing often will result when a fishery resource is both *common property* and *open access*. *Biological overfishing* has been defined as harvesting that reduces a fish stock to a level below the stock level that supports maximum sustainable yield or, in the notation of previous chapters, $X_t < X_{MSY}$ (Clark, 1990). By a *common-property resource*, I mean a resource that is not recognized as "private property" until it is captured. *Open access* is a situation in which fishers face no regulations in terms of either their level of harvest or entry or exit to or from the fishery.

Overfishing has been the usual result when a common-property fishery is harvested under conditions of open access. It has occurred on fishing, sealing, and whaling "grounds" going back to the seventeenth century, if not before. In the nineteenth century one sees the first attempts by individual nation states or two or more nations via international treaty to implement management policies in the hopes of avoiding severe overfishing. We will see that these traditional management policies often were unable to prevent persistent overfishing. Policies such as enforcing a *total allowable catch* (TAC), if they did prevent overfishing, often resulted in other undesirable side effects.

The failure of traditional management policies recently has led
to a willingness on the part of some coastal nations to experiment
with bioeconomic, or "incentive-based," policies, such as *individual
transferable quotas* (ITQs). ITQ programs have been established in
Australia, New Zealand, Iceland, Canada, and, to a limited extent,
the United States. In such programs, fishery managers set a TAC
for the current year or season, and shares of that TAC then are distributed among a limited number of licensed fishers. The TAC may
vary from year to year depending on fluctuations in the estimated
stock. (Recall our stochastic escapement model in Chapter 2, where
$Y_t = \max[0, X_t - S^*]$.) Fishers holding an ITQ are allowed to fish or
sell all or a portion of their ITQ to another licensed fisher during the
year that the TAC and the ITQ shares are in force.

High levels of uncertainty, when estimating stock size, the level of
total harvest (legal plus illegal), discards (fish discarded while a vessel
is at sea), and more generally, the risk of stock collapse, have led to
another management policy: *marine protected areas* or *marine reserves*.
Marine reserves are viewed by many as the appropriate precautionary
way to deal with the "unknowable uncertainties" that are present in
real-world marine fisheries. Marine reserves are "no-fishing zones"
where commercial fishing is prohibited. We will examine some of the
spatial and economic aspects of marine reserves.

3.1 NET GROWTH

In Equation (1.1) I introduced a difference equation to describe the
change in the biomass of a renewable resource when going from period
t to period $t + 1$. The function $F(X_t)$ was referred to as a *net-growth
function*. This function indicates the amount of new net biomass as
a function of current biomass X_t. Harvest was subtracted from net
growth to determine $X_{t+1} - X_t$, which could be positive, zero, or negative. There are numerous functional forms that might be used to
describe net biological growth. We have already employed one form,
$F(X) = rX(1 - X/K)$, which we called the *logistic growth function*,
where $r > 0$ was referred to as the *intrinsic growth rate* and $K > 0$
was called the *environmental carrying capacity*. Here are four other

possible functional forms.

$$F(X) = rX(1 - X/K)^{\beta} \tag{3.1a}$$

$$F(X) = X(e^{r(1-X/K)} - 1) \tag{3.1b}$$

$$F(X) = rX \ \ln(K/X) \tag{3.1c}$$

$$F(X) = rX(X/K_1 - 1)(1 - X/K_2) \tag{3.1d}$$

I will refer to the form in Equation (3.1a) as the *skewed logistic* because the parameter $\beta > 0$ will affect the skew of this net-growth function. Figure 3.1 shows this function for $\beta = 0.5, \beta = 1$, and $\beta = 2$ when $r = 1$ and $K = 1$.

Equation (3.1b) is sometimes referred to as the *exponential net-growth function* or the *exponential logistic*. Equation (3.1c) is the *Gompertz net-growth function*. Equation (3.1d) is a net-growth function exhibiting *critical depensation*, where it is assumed that $K_2 > K_1 > 0$.

Plots of these four net-growth functions are shown in Figure 3.2 for $r = 1, K = 1, \beta = 1, K_1 = 0.25$, and $K_2 = 1$. Points where $F(X) = 0$

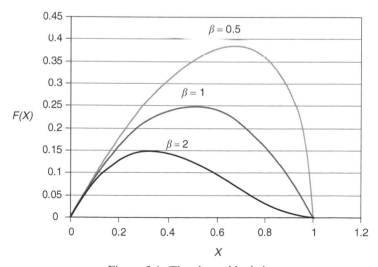

Figure 3.1. The skewed logistic.

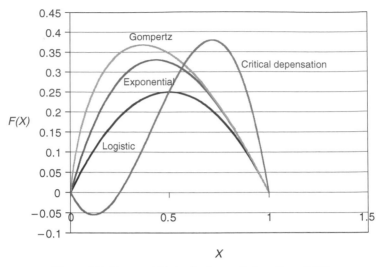

Figure 3.2. Four net biological growth functions $F(X)$.

correspond to steady-state equilibria in the unharvested or *pristine
fishery*. The skewed logistic, exponential, and Gompertz net-growth
functions have steady states at $X = 0$ and $X = K$, whereas the function
exhibiting critical depensation has steady states at $X = 0$, $X = K_1$,
and $X = K_2$. For the skewed logistic, exponential, and Gompertz net-
growth functions, $F(X) > 0$ for $K > X > 0$. This will imply, when
starting from an initial condition $X_0 > 0$, that $X_t \to K$ as $t \to \infty$
provided that $|1 + F'(K)| < 1$. [Recall our discussion in Chapter 1.
Here, $X_{t+1} = G(X_t) = X_t + F(X_t)$. For $K > 0$ to be locally stable,
$|G'(K)| = |1 + F'(K)| < 1$.]

For Equation (3.1d), the steady state at $X = K_1$ is unstable. If the
stock were displaced slightly to the left of K_1, net growth would be
negative [$F(X) < 0$], and a process leading to extinction would result.
Alternatively, if the stock were displaced slightly to the right of K_1,
net growth would be positive [$F(X) > 0$], and the stock would grow
toward K_2. The instability of K_1, where $X_t < K_1$ leads to extinction,
results in $X = K_1$ being referred to as the *minimum viable population*
or *critical population level*. When there is harvesting, if net growth
exhibits critical depensation, you probably would not want to run the
risk of reducing the stock below K_1.

In the logistic ($\beta = 1$), exponential, and Gompertz net-growth functions, the intrinsic growth rate $r > 0$ will influence the local stability of K. For the logistic function, the local stability condition requires $|G'(K)| = |1 - r| < 1$, and we see that K is stable ($X_t \rightarrow K$ from $X_0 > 0$) when $0 < r < 2$.

Spreadsheet S3.1 shows the values for X_t, for $t = 0, 1, \ldots, 30$, when starting from $X_0 = 0.4$, with $X_{t+1} = (1 + r - rX_t/K)X_t$ when $K = 1$ and $r = \{1.9, \ 2.2, \ 2.55, \ 2.9\}$.

For the logistic net-growth function, we know that if $r > 2$, K will not be stable and will not be reached from $X_0 > 0$, but we don't know the type of dynamic behavior that might be exhibited by $X_{t+1} = (1 + r - rX_t/K)X_t$. It turns out that our discrete-time logistic equation is capable of some very interesting behavior. In the four figures contained in Spreadsheet S3.1 we see *overshoot with oscillatory convergence* when $r = 1.9$, *two-point cycles* when $r = 2.2$, *four-point cycles* when $r = 2.55$, and what is called *deterministic chaos* when $r = 2.9$. This progression of behavior can occur for other net-growth functions as well, where 2^n-point cycles emerge as r is increased. When r exceeds a certain value, n becomes sufficiently large that the number of points in the cycle approaches infinity, and the time path for X_t looks like it is fluctuating randomly, even though there is no random variable at work within our difference equation – hence the name *deterministic chaos*. The take-home from Spreadsheet S3.1 is that nonlinear difference equations (also called *iterative maps*) are capable of very complex dynamic behavior including cycles and deterministic chaos.

3.2 FISHERY PRODUCTION FUNCTIONS

In this text, a *fishery production function* will relate harvest in period t to the fish stock and *fishing effort* also in period t. Harvest is regarded as the output and the fish stock and effort are regarded as inputs. In general, the production function will be written as $Y_t = H(X_t, \ E_t)$. One normally expects such production functions to be concave, with positive first partial derivatives $[\partial H(\bullet)/ \partial X_t > 0, \ \partial H(\bullet)/\partial E_t > 0]$, a nonnegative, mixed second partial $[\partial^2 H(\bullet)/\partial X_t \partial E_t = \partial^2 H(\bullet)/\partial E_t \partial X_t \geq 0]$, and nonpositive, pure second partials $[\partial^2 H(\bullet)/\partial X_t^2 \leq 0, \ \partial^2 H(\bullet)/\partial E_t^2 \leq 0]$. Two frequently

	A	B	C	D	E	F	G	H	I	J	K
1	S3.1 The Logistic Net Growth Function with Four Values of r										
2											
3	$K =$	1									
4	$X(0) =$	0.4									
5											
6	t	$r = 1.9$	$r = 2.2$	$r = 2.55$	$r = 2.9$						
7	0	0.4	0.4	0.4	0.4						
8	1	0.856	0.928	1.012	1.096						
9	2	1.0902016	1.0749952	0.9810328	0.7908736						
10	3	0.903359536	0.897632344	1.028481786	1.270511992						
11	4	1.069231597	1.097787086	0.953784641	0.273814677						
12	5	0.928584836	0.858349079	1.066187364	0.850451256						
13	6	1.054583409	1.125838141	0.886238629	1.219284616						
14	7	0.94521417	0.814156707	1.143328919	0.443910576						
15	8	1.043604422	1.147028947	0.725455069	1.159787108						
16	9	0.957143464	0.77600674	1.233338599	0.622361928						
17	10	1.035081185	1.158411355	0.499485572	1.303941848						
18	11	0.966088623	0.754699228	1.136984897	0.154606613						
19	12	1.028335274	1.161981495	0.739823012	0.533646498						
20	13	0.972972766	0.747898595	1.230659565	1.255363446						
21	14	1.022936615	1.162700425	0.506807894	0.325699033						
22	15	0.978357479	0.746522347	1.144189708	0.962594634						
23	16	1.018588311	1.162821158	0.723489739	1.067012627						
24	17	0.982614022	0.746291005	1.233623197	0.859653002						
25	18	1.015073063	1.162840635	0.498705559	1.209537185						

The Logistic with $K = 1$, $r = 1.9$

The Logistic with $K = 1$, $r = 2.2$

Spreadsheet S3.1

80

19	0.986002568	0.746253679	1.136201286	0.474552437
20	1.012225425	1.162843755	0.74?583492	1.197674459
21	0.988713141	0.746247699	1.230258904	0.511100472
22	1.009916126	1.162844255	0.50?89?834	1.235743132
23	0.990888661	0.746246742	1.14324?695	0.390921057
24	1.008042474	1.162844335	0.721085031	1.081416231
25	0.992638879	0.746246588	1.233944624	0.826086212
26	1.006522055	1.162844347	0.49782411	1.242722781
27	0.994049329	0.746246564	1.1?5312037	0.367975107
28	1.005288324	1.162844349	0.743577506	1.042426448
29	0.995187373	0.74624656	1.229785002	0.914169739
30	1.004287358	1.162844435	0.5?9187599	1.141713678

|G'(K)| =	0.9	1.2	1.55	1.9
Behavior	Convergence	2-Point Cycle	4-Point Cycle	Chaos

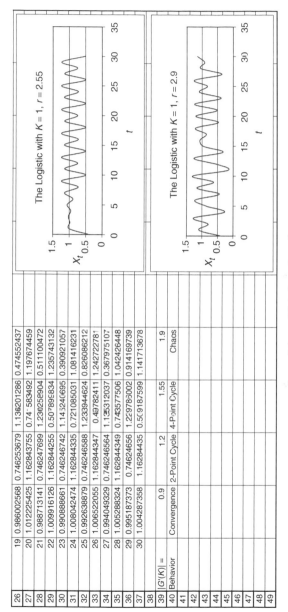

Spreadsheet S3.1 (*continued*)

81

encountered functional forms are

$$Y_t = qX_tE_t \qquad\qquad (3.2a)$$

$$Y_t = X_t(1 - e^{-qE_t}) \qquad\qquad (3.2b)$$

where $q > 0$ is called a *catchability coefficient*. Production function (3.2a) is a special case of the Cobb-Douglas form $Y_t = qX_t^\alpha E_t^\beta$, where $\alpha = \beta = 1$. It is often referred to as the *catch-per-unit-effort* (CPUE) production function because it was originally the result of the assumption that catch per-unit effort Y_t/E_t was proportional to the stock X_t with $q > 0$ being the constant of proportionality.

I will refer to Production function (3.2b) as the *exponential production function*. Note that as $E_t \rightarrow \infty, Y_t \rightarrow X_t$. The exponential production function might be regarded as more realistic, but either production function (or the more general Cobb-Douglas production function) is best viewed as an approximation to harvest technology and the way fish distribute themselves within the marine environment. Thus the choice between Production function (3.2a) and (3.2b) and other functional forms should be decided by the available time-series data.

3.3 THE YIELD-EFFORT FUNCTION

Consider a single-species fishery where the amount harvested in period t is given by the general production function $Y_t = H(X_t, E_t)$. With harvest, the resource stock changes according to $X_{t+1} - X_t = F(X_t) - Y_t$. If we substitute the production function into this equation and evaluate it at steady state (where $X_{t+1} = X_t = X$), we conclude that $F(X) = H(X, E)$. This is nothing more than a restatement of our earlier observation that harvest must equal net growth at steady state. Suppose that we can solve this last equation for X as a function of E, say, $X = G(E)$. If we take this function and substitute it into the production function, we would have $Y = H[G(E), E] = Y(E)$, where $Y(E)$ is called the *yield-effort function*. It gives the steady-state relationship between harvest (or yield) and fishing effort. This function might be useful in the "long-run management" of a fishery, and it has the potential to be estimated with appropriate time-series data on effort and harvest.

Suppose that we adopt the logistic form $F(X) = rX(1 - X/K)$ and the CPUE production function $Y = H(X, E) = qXE$. Then the

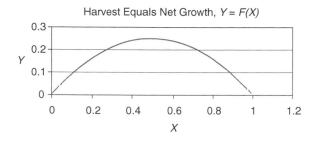

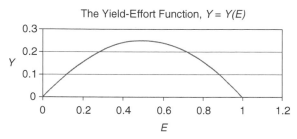

Figure 3.3. The functions $Y = F(X)$ and $Y = Y(E)$.

steady-state condition $H(X, E) = F(X)$ implies $X = K[1 - (q/r)E]$, and the yield-effort function takes the form $Y = Y(E) = qKE[1 - (q/r)E]$. The logistic net-growth function and the yield-effort function are plotted in Figure 3.3. The figure consists of Excel charts drawn when $r = 1$, $K = 1$, and $q = 1$ for $1 \geq X \geq 0$ and $1 \geq E \geq 0$. While they appear the same (they are both quadratics, and both have a maximum at $Y_{MSY} - rK/4$), the net-growth function shows the steady-state relationship between X and Y, whereas the yield-effort function shows the steady-state relationship between E and Y.

Measuring fishing effort E_t is problematic. In a fishery where similar vessels pull identical nets through the water (a trawl fishery), one might ideally measure effort as the total number of hours nets were deployed and actively fishing during the year or season. In a troll or longline fishery, one might measure effort as the total number of "hook hours" by a fleet, again in a season or year. In fixed-gear fisheries (i.e., gillnet, lobster, and crab), effort might be measured as the total number of units deployed (i.e., nets, traps. or pots), assuming that they are fishing continuously throughout the season or year. Unfortunately, there is typically some vessel diversity within a fleet, records are not required or kept on the number of hours a particular gear was actively fishing, and snags or improper deployment may reduce the effectiveness of a particular set. Often fishery scientists have to settle for the data available, which might be days from port or simply the number of vessels in a fleet (with no record of the number or length of trips during a season or year). Fishers typically are reluctant to reveal information on the time, location, and extent of their fishing effort, making time-series data on the ideal measure of effort unavailable. Even with less than ideal data, there seems to be conclusive evidence as to what happens when a common-property fishery is harvested under open-access conditions.

3.4 THE STATIC MODEL OF OPEN ACCESS

With the yield-effort function $Y = Y(E)$, we can analyze the long-run equilibrium in an open-access fishery. Suppose that the per-unit dockside price is $p > 0$. Then the steady-state revenue from yield $Y = Y(E)$ is simply $R = pY(E)$. This revenue function will look identical to the yield-effort function, but the vertical axis now will measure dollars (\$) or whatever the appropriate "coin of the realm" is. Suppose further that the cost of fishing is given by the simple linear equation $C = cE$, where $c > 0$ is the unit cost of effort. Both the revenue and the cost equations are plotted in Figure 3.4. They intersect at $E = E_\infty$, which is referred to as the *open-access equilibrium level of effort*. At $E = E_\infty$, revenue equals cost, and net revenue, or *rent*, is zero ($\pi = R - C = 0$). The zero-profit condition is, in theory, encountered in all competitive industries, where it is viewed as the healthy outcome of socially desirable competitive forces. This is *not* the case in a common-property, open-access fishery.

At $E = E_\infty$, the cost of effort (including compensation to vessel owners and crew) is being covered, but there is nothing left to pay the other important factor of production – the fish stock! Because access is free, the fish stock is reduced until it is worthless, in the sense that at the corresponding equilibrium stock, $X = X_\infty$, effort cannot be expanded without incurring a net financial loss. The open-access equilibrium (X_∞, E_∞, Y_∞) is frequently described as having "too many vessels chasing too few fish." Open-access harvest Y_∞ is often considerably smaller than what could be sustainably harvested at larger steady-state biomass levels. The open-access equilibrium is also non-optimal because if effort could be reduced, the positive net revenues

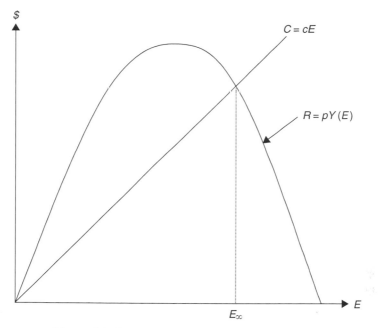

Figure 3.4. Open-access equilibrium level of effort.

that would result could more than financially compensate the fishers who reduced effort or left the fishery entirely.

This simple static model would seem consistent with the observed outcome of open-access regimes throughout history and across cultures. In addition to fish stocks, case studies describing the depletion of wildlife, forests, groundwater, and grassland also could be described. What the static model does not do is describe the dynamics of the resource and the harvesting industry from an initial condition where the resource is often abundant. It will turn out that the open-access equilibrium described by the static model may not be reached (it is not locally stable) and that the resource might be driven to extinction along an "approach path."

3.5 THE DYNAMIC MODEL OF OPEN ACCESS

The dynamic model of open access will consist of two difference equations, one describing the change in the resource when harvested and the other describing the change in fishing effort. Substituting the fishery production function into Equation (1.1) will give us $X_{t+1} - X_t = F(X_t) - H(X_t, E_t)$, which we will use as the first equation. The second equation, describing effort dynamics, is more speculative because it seeks to explain the economic behavior of fishers. There are many possible models, but perhaps the simplest might hypothesize that effort is adjusted in response to last year's profitability. While such a model might be criticized as viewing fishers as myopic, the empirical predictions of the model seem consistent with sealing and whaling in the nineteenth century.

If the per-unit price is $p > 0$ and the per-unit cost of effort is $c > 0$, then profit, or net revenue, in period t may be written as $\pi_t = pH(X_t, E_t) - cE_t$. If profit in period t is positive, we would think that effort in period $t+1$ would be expanded. If this response were proportional to net revenue, we could write $E_{t+1} - E_t = \eta[pH(X_t, E_t) - cE_t]$, where $\eta > 0$ is called an *adjustment* or *stiffness parameter*.

We can write our two difference equations in iterative form as the *dynamical system*

$$X_{t+1} = X_t + F(X_t) - H(X_t E_t)$$
$$E_{t+1} = E_t + \eta[pH(X_t E_t) - cE_t] \tag{3.3}$$

With functional forms for $F(\bullet)$ and $H(\bullet)$, parameter values for η, p, and c, and initial values for X_0 and E_0, we could simulate (iterate) System (3.3) forward in time and observe the dynamics of X_t and E_t. System (3.3) is likely to be nonlinear and thus has the potential for periodic and chaotic behavior. This raises the question of whether the system will ever reach the equilibrium identified in the static open-access model.

To illustrate the potential behavior of the dynamic open-access system, lets specify logistic growth and the CPUE production function so that System (3.3) can be written as

$$X_{t+1} = [1 + r - rX_t/K - qE_t]X_t$$
$$E_{t+1} = [1 + \eta(pqX_t - c)]E_t \tag{3.4}$$

The parameters for System (3.4) are r, K, q, η, p, and c. With initial values X_0 and E_0, we can simulate this system in a spreadsheet and observe the behavior of X_t and E_t. Before presenting the simulation results for this system, it will be useful to derive analytic expressions for the open-access equilibrium.

First note that in steady state. $\pi = pqXE - cE = 0$ implies $X_\infty = c/(pq)$, and using the yield-effort function, we also know that $pqKE[1 - (q/r)E] = cE$. Solving this last expression for E yields $E_\infty = r(pqK - c)/(pq^2K)$, which is positive provided that $pqK > c$. In the numerical analysis of System (3.4), we can calculate X_∞ and E_∞ in advance. They will provide a reference by which to judge convergence. The point $X_\infty = 0, E_\infty = 0$ is also an equilibrium, one in which both the resource and harvesters go extinct. Barring species reintroduction, this equilibrium is stable and may be the ultimate destination of (X_t, E_t) if other equilibria are unstable. We now examine this possibility numerically.

Figure 3.5 shows the results of two open-access simulations. In Figure 3.5a, the parameter set is $c = 1, \eta = 0.3, K = 1, p = 200,$

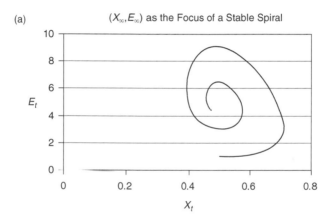

(a) (X_∞, E_∞) as the Focus of a Stable Spiral

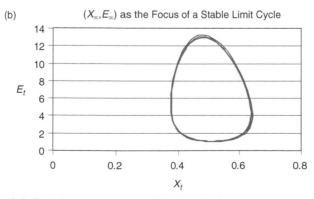

(b) (X_∞, E_∞) as the Focus of a Stable Limit Cycle

Figure 3.5. Spiral convergence and limit cycles in open-access systems.

$q = 0.01$, and $r = 0.1$. The initial values are $X_0 = 0.5$ and $E_0 = 1$. We show the evolution of the point (X_t, E_t) by constructing what is called the *phase-plane diagram* for System (3.4). The results, for $t = 0, 1, 2, \ldots, 100$, reveal a slow counterclockwise spiral converging to $X_\infty = 0.5$ and $E_\infty = 5$. We would infer from this simulation that $(X_\infty, E_\infty) = (0.5, 5)$ is locally stable and that the initial condition is in the *basin of attraction* leading to (X_∞, E_∞).

In Figure 3.5b, η has been increased to one, whereas all other parameter values and the initial conditions are unchanged. The values of X_∞ and E_∞ are unchanged, but instead of counterclockwise spiral convergence, (X_∞, E_∞) would appear to be the *focus of a stable-limit cycle*. The fish stock and the level of effort change to keep the point (X_t, E_t) in perpetual counterclockwise motion on the closed orbit defining the stable-limit cycle. The open-access equilibrium in this case is never reached.

What would happen if the net-growth function exhibited critical depensation, and System (3.4) became

$$X_{t+1} = [1 + r(X_t/K_1 - 1)(1 - X_t/K_2) - qE_t]X_t$$
$$E_{t+1} = [1 + \eta(pqX_t - c)]E_t \tag{3.5}$$

This is a more complex system. It is capable of equilibria that are (1) reached by spiral convergence, (2) never reached because they are the foci of stable-limit cycles, and (3) never reached because of overshoot that leads to extinction. In steady state, System (3.5) implies $X_\infty = c/(pq)$ and $E_\infty = (r/q)(X_\infty/K_1 - 1)(1 - X_\infty/K_2)$, which will again serve as reference points for numerical simulation. The behavior of System (3.5) will depend on the relationship of $X_\infty = c/(pq)$ to $X_H = (K_1 + K_2)/2$. If $K_2 > X_\infty > X_H$, we observe counterclockwise spiral convergence to (X_∞, E_∞). If $X_\infty = X_H$, (X_∞, E_∞) is the focus of a limit cycle. If $X_\infty < X_H$, the system overshoots (X_∞, E_∞) and converges to extinction $(0, 0)$. System (3.5) is said to undergo a *Hopf bifurcation* at $X_\infty = X_H$, where the limit cycle is a transitional behavior between spiral convergence and extinction. These behaviors are shown in Figure 3.6.

In Figure 3.6 we vary the cost parameter c while maintaining $r = 0.1$, $K_1 = 0.1$, $K_2 = 1$, $q = 1$, $p = 3$, $\eta = 0.3$, $X_0 = 0.9$, and $E_0 = 0.1$. In Figure 3.6a, $c = 2$, yielding $X_\infty = c/(pq) = 0.67$, which is greater than $X_H = (K_1 + K_2)/2 = 0.55$, and (X_∞, E_∞) is the focus of a stable

(a)

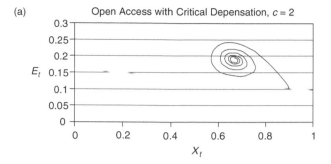

(b)

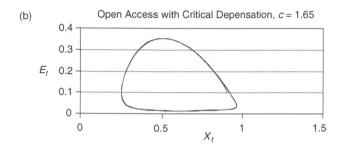

(c)

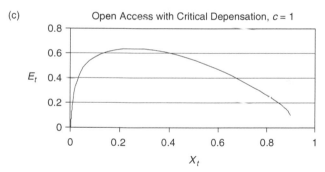

Figure 3.6. Open access with critical depensation.

spiral. In Figure 3.6b, $c = 1.65$, yielding $X_\infty = c/(pq) = 0.55$, which is precisely equal to $X_H = (K_1 + K_2)/2 = 0.55$, and (X_∞, E_∞) is the focus of a stable limit cycle. In Figure 3.6c, $c = 1$, yielding $X_\infty = c/(pq) = 0.33$, which is less than $X_H = (K_1 + K_2)/2 = 0.55$, and the system overshoots (X_∞, E_∞) on its way to extinction. An increase in price $p > 0$ or catchability $q > 0$ or a reduction in harvest cost $c > 0$ might result in $X_\infty < X_H$.

In the last half of the nineteenth century, the passenger pigeon came under intensive harvesting as a result of extension of the railroad to the U.S. Midwest and introduction of the telegraph. The railroad allowed pigeons harvested in the Midwest to be packed in ice and shipped to markets on the more densely populated East Coast. The telegraph allowed the hunters to quickly communicate the location of nesting sites where the birds would congregate in huge numbers. While the formation of huge flocks at nesting sites may have been a good evolutionary strategy against natural predators, it made the passenger pigeon easy prey to rent-seeking "pigeoners" toting shotguns and nets. Reduced shipping and communication costs may have caused $X_\infty = c/(pq)$ to fall below $X_H = (K_1 + K_2)/2$. The passenger pigeon was hunted under conditions of open access and is believed to have gone extinct in the wild by 1901. The last passenger pigeon died in the Cincinnati Zoo in 1914.

3.6 REGULATED OPEN ACCESS

Homans and Wilen (1997) developed a model of *regulated open access* in which a total allowable catch (TAC) served as an upper bound on harvest during any particular year. Management authorities would monitor harvest, and when cumulative harvest equaled the TAC, the season was over. If access to the fishery was open or of nominal cost, the imposition of a TAC created a *race for the fish*, where individual fishers tried to capture as much of the TAC for themselves before the season was closed. One might predict that the fishing season would become compressed over time and that a large amount of fish would be landed during progressively shorter seasons. This, in turn, would lead to falling dockside prices because fish had to be frozen. The fisher would lose the price premium normally associated with the marketing of fresh (not previously frozen) fish. It also might be the case that in their race for the fish, fishers would take ill-advised risks (overloading a boat in heavy seas) that could result in capsizing and loss of human life.

This is pretty much the description of the Alaskan halibut derby as it existed prior to the introduction of individual transferable quotas in 1995. Timothy Egan, in an article appearing on May 8, 1991, in the *New York Times*, provides a description of the preparations for a one-day halibut derby by vessels working out of Seward, Alaska.

At the stroke of noon today, about 4,000 commercial fishermen lowered enough baited-hook lines into the water to circle the globe. In one of the most intense food-gathering rituals in North America, they have, according to current regulations, only 24 hours to catch as much halibut as human endurance, or greed, will allow.

To some crew members, who fly here from Chicago, fish for a day, and return home with $20,000, the derby is a vestige of pure American capitalism. To others, who labor without sleep or balance on a boat that may come back empty-handed, the derby is a marathon of misery. . . .

The Pacific halibut, somewhat similar to Atlantic flounder, is a huge, small-eyed, ugly fish, some of which weigh up to 400 pounds. Fresh from the water, it tastes better than lobster to many palates. The halibut were fished during World War II to provide vitamin A to help pilots improve their night vision. Prized by West Coast restaurants, the catch will bring fishermen up to $2 a pound, far more than most species of salmon will bring. . . . But a 250-pound halibut, flopping around on a small deck in high seas, is not a thing of sport or great taste; it is like a prizefighter gone mad in a crowded elevator [Egan, 1991].

Since 1923, the Pacific halibut fishery has been managed by the International Pacific Halibut Commission (IPHC), a joint U.S.–Canadian commission. The IPHC employs biologists and statisticians to collect data and develop models that can be used to predict the halibut stock in 10 regulated areas along the coasts of the Province of British Columbia and the State of Alaska, as shown in the map below.

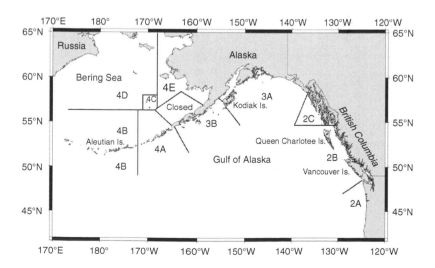

TACs were specified for each open area. They did a reasonable job of maintaining the halibut population at high levels and avoiding the overfishing associated with pure open access. In the 1980s and early 1990s, higher stocks supported larger TACs, and positive profits attracted more vessels to the fishery. Season length, determined by the time it would take for cumulative catch to reach the TAC, started to decline. The season, which lasted six months in the 1970s, had been reduced to two days by 1991 when Timothy Egan was reporting on the fishery.

Homans and Wilen (1997) developed a bioeconomic model that incorporated the economic incentives that were created when a TAC was imposed on a fishery with zero or nominal costs of entry. The halibut fishery was a perfect case study. The IPHC had extensive time-series data on estimated biomass, harvest, and fishing effort, as measured by skate soaks (a *skate soak* is a 1,800-foot-long weighted cable with baited C-hooks every 18 feet that is lowered to the ocean floor, left to "soak" while catching fish, and then retrieved).

Their model is based on the following equations:

$$X_{t+1} - X_t = aX_t - bX_t^2 - X_t(1 - e^{-qE_tT_t})$$
$$\pi_t = pX_t(1 - e^{-qE_tT_t}) - vE_tT_t - fE_t \qquad (3.6)$$
$$\text{TAC}_t = c + dX_t = X_t(1 - e^{-qE_tT_t})$$

where X_t is the biomass of halibut at the start of the season in year t, E_t is an index of effort committed to the season in year t, T_t is the length of the season (in days) in year t, and TAC_t is the total allowable catch set by management authorities using a linear TAC policy, where $\text{TAC}_t = c + dX_t$.

It is assumed that the TAC equals actual harvest in every year so that $\text{TAC}_t = X_t(1 - e^{-qE_tT_t})$. The parameters $v > 0$ and $f > 0$ are variable and fixed cost coefficients, respectively. In the linear TAC policy, c might be positive, negative, or zero, whereas $d > 0$.

The level of effort and the length of the fishing season are assumed to drive net revenue (rent) to zero during each season so that $\pi_t = 0$. Solving $\text{TAC}_t = X_t(1 - e^{-qE_tT_t})$ for T_t yields

$$T_t = [1/(qE_t)] \ln\left[\frac{X_t}{(X_t - \text{TAC}_t)}\right] \qquad (3.7)$$

Substituting Equation (3.7) into $\pi_t = 0$ and doing some careful algebra, you can obtain an equation for E_t that depends on X_t and TAC_t and takes the form

$$E_t = \frac{p}{f}\text{TAC}_t - [v/(fq)]\ln\left[\frac{X_t}{(X_t - \text{TAC}_t)}\right] \tag{3.8}$$

Equations (3.7) and (3.8) also hold in steady state where halibut biomass is unchanging because $c + dX = aX - bX^2$. This implies that biomass in the regulated open-access equilibrium is given by the positive root of a quadratic taking the form

$$X = \frac{a-d}{2b} + \sqrt{\left(\frac{a-d}{2b}\right)^2 - \frac{c}{b}} \tag{3.9}$$

provided that $a > d$ and $[(a-d)/(2b)]^2 > (c/b)$. With estimates of a, b, c, and d, Homans and Wilen can solve Equation (3.9) for X. The equilibrium TAC is given by $\text{TAC} = c + dX$. Given X and TAC, you can obtain equilibrium E from Equation (3.8) and then, given E, TAC, and X, the equilibrium season length T from Equation (3.7).

For the sake of comparison, Homans and Wilen assume that the season length under pure open access will be given by the value of T that maximizes effort (see Homans and Wilen, 1997, Figure 1). This level of effort $T_{\max}$ is given by the equation

$$T = T_{\max} = \frac{1}{qE}\ln\left(\frac{pqX}{v}\right) \tag{3.10}$$

Substituting this last equation for T into the steady-state relationship where harvest equals net growth yields

$$X(1 - e^{-\ln(pqX/v)}) = aX - bX^2 \tag{3.11}$$

Some careful algebra leads to a quadratic equation where the pure open-access equilibrium stock is given as the positive root

$$X = \frac{a-1}{2b} + \sqrt{\left(\frac{a-1}{2b}\right)^2 + \frac{v}{bpq}} \tag{3.12}$$

Table 3.1. *Regulated and Pure Open Access in Area 3 of the Pacific Halibut Fishery*

Parameters

$a = 0.3119$	$b = 0.00075$	$c = 16.417$	$d = 0.0575$
$q = 0.000975$	$v = 0.07848$	$f = 2.0993$	$p = 1.95$

Regulated Open Access

$X = 252.51 \times 10^6$ lb	$Y = 30.94 \times 10^6$ lb	$E = 23.73$ (index of fishing capacity)	$T = 5.65$ days

Pure Open Access

$X = 56.51 \times 10^6$ lb	$E = 2.11$ (index of fishing capacity)	$T = 152.99$ days	$Y = 15.23 \times 10^6$ lb

Knowing the above value for X, one can solve the zero-rent equation $\pi = 0$ for E, yielding

$$E = (p/f)X[1 - v/(pqX)] - [v/(fq)] \ \ln[pqX/v] \tag{3.13}$$

With values for X and E, you can go back to Equation (3.10) and compute $T = T_{max}$, and then with values for X, E, and $T = T_{max}$, you can compute

$$Y = X(1 - e^{-qE\bullet T}) \tag{3.14}$$

Homans and Wilen estimated the bioeconomic parameters for Area 3 of the Pacific halibut fishery for the period 1935–1977. These parameter estimates and the calculated values of X, Y, E, and T at the regulated open-access equilibrium and the values of X, E, T, and Y at the pure open-access equilibrium are given in Table 3.1.

The first thing to note is that the model of regulated open access predicts an equilibrium where the fishing season has been reduced to $T = 5.65$ days. The binding TAC results in an equilibrium harvest of $Y = 30.94 \times 10^6$ pounds from a steady-state stock of $X = 252.51 \times 10^6$ pounds. The effort index of $E = 23.73$ is high relative to the index under pure open access, where $E = 2.11$. This makes sense because the harvest of $Y = 30.94 \times 10^6$ pounds in less than six days requires more than 10 times the effort capacity of pure open access, where the season is more than 25 times longer at $T = 152.99$ days. Note also that the TAC does maintain the fish stock at a much higher level, $X = 252.51 \times 10^6$ pounds compared with the pure open-access equilibrium stock ot $X = 56.51 \times 10^6$ pounds.

3.7 MAXIMIZATION OF STATIC RENT

The economic *in*efficiency of open access was recognized by the mid-1950s. The policy prescription that was proposed at that time was either "sole ownership" (privatization) of the resource or a limitation on effort to the level that would be adopted by a sole owner seeking to maximize static rent, or profit. The rent-maximizing level of effort is shown in Figure 3.7, where the revenue function $R(E) = pY(E)$ and cost equation $C = cE$ that were used to identify the open-access equilibrium level of effort E_∞ in Figure 3.4 have been redrawn.

A sole owner, with the exclusive right to harvest the fish stock, would invest in a fleet or hire vessels so that effort maximized rent $\pi = pY(E) - cE$. The simple first-order condition $d\pi/dE = 0$ implies

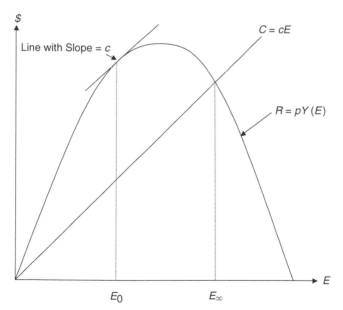

Figure 3.7. Open-access and static rent-maximizing equilibria.

that $pY'(E) = c$, where $Y'(E)$ is the first derivative of the yield-effort function and $pY'(E)$ is marginal revenue. Thus the level of effort that maximizes rent satisfies the familiar economic dictum that marginal revenue should equal marginal cost.

Graphically, the rent-maximizing level of effort is identified by finding the point where the revenue curve has a slope of $c > 0$, the marginal cost of effort, and dropping a vertical to the E axis. This occurs at E_0 in Figure 3.7. At E_0, the vertical distance between $R(E) = pY(E)$ and $C = cE$ is maximized.

Auctioning off permanent access to a fishery to the highest-bidding sole owner was not a politically acceptable solution to the problem of open access. A more feasible, although still controversial, policy that emerged from the analysis of the rent-maximizing sole owner was *limited entry*. If fishery managers could somehow remove excess vessels so that effort was reduced from E_∞ to E_0, they would maximize the static net value of the fishery once the stock reached the associated equilibrium at X_0. If E_0 corresponded to some number of vessels, management authorities could auction off licenses granting seasonal or permanent access to the resource. In theory, they would then capture all or a portion of the discounted static rent. Such revenues might be earmarked for enforcement, management, research, or habitat improvement.

The problem became how to encourage the appropriate number of vessels to leave the fishery and how to keep the remaining vessels from investing in vessel improvements that would increase "fishing power," or de facto effort. The increase in de facto effort that results from increasing engine size, hold capacity, electronics, or other inputs is called *capital stuffing*. Several countries, including Canada, instituted vessel buyout programs, where federal or provincial funds were used to buy vessels from owners participating in "overcapitalized" fisheries. After purchase, the government might sell the vessel for scrap metal or resell it, with the restriction that it could never participate in the fishery it was paid to leave. Vessel buyout programs may become prohibitively expensive if potential entrants to an open-access fishery anticipate that a buyout program and limited entry will be introduced in the near future.

The vessels remaining in the limited-entry fishery usually were given a license, and only licensed vessels were allowed access to the resource.

Provisions frequently allowed a license holder to sell his or her license on retiring from the fishery. If the buyout program was successful (with no subsequent capital stuffing), and remaining vessels were making profits, the market price for a license would reflect the expected present value of profits. In his discussion of the halibut derby, Timothy Egan notes that licenses in the some of the Alaskan limited-entry salmon fisheries were selling for as much as $250,000 in 1991.

3.8 PRESENT-VALUE MAXIMIZATION

It will turn out that static rent maximization, with equilibrium effort at E_0, is not optimal if your objective is maximization of the present value of net revenue with a positive rate of discount. It also turns out that the abstract exercise of present-value maximization reveals an important management concept that does not even arise in a static model. Thus, from both a theoretical and a practical perspective, it is important to revisit the dynamic optimization problem posed in Chapter 1 to illustrate the method of Lagrange multipliers. We have already done quite a bit of the tedious spade work in that chapter, so in this section we can concentrate on the economic and management implications.

Recall from Chapter 1 that $\pi_t = \pi(X_t, Y_t)$ represented the net benefits in period t of harvest Y_t from a stock of size X_t. The harvested resource changed according to $X_{t+1} - X_t = F(X_t) - Y_t$, and the initial stock was given by X_0. Maximizing the present value of net benefits over an infinite horizon led to the problem

$$\underset{\{Y_t\}}{\text{Maximize}} \ \pi = \sum_{t=0}^{\infty} \rho^t \pi(X_t, Y_t)$$

$$\text{Subject to} \ X_{t+1} - X_t = F(X_t) - Y_t$$

$$X_0 > 0 \ \text{given}$$

The Lagrangian for this problem was given in Equation (1.14) and the first-order necessary conditions in Equations (1.15) through (1.17). In steady state, the first-order conditions collapsed to three equations, Equations (1.21) through (1.23), in three unknowns, X, Y, and λ. It was possible to eliminate the term $\rho\lambda$, and after some algebra, we obtained a two-equation system that we rewrite for convenience as

$$F'(X) + \frac{\partial \pi(\bullet)/\partial X}{\partial \pi(\bullet)/\partial Y} = \delta$$

$$Y = F(X)$$

We referred to the first of these equations as the *fundamental equation of renewable resources* and noted that it required the steady-state levels of X and Y to equate the "resource's own rate of return" (the left-hand side) to the rate of discount δ. By the implicit function theorem, this equation implied a curve $Y = \phi(X)$ in $X - Y$ space, which we could plot along with $Y = F(X)$ to identify the optimal levels X^* and Y^* (see Figure 1.3).

For the case where $F(X) = rX(1 - X/K)$, $Y = H(X, E) = qXE$, and $C = cE$, we can solve the production function for $E = Y/(qX)$, and on substitution into the cost equation, we obtain the cost function $C = cY/(qX)$ (where all the functions are evaluated at steady state). This permits us to write net revenue as $\pi = pY - cY/(qX) = [p - c/(qX)]Y$, which has the partial derivatives $\partial \pi(\bullet)/\partial X = cY/(qX^2)$ and $\partial \pi(\bullet)/\partial Y = p - c/(qX)$. The derivative of the net-growth function is $F'(X) = r(1 - 2X/K)$. Substituting these derivatives into the fundamental equation of renewable resources yields

$$r(1 - 2X/K) + \frac{cY}{X(pqX - c)} = \delta \qquad (3.15)$$

Solving Equation (3.15) for Y, we obtain

$$Y = \phi(X) = \frac{X(pqX - c)[\delta - r(1 - 2X/K)]}{c} \qquad (3.16)$$

We see that $Y = \phi(X)$ depends on the entire set of bioeconomic parameters: c, δ, K, p, q, and r. Changes in any of these parameters will cause $Y = \phi(X)$ to shift in $X - Y$ space, as was implied by the curves $\phi_i(X)$, $i = 1, 2, 3$, in Figure 1.3. In Figure 3.8, $Y = \phi(X)$ and $Y = F(X) = rX(1 - X/K)$ are plotted for the parameter values $r = 0.1$, $K = 1$, $c = 1$, $p = 200$, $q = 0.01$, and $\delta = 0.05$.

Recall that one of the conclusions drawn from Figure 1.3 was that the intersection of $Y = \phi(X)$ and $Y = F(X)$ could result in the optimal stock lying above or below the stock supporting maximum sustainable yield X_{MSY}. We should have expected this. When

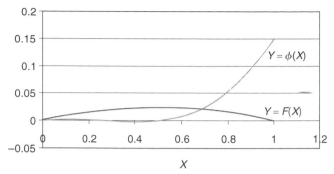

Figure 3.8. A plot of $Y = \phi(X)$ and $Y = F(X) = rX(1 - X/K)$.

$Y = F(X) = rX(1-X/K)$, the stock supporting maximum sustainable yield was $X_{MSY} = K/2$, and if we have an objective that maximizes the present value of net benefit (in this case net revenue), then the optimal stock should depend on the economic parameters $c, \delta, p,$ and q as well.

By substituting $Y = rX(1-X/K)$ for Y on the left-hand side (LHS) of Equation (3.15), we end up with a single equation in X that, after an algebraic tussle, has an explicit solution

$$X^* = \left(\frac{K}{4}\right)\left[\left(\frac{c}{pqK}+1-\frac{\delta}{r}\right)+\sqrt{\left(\frac{c}{pqK}+1-\frac{\delta}{r}\right)^2+\frac{8c\delta}{pqKr}}\right]$$

$$(3.17)$$

Equation (3.17) is the positive root of a quadratic expression (the negative root, not making any economic sense, is discarded). While notationally cumbersome, it has the advantage, when programmed on a spreadsheet, of permitting calculation of the optimal stock without having to solve for X^* using Solver. For the parameter values underlying Figure 3.8, we can program Equation (3.17) and calculate $X^* = 0.6830127$. This is the numerical for X where $Y = \phi(X)$ intersects $Y = F(X)$ and where $Y^* = F(X^*) = \phi(X^*) = 0.021650635$. Numerically, one could change any of the parameters and observe how X^* changes (thus performing *numerical comparative statics*). Knowing X^* and Y^*, one also can calculate $E^* = Y^*/(qX^*)$ and $\lambda^* = (1 + \delta)[p - c/(qX^*)]$, thus obtaining values for all the variables at the bioeconomic optimum.

If you took the appropriate derivatives of the expression for X^* in Equation (3.17), or if you programmed Equation (3.17) on a spreadsheet, you would conclude that $dX^*/dr > 0$, $dX^*/dK > 0$, $dX^*/dc > 0$, $dX^*/dp < 0$, $dX^*/dq < 0$, and $dX^*/d\delta < 0$. In words, if r, K, or c increase, the optimal stock increases. If p, q, or δ increase, the optimal stock decreases.

We are now in a position to explain the logic behind the subscripts used in identifying the pure open-access and rent-maximizing levels of effort in Figure 3.7. For $\infty > \delta > 0$, $E_\infty > E^* > E_0$. In words, the open-access level of effort will exceed the optimal level of effort, which will exceed the rent-maximizing level of effort, for a finite and positive rate of discount. Further, as $\delta \to \infty$, $E^* \to E_\infty$, and as $\delta \to 0$, $E^* \to E_0$ – hence the subscripts.

That E^* approaches E_∞ as the discount rate goes to infinity has an interesting interpretation. In open access, individual fishers are caught in something of a dilemma. Collectively, they know that by harvesting less today, they would leave a larger fish stock, which would support larger sustainable yields in the future, but unless they can trust all fishers to cooperate in such a conservation strategy, they would only be leaving fish that another fisher will harvest, and their individual effort at building the stock will be for naught. The game-strategic aspects of conservation make stock maintenance above X_∞ an unlikely and unstable outcome under pure open access, with the result that individual fishers appear to behave as if "there were no tomorrow," or more precisely, that they employ an infinite discount rate to evaluate the effectiveness of individual conservation.

At the other extreme, if $\delta \to 0$, then a dollar's worth of net benefit is valued the same regardless of when it occurs, and it is optimal to maximize sustainable rent. Note that in steady state, $X_0 > X^*$ when $\delta > 0$. Present value always can be increased by harvesting $(X_0 - X^*)$, thus increasing present value in the near term to an extent that will more than offset the small reduction in sustainable net benefits once you reach X^*.

The preceding discussion has been an attempt to compare three steady-state equilibria: pure open access, static rent maximizing, and the bioeconomic optimum. For a positive but finite rate of discount, it will be the case that $E_\infty > E^* > E_0$ and $X_0 > X^* > X_\infty$. The relationship of Y_∞ to Y_0 and Y^* is ambiguous because of the nonlinear net-growth function, which usually will have a single maximum at X_{MSY}. It is possible that $Y_\infty > Y_0$. For example, when $F(X) = rX(1 - X/K), H(X, E) = qXE$, and $C = cE$, some algebra will reveal that

$$X_\infty = \frac{c}{pq} \tag{3.18}$$

$$E_\infty = \frac{r(pqK - c)}{pq^2 K} \tag{3.19}$$

$$Y_\infty = \frac{cr(pqK - c)}{p^2 q^2 K} \tag{3.20}$$

$$E_0 = \frac{r(pqK - c)}{2pq^2 K} = \frac{E_\infty}{2} \tag{3.21}$$

$$Y_0 = \frac{r(pqK - c)(pqK + c)}{4p^2 q^2 K} = \frac{(pqK + c)Y_\infty}{4c} \tag{3.22}$$

$$X_0 = \frac{pqK + c}{2pq} = \frac{K + X_\infty}{2} \tag{3.23}$$

In Spreadsheet S3.2 we calculate $(X_\infty, E_\infty, Y_\infty)$, (E_0, Y_0, X_0), and (X^*, Y^*, E^*) for the base-case parameter set $r = 0.1$, $K = 1$, $q = 0.01$, $p = 200$, $c = 1$, and $\delta = 0.05$. Only the bioeconomic optimum depends on δ, and we see that the bioeconomic optimum is identical with the rent-maximizing optimum when $\delta = 0$ and essentially identical to the open-access equilibrium when $\delta = 500$ (an approximation of $\delta \to \infty$).

With a comparative sense of the open-access, rent-maximizing (sole owner), and bioeconomic (present-value-maximizing) equilibria, we now return to the concept of *user cost* to see the crucial role it plays in moving from open access to a bioeconomic optimum. In Chapter 1, Equation (1.18) required $\partial \pi(\bullet)/\partial Y_t = \rho\lambda_{t+1}$. This equation was interpreted as equating the marginal net benefit from harvest in period t to the discounted value of an additional fish in the water in period $t + 1$, where the latter term was referred to as *user cost*. From the recursive structure of the first-order conditions, it can be shown that λ_{t+1} reflects the discounted value that the additional fish (or marginal unit of biomass) contributes in $t + 1$ *and* over the entire (possibly infinite) future horizon. Thus user cost reflects the discounted future benefit that an increment in the stock in period $t+1$ will provide through additional biological growth and cost savings into the indefinite future.

	A	B	C	D
1	Spreadsheet S3.2			
2	$r =$	0.1	0.1	0.1
3	$K =$	1	1	1
4	$q =$	0.01	0.01	0.01
5	$p =$	200	200	200
6	$c =$	1	1	1
7	$\delta =$	0.05	0	500
8				
9	$X_\infty =$	0.5	0.5	0.5
10	$E_\infty =$	5	5	5
11	$Y_\infty =$	0.025	0.025	0.025
12				
13	$E_0 =$	2.5	2.5	2.5
14	$Y_0 =$	0.01875	0.01875	0.01875
15	$X_0 =$	0.75	0.75	0.75
16				
17	$X^* =$	0.683012702	0.75	0.500049995
18	$Y^* =$	0.021650635	0.01875	0.025
19	$E^* =$	3.169872981	2.5	4.99950005

Spreadsheet S3.2

Individual fishers, while perhaps aware of the potential benefit of a positive increment to the fish stock, may feel helpless to effectively increase the stock in the face of harvesting by other competitive fishers. Each fisher is presumably adopting a level of effort that equates the marginal value product of effort to marginal cost, and no weight is given to user cost. We will see that the success of actual management policies in avoiding the excesses of open access may critically depend on their ability to introduce user cost into the decision calculus of individual fishers.

3.9 TRADITIONAL MANAGEMENT POLICIES

There are at least six regulations that have been used in an attempt to avoid stock depletion under open access. Collectively, they might be regarded as traditional management policies. They are (1) closed seasons, (2) gear restrictions, (3) size restrictions, (4) trip or "bag" limits,

(5) total allowable catch (TAC), and (6) limited entry. We discussed certain aspects of some of these policies earlier in this chapter. Let's examine them in greater detail.

A *closed season* specifies a period of time when harvest of the resource is illegal. The closed season may correspond to a critical stage in the life history of a species when harvest might be particularly disruptive to survival or spawning (reproduction). For example, the commercial harvest of Pacific salmon in North America is prohibited when salmon enter the rivers and streams leading to their spawning grounds. The harvest of shellfish is often closed during the spring months when warming waters induce spawning, which will determine, in part, the set, survival, and size of future cohorts. It is also the case that a closed season may effectively reduce effort below E_∞, which would have occurred with no closed season. This is not a certainty because rent seeking by fishers simply may reallocate greater effort to the open season, when harvest is legal.

Gear restrictions are often imposed to deliberately reduce the efficiency of fishers or to prevent adverse impacts to the supporting ecosystem. In trawl fisheries, such as the groundfishery off the coast of New England in the United States, regional management authorities have set a minimum mesh size for the nets pulled by fishing vessels. By keeping mesh size at or above a minimum, it is hoped that juveniles would escape harvest as the net is being pulled along the sandy and relatively shallow bottom on Georges Bank. In Maryland, watermen harvesting oysters from Chesapeake Bay are restricted to pulling dredges using only sail power in boats called *skipjacks*. In the bays on southern Long Island, the harvest of hard clams is restricted to hand-pulled rakes or tongs. In these two shellfisheries, the restrictions that preclude diesel-powered vessels pulling larger dredges with vacuum pumps are thought to preserve the viability of the benthic ecosystem and thus the ability to grow future "crops" of oysters and clams.

In the Alaskan drift-net fishery in Bristol Bay, vessels are restricted to be no more than 32 feet in overall length. This has resulted in some interesting naval architecture, as can be seen in Figure 3.9. In this photograph, by Norm Van Vactor, both vessels are the same length. The bow of the *Ann Marie* has been flattened, and the hold capacity, engine horsepower, and in all likelihood, onboard electronics have been increased and upgraded. While the vessels are the same length, which

Resource Economics

Figure 3.9. Limited entry and gear restrictions may lead to capital stuffing.

one do think would result in greater de facto effort per day fished? The *Ann Marie* is an example of what we previously referred to as *capital stuffing*. If restrictions and/or limited entry create positive profits for vessels in the fishery, those profits are often used to invest in vessel modifications that increase the ability of the owner to catch more fish.

In the short run, gear restrictions are sometimes viewed as increasing the cost of effort $c > 0$ to a level above what it would be if there were no restrictions. This would result in a pivoting of the cost ray in Figure 3.4 upward and to the left, resulting in a lower open-access level of effort. If gear restrictions result in $c' > c > 0$, then in our static model of pure open access, $E'_\infty < E_\infty$.

Size limits often set a minimum legal harvest size for an individual fish or shellfish. They are designed to prevent the harvest of fish or shellfish before they reach sexual maturity and have had a chance to contribute to spawning and recruitment. Minimum size limits exist in the lobster fishery off the coast of Maine, where egg-bearing females are also supposed to be released. Some biologists are now advocating *maximum* size limits on the theory that stock abundance critically depends on "fat old females" (FOFs). FOFs are often significantly more fecund than younger females, and their value in the water is thought to be considerably greater than on the dock.

Trip limits are similar to "bag" limits in recreational hunting and fishing. In some fisheries, vessels might be limited in the number of pounds they can land on return to port. This may create an incentive to discard smaller fish until the trip limit is comprised of fewer but larger fish *if* large fish command a higher price per pound. The process of discarding smaller or lower-valued fish to maximize the dockside value of a trip limit is called *high-grading*. If the discarded fish die, then fishing mortality is greater than what would be indicated by harvest data.

We have already discussed TACs in the context of Homans and Wilen's model of regulated open access. In the case of the Pacific halibut, we saw that while a TAC might sustain a larger fish stock than under pure open access, it usually results in a "race for the fish" and leads to a compression of the fishing season. This, in turn, results in a flood of fish hitting the market during a short period of time and fishers losing the price premium normally associated with the marketing of fresh fish.

We also have discussed *limited entry* as an attempt to reduce effort by limiting the number of vessels with access to a fishery. Instituting a limited-entry program may require a program to "buy out" excess vessels. If such a program is anticipated, it may cause even more vessels to enter the fishery.

3.10 BIOECONOMIC OR INCENTIVE-BASED MANAGEMENT POLICIES

There are two bioeconomic management policies that economists have advocated based on the concept of user cost. They are landings taxes and the previously described ITQs. Recall, for the general renewable-resource model, that $\partial L/\partial Y_t = \partial \pi(\bullet)/\partial Y_t - \rho \lambda_{t+1} = 0$ or $\partial \pi(\bullet)/\partial Y_t = \rho \lambda_{t+1}$, where $\rho \lambda_{t+1}$ was the discounted marginal value of having one more fish in the water in period $t + 1$. Also recall that $\partial \pi(\bullet)/\partial Y_t$ was the net marginal benefit of harvesting one more fish today, in period t. For an individual price-taking (competitive) fisher, the marginal net benefit of harvesting an additional fish would be $\partial \pi(\bullet)/\partial Y_t = p - MC_t$, where $p > 0$ is the ex-vessel or dockside price per fish and $MC_t > 0$ is the marginal cost, to the fisher, of harvesting that fish. The competitive fisher, who is helpless to conserve the resource by himself or herself, would logically harvest until $p = \text{MC}_t$ and ignore user cost $\rho\lambda_{t+1}$. This is not optimal from a bioeconomic perspective. What is needed is a way to introduce $\rho\lambda_{t+1}$ into the decision calculus of the competitive fisher.

Economists have long been advocates of taxes to internalize externalities, and in 1974, Gardner Brown discussed the use of a *landings tax* to induce optimal harvest by competitive fishers. If fishery managers could estimate user cost, perhaps by estimating the cost function of a representative fisher and then solving a dynamic optimization problem, and if they could pass a law that would allow them to impose a landings tax at rate $\tau \approx \rho\lambda^*$, then fishers seeking the level of harvest that would equate the after-tax unit price to marginal cost would, in theory, set their level of harvest so that $p - \tau = \text{MC}_t$. Thus a landing tax, which would have the same dimension as $p > 0$, has the potential to induce optimal harvest.

In the mid-1970s, the U.S. Congress was considering an extension of territorial waters, outward from the U.S. coastline, to 200 miles and simultaneously reforming the way in which the fisheries in those waters would be managed. Lobbyists for the fishing industry, aware of economists' penchant for taxes to correct for externalities, were able to introduce language in the Fisheries Conservation and Management Act (FCMA) of 1976 that explicitly prohibited the use of taxes to manage fisheries. While the FCMA ruled out the use of taxes, it did not rule out the use of individual transferable quotas (ITQs).

In 1995, ITQs were introduced as a way to manage the Pacific halibut fishery, bringing an end to the halibut derby, as described previously by Timothy Egan. ITQs were described briefly in the introduction to this chapter. We now examine them in greater detail.

Suppose that fishery managers have set a limit on the number of vessels that can participate in a particular fishery. Let the total number of vessels be N, and let i be a vessel index number, $i = 1, 2, \ldots, N$. Each vessel is awarded (or may be required to purchase at auction) a share s_i of the total allowable catch. The TAC is likely to vary from year to year and is now denoted TAC_t. The shares must sum to one, that is, $\sum_{i=1}^{N} s_i = 1$. Once the TAC_t is announced, fishers holding a license and a share in the fishery know they have the option to harvest

$y_{i,t} = s_i \text{TAC}_t$ in year t. Fishers are not obligated to harvest $y_{i,t}$. If they wish, they can sell some or all of their individual transferable quota in year t to another licensed fisher. In theory, a market for ITQs and a market clearing price will develop where fishers who want to harvest more than their individual quota will be looking to buy, and those who want to harvest less will be looking to sell.

If $y_{i,t} = s_i \text{TAC}_t$ is the amount of fish (say, pounds) that the ith fisher has the option to harvest in period t, then the possibility of *not* fishing but rather selling $y_{i,t}$ in the ITQ market adds an opportunity cost to fishing. If the ITQ market clears at the price P_t^{ITQ}, then economic theory would suggest that $P_t^{\text{ITQ}} \approx p - \text{MC}_t \approx \rho\lambda_{t+1}$, and the ITQ-endowed fisher has to think whether he or she is better off fishing his or her quota or selling it. If shares are granted in perpetuity, they can create a class of fishers who have a long-term stake in managing the fishery so as to maximize the value of "their" property. If the stock is overfished, stock-dependent fishing costs will be high, the TAC likely will be low, and the value of ITQ, given by P_t^{ITQ}, will be low as well. Figure 3.10 shows TAC and quota demand curves when the fish stock is low, say, at X_0, and when it is at the steady-state optimal stock X^*, where $\text{TAC}^* = Y^* = F(X^*)$.

If management authorities can astutely set the TAC over time so as to guide the stock from X_0 to X^*, then $P_0^{\text{ITQ}} \to P^{\text{ITQ}*} = \rho\lambda^*$, and the bioeconomic optimum can be sustained in a limited-entry ITQ fishery. ITQs also have the potential to induce dynamic efficiency in a fishery.

Are there any negative aspects to limited entry and ITQs? ITQs work best in a well-defined single-species fishery. They do not work well in a multispecies fishery where the gear is nonselective. The Pacific halibut is pretty good example of a well-defined single-species fishery, whereas the groundfishery for cod, haddock, and flounder off the New England coast is not. Some economists also worry about the incentive to high-grade an ITQ if larger fish command a price premium. Perhaps the strongest criticism of ITQ programs is that they may create a wealthy group of ITQ-holding fishers. Those fishers who were *not* initially selected to be in the limited group of N fishers who were allocated shares of a TAC and who are just scraping by in poorly managed or open-access fisheries will not be fans of fishery management via ITQs. The article by John Tierney (2000), in the following box, does a

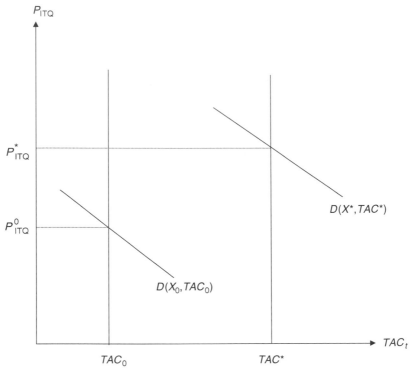

Figure 3.10. ITQ market prices when $X_0 < X^*$ and $TAC_0 < TAC^* = Y^*$.

great job of comparing a more or less open-access lobster fishery off the coast of Rhode Island with a similar ITQ fishery in Australia. Do equity issues outweigh the benefits of efficient resource management? Should the fishers fortunate enough to be members of a limited-entry ITQ fishery pay additional taxes? What do you think?

A Tale of Two Fisheries[*]

by
John Tierney

John Sorlien, a lean, sunburned fisherman in rubber overalls, was loading his boat along the wharf at Point Judith, R.I., not far from

---

[*] Published in the *New York Times Magazine* on August 27, 2000.

the spot where the "Tuna Capital of the World" sign stood three decades ago. Back then, you could harpoon giant bluefins right outside the harbor. Today, you would have a hard time finding one within 20 miles. Since the early 1970s, the tuna have declined – along with cod, swordfish, halibut and so many other species in the ruined fisheries of the Northeast. Sorlien, like the other fishermen in this harbor just west of Newport, is surviving thanks to New England's great cash crop, lobsters, but he wonders how much longer they'll be around. "Right now, my only incentive is to go out and kill as many fish as I can," Sorlien said. "I have no incentive to conserve the fishery, because any fish I leave is just going to be picked by the next guy."

Like the men who wiped out the buffaloes on the Great Plains in the 19th century, Sorlien is a hunter-gatherer who has become too lethal for his range. He is what's known in the business as a highliner – a fisherman who comes back with big hauls – but every season the competition gets tougher. When he got started 16 years ago, at the age of 22, he used a small boat and set traps within three miles of shore. These days, he doesn't even bother looking in those waters, which fishermen now refer to as "on the beach." He has graduated to a 42-foot boat and often goes 70 miles out to sea for lobsters, which can mean leaving the dock at midnight and not returning until 10 the following night. Each year, he has had to go farther and haul more traps just to stay even.

Sorlien was starting the season on this May morning by loading hundreds of the traps onto his boat, the *Cindy Diane*. The four-foot-long steel cages, each baited with a dangling skate fish, would spend the next eight months at sea. Sorlien would be tending 800 of them in all. On a typical day, he would haul 300, sometimes 400, up from the ocean floor to remove lobsters and insert fresh bait. As he stacked one 40-pound trap after another on deck, it was easy to see why he and so many other lobstermen have back problems. "My chiropractor says he can always tell when it's lobster season," Sorlien said.

The chiropractor is treating the consequence of what fishery scientists call "effort creep." Over the years, as Sorlien got a bigger boat and gradually doubled the number of his traps in the water, other lobstermen were doing the same. It was an arms race with no winners and some definite losers: the lobsters. Their life expectancy plummeted. "Lobsters used to live for 50 or 75 years," recalled Robert Smith, who has been lobstering at Point Judith since 1948. "When I started, it was not unusual to get a 30-pound lobster. It's been 20 years since I got one that was even 20 pounds." Last year, the biggest one he caught was four pounds, and that was an anomaly. Most lobsters don't even make it to two pounds. Biologists estimate that 90 percent of lobsters are caught within a year after they reach the legal minimum size at about age 6.

"If you translate that to the human population," Sorlien said, "it means that our industry is relying almost entirely on a bunch of 13-year-olds to keep us going. That doesn't seem too healthy. If we get some kind of environmental disruption that interferes with reproduction one year, we'll end up with nothing to catch for a whole season. We just go from year to year not knowing what to expect. I don't have a clue what kind of year this will be for me. It's like we're backing up to the edge of a cliff blindfolded, and we don't know if we're 50 feet away or have two wheels over the edge."

The obvious remedy would be to restrict the amount of fishing going on, as lobstermen have traditionally done in some communities. They have created informal local groups – called harbor gangs by anthropologists – in which they divvy up the nearby seabed, determining who can fish where, how long the season will be and how many traps each man can use.

The harbor gangs are built around the management principles of Tony Soprano. If a fishing trawler drags a net through their waters, destroying their traps, the lobstermen may dump an old car onto the seabed, which will rip the trawler's net the next time it's dragged. If an outside lobsterman intrudes, he might find a threatening note inside a bottle in one of his lobster traps or attached to the buoy above the traps. He might find that someone has removed his lobsters and left the traps conspicuously open or maybe applied a chain saw to the steel cages. More commonly, the intruder will find that the rope from the buoy has been cut, leaving the traps lost on the seabed. If he doesn't take the hint, his boat might be burned or sunk. Last summer, the Coast Guard barely rescued a lobster boat in Rockport, Me., that was going down. The owner, Robert Crowe, a newcomer to those fishing grounds, said someone had gone on board at night and destroyed the boat's battery, smashed the windows and beaten the engine with a hammer. "It's a lobster war," he explained.

The gang tactics yield both biological and economic benefits, as James M. Acheson reported in his 1988 book, *The Lobster Gangs of Maine.* Acheson, an anthropologist at the University of Maine, found that the lobstermen who most avidly defended their turf were able to make more money with less effort because the lobsters in their waters were larger and more plentiful. But the tactics generally work only in waters close to the gang's home. The open ocean is harder to defend. One small patch 20 miles offshore has been divvied up by a few lobstermen from Point Judith, but that's an exceptional case. It took several years and several thousand broken traps for the lobstermen and trawler captains to negotiate who got to fish where and when. And their arrangement is respected by outsiders mainly because one of the lobstermen has an especially fearsome reputation for protecting his turf.

Most stretches of open ocean are governed by state and federal governments, which is why the fish are in so much trouble. Tuna do not vote. Lobsters do not make campaign contributions. There may be future benefits from limiting this year's catch, but politicians don't want the fishing industry to suffer while they're up for re-election. Even when fish populations start to decline, officials are reluctant to impose strict limits. Instead, they have often tried to help struggling fishermen with subsidies, which merely encourage more overfishing.

The Canadian and American governments devastated one of the world's most productive fisheries, the Georges Banks off the coast of New England, by helping to pay for bigger boats. Now, even as scientists urge limits on lobstering, state and federal governments continue to offer tax breaks and other incentives to the lobstermen at Point Judith. John Sorlien was docked at a wharf financed by the taxpayers of Rhode Island. "It's not a sane system," Sorlien said. "We work with the government to break fisheries, and then we ask the government to subsidize us when the fish disappear."

As he got ready to take his traps to sea, he was listening to a plan for saving the fisheries. Sorlien, the president of the Rhode Island Lobstermen's Association, was being lobbied by one of his members, Richard Allen. It was gentle lobbying – New England lobstermen have not lost their classic laconic style – but there was no mistaking Allen's dedication to his cause. At 54, he has been lobstering for nearly 30 years and preaching reform for a decade. He expounded as Sorlien hosed the deck of the stinking juice from the lobster bait. "Dick is the messiah," Sorlien said with a smile. "His ideas have gotten him in a lot of trouble. Most of the guys don't agree with him. For a while, I didn't want to accept his ideas. But now I'm starting to think he's found the way."

Allen first found the way in the academic literature of fishery management, and then he saw it in operation. He journeyed to a port in Australia and returned with stories of a place with thriving lobsters, plenty of fat tuna, lots of prosperous fishermen – and no Soprano strong-arm tactics. It sounded like the maritime version of the Happy Hunting Grounds.

On the way into Port Lincoln, a little fishing town on a remote peninsula of Australia's southern coast, you pass an elaborate 20-foot-high black gate adorned with a gold crown. Below the crown is a sign in gold script: "Mansion de Braslov." The mansion is a red brick pile perched on the hillside, with a pink balustrade overlooking the water and a grand staircase attended by statues of two nymphs. It is the house that tuna built.

Locals call it the "Dynasty" house, as opposed to the "Dallas" house up the hill, which was built by another tuna oligarch who is said to have spent $50,000 just to get the plans for the mansion that appeared on the show. Nearby is a pink stucco house with 127,000 square feet. One fisherman with a stable of racehorses made news recently by spending $200,000 at an auction for an antique racing trophy. Another bought a mammoth yacht that had once belonged to Alan Bond, the financier.

Fishing has been very good to Port Lincoln. The fishermen have gleaming $600,000 boats in a pristine private marina flanked by new white stucco town houses. Compared with the decaying public wharfs in Point Judith, Port Lincoln feels like Palm Beach. The town's 13,000 inhabitants are said to include the highest number of millionaires per capita in the southern hemisphere. That, at least, is a factoid you keep hearing there. No one seems to know exactly where it comes from (there is no Southern Hemisphere Millionaire Census Bureau), but as the locals say, "You wouldn't be far wrong."

These millionaires are generally not the sort profiled by Robin Leach. Except for a half-dozen or so in mansions, they live in nice ranch houses. They are men like Daryl Spencer, who dropped out of school at 15 to work as a house painter. One morning, a friend asked him to fill in as a deckhand on a lobster boat. He kept working on the boats for four years and saved up $10,000 for the down payment on a house.

"I told my captain I needed a day off to go look at houses," Spencer recalled, "and he told me I should buy a boat instead. I said I couldn't afford a boat. He said: 'How about half a boat? I'll be your partner.' I wasn't sure – in those days lobstering wasn't a sought-after job. But my wife and I decided to hold off on the house."

Today, they have a house on a hilltop with a sweeping view of the harbor. They also own a thoroughbred racehorse. Lobstering turned out to be an excellent job thanks to a system of quotas that was pioneered in Australia and New Zealand. It is basically a version of the New England harbor gangs, run by the lobstermen under government supervision. The government started it in the 1960s by setting a limit on the total number of traps used by the fleet in Port Lincoln. Licenses for those traps were assigned to the working fishermen, and from then on, any newcomer who wanted to set a trap in those waters had to buy a license from someone already in the business. It's like New York's taxicab system, which has a fixed number of taxi licenses or "medallions": a newcomer who wants to own a cab must buy a medallion from someone who is retiring.

When Spencer got his own boat in 1984, he bought his first trap licenses for $2,000 apiece in Australian dollars. Nowadays, they would sell for $35,000, which means that Spencer's are worth a total of $2.1 million, or about $1.2 million in American dollars. He has done well by doing good: his licenses have become more valuable because the lobstermen are conservationists. They pay for scientists to monitor the fishery, and they have imposed strict harvesting limits that allow the lobsters to grow into sizable adults. The Australians are not any more altruistic than the Rhode Islanders – they too have mortgages to pay – and in the old days they used to howl when anyone suggested reducing their catch. But they began taking the long view as soon as they saw the rising price of their licenses for their lobster pots, as they call the traps. Like any property owner, they began thinking about resale value. "Why hurt the fishery?" Spencer said. "It's my retirement fund. No one's going to pay me $35,000 a pot if there are no lobsters left. If I rape and pillage the fishery now, in 10 years my licenses won't be worth anything."

Besides building up nest eggs, Port Lincoln's lobstermen have made their own jobs easier. In the old free-for-all days, lobstermen used to work every day of the seven-month season, including Christmas and Easter. "I once spent 10 days at sea with a dislocated hip," Spencer recalled. "I wasn't about to lose two days' income coming back to the doctor when my boat wasn't full." Now, he would go to the doctor and use up a couple of the off-days that each lobsterman is required to take during the season. While Rhode Island lobstermen are sometimes on the water 240 days per year, the Australians are not allowed to work more than 187 days of their 211-day season. And their days are a lot easier on the back, as a young lobsterman, Hubert Hurrell, demonstrated one March morning in his appropriately named boat, *Fine Time.*

Hurrell and I left the dock at 7:30 a.m. and sped out to his traps in barely an hour, cruising at 22 knots in his 60-foot boat. It was faster than Sorlien's and had twice as much room on deck and below. The wheelhouse and staterooms had the space and amenities you expect to find on yachts, not lobster boats. There was a television and VCR, a video-game player and a wraparound console with six screens showing data from computers, instruments and satellites. "We could virtually shut the window and fish just by looking at these," Hurrell said, pointing to the color images of the ocean floor and the locations of his traps.

He shook his head and winced when he heard about the 800 traps tended by the typical lobsterman in Rhode Island. In Port Lincoln, the lobstermen have limited themselves to 60 traps each. Hurrell had a larger boat than Sorlien not because he needed the space but because he could afford the luxury. It took Hurrell and his deckhand just an hour to raise their 60 traps and to extract an assortment of lobsters, including some hefty long-lived ones. After a leisurely lunch, they dropped the traps back into the water and were back on shore by 3. It was not quite an eight-hour day, and Hurrell was satisfied with the financial results. "No worries, mate," he said, which was not a bad summary of the prevailing view among the scientists who study the lobsters.

"Fishing may be the only economic activity in which you can make more money by doing less work," said Rick McGarvey, a biologist who monitors the fishery for the South Australian government. "By fishing less, the fishermen leave more lobsters out there to produce more eggs, which will make it easier for them to catch lobsters in the future. It's a win-win for the fish and the fishermen. The lobsters are thriving and the fishermen are spending more time at home with their families."

The system also makes McGarvey's job easier because he is spared the controversies that American scientists endure when they try to protect a fishery. In New England, a proposed conservation measure typically inspires a decade of battling that leads, at best, to an ineffectual compromise. In South Australia, the lobstermen act quickly to prevent overfishing, sometimes imposing stricter limits than the ones suggested by scientists. "We don't have to fight with the lobstermen," McGarvey said. "The old philosophy of fishery scientists was, 'We're philosopher kings and the fishermen are children who don't know what's good for themselves or the fish, so we have to impose regulations.' Now we just tell them what our research shows about the fishery, and they do a great job of regulating themselves."

Other researchers have documented similar success stories around the world, including many from traditional societies that have used property rights to protect the environment. In the South Pacific, where coral reefs have been destroyed by fishermen using dynamite and cyanide, the best-preserved reefs are the ones controlled by local villagers and closed off to outsiders. Japanese fishing villages have long prevented overfishing in local waters by using versions of harbor gangs. Louisiana's privately leased oyster beds are much healthier than the public ones in Mississippi. These results have won over most academic experts on fisheries. Last year, Australian-style quotas were endorsed in a report to Congress by the National Research Council, an arm of the National Academy of Sciences.

Property rights enable fishermen to avoid what ecologists call the tragedy of the commons: the destruction of a common resource because it is open to all. Just as the closely tended herds of cattle thrived on the same plains where the buffaloes perished, fish stand a better chance of surviving if they belong to someone instead of everyone.

The lobstermen of Port Lincoln have managed to work out only a primitive system of property rights – they each own a percentage of the traps used, not a patch of the ocean – and they are dealing with just one relatively immobile species in coastal waters. What about all the fish that migrate vast distances in the open ocean? How could you turn them into private property? It is not a simple proposition, but the lure of profits is inspiring innovation. Already, for instance, there are property owners in Port Lincoln tending herds of wild tuna.

It was feeding time for the tuna, and Brian Cuddeford was chugging out of the Port Lincoln harbor with eight tons of frozen herrings and anchovies stacked on the deck. The herrings were from England; the anchovies, from California. These tuna were accustomed to imported delicacies. "It's like room service for the fish, with the full white-glove treatment," Cuddeford said. "They're getting fed twice a day. In the wild, they were probably eating once a week."

The tuna fishermen of Port Lincoln used to go out to sea with empty decks and catch as many tuna as they wanted. They returned with a boatload of dead fish and dumped them into unrefrigerated trucks bound for a canning factory. The fishermen collected about $600 per ton. Today, the tuna ranchers make more than that for a single fish. "You're getting more dollar for your product, so you don't have to catch as many," Cuddeford said. "You don't have to be so greedy."

The ranchers still fish for their tuna in the wild, but with restrictions. Because tuna were decimated by the old open system, in the 1980s the government imposed limits on the annual catch. Now each fisherman owns what is called an individual transferable quota – the right to catch a certain percentage of the yearly haul. These quotas, which can be bought or sold like stock shares, are not cheap, so fishermen have changed their strategy. No longer able to slaughter fish at will, they have looked for ways to make the most of each fish. The result has been the world's premier tuna ranches.

When the tuna are first caught in a net far out at sea, they are shepherded by the thousands into floating pens. The pens are slowly towed to Port Lincoln in an enormous tuna drive that lasts about two weeks. Once the pens are anchored in a bay near Port Lincoln, it is the ranch hands' job to produce a fish good enough to become sashimi in Tokyo. "It's just like a feeding lot to fatten up cattle," Cuddeford said as he pulled up one of the pens, which consisted of a closed net dangling more than 40 feet below the surface. The net was attached to what looked like a huge inner tube, a floating ring of rubber about 200 feet in circumference. Cuddeford tossed in the frozen blocks of herrings and anchovies. As the blocks began melting, you could see the flashes of blue fins below the surface as the tuna snapped up their meals.

"We're giving them herring to get the oil content up in the meat," Cuddeford explained. "A bit more oil changes the color. The Japanese are fussy. They eat with their eyes." The tuna would be fed for several months as the ranchers monitored their weight and watched the price of tuna on the Tokyo market. At a propitious time, divers would jump into the pen and guide the fish – gently, because any bruise would mean a lower price – on to a boat, which would whisk them to shore and on to an airplane for Tokyo. The 2,200 tuna in this pen were worth more than $2 million. At night, armed guards patrolled the waters for larcenous humans and hungry seals.

Such ranching isn't practical yet for most species of fish – the tuna pens are economical only because bluefins are worth so much – but marine scientists are studying other ways to homestead the oceans. They have identified genetic markers and various features on fish that could serve as the equivalent of cattle brands. They can tell, for instance, exactly where a salmon spawned by examining its scales for the unique chemical signature of the stream where it was born. They have experimented with new kinds of underwater pens that use sound waves to mark their borders. Surveillance satellites can monitor who is fishing and what they are catching anywhere on the planet, which should soon make it technologically feasible for a quota system to be enforced throughout the world.

But there are, of course, a few political problems in persuading hunter-gatherers to become homesteaders. The biggest is how to divide up the range. Do you allocate the quotas and licenses equally among all working fishermen or according to how many fish each has been catching? Do you calculate each one's catch by considering the past year or the past 10 years? Do locals get first dibs on fishing rights? During Australia's debate over these questions, lobstermen were suing the government and slugging each other in pubs. Two decades later, some of their wives still aren't speaking at the grocery store.

Those disputes were relatively simple compared with the ones in America, where the fishing industry is older and larger. In the mid-1990s, the federal government successfully introduced Australia-style quotas in a few fisheries. But then Alaska's politicians got worried that fishermen from Seattle would end up with most of the quotas in their waters, so in 1996 they persuaded Congress to declare a national moratorium on any new quotas. The moratorium could end soon, which gives hope to Richard Allen, the Rhode Island lobsterman who has been preaching the

Port Lincoln gospel. But he has no illusions about the political difficulties of setting up a quota system. Over the past decade, he figures he has spent 5,000 hours serving on advisory commissions and meeting with lobstermen, politicians, bureaucrats and environmentalists.

"Most people start with the feeling that the ocean should be open to anyone who wants to fish," Allen said. "They complain that it's unfair to lock anyone out of the fishery. My answer is that with the current system, we already have fisheries that we're all locked out of. I can't go out and fish for halibut or swordfish – there aren't any left. I would rather have a healthy fish stock and the option to buy access to it." Allen has been gradually winning converts on the wharfs in Point Judith, but it hasn't been easy.

"We're our own worst enemy," Sorlien said. "We're like the cattlemen in the range wars who shot at each other because they were claiming the right to the same property. Somewhere along the line, they figured out it made more sense to divide up the land and set up a system of property rights. That's the rational solution for us, but we can't bring ourselves to go through the pain of allocating each person a share. We're so far away from being South Australia."

Quotas have been gaining support among conservationists, notably at the Environmental Defense Fund, but they still face strong opposition from Greenpeace and other critics who fear that corporations will take over public waters. Once property rights are established, the same economic forces working against family farms could induce local fishermen to sell out to companies with big boats. While economists appreciate the increased efficiency of the bigger boats – less labor, fuel and capital expended per fish – others worry about the lost jobs and the impact on fishing towns. But it is possible to set up a quota system and still protect small-time operators, as the lobstermen in Port Lincoln did by putting a limit on the number of trap licenses that any one person can own.

As a result, there are still plenty of independent lobstermen in Port Lincoln; they just make more money doing easier work. Allen was explaining this to Sorlien and his deckhand, James West, as they stacked lobster traps that morning in May. They looked incredulous when Allen described the huge new boats in Port Lincoln being used to haul just 60 traps.

"Sixty traps?" West said. "Man, I'd be happy if we could get by with 200." He listened approvingly to Allen's description of the Australian system, but he didn't like the part about newcomers having to buy their way into the fishery. West, who had been working as a deckhand for 11 years, was hoping soon to get his own boat. "I don't want the door shut on me," he said. "I've put a lot of time into this business. That's not fair."

Allen said that there would be special help for young people in West's position, but he conceded that there would be an expense. "You'd have to pay some money up front," he said. "But think of all the costs you'd avoid by using fewer traps. You'd be burning less fuel and using less bait. Think of what you'd be buying into – a business with a future."

The deckhand was starting to come around. "Well, I like that idea," West said. "I don't want to buy a boat and hear that in 10 years it'll be worthless because you won't be able to make a dime lobstering."

The captain was still thinking about all the traps he wouldn't have to stack. "Imagine that – just 60 traps," Sorlien said. He had been working for six hours, since 5:30 a.m., and the workday wasn't even half over. "You'd be done for the day now. You could be home counting your money, and you wouldn't have to worry about where the next lobster was coming from."

3.11 MARINE RESERVES

Fishery management is made difficult because of fluctuations in the marine environment that influence mortality, growth, and recruitment in commercial fisheries. These seemly random fluctuations turn dynamic equations, such as our difference equation describing the change in a fish stock, into what mathematicians call *stochastic processes*. The management problem now becomes a stochastic optimization problem that might be solved using stochastic dynamic programming, provided that the random variables are statistically independent and drawn from distributions that are identical over time (and thus time-invariant). The problem then becomes a question of knowing the functional forms of the equations in the bioeconomic model and estimating the parameters in those equations and the distributions of the random variables driving the stochastic processes. I have already admitted that all models are abstractions, and now I have to admit that it is probably impossible to know the functional forms, parameters, and distributions of the best or most appropriate model. Lauck et al. (1998) refer to this as a situation of *irreducible uncertainty*. In such a world, perhaps the most appropriate policy is to follow a *precautionary principle*, where actions, such as harvest rates, are set at levels that keep the subjective probability of a catastrophic outcome (e.g., collapse of a fish stock) at some very small level (perhaps 0.001). The problem, of course, is to estimate how the probability of catastrophe depends on the scale of the action. In fisheries, many biologists are convinced that the best way to reduce the risk of a harvest-induced stock collapse is through establishment of areas where fishing is prohibited. These "no-fish" areas are often called *marine reserves* or *marine protected areas*.

Marine reserves might be permanent or temporary, part of a system where areas are opened and closed rotationally within a larger marine ecosystem. Permanent marine reserves are often designated as a way of protecting unique ecosystems, such as coral reefs, or systems containing endangered species (e.g., Gray's Reef off the coast of Georgia, where the North Atlantic right whale, *Eubalaena glacialis*, has its calving grounds). In 2004, the U.S. National Marine Sanctuary Program listed a total of 14 marine protected areas (MPAs) – four in California; one in American Samoa; one in Florida; one in Georgia; two in Hawaii; and one each in Louisiana, Massachusetts, Michigan, North Carolina, and Washington. Permanent MPAs are comparable to the U.S. system of national parks, where landscapes and terrestrial ecosystems are preserved and protected from human impact and alteration. Marine reserves, whether permanent or rotational, might play a role in restocking and reducing the fluctuations of commercial species that are harvested from areas that remain open to fishing (see Conrad, 1999). The optimal location and size of marine reserves might be determined within a dynamic-spatial model.

We will look at a model of rotational marine reserves that is a simplification of a more complex model developed by Valderrama and Anderson (2007) for the Atlantic sea scallop (*Placopecten magellanicus*). The model provides a nice introduction to Chapter 4, which will examine the optimal rotation for even-aged trees grown in a forest plantation.

Consider a very small patch of ocean bottom, suitable for growing a single sea scallop. Sea scallops exhibit rapid growth in shell size and the size of the adductor muscle, which they use to open and close the two halves of their distinctive, fan-shaped shell. (See the box below for a description of both the sea and bay scallop, along with culinary advice on their preparation.)

The Scallop: Description and Culinary Guide from the University of Delaware Sea Grant Program

The Scallop

The scallop is possibly best known for its beautiful and distinctive shell. It has been captured in works of art by Titian, Botticelli, and many others. Buildings in ancient Pompeii were decorated with scallop-shell ornaments.

Scallops are bivalve mollusks with scallop-edged, fan-shaped shells. The shells are further characterized by radiating ribs or grooves and concentric growth rings. Near the hinge, where the two halves (shells) meet, the shell is flared out on each side forming small "wings". Just inside the shell, along the edge of the mantle, is a row of short sensory tentacles and a row of small blue eyes. (Maybe you've heard of the book *Stalking the Blue-Eyed Scallop*, by Euell Gibbons). The shells are opened and closed by a single, over-sized adductor muscle which is sometimes referred to as the "eye".

The eye, or adductor muscle, is the part of the scallop we eat here in the U.S. In Europe, the entire scallop is eaten. The adductor muscle is more developed in the scallop than in oysters and clams because scallops are active swimmers. They glide freely through the water and over the sea floor by snapping their shells together.

Scallops are primarily harvested by dredging and are shucked soon after capture. They cannot hold their shells closed; therefore, once they are out of the water, they lose moisture quickly and die. Consequently, they're shucked on board the fishing vessel, placed in containers, and refrigerated.

Culinary Description and Preparation of
Sea Scallops and Bay Scallops

The sea scallop (*Plactopecten magellanicus*) is the largest of the scallops. You usually get approximately 20–40 in one pound. They can be bought fresh or frozen. Scallops freeze well, so if they are on sale or you buy too many, freeze them for later use. The raw meats are creamy white in color and sometimes slightly orange due to the food (algae) they consume. Scallops have a distinct, sweet odor when they are fresh.

There are many ways to prepare scallops. Always take care not to overcook them; they toughen easily. As soon as they lose their translucence and turn opaque, they are done. Sea scallops may be broiled, kabobed, stir-fried, baked, or microwaved. There are many recipes for scallops. If you plan to put them in a sauce, it's best to cook the scallops and the sauce separately and then combine them; otherwise, water will cook out of the scallops and make your sauce runny.

The bay scallop (*Argopecten irradians*) resides in bays and estuaries from New England to the Gulf of Mexico. Its muscle reaches about one half inch in diameter. You usually find about 50–90 in one pound. Bay scallop meats are white with some pink coloration, on occasion, due to the food (algae) they consume.

You need to be especially careful when cooking bay scallops. Because of their size, they tend to overcook very easily and will become tough. They are sweet and tender yet firm when cooked properly. Bay scallops may be baked, sautéed, stir-fried, or microwaved. If you need cooked scallops for a seafood salad, simply wash and dry one pound, then wrap them deli-sandwich style in a microwaveable paper towel, and microwave on HIGH for 3 minutes. You will have perfectly cooked scallops. Or else, you may prefer a more traditional recipe such as Coquilles Saint-Jacques, a creamy scallop recipe found in many cookbooks. This favorite can even be used as an appetizer before an elegant repast.

Let $N(T)$ denote the net revenue from harvesting a sea scallop of age $T = 1, 2, 3, \ldots$. Let $\delta > 0$ be the discount rate and $m > 0$ be the annual mortality rate. Our discrete-time discount factor is again $\rho = 1/(1 + \delta)$, and the mortality rate will influence expected revenue. We want to determine the age at which to harvest our scallop, start rearing the next scallop, and so on *ad infinitum*. The present value of our small patch of ocean floor devoted to growing scallop after scallop, all harvested at expected age T, will be given by the expression

$$\pi(T) = N(T)\rho^T[1 + \rho^T + (\rho^T)^2 + (\rho^T)^3 + \cdots] \qquad (3.24)$$

Since $1 > \rho > 0$, the infinite series $[1 + \rho^T + (\rho^T)^2 + (\rho^T)^3 + \cdots]$ converges to $1/(1 - \rho^T)$. [This is precisely what was happening in Equation (1.10) in Chapter 1.] We therefore can write the present value of our small patch of ocean floor as

$$\pi(T) = \frac{N(T)\rho^T}{(1 - \rho^T)} = \frac{N(T)}{(\rho^{-T} - 1)} = \frac{N(T)}{[(1 + \delta)^T - 1]} \qquad (3.25)$$

Biologists have studied the growth in shell height and weight of the adductor muscle. They have found that the *Von Bertalanffy equation* gives a very good fit for shell height as a function of age. This equation may be written as

$$S(T) = S_\infty(1 - e^{-kT}) \qquad (3.26)$$

where $S(T)$ is expected shell height at age T, $S_\infty = 152.46$ is the asymptotic maximum shell height in millimeters (mm), and $k = 0.4$ is a growth rate. These parameter estimates are for Georges Bank, a major scalloping grounds off the New England coast.

The relationship between shell height and weight of the adductor muscle is modeled by the equation

$$W(T) = e^{a + b \ln[S(T)]} = e^{a + b \ln[S_\infty(1 - e^{-kT})]} \qquad (3.27)$$

where $W(T)$ is the weight of the adductor muscle of a surviving scallop in grams. Biologists have estimated the parameter values for Georges Bank as $a = -11.6$ and $b = 3.12$. To keep things simple, we adopt a constant per-gram price of $p > 0$ and a constant cost for harvest of a single scallop of any age of $c > 0$. Expected net revenue, should the scallop survive to T, is

$$N(T) = (1 - m)^T p e^{a + b \ln[S_\infty(1 - e^{-kT})]} - c \qquad (3.28)$$

and our expression for expected present value becomes

$$\pi(T) = \frac{(1-m)^T p e^{a+b\ln[S_\infty(1-e^{-kT})]} - c}{(1+\delta)^T - 1} \tag{3.29}$$

With parameter values for p, a, b, S_∞, k, c, δ, and m, we can use Solver to find the integer value for T that maximizes $\pi(T)$. This is done in Spreadsheet S3.3, where $p = 0.013$ ($/gram) and $c = 0.003$ ($/scallop). The optimal age at harvest, in this simplified model, is $T^* = 4$ years when shell height is approximately 121.68 millimeters and the adductor muscle has an expected weight of 29.38 grams. The expected present value of our tiny patch of ocean floor is $1.15. There is quite a large area of ocean floor suitable for sea scallops, and in 2006, the value of the U.S. harvest was estimated to be almost $386 million, making the Atlantic sea scallop fishery one of the most valuable in the world.

Valderrama and Anderson (2007), in a multiple-cohort model where older and larger scallops command a price premium, found that the optimal rotation on Georges Bank was to open a closed area for scalloping every sixth year and then allow intensive harvest for approximately two years, after which time the area is closed for another five

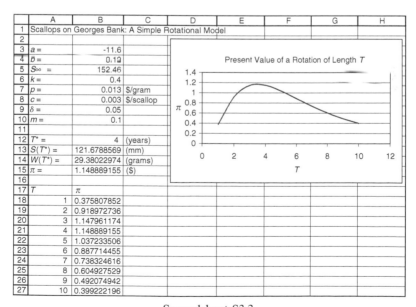

	A	B	C	D	E	F	G	H
1	Scallops on Georges Bank: A Simple Rotational Model							
2								
3	$a =$	-11.6						
4	$b =$	0.12						
5	$S_\infty =$	152.46						
6	$k =$	0.4						
7	$p =$	0.013	$/gram					
8	$c =$	0.003	$/scallop					
9	$\delta =$	0.05						
10	$m =$	0.1						
11								
12	$T^* =$	4	(years)					
13	$S(T^*) =$	121.6788569	(mm)					
14	$W(T^*) =$	29.38022974	(grams)					
15	$\pi =$	1.148889155	($)					
16								
17	T	π						
18	1	0.375807852						
19	2	0.918972736						
20	3	1.147961174						
21	4	1.148889155						
22	5	1.037233506						
23	6	0.887714455						
24	7	0.738324616						
25	8	0.604927529						
26	9	0.492074942						
27	10	0.399222196						

Spreadsheet S3.3

years. This optimal rotation would suggest that Georges Bank should
be partitioned into six scalloping grounds, with vessels allowed to harvest each area every sixth and possibly seventh year. The New England
Fishery Management Council is currently managing the sea scallop
fishery on Georges Bank using a combination of three closed or limited-
access areas, a limit on effort (days at sea), and a dredge ring size of 4
inches, which allows smaller scallops to escape harvest.

3.12 EXERCISES

E3.1 Consider the fishery management problem that seeks to

$$\text{Maximize } \pi = \sum_{t=0}^{\infty} \rho^t [p Y_t - (c/2) Y_t^2 / X_t]$$
$$\{Y_t\}$$
$$\text{Subject to} X_{t+1} - X_t = r X_t (1 - X_t/K) - Y_t$$
$$X_0 > 0 \quad \text{given}$$

The associated Lagrangian may be written as

$$L = \sum_{t=0}^{\infty} \rho^t \{ [p Y_t - (c/2) Y_t^2 / X_t]$$
$$+ \rho \lambda_{t+1} [X_t + r X_t (1 - X_t/K) - Y_t - X_{t+1}] \}$$

(a) What are the first-order necessary conditions?
(b) Evaluate the first-order conditions in steady state, and show
    that they imply the following two-equation system:

$$Y = \phi(X) = X[r(1 - 2X/K) - \delta]$$
$$+ \sqrt{\{X[r(1 - 2X/K) - \delta]\}^2 - (2pX^2/c)[r(1 - 2X/K) - \delta]}$$
$$Y = F(X) = rX(1 - X/K)$$

(c) Show that $F(X) = \phi(X)$ further implies that

$$X^* = \frac{B + \sqrt{B^2 - 4C}}{2A}$$

where

$$A = 1$$

$$B = \left(\frac{2K}{3cr}\right)(2cr - c\delta - 2p)$$

$$C = -\left(\frac{2K^2}{3cr}\right)(p - cr/2 - \delta p/r + c\delta).$$

(d) For $r = 1$, $K = 1$, $c = 3$, $p = 1$, and $\delta = 0.05$, construct a spreadsheet and confirm that $B = 0.85555556, C = 0.08888889$, $X^* = 0.73454306, Y^* = 0.19498955$, and that the plots of $Y = F(X) = rX(1 - X/K)$ and $Y = \phi(X)$ look as follows. *Note:* $Y = \phi(X)$ is an imaginary number for $0.47 \geq X \geq 0.15$.

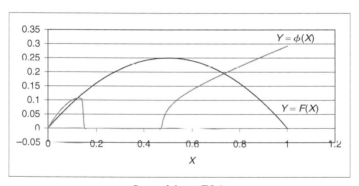

Spreadsheet E3.1

E3.2 Suppose that X_t represents the amount of water (in acre-feet) in an underground aquifer and W_t the amount of water pumped (also in acre-feet) from the aquifer, both in period t. Suppose that there is a *constant rate of recharge* $R > 0$ (in acre-feet) into the aquifer in each period so that the change in the amount of water in the aquifer is given by the difference equation $X_{t+1} - X_t = R - W_t$. The net benefit from water pumped from the aquifer in period t is given by the function $\pi(X_t, W_t) = aW_t - (b/2)W_t^2 - cW_t/X_t$, where $a > b > 0$ and $c > 0$ are parameters. The groundwater management problem might be stated as

$$\text{Maximize}_{\{W_t\}} \pi = \sum_{t=0}^{\infty} \rho^t [aW_t - (b/2)W_t^2 - cW_t/X_t]$$

$$\text{Subject to } X_{t+1} - X_t = R - W_t$$

$$X_0 > 0 \quad \text{given}$$

(a) What is the Lagrangian for this problem?

(b) What are the first-order conditions for the optimal trajectories for W_t, X_t, and λ_t?

(c) Evaluate the first-order conditions in steady state, and show that they imply the two-equation system

$$W = \phi(X) = \frac{\delta(aX - c)X}{\delta bX^2 + c}$$

$$W = R$$

(d) What is the analytic expression for X^*? *Hint:* It is the positive root of a quadratic equation.

(e) For $a = 100, b = 0.001, c = 812,500$. $R = 35,000$ (acre-feet), and $\delta = 0.05$, plot $W = \phi(X)$ for $200,000 \geq X \geq 0$ and $W = R = 35,000$. What is the numerical value for X^*?

E3.3 This exercise is a continuation of Exercise E3.2, where you solved for the optimal steady-state stock of water to maintain in an aquifer. In this exercise we keep the same parameter values that were given in part (e) of Exercise E3.2, but now we give you an initial condition, $X_0 = 200,000$ acre-feet and ask you to use Excel's Solver to find the approximately optimal approach path from X_0 to X^*. The horizon where Solver gets to choose W_t is $t = 0, 1, 2, \ldots, 19$. For $t = 20, 21, \ldots, \infty$, the groundwater stock is maintained by requiring $W_t = R$ (you are only allowed to pump recharge for $t = 20, 21, \ldots, \infty$).

(a) What is the final function for this problem?

(b) Set up an initial spreadsheet with $W_t = 35,000$ for $t = 0, 1, 2, \ldots, 19$. What are the values for $X_{20}, \psi(X_{20})$, the final function, and π, discounted net revenue, on your initial spreadsheet?

(c) Ask Solver to maximize π by changing W_t from the initial guess $W_t = 35{,}000$ for $t = 0, 1, 2, \ldots, 19$. What are the values for X_{20}, $\psi(X_{20})$, the final function, and π, discounted net revenue, on the optimized spreadsheet?

E3.4 Consider a fishery where $X_{t+1} - X_t = rX_t(1 - X_t/K)^\beta - Y_t$, $\pi(X_t, Y_t) = \ln[Y_t]$, and you wish to

$$\underset{\{Y_t\}}{\text{Maximize}} \sum_{t=0}^{\infty} \rho^t \ln(Y_t)$$

$$\text{Subject to } X_{t+1} - X_t = rX_t(1 - X_t/K)^\beta - Y_t$$

$$X_0 > 0 \text{ given}$$

(a) What is the Lagrangian expression for this problem? What are the first-order conditions?

(b) Evaluating the first-order conditions in steady state, derive the implicit expression $G(X)$, where $G(X) = 0$ at $X = X^*$, the steady-state optimal biomass.

(c) What are the values for X^* and Y^* when $r = 1$, $K = 1$, $\beta = 0.5$, and $\delta = 0.04$?

E3.5 In some fisheries, recruitment to the adult fishable population depends on the escapement of adults $(\tau + 1)$ periods earlier. Specifically, consider a fishery where the adult population in period $t + 1$ is determined by $X_{t+1} = (1 - m)(X_t - Y_t) + F(X_{t-\tau} - Y_{t-\tau})$, where $1 > m > 0$ is the per-period mortality rate for adults, $(X_t - Y_t)$ is adult escapement in period t, and $F(X_{t-\tau} - Y_{t-\tau})$ is a net-growth or recruitment function where new recruits to the adult population in period $t + 1$ depend on adult escapement in $t - \tau$. The problem of interest seeks to

$$\underset{\{Y_t\}}{\text{Maximize}} \pi = \sum_{t=0}^{\infty} \rho^t \pi(X_t, Y_t)$$

$$\text{Subject to } X_{t+1} = (1 - m)(X_t - Y_t) + F(X_{t-\tau} - Y_{t-\tau})$$

Derive the analogue to the fundamental equation of renewable resources, which in Chapter 1 took the form

$$F'(X) + \frac{\partial \pi(\bullet)/\partial X}{\partial \pi(\bullet)/\partial Y} = \delta$$

In this problem, with lagged recruitment, write your analogue expression so that $(1 + \delta)$ is isolated on the right-hand side.

E3.6 Let X_t be the number of adult (sexually mature) blue whales in the southern ocean and E_t the number of factory vessels harvesting whales. A plausible model for the dynamics of the blue whale population takes the form

$$X_{t+1} = (1 - m)(1 - qE_t)X_t + r(1 - qE_{t-\tau})$$
$$\times X_{t-\tau}\{1 - [(1 - qE_{t-\tau})X_{t-\tau}/K]^\alpha\}$$

where

$$E_t = \begin{cases} E_{\max} \text{ if } pqX_t - c > 0 \\ E_{\min} \text{ if } pqX_t - c \le 0 \end{cases}$$

In the preceding equations and inequalities, $1 > m > 0$ is the natural mortality rate for adult blue whales, $q > 0$ is a catchability coefficient, $r > 0$ is an intrinsic growth rate, $K > 0$ is a parameter that, in part, determines the carrying capacity for blue whales in the southern ocean, $\alpha > 1$ is a skew parameter, $E_{\max} > 0$ is the maximum number of factory vessels available during the period of analysis, $E_{\min} = 0$ is the minimum number of factory vessels available, $p > 0$ is the value of products obtainable from an adult blue whale, and $c > 0$ is the cost of operating a factory vessel and associated catcher boats during a whaling season in the southern ocean.

We are interested in simulating the blue whale population, effort, and harvest from 1946 until 1965 when the International Whaling Commission (IWC) banned the harvest of blue whales in the southern ocean. The equation describing the dynamics of the blue whale is a model with *lagged recruitment*. Blue whales are assumed to reach sexually maturity at age τ, and thus the recruits to the adult population in period $t + 1$ depend on the number of adults that escaped harvest in period $t - \tau$. Lagged recruitment is given by the term $F(S_{t-\tau}) = r(1 - qE_{t-\tau})X_{t-\tau}\{1 - [(1 - qE_{t-\tau})X_{t-\tau}/K]^\alpha\}$, where $S_{t-\tau} = X_{t-\tau} - Y_{t-\tau} = (1 - qE_{t-\tau})X_{t-\tau}$.

Suppose that $X_t = 102,233$ and $E_t = 0$ for the years $t = 1939, 1940, \ldots, 1945$. In 1946, assume that $E_{1946} = 19$, and for the years 1947 through 1964, the levels for E_t were determined by the *if statement* below the equation for X_{t+1}. Assume that $r = 0.05$, $m = 0.03, K = 150,000, \tau = 6, \alpha = 2.39, c = 400,000, p = 20,000$, $q = 0.01 \quad E_{max} = 27$, and $E_{min} = 0$. Set up a spreadsheet that simulates X_t for $t = 1946, \ldots, 1965$ and E_t and $Y_t = qX_tE_t$ for $t = 1946, \ldots, 1964$. What is the value of X_{1965}, the blue whale population in the southern ocean in 1965?

E3.7 With the moratorium on the harvest of blue whales in the southern ocean, the equation for population dynamics becomes

$$X_{t+1} = (1 - m)X_t + rX_{t-\tau}[1 - (X_{t-\tau}/K)^\alpha]$$

(a) What is the expression for X_{SS}, the steady-state population of blue whales in the southern ocean when they are no longer harvested?

(b) What is the necessary and sufficient condition for the stability of X_{SS}? (After substituting your expression for X_{SS} into the stability condition, the inequality for stability will depend on a constant and the parameters α, r, and m.)

(c) For $r = 0.05, m = 0.03, K = 150,000, \tau = 6$, and $\alpha = 2.39$, what is the numerical value for X_{SS}? Is X_{SS} locally stable? Why?

(d) Assume that $X_t = 2,000$ for $t = 1959, \ldots, 1965$ and that $r = 0.05, m = 0.03, K = 150,000, \tau = 6$, and $\alpha = 2.39$. Simulate and plot the population of blue whales in the southern ocean from 1959 through 2007. What is the value for X_{2007}?

4

The Economics of Forestry

This chapter will examine the economics of even-aged forestry and the optimal inventory of old-growth forest. By an *even-aged forest*, I mean a forest consisting of trees of the same species and age. Such a forest might be established by a lightning-induced fire or by humans after clearcutting a stand of trees. The first nonnative settlers in western Washington and Oregon encountered vast stretches of even-aged forest (predominantly Douglas fir) that had been established by natural ("volunteer") reseeding following a fire. Today, silvicultural practices by forest firms are specifically designed to establish an age-structured forest inventory, or *synchronized forest*, where tracts of land contain cohorts ranging in age from seedlings to "financially mature" trees, that provides the forest firm with a more or less steady flow of timber to its mills.

In western Washington and Oregon in the mid-1800s, most forest stands contained trees over 200 years old with diameters in excess of five feet. Collectively, these forests constituted a huge inventory of old-growth timber that was used in the construction of houses and commercial buildings, the building of ships, and the manufacture of railroad ties, telegraph poles, furniture, musical instruments, and a plethora of other items. In the 1850s, the old-growth forests of the Pacific Northwest must have seemed limitless and inexhaustible, but by the 1920s, foresters were already contemplating the end of this period of "old-growth mining" and the establishment of a forest economy based on the sustainable harvest of timber from even-aged forest "plantations."

An obvious question would be, "When should we cease the cutting of old-growth forest and preserve what's left?" This question was a controversial policy issue in the Pacific Northwest and Alaska, where most of the remaining old-growth forest resides on land owned by the federal government. The remaining inventory of old-growth forest provides a valuable flow of amenity services as a result of its ability to provide (1) sites for hiking and camping, (2) habitat for wildlife, (3) watershed protection, and (4) what we refer to as *option value*.

In determining the optimal age at which to cut an even-aged stand of trees, I will take the perspective of a private, present-value-maximizing individual or firm. When trying to determine the optimal inventory of old-growth forest to preserve, I will take the perspective of a social forester or planner who seeks to balance the flow of nontimber amenity value with the desire for net revenue and jobs in the forest economy. Many of these same issues arise in management of the mixed-hardwood forests of the north-central and northeastern United States and in the tropical forests found in developing countries. The management of these forests is more complex because it involves multispecies management with interspecific competition for light, water, and nutrients in the case of temperate forests or the potential instability of soils in the case of tropical forests.

4.1 THE VOLUME FUNCTION AND MEAN ANNUAL INCREMENT

Consider a parcel of land that has been cleared of trees recently by fire or cutting. Supposed that the parcel is reseeded (restocked) by windblown seed from neighboring trees or by seedlings planted by a forest firm. Taking the date of reseeding as $t = 0$ and treating time as a continuous variable, let $Q = Q(t)$ denote volume of merchantable timber at instant $t > 0$. *Merchantable volume* is the volume of wood that has commercial value. A plausible shape for this volume function is shown in Figure 4.1.

This figure shows the volume of merchantable timber increasing until about $t = 86$, after which time volume decreases as a result of disease and decay (senescence). In reality, merchantable volume may not become positive until five or more years after reseeding. The functional

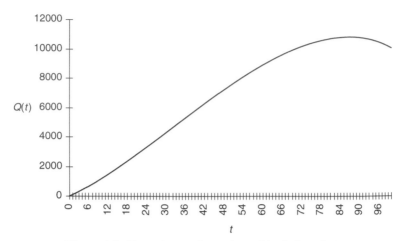

Figure 4.1. The volume of merchantable timber $Q(t)$.

form used in drawing Figure 4.1 is a cubic given by

$$Q(t) = at + bt^2 - dt^3 \qquad (4.1)$$

where $a = 100$, $b = 2$, and $d = 0.02$. Another functional form that is used frequently to approximate merchantable volume is the exponential

$$Q(t) = e^{a-b/t} \qquad (4.2)$$

where $b > a > 0$. As $t \to \infty$, $Q(t) \to e^a$, and there is no decline in the volume of merchantable timber when using this functional form.

Foresters have long been interested in the appropriate time to wait before a recently replanted parcel should be cut and replanted again. The interval between cuttings is called the *rotation length*. Foresters also were aware that it might be desirable to arrange a more or less steady annual timber harvest from a large forest. This presumably would permit a more or less steady annual employment for loggers and mill workers. It might be possible to organize a large forest into some number of smaller parcels ranging in age from zero (just replanted) to age T (about to be cut), where T is rotation length.

Suppose that one wished to maximize the average annual yield from a rotation of length T. This means that every T years you would cut the representative parcel, obtaining an average annual volume $Q(T)/T$. Early foresters called this average annual volume the *mean*

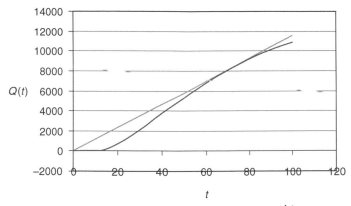

Figure 4.2. The volume function $Q(t) = e^{a-b/t}$.

annual increment (MAI) and sought the rotation that would maximize it. Taking the derivative, $d[Q(T)/T]/dT$, and setting it equal to zero results in the expression $Q(T)/T = Q'(T)$. This says that the rotation that maximizes MAI must equate the average product from waiting $[Q(T)/T]$ with the marginal product from waiting $[Q'(T)]$. Graphically, this rotation can be identified by finding where a ray from the origin is just tangent to the volume function. For the cubic volume function given in Equation (4.1), the rotation-maximizing MAI will be $T = b/(2d)$. For the exponential function in Equation (4.2), this rotation is simply $T = b$, Figure 4.2 shows a plot of Equation (4.2) for $a = 10$ and $b = 70$ and draws in the ray from the origin that is tangent at $T = 70$.

The rotation that maximizes average annual volume is analogous to the stock level that maximized sustainable yield in the fishery. While at first blush it may seem a desirable rotation (it maximizes the volume harvested over an infinite horizon), it similarly ignores any economic considerations, such as the net price for timber, the cost of replanting, and the discount rate.

4.2 THE OPTIMAL SINGLE ROTATION

Suppose that a parcel of land has been reseeded recently, and you are to maximize the net present value of this single stand. After this stand is cut, the land will be converted to some other use in which you have no financial stake. How long should you wait before harvesting this single stand?

Let $p > 0$ denote the *net* price per unit volume at harvest, which is assumed known and constant. With time a continuous variable, we will use $e^{-\delta t}$ as the appropriate factor for calculating the present value of a financial reward at instant $t > 0$. (See Chapter 1 for a discussion of continuous-time discounting.) With no replanting, the net present value of a single rotation of length T is given by $\pi_s = pQ(T)e^{-\delta T}$. The optimal single rotation can be found by solving $d\pi_s/dT = pQ(T)e^{-\delta T}(-\delta) + pQ'(T)e^{-\delta T} = 0$, which implies

$$pQ'(T) = \delta pQ(T) \tag{4.3}$$

This equation has an important economic interpretation. On the left-hand side (LHS), the term $pQ'(T)$ is the marginal value of allowing the stand to grow an increment (dT) longer. On the right-hand side (RHS), the term $\delta pQ(T)$ is the marginal cost of allowing the stand to grow an increment longer. It represents the foregone interest payment on not cutting the stand now. Thus the optimal single rotation will balance the *marginal value of waiting* with the *marginal cost of waiting*.

We could have canceled $p > 0$ from both sides of Equation (4.3) and written the first-order condition as $Q'(T)/Q(T) = \delta$. The interpretation of this equivalent equation is that the optimal single rotation equates the percentage rate of increase in volume $[Q'(T)/Q(T)]$ with the discount rate. For the exponential volume function in Equation (4.2), the optimal single rotation has an analytic (explicit) expression given by $T = \sqrt{b/\delta}$. It normally will be the case that the optimal single rotation is shorter than the rotation that maximizes mean annual increment.

4.3 THE FAUSTMANN ROTATION

Suppose now that the parcel of land has just been reseeded, and you are asked to determine the optimal rotation if the parcel is to be devoted to rotational (even-aged) forestry in perpetuity. Suppose that $c > 0$ is the cost of replanting the parcel and that p, c, δ, and $Q(t)$ are unchanging over all future rotations. In this unlikely stationary environment, the optimal rotation is constant, and the pattern of cutting and replanting leads to the "sawtoothed" time profile for $Q(t)$ shown in Figure 4.3.

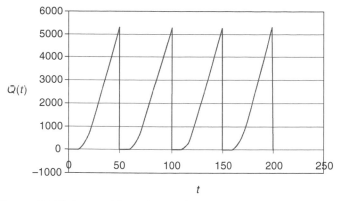

Figure 4.3. Volume with cutting and reseeding every $T = 50$ years.

This figure was drawn using the exponential volume function with $a = 10$ and $b = 70$ and arbitrarily imposing a rotation of 50 years. From an economic perspective, we may ask what is the optimal rotation?

Recall that we are assuming that the parcel has been reseeded recently and that cost has been "sunk." What is the expression for the present value of net revenues from an infinite series of rotations all of length T? At the end of each rotation we would receive the same net revenue of $[pQ(T) - c]$. This would be obtained at $T, 2T, 3T, \ldots$, and so on *ad infinitum*. The present value of this infinite series will equal

$$
\begin{aligned}
\pi &= [pQ(T) - c]e^{-\delta T}(1 + e^{-\delta T} + e^{-2\delta T} + e^{-3\delta T} + \cdots) \\
&= \frac{[pQ(T) - c]e^{-\delta T}}{1 - e^{-\delta T}} \qquad\qquad (4.4) \\
\pi &= \frac{[pQ(T) - c]}{e^{\delta T} - 1}
\end{aligned}
$$

Note that the infinite series $(1 + e^{-\delta T} + e^{-2\delta T} + e^{-3\delta T} + \cdots)$ converges to $1/(1 - e^{-\delta T})$ when $1 > e^{-\delta T} > 0$, and Equation (4.4) is obtained by multiplying the top and bottom of the preceding expression by $e^{\delta T}$. The Faustmann rotation is the value of T that maximizes π. It is named after Martin Faustmann, who correctly formulated this problem way back in 1849. The problem was solved by another German, Max Robert Pressler, in 1860. The optimal rotation must satisfy $d\pi/dT = 0$. The derivative and subsequent algebra are tedious but ultimately lead to a logical expression with a nice economic interpretation. First, note that

$$\frac{d\pi}{dT} = [pQ(T) - c](-1)(e^{\delta T} - 1)^{-2}e^{\delta T}\delta + (e^{\delta T} - 1)^{-1}pQ'(T) = 0$$

implies that

$$pQ'(T) = \frac{\delta[pQ(T) - c]e^{\delta T}}{e^{\delta T} - 1} = \frac{\delta[pQ(T) - c]}{1 - e^{-\delta T}}$$

Multiplying both sides by $1 - e^{-\delta T}$ and transposing yields

$$pQ'(T) = \delta[pQ(T) - c] + pQ'(T)e^{-\delta T}$$

Now we make use of a critical observation. The second term on the RHS is equal to $\delta\pi$ because

$$pQ'(T)e^{-\delta T} = \frac{\delta[pQ(T) - c]e^{\delta T}e^{-\delta T}}{e^{\delta T} - 1} = \frac{\delta[pQ(T) - c]}{e^{\delta T} - 1} = \delta\pi$$

This permits us to finally write

$$pQ'(T) = \delta[pQ(T) - c] + \delta\pi \qquad (4.5)$$

On the LHS, $pQ'(T)$ is once again the marginal value of waiting. It is the incremental return from delaying the cutting of the current stand by dT. On the RHS, $\delta[pQ(T) - c]$ is the interest payment if the current stand were cut at instant T. This is the only opportunity cost from delaying the cutting of the current stand. It is not the only opportunity cost. The term $\delta\pi$ is the cost of incrementally delaying all future stands. An alternative and valid interpretation of $\delta\pi$ is that it is the interest payment if you sold the land (after cutting the current stand and replanting) to another present-value-maximizing forester. Thus, by delaying the cutting of the current stand, you forego the interest payments on the net revenue of the current stand and the interest payment on the sale of the recently reseeded land.

How does the Faustmann rotation, which must satisfy Equation (4.5), compare with the optimal single rotation of the preceding section? Intuitively, delay in the infinite rotation problem incurs an additional opportunity cost ($\delta\pi$). Thus it is typically the case that the Faustmann rotation will be *shorter* than the optimal single rotation. For high rates of discount, the Faustmann rotation may be only slightly less than the optimal single rotation. Why? What happens to $\delta\pi$ as δ increases? Remember that π depends on δ!

Another interesting concept is given by the term $\pi(T^*) - c$, where T^* is the Faustmann rotation. Recall that π was the present value of all future rotations given that the cost of planting the current stand had been paid (sunk). We know that T^* maximizes π. The term $\pi(T^*) - c$ is called the *land expectation* or *site value*. It is the value of bare land devoted to forestry. After cutting the current stand but before replanting, $\pi(T^*) - c$ must be positive to make replanting worthwhile. In other words, the expected value of land with freshly planted seedlings $[\pi(T^*)]$ must exceed the cost of those seedlings to make reseeding a worthwhile thing to do. If $\pi(T^*) - c < 0$, the landowner probably would devote the land to an alternative use.

4.4 AN EXAMPLE

To illustrate the concepts encountered thus far, let's consider a numerical example. Table 4.1 reports the volume of merchantable timber (in board feet) from even-aged stands of Douglas fir grown on 14 different site classes in the Pacific Northwest. The site-class index runs from 80 (a low-quality site) to 210 (a high-quality site). Volume for each site class is reported in 10-year increments for stands ranging in age from 30 to 160 years.

Consider site class 140. Suppose that we wish to fit the exponential volume function to the merchantable volume for this site class. Taking the natural log of both sides of Equation (4.2), we obtain $\ln[Q(t)] = a - b/t$. Taking the natural log of the volume data under site class 140 in Table 4.1 and regressing it on $1/t$ results in the following ordinary least squares (OLS) equation:

$$\ln Q(t) = 12.96 - 196.11/t \qquad \text{Adjusted } R^2 = 0.96 \qquad (4.6)$$
$$(71.51) \ (-16.72)$$

where the t-statistics are given in parentheses. The transformed data and the regression results are reported in greater detail in Spreadsheet S4.1.

For the exponential volume function, we saw that the rotation-maximizing average annual volume (or MAI) was simply $T = b = 196.11$ years. We also determined that the rotation-maximizing present value of a single rotation was $T_s = \sqrt{b/\delta}$. If the discount rate is $\delta = 0.05$, then the optimal single rotation is $T_s = 62.63$.

Table 4.1. *Merchantable Volume (Board Feet per Acre) for Douglas Fir by Age and Site Class*

Age (yrs)	Site-Class Index													
	80	90	100	110	120	130	140	150	160	170	180	190	200	210
30	0	0	0	0	0	0	300	900	1,500	2,600	4,000	6,000	8,000	10,500
40	0	0	0	200	1,200	2,600	4,500	6,500	9,000	11,900	15,500	19,600	24,400	29,400
50	30	200	1,600	3,300	5,500	8,400	12,400	17,000	22,200	27,400	32,700	38,400	44,100	50,000
60	1,100	2,600	4,800	8,100	12,500	18,000	23,800	29,600	36,200	42,800	49,300	55,900	62,000	68,300
70	2,400	5,300	9,000	14,000	20,600	27,900	35,200	42,500	50,000	57,200	64,600	71,500	78,200	85,000
80	4,400	8,600	13,900	20,100	28,600	37,000	45,700	54,300	62,100	70,000	78,000	85,400	92,500	99,800
90	6,900	12,000	18,600	26,000	35,700	45,200	55,000	64,000	72,900	81,000	89,200	97,200	104,800	112,300
100	9,600	15,400	22,800	31,400	42,000	52,400	62,800	72,400	81,800	90,400	98,900	107,100	115,100	122,900
110	12,200	18,900	26,700	36,300	47,500	58,500	69,400	79,400	89,200	98,300	107,000	115,200	123,700	131,200
120	14,700	21,800	30,400	40,700	52,400	63,900	75,000	85,500	95,500	105,100	114,100	122,500	131,100	139,000
130	17,000	24,600	33,800	44,700	56,700	68,700	80,000	91,000	101,100	111,000	120,000	128,900	137,700	146,100
140	19,200	27,200	36,800	48,300	60,600	72,900	84,500	95,900	106,200	116,300	125,500	134,500	143,500	152,000
150	21,300	29,600	39,700	51,600	64,000	76,600	88,600	100,300	111,000	121,200	130,700	139,500	148,700	157,200
160	23,300	31,900	42,200	54,600	67,100	80,100	92,400	104,400	115,400	125,700	135,400	144,400	153,500	162,000

	A	B	C	D	E	F	G
1	Site Class 140 Estimation of Exponential Volume Function						
2							
3	t	Q	lnQ	1/t			
4	30	300	5.703782475	0.033333333			
5	40	4500	8.411832676	0.025			
6	50	12400	9.425451752	0.02			
7	60	23800	10.07744086	0.016666667			
8	70	35200	10.46880136	0.014285714			
9	80	45700	10.72985358	0.0125			
10	90	55000	10.91508846	0.011111111			
11	100	62800	11.04771035	0.01			
12	110	69400	11.14764215	0.009090909			
13	120	75000	11.22524339	0.008333333			
14	130	80000	11.28978191	0.007692308			
15	140	84500	11.34450681	0.007142857			
16	150	88600	11.39188714	0.006666667			
17	160	92400	11.43388226	0.00625			
18							
19	Regression of lnQ on 1/t						
20	Multiple R	0.979197246					
21	R Square	0.958827247					
22	Adjusted R Square	0.955396184					

Spreadsheet S4.1

141

		Coefficients / df	Sum of Squares	Mean Square	F	Significance F		Upper 95%
23	Standard Error	0.335296225						
24	Observations	14						
25								
26	Analysis of Variance							
27		df	Sum of Squares	Mean Square	F	Significance F		
28	Regression	1	31.41731233	31.41731233	279.4548829	1.11887E-09		
29	Residual	12	1.3490827	0.112423558				
30	Total	13	32.76639503					
31								
32		Coefficients	Standard Error	t Statistic	P-value	Lower 95%		Upper 95%
33								
34	a	12.96393602	0.181288031	71.51015962	2.90929E-18	12.56894334		13.3589287
35	minus b	−196.1058676	11.73099196	−16.7169041	3.60089E-10	−221.6655029		−170.5462323
36								
37	a =	12.96						
38	b =	196.11						
39	c =	180						
40	p =	0.65						
41	d =	0.05						
42								
43	T* =	61.66099325						
44	π =	542.8416146						

Spreadsheet S4.1 (*continued*)

At the bottom of Spreadsheet 4.1 we entered an initial guess for the Faustmann rotation ($T^* = 50$, no longer shown) in cell $B$43. The expression for π, as given in Equation (4.4), was programmed into cell $B$44. The cost of replanting was set at $c = \$180$ per acre, the net price per board foot for timber was $p - \$0.65$, and the discount rate was kept at $\delta = 0.05$. Excel's Solver was summoned to maximize π by changing the initial guess for T^*. The optimal (Faustmann) rotation, to which Solver quickly converged, was $T^* = 61.66$ (now in cell $B$43), which is only slightly less than the optimal single rotation of $T_s = 62.63$. The maximized value of π is $\$542.84$ per acre, which exceeds the cost of replanting, $c = \$180$ per acre, implying that rotational forestry is viable on site class 140 land.

4.5 TIMBER SUPPLY

The Faustmann model can be used to analyze the supply response of a forest company to changes in p, c, and δ. We will define the *short-run supply response* to be the change in the volume of timber cut as the result of a change in the rotation length. The *long-run supply response* will be the result of a change in (1) the average annual volume $Q(T)/T$ and (2) the amount of land devoted to forestry. Because the long-run supply response depends on two factors, the net *qualitative* effect of a change in p or c will be ambiguous.

To determine whether the timber supply will increase or decrease in either the short run or the long run, we need to know the comparative statics of the rotation length T and the rent or interest income on forest land $\delta\pi$ for changes in p, c, and δ. In deriving Equation (4.5), we saw that

$$pQ'(T) = \frac{\delta[pQ(T) - c]}{1 - e^{-\delta T}}$$

Dividing both sides by p yields

$$Q'(T) = \frac{\delta[Q(T) - c/p]}{1 - e^{-\delta T}}$$

or

$$\frac{Q'(T)}{[Q(T) - c/p]} = \frac{\delta}{1 - e^{-\delta T}} \tag{4.7}$$

The comparative static results we derive assume that $Q'(T) > 0$, $Q''(T) < 0$, and that all Faustmann rotations before and after a change in p, c, or δ are less than the rotation that maximizes average annual volume. This last assumption is important in determining the long-run supply response.

Carefully examine Equation (4.7), which must be satisfied by the Faustmann rotation. Suppose that p increases. How will the Faustmann rotation change in order to reestablish the equality of Equation (4.7)? An increase in p will *increase* the denominator of the LHS and thus reduce the LHS overall. To reestablish Equation (4.7), we must increase $Q'(T)$, which, given our assumptions, can be done only by *shortening* the Faustmann rotation from its previous value. Thus, if price increases from p_1 to p_2 $(p_2 > p_1)$, the Faustmann rotation will decrease from T_1 to T_2 $(T_2 < T_1)$. Since the Faustmann rotation *decreases* with an *increase* in price, we write $dT/dp < 0$.

A change in c will have the opposite effect on rotation length. In fact, it is legitimate to simply regard (c/p) as a single parameter, the cost-price ratio. Increases in p decrease the cost-price ratio, whereas increases in c increase it's value. By similar reasoning, if c increases, the denominator of the LHS of Equation (4.7) decreases, and we need to decrease $Q'(T)$ to reestablish equality. To decrease $Q'(T)$, we would move to a *longer* rotation. Since an increase in c lengthens the rotation, we write $dT/dc > 0$.

Finally, consider an increase in the discount rate δ, which only appears on the RHS of Equation (4.7). As the discount rate increases, the RHS will increase because the numerator is increasing linearly in δ, whereas the denominator is asymptotically increasing to unity. To reestablish the equality of Equation (4.7), we need to increase $Q'(T)$ on the LHS of Equation (4.7), which can be done only by *decreasing* T. This implies that $dT/d\delta < 0$.

The short-run supply response of forest firms can be inferred from these comparative results. In particular, if p, c, or δ change so that the new rotation is shorter than the old (prechange) rotation, then forest firms will find themselves with "overmature" timber, which they will cut, increasing the volume (and thus supply) of timber flowing to the market. Increases in p or δ will result in a short-run *increase* in timber supply, whereas an increase in c *reduces* short-run supply because the new, longer rotation will necessitate a delay in cutting stands that were almost financially mature under lower replanting costs.

In the long run, timber supply will depend on the average annual volume per acre, $Q(T)/T$, and on the number of acres devoted to forestry. The number of acres in forestry is thought to depend on $\delta\pi$, the rental value (or interest income from the sale) of forest land. Any change in p, c, or δ that increases $\delta\pi$ will, in theory, serve to attract more land to forestry. We can write $\delta\pi = \delta[pQ(T) - c]/(e^{\delta T} - 1)$. By inspection, an increase in p will increase $\delta\pi$, whereas an increase in c will lower $\delta\pi$. Thus an increase in p makes it more attractive to devote land to forestry, whereas an increase in c makes existing forest land less profitable, and some will be converted to other land uses.

An increase in δ will *reduce* $\delta\pi$! This occurs because π depends on δ and will decrease *exponentially* with increases in δ. Since an increase in δ will lower $\delta\pi$, land devoted to forestry becomes less valuable and more susceptible to conversion.

Thus, what are the long-run supply implications of a change in p, c, or δ? An increase in p leads to a shorter rotation and a lower average annual volume, $Q(T)/T$. This would tend to reduce long-run supply. However, an increase in p will increase $\delta\pi$ and make forest land financially more attractive. The net effect will depend on the relative strength of these two forces, which is an *empirical question*. Qualitatively, the long-run supply effect of an increase in p is said to be ambiguous.

The long-run supply implications of an increase in c (replanting cost) are also ambiguous. Why? An increase in c causes forest firms to adopt a longer rotation. This will increase $Q(T)/T$, which would tend to increase long-run supply. However, an increase in c will reduce $\delta\pi$, making forest land less profitable and reducing the amount of land devoted to forestry. Again, the average annual volume effect and the forest land value effect work at cross purposes, and the net effect cannot be determined by a qualitative analysis using comparative statics.

Finally, an increase in the discount rate δ will have an *unambiguous* long-run supply effect. An increase in δ will shorten the rotation of forest firms and will reduce average annual volume $Q(T)/T$. An increase in δ also will reduce $\delta\pi$ and make land devoted to forestry less valuable. Both effects work to reduce the long-run supply of timber. The

Table 4.2. *The Effect of Changes in p, c, and δ on the*
Faustmann Rotation, Short-Run Timber Supply, Q(T)/T,
δπ, and Long-Run Timber Supply

	p	c	δ
T	$-$	$+$	$-$
Short-run supply	$+$	$-$	$+$
$Q(T)/T$	$-$	$+$	$-$
$\delta\pi$	$+$	$-$	$-$
Long-run supply	?	?	$-$

change in rotation length T, short-run timber supply $Q(T)/T$, $\delta\pi$, and long-run timber supply are summarized in Table 4.2.

A plus sign indicates that an increase in the parameter will increase the variable in question, a negative sign indicates that an increase in the parameter will reduce the variable in question, and a question mark indicates that the effect is qualitatively ambiguous. For example, a negative sign in the T row under p means $dT/dp < 0$; the plus sign in the row "Short-Run Supply" below p means that an increase in p will increase the short-run supply of timber; and so on. Study Table 4.2 to make sure that the entries are consistent with your understanding of the Faustmann model.

4.6 THE OPTIMAL STOCK OF OLD-GROWTH FOREST

When the first white settlers arrived in the Pacific Northwest in the mid-1800s, they found vast tracts of even-aged forest, the result of lightning-induced forest fires and natural reseeding. Most of these tracts contained trees in excess of 200 years old. Western Washington, Oregon, and northern California were seen as a huge inventory of old-growth timber. At the time, there was not much concern for conservation. One-hundred and sixty years later, less than 10% of the old-growth inventory remains. Old-growth forest is thought to convey a variety of nontimber benefits, or *amenity values*, in the form of habitat for wildlife, watershed protection, and sites for hiking and camping. Let's consider a model that addresses the question, "When should we stop cutting old-growth forest and preserve what's left?"

Suppose that the flow of nontimber amenities in period t is a function of the remaining stock of old-growth forest, as given by the function

$A_t = A(X_t)$, where A_t is the value (\$) of the amenity flows from an old-growth stock X_t measured in hectares. We will assume that $A'(\bullet) > 0$ and $A''(\bullet) < 0$. Suppose further that it is not possible to recreate old-growth forest, in the sense that the evolutionary processes that created the current "old-growth ecosystem" would not be operable after cutting. In other words, while it may be possible to regrow a stand of 200-year-old trees, the forest ecosystem 200 years after cutting would have a different composition of species (flora and fauna) than if the current old-growth stand were preserved. If this perspective is legitimate, the stock of old-growth forest becomes a *nonrenewable resource*, with dynamics given by $X_{t+1} = X_t - h_t$, where h_t is the number of hectares of old-growth forest cut in period t.

What is gained by cutting a hectare of old-growth forest? Suppose that each hectare contains timber that has a net revenue of $N > 0$ after logging. After the old-growth timber is harvested, assume that the hectare is replanted and becomes a *permanent* part of the new-growth forest inventory, which is optimally managed under a Faustmann rotation with a present value of $\pi > 0$ per hectare. If X_0 is the initial stock of old-growth forest and Y_0 the initial stock of new-growth forest, then the stock of new-growth forest in period t is simply $Y_t = (Y_0 + X_0 - X_t)$.

Suppose that the welfare flow in the forest economy in period t is given by

$$W_t = A(X_t) + Nh_t + \delta\pi(Y_0 + X_0 - X_t) \qquad (4.8)$$

Note that the welfare flow consists of the amenity flow $A(X_t)$, the one-time net revenue (stumpage) flow from cutting old-growth timber Nh_t, and the rental or interest income from the accumulated stock of new-growth forest $\delta\pi(Y_0 + X_0 - X_t)$, where $\delta\pi$ is a given constant because the new-growth forest is optimized via a Faustmann rotation for a discount rate of δ.

At some point the forest economy will cease the harvesting of old-growth forest because (1) none is left or (2) what's left is more valuable preserved. When this happens, the forest economy has reached a steady state with $h_t = 0$ and $X_t = X^* \geq 0$. Let's assume that the forest economy does decide to preserve some old-growth forest ($X^* > 0$). How many hectares should be preserved? Consider the problem seeking to maximize the present value of welfare subject to old-growth dynamics:

$$\text{Maximize} \sum_{t=0}^{\infty} \rho^t [A(X_t) + Nh_t + \delta\pi(Y_0 + X_0 - X_t)]$$

Subject to $X_{t+1} = X_t - h_t$

Given $\quad X_0 > 0 \quad$ and $\quad Y_0 \geq 0$

This problem has the associated Lagrangian

$$L = \sum_{t=0}^{\infty} \rho^t [A(X_t) + Nh_t + \delta\pi(Y_0 + X_0 - X_t)$$

$$+ \rho\lambda_{t+1}(X_t - h_t - X_{t+1})]$$

The first-order necessary conditions include

$$\frac{\partial L}{\partial h_t} h_t = \rho^t(N - \rho\lambda_{t+1})h_t = 0 \qquad h_t \geq 0$$

$$\frac{\partial L}{\partial X_t} = \rho^t[A'(X_t) - \delta\pi + \rho\lambda_{t+1}] - \rho^t\lambda_t = 0 \qquad X_t > 0$$

In steady state, where the forest economy chooses to preserve some positive amount of old-growth forest, it will be the case that both $h = 0$ and $\rho\lambda = N$. This implies that $\lambda = (1 + \delta)N$. Evaluating the last expression in steady state implies that

$$A'(X) - \delta\pi + N - (1 + \delta)N = 0$$

or

$$A'(X) = \delta(\pi + N) \qquad\qquad (4.9)$$

This is one equation in one unknown, the optimal stock of old-growth forest X^*. The economic interpretation is straightforward. It says cut old-growth forest until the *marginal amenity value* $A'(X)$ is equal to the interest payment on the sum of the present value of an additional hectare of new-growth forest and the net revenue from cutting one more hectare of old-growth timber $\delta(\pi + N)$. It also can be shown that the approach from $X_0 > X^*$ to X^* will be "most rapid." If $h_{\max}$ is the maximum rate at which old-growth can be cut, then there will be an interval $\tau > t \geq 0$ where $h_t^* = h_{\max}$, implying that $\tau = (X_0 - X^*)/h_{\max}$.

Marginal amenity value is difficult to measure. It would include the incremental benefits of habitat, watershed protection, and recreation that an additional hectare of old-growth forest would provide, per period. The term $\delta(\pi + N)$ can be regarded as the *opportunity cost of preservation*. It is the interest payment foregone by not cutting another hectare of old-growth forest. It is more amenable to measurement. In fact, if one can estimate $\delta(\pi + N)$, one would have a lower-bound value that $A'(X)$ must *exceed* in order to justify the preservation of all remaining old-growth forest.

Table 4.3 contains estimates of $\delta(\pi + N)$ for four important commercial species on high-quality sites in coastal British Columbia *circa* 1990. The per-hectare market value for old-growth timber provided a considerable incentive for logging. A mixed stand of old-growth cedar/hemlock would yield a net revenue of $50,199 (Canadian dollars) in 1990. The Faustmann rotations, for $\delta = 0.04$ and $\delta = 0.06$, are given in the third and fourth columns and range from 52 to 79 years. The present value of all future rotations for a recently replanted hectare are given for both discount rates in the fifth and sixth columns. Finally, the opportunity cost of old-growth preservation $\delta(\pi + N)$ is given for $\delta = 0.04$ and $\delta = 0.06$ in the last two columns. If marginal amenity value per hectare per year exceeded these values, then the remaining old-growth forest in British Columbia should be preserved.

It is interesting to note that as the discount rate increases from $\delta = 0.04$ to $\delta = 0.06$, π decreases, as expected, but the overall opportunity cost $\delta(\pi + N)$ *increases*. This happens because the net revenue from cutting old-growth timber is so large, relative to π, that the increased interest payment on N more than offsets the decline in $\delta\pi$. For higher discount rates, land expectations or site value $(\pi - c)$ may became negative, indicating that forest firms would have no interest in replanting. Their *only* interest would be in the value of standing old-growth timber.

4.7 EXERCISES

E4.1 Consider a parcel of land that contains an even-aged stand of trees currently of age A in $t = 0$. You have to decide how much longer to allow this stand to grow given that when you cut the stand, you incur a cost of $c > 0$ independent of the age of the stand, and you plan to sell the land for a previously contracted price of $v > 0$.

Table 4.3. *Opportunity Cost of Old-Growth Forest Preservation on High-Quality Sites in Coastal British Columbia, circa 1990*

N Species	Net Revenue from Standing Old-Growth	Faustmann Rotation When $\delta = 0.04$ or $\delta = 0.06$		π When $\delta = 0.04$ or $\delta = 0.06$		Opportunity Cost $\delta(\pi + N)$ When $\delta = 0.04$ or $\delta = 0.06$	
Douglas fir	$24,517	76 yrs	69 yrs	$718	$162	$1,009	$1,480
Cedar/hemlock	$50,199	57 yrs	52 yrs	$2,222	$707	$2,096	$3,054
Balsam	$17,383	62 yrs	57 yrs	$735	$211	$724	$1,055
Spruce	$48,313	79 yrs	70 yrs	$527	$116	$1,953	$2,905

Note: (1) N, π, and $\delta(\pi + N)$ are in 1990 Canadian dollars per hectare. N is a "one-time" net revenue, π is a present value, and $\delta(\pi + N)$ is an annual interest payment.
(2) The Faustmann rotations were calculated after fitting a cubic polynomial to net value at harvest and then maximizing the present value of an infinite series of even-aged rotations.
Source: Conrad and Ludwig (1994).

If the trees are allowed to grow another T years, the volume of merchantable timber will be $Q(T) = e^{a-b/(A+T)}$. The unit price of timber, also independent of T, is given by $P > 0$. You seek the value of T that will maximize $\pi(T) = (Pe^{a-b/(A+T)} - c + v)e^{-\delta T}$. Suppose that $a = 13$, $b = 185$, $A = 40$, $P = 1.78$, $c = 1,000$, $\delta = 0.05$, and $v = 2,000$. What is the value of T that maximizes $\pi(T)$? Plot $\pi(T)$ for $T = \varepsilon, 1, 2, \ldots, 50$, $\varepsilon = 0.0001$, to make sure that you have found a global maximum.

E4.2 You are the manager of a forest products company with land recently planted ($t = 0$) with a fast-growing species of pine. The merchantable volume of timber at instant $t \geq 0$ is given by $Q(t) = \alpha t + \beta t^2 - \gamma t^3$, where $\alpha = 10$, $\beta = 1$, and $\gamma = 0.01$.

(a) What is the maximum volume, and when does it occur? What rotation length maximizes mean annual increment $[Q(T)/T]$, and what is the associated volume?

(b) If the net price per unit volume is $p = 1$ and the discount rate is $\delta = 0.05$, what is the optimal *single rotation* T_S, volume at harvest $Q(T_S)$, and present value $\pi_S(T_S)$?

(c) If the cost of replanting is $c = 150$, what is the optimal Faustmann rotation T^*, volume at the Faustmann rotation $Q(T^*)$, and present value $\pi(T^*)$?

(d) If the price increases to $p = 2$, what are the new values for T_S and T^*? Do the new values make sense relative to their values when $p = 1$?

E4.3 Suppose that the inventory of old-growth forest yields an amenity value given by $A_t = a \ln(X_t)$, where $a > 0$ and $\ln(\bullet)$ is the natural log operator. As in Section 4.6, let $\delta > 0$ denote the discount rate, $N > 0$ the net revenue from old-growth timber, and π the present value of recently replanted land under the optimal Faustmann rotation.

(a) What is the expression defining X^*, the optimal old-growth inventory to preserve?

(b) Suppose that the initial stock of old-growth forest has been normalized to $X_0 = 1$ and that you estimate $a = 615$, $\delta = 0.05$, $\pi = 1,000$, and $N = 40,000$. What is the value for X^*?

(c) If the maximum rate at which old-growth can be cut is $h_{max} = 0.01$, how many years of "old-growth mining" will be allowed before the forest economy must obtain all its timber from new-growth forest under the Faustmann rotation?

E4.4 A private woodlot owner receives an amenity flow $A(t)$ while growing trees, where $A'(t) > 0$, $A''(t) < 0$, $A(0) = 0$, and the woodlot was replanted at $t = 0$. Suppose that she is interested in both the amenity flow and the present value of net revenue from a *single rotation*. She wishes to maximize

$$\pi = pQ(T)e^{-\delta T} + \int_0^T A(t)e^{-\delta t}dt$$

(a) What is the first-order condition defining the optimal single rotation with nontimber amenity benefits? *Hint:* The derivative of the integral with respect T is simply $A(T)e^{-\delta T}$.

(b) What is the marginal value of waiting? What is the marginal cost of waiting?

(c) If $Q(t) = e^{a-b/T}$, where $b > a > 0$, and $A(t) = vt - wt^2$, where $v > w > 0$, what is the implicit expression, $G(T) = 0$, that must be satisfied by the single rotation maximizing π?

(d) If $a = 15$, $b = 180$, $\delta = 0.05$, $p = 1$, $v = 173.167$, and $w = 0.0025$, what is the value for the rotation-maximizing π? Denote this rotation T_A.

(e) How does T_A compare with T_S, the optimal single rotation, when no amenity value is present?

5

The Economics of Nonrenewable Resources

5.0 INTRODUCTION AND OVERVIEW

Nonrenewable resources do not exhibit significant growth or renewal over an economic time scale. Examples include coal, oil, natural gas, and metals such as copper, tin, iron, silver, and gold. I noted in Chapter 1 that a plant or animal species might be more appropriately viewed as a nonrenewable, as in Chapter 4, where the stock of old-growth forest was modeled as a nonrenewable resource. In Chapter 2, in the mine manager's problem, I developed a finite-horizon model of a nonrenewable resource to show how Solver might be used to determine the optimal extraction path.

If the initial reserves of a nonrenewable resource are known, the question becomes, "How should they be extracted over time?" Is complete depletion (exhaustion) ever optimal? Is it ever optimal to abandon a mine or well with positive reserves? Does the time path of extraction by a competitive firm differ from that of a price-making monopolist or cartel? If exploration allows a firm to find (acquire) more reserves, what is the optimal risky investment in exploration?

In working through the various models of this chapter, an economic measure of *resource scarcity* will emerge that is different from standard measures based on physical abundance. From an economic perspective, scarcity should reflect *net marginal value* (marginal value less the marginal cost of extraction). The Lagrange multiplier or shadow price encountered in our models of renewable resources will provide the appropriate economic measure of scarcity.

When a commodity is scarce from an economic perspective, it commands a positive rent; that is, market price exceeds the marginal cost of production. Exploration by firms supplying the commodity, research and development of potential substitutes, and conservation or substitution by consumers wishing to avoid high prices will set in motion market forces that may offset a decline in physical abundance. Economists view scarcity as a constantly changing dynamic condition where ingenuity and adaptive behavior allow society to escape the pinch of scarcity in one resource, only to face it in another.

Not all scientists share the economist's optimism about the ingenuity and adaptability of *Homo economicus* or at least his ability to extend that ingenuity to the protection of environmental quality and the preservation of natural environments. Our discussion of the economic notion of scarcity leads to an entertaining and provocative article by John Tierney (1990) describing a bet between ecologist Paul Ehrlich and economist Julian Simon. That bet took place between 1980 and 1990. Would the outcome of that bet be the same for the decade 2000 to 2010?

When a society is free from the threat of starvation and war, resources might be devoted to protecting environmental quality and preserving natural areas. Can nutritional security and political stability be established in less developed countries in time to allow investment in and preservation of their natural environments?

5.1 A SIMPLE MODEL

Suppose that a nonrenewable resource has known initial reserves given by R_0. Denote the level of extraction in period t by q_t. With no exploration and discovery, the dynamics of remaining reserves are given by the simple difference equation $R_{t+1} = R_t - q_t$, where R_t and q_t have the same unit of measure, say, metric tons.

To keep things simple, suppose that society only values extraction q_t according to the utility function $U(q_t)$, where $U'(q_t) > 0$ and $U''(q_t) < 0$ guarantee strict concavity. If we also assume that $U'(0) \rightarrow \infty$, it will guarantee some positive (though perhaps vanishingly small) level of extraction in every period. Utility is discounted by the factor $\rho = 1/(1 + \delta)$, where, as before, $\delta > 0$ is the discount rate, and society's objective is to select the extraction schedule that maximizes discounted utility subject to the dynamics of remaining reserves.

What is the relevant horizon? For our first simple problem, let's suppose that the relevant economic horizon is $t = 0, 1, 2, \ldots, T$, where T is finite and given. In subsequent problems, we will treat T as an unknown that must be optimally determined.

With $U_t = U(q_t)$ and T given, I argued in Section 2.8 (the mine manager's problem) that the shadow price on remaining reserves in period $T + 1$ should be zero so that $\lambda_{T+1} = 0$. In this first model, we will have no incentive to save or conserve the resource beyond $t = T$, and exhaustion ($R_{T+1} = 0$) will be optimal. This permits us to dispense with the difference equation for remaining reserves and to substitute the single constraint

$$R_0 - \sum_{t=0}^{T} q_t = 0 \tag{5.1}$$

Equation (5.1) requires that cumulative extraction exhausts initial reserves. Maximization of discounted utility subject to the exhaustion constraint leads to the Lagrangian

$$L = \sum_{t=0}^{T} \rho^t U(q_t) + \mu \left(R_0 - \sum_{t=0}^{T} q_t \right) \tag{5.2}$$

where $\mu > 0$ is a Lagrange multiplier that will be interpreted as the marginal value of a small increase in R_0. Let's assume that $U'(0) \to \infty$, so $q_t^* > 0$ for $T \geq t \geq 0$, and exhaustion *before* $T + 1$ will not be optimal. The first-order conditions for maximization of discounted utility require

$$\frac{\partial L}{\partial q_t} = \rho^t U'(q_t) - \mu = 0 \tag{5.3}$$

and

$$\frac{\partial L}{\partial \mu} = R_0 - \sum_{t=0}^{T} q_t = 0 \tag{5.4}$$

Equation (5.3) must hold for $t = 0, 1, 2, \ldots, T$ and implies

$$U'(q_0) = \rho U'(q_1) = \rho^2 U'(q_2) = \cdots = \rho^T U'(q_T) = \mu \tag{5.5}$$

Equation (5.5) implies that discounted utility is maximized by scheduling extraction so that discounted marginal utility is equal in every period, where $\mu = \partial L / \partial R_0$ is the shadow price on initial reserves R_0.

Consider two adjacent periods, t and $t + 1$. Equation (5.5) implies that $\rho^t U'(q_t) = \rho^{t+1} U'(q_{t+1})$, or $U'(q_{t+1}) = (1 + \delta) U'(q_t)$. The implication of this last expression is that the marginal utility of extraction must be growing at the rate of discount or, more generally,

$$U'(q_t) = (1 + \delta)^t U'(q_0) \tag{5.6}$$

Finally, note that Equations (5.3) and (5.4) constitute a system of $(T+2)$ equations in $(T+2)$ unknowns, hopefully permitting us to solve for $q_t, t = 0, 1, 2, \ldots, T$, and $\mu > 0$.

5.2 HOTELLING'S RULE

Suppose that both *spot* and *futures markets* exist for q_t. A *spot price* is the price you would pay in period t for delivery of a unit of q_t in period t. When we walk out of a grocery store, we have paid spot prices for the items purchased. We will denote the spot price for q_t as p_t. A futures price is what you would pay today ($t = 0$) for delivery of a unit of q_t in period $t > 0$. If we denote the futures price as $p_{0,t}$, then, in theory, $p_{0,t} = \rho^t p_t$. Let's suppose that our perfect markets operate so that $U'(q_t) = p_t$. Then we can substitute $p_t = U'(q_t)$ and $p_0 = U'(q_0)$ into Equation (5.6) to obtain

$$p_t = (1 + \delta)^t p_0 \tag{5.7}$$

Equation (5.7) says that price is rising at the rate of interest. Harold Hotelling, a brilliant economist, writing in 1931, presumed that a competitive industry comprised of present-value-maximizing mine owners with access to perfect futures markets would choose to extract their initial reserves so that price would rise at the rate of discount. If they did not, they couldn't be maximizing present value because a reallocation of extraction from a period with a lower discounted price to a period with a higher discounted price would increase present value. From Hotelling's perspective, competitive mine owners, maximizing the present value of their initial reserves, would be forced to extract so that price rose at the rate of interest. An equivalent way of expressing

Hotelling's rule is to note that Equation (5.7) implies $p_{t+1} = (1+\delta)p_t$, which can be manipulated algebraically to yield

$$\frac{p_{t+1} - p_t}{p_t} = \delta \tag{5.8}$$

This version of Hotelling's rule says that the capital gain on an extractable unit of q_t in the ground (the left-hand side) must equal the rate of discount in order to remain indifferent between extracting that unit in period t versus period $t + 1$.

This is the simplest form of Hotelling's rule, and it implicitly assumes that there are no costs of extraction. If extraction costs depend on q_t and R_t, we will get modifications of Equation (5.8). Before we examine more complex models, let's flesh out the implications of Hotelling's rule for different inverse demand curves.

5.3 THE INVERSE DEMAND CURVE

By an *inverse demand curve*, I mean a function-mapping aggregate quantity to market price. In general, we will write $p_t = D(q_t)$, where p_t is the unit (spot) price for q_t in period t given that the aggregate quantity q_t is supplied to the market. We will assume that $D(q_t)$ does not increase with increases in q_t $[D'(q_t) \leq 0]$, and we will often assume that price decreases with increases in q_t $[D'(q_t) < 0]$. Two functional forms we will use in our analysis of nonrenewable resources are the linear inverse demand curve given by

$$p_t = a - bq_t \tag{5.9}$$

and the constant-elasticity inverse demand curve given by

$$p_t = aq_t^{-b} \tag{5.10}$$

where $a > 0$ and $b \geq 0$ are parameters. The linear inverse demand curve has an intercept of $a > 0$ on the price axis and an intercept of $a/b > 0$ on the quantity axis when $b > 0$ (Figure 5.1).

The elasticity of demand in period t is given by the general expression

$$\eta_t = \left| \frac{\dfrac{dq_t}{q_t}}{\dfrac{dp_t}{p_t}} \right| = \left| \frac{p_t}{q_t} \frac{1}{(dp_t/dq_t)} \right| \tag{5.11}$$

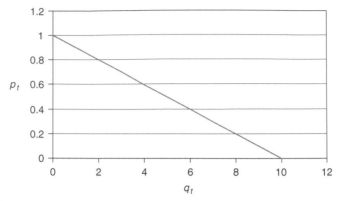

Figure 5.1. The linear inverse demand curve when $a = 1$ and $b = 0.1$.

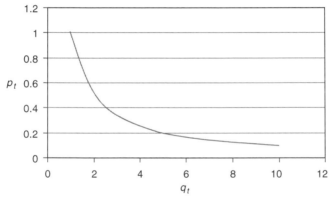

Figure 5.2. The constant-elasticity inverse demand curve when $a = 1$ and $b = 1$.

For the linear inverse demand curve, you can show that $\eta_t = |1 - a/(bq_t)|$. As $q_t \rightarrow 0, \eta_t \rightarrow \infty$. When $q_t = a/(2b), \eta_t = 1$, and when $q_t = a/b, \eta_t = 0$.

The constant-elasticity inverse demand curve, with $a > 0$ and $b > 0$, is convex to the origin, with the q_t and p_t axes serving as asymptotes (Figure 5.2). The elasticity of demand does not depend on q_t and is given by $\eta_t = |-1/b|$.

What will be the level of extraction and price (over time) under Hotelling's rule when the competitive market is characterized by the linear or constant-elasticity inverse demand curve? Would the extraction and price paths differ if all reserves of the nonrenewable resource were controlled by a price-making monopolist? We will analyze the competitive industry first.

5.4 EXTRACTION AND PRICE PATHS IN THE COMPETITIVE INDUSTRY

Let's first consider a competitive mining industry facing a linear inverse demand curve for aggregate output q_t. An important characteristic of the linear demand curve is that the implied maximum or *choke-off price* occurs at the intercept where $p_t = a$ when $q_t = 0$. Such an upper bound may result from the existence of a superabundant substitute, available at a constant marginal cost, $MC_s = a$. In scheduling their production, each competitive firm is assumed to know about this backstop/substitute, and that price will reach the intercept when all reserves have been collectively exhausted. Suppose exhaustion occurs in $t = T$. At that time, remaining reserves and extraction fall to zero $(R_T = q_T = 0)$. The date of exhaustion T is unknown and must be determined along with the competitive extraction and price paths.

With knowledge of the choke-off price, and optimizing so as to equate the discounted price in each period, price will rise at the rate of discount until $p_T = a$. Knowing where price will end up, and knowing its rate of increase, implies $p_T = a = (1 + \delta)^T p_0$. We can solve for the initial price $p_0 = a(1 + \delta)^{-T}$, which upon substitution into Equation (5.7) implies

$$p_t = a(1 + \delta)^{t-T} \tag{5.12}$$

This is the price path p_t. With the linear inverse demand curve we also have $p_t = a - bq_t$. Equating these two expressions and solving for q_t yields the extraction path

$$q_t = (a/b)[1 - (1 + \delta)^{t-T}] \tag{5.13}$$

The only problem with the price and extraction paths is that we don't know the date of exhaustion T. With no reserve-dependent extraction costs, exhaustion will be optimal, and cumulative extractions, from $t = 0$ to $t = T - 1$, must equal initial reserves, R_0, implying

$$\sum_{t=0}^{T-1} q_t = \sum_{t=0}^{T-1} (a/b)[1 - (1 + \delta)^{t-T}] = R_0 \tag{5.14}$$

We can do some algebra on this last expression and show that it will imply a single equation in the unknown T. The algebra is identical to what was required in Exercise E1.4. In this case, you will obtain the expression $\sum_{t=0}^{T-1}(1 - \rho^{T-t}) = bR_0/a$ as being equivalent to Equation (5.14). We know that the series $\sum_{t=0}^{\infty}\rho^t$ converges to $1/(1 - \rho)$ when $1 > \rho > 0$. We can use this result to show that $\sum_{t=0}^{T-1}[1 - \rho^{T-t}]$ equals $T - [\rho/(1 - \rho)](1 - \rho^T)$. This leads to an implicit equation in the unknown T that can be written as $G(T) = \delta T - 1 + \rho^T - \delta bR_0/a$, and the optimal date of extraction is T^*, where $G(T^*) = 0$. This can be found in a numerical example by using Solver. There is one problem. We are in discrete time where $t = 0, 1, 2, \ldots$. The zero of $G(T)$ may not be an integer. In such a case, you might round T^* to the nearest integer.

Figures 5.3 and 5.4 show price and extraction paths when $a = 1$, $b = 0.1$, $\delta = 0.05$, and $R_0 = 75$. The value of T satisfying $G(T) = \delta T - 1 + \rho^T - \delta bR_0/a = 0$ is $T = 19.94$, which we round up to $T = 20$. The extraction path is concave from below, starting at $q_0 = 6.22$ and declining to $q_{20} \approx 0$. The price path is convex from below starting at $p_0 = 0.38$ and rising at the rate of discount to $p_{20} = 1$.

The derivation of competitive extraction and price paths for the constant-elasticity inverse demand curve [Equation (5.10)] are made difficult by the lack of a choke-off price. Recall that the q_t and p_t axes were asymptotes for the constant-elasticity curve. With no choke-off price, price will rise without bound as the rate of extraction becomes infinitesimal. While we have no finite terminal price, we do know that

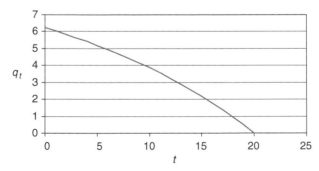

Figure 5.3. The competitive extraction path for the linear inverse demand curve when $a = 1$, $b = 0.1$, $\delta = 0.05$, and $R_0 = 74$.

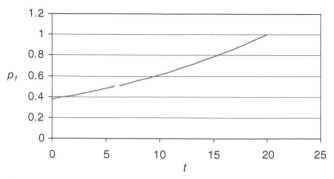

Figure 5.4. The competitive price path for the linear inverse demand curve when $a = 1$, $b = 0.1$, $\delta = 0.05$, and $R_0 = 75$.

price will rise at the rate of discount so that $p_t = (1 + \delta)^t p_0$. Equating this last expression to $p_t = a q_t^{-b}$ and solving for q_t yields

$$q_t = \left[\frac{a}{(1 + \delta)^t p_0} \right]^{1/b} \tag{5.15}$$

As $t \to \infty$, $q_t \to 0$ and $p_t \to \infty$, as we surmised from Figure 5.2. Assuming exhaustion as $t \to \infty$, we can equate cumulative extraction (in the limit) to initial reserves and use the resulting expression to solve for p_0. Specifically, it can be shown that

$$\sum_{t=0}^{\infty} \left[\frac{a}{(1 + \delta)^t p_0} \right]^{1/b} = \frac{[a(1 + \delta)/p_0]^{1/b}}{(1 + \delta)^{1/b} - 1} = R_0 \tag{5.16}$$

Solving for p_0 yields

$$p_0 = \frac{a(1 + \delta)}{\{R_0[(1 + \delta)^{1/b} - 1]\}^b} \tag{5.17}$$

When this last expression is evaluated for the same parameter values used to illustrate the linear inverse demand curve ($a = 1$, $b = 0.1$, $\delta = 0.05$, and $R_0 = 75$), one obtains $p_0 = 0.7142$. The competitive extraction and price paths in this case are shown in Figures 5.5 and 5.6.

With the implications of Hotelling's rule fleshed out for a competitive mining industry facing either a linear or constant-elasticity inverse demand curve, we can now ask, "How would the extraction

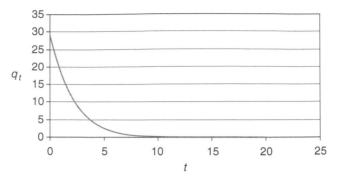

Figure 5.5. The competitive extraction path for the constant-elasticity inverse demand curve when $a = 1$, $b = 0.1$, $\delta = 0.05$, and $R_0 = 75$.

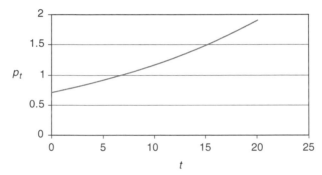

Figure 5.6. The competitive price path for the constant-elasticity inverse demand curve when $a = 1$, $b = 0.1$, $\delta = 0.05$, and $R_0 = 75$.

and price paths differ if all reserves were controlled by a monopolist?" The question is of interest because of the existence of the Organization of Petroleum Exporting Countries (OPEC) .

OPEC was formed on September 14, 1960, with five founding members: Saudi Arabia, Kuwait, Iran, Iraq, and Venezuela. The current membership (2008) also includes Qatar, Indonesia, Libya, the United Arab Emirates, Algeria, Nigeria, and Ecuador. Its original purpose was to try to obtain higher prices for oil sold to the "seven sisters": Esso, Royal Dutch Shell, Anglo-Persian Oil Company, Socony, Socal, Gulf Oil, and Texaco, which were the major oil companies that dominated production, refining, and distribution at that time. By 1970, OPEC had begun to exert considerable control over production by its members, and this, in turn, had a significant influence on the market price for crude oil.

On October 17, 1973, OPEC announced that it would no longer ship oil to nations that were supporting Israel in the Yom Kippur War. These nations included the United States, its allies in Europe, and Japan. The OPEC oil embargo set off a series of price increases that were subsequently exacerbated by the Iranian Revolution (1979) and the Iran–Iraq War (1980–1988). In January 1981, the nominal price of oil in the United States reached $38.85 per barrel. In real terms (using the April 2008, adjusted consumer price index) this was equivalent to a price of $95.08 per barrel; more than seven times the real price of oil in 1973.

The price increases in crude oil between 1973 and 1981 resulted in the greatest "peaceful" transfer of wealth from the industrialized economies of North America, Europe and Asia to OPEC members. By the early 1980s, however, a combination of energy conservation, new (non-OPEC) sources of crude oil, and a worldwide economic recession, resulted in a reduced demand for oil. Saudi Arabia, which had frequently reduced its quota to maintain price while other members were producing in excess of their agreed quota, finally grew tired of what it regarded as greedy, undisciplined overproduction, and decided that it would produce at its full quota and let the price find a new, lower market equilibrium. By July 1986, the nominal price of oil had fallen to $10.91 per barrel (the real price, again from the perspective of April 2008, was $21.27 per barrel). From August 1986 through August of 1990, the real price of crude was relatively stable, fluctuating between $22 and $36 per barrel. Real prices increased with Iraq's invasion of Kuwait and the start of the First Gulf War (August 1990–February1991). In October 1990, the real price spiked to $52.69 per barrel, but by February 1991, the real price had fallen below $30 per barrel. Real prices ranged between $21 and $32 per barrel from February 1991 through December 1997, providing stable energy costs as most of the industrialized countries experienced economic growth and low unemployment. In January 1998, the U.S. real price of crude averaged $18.90 per barrel. Through 1998, the price drifted downward reaching a real-price low of $12.20 in December of that year. Since January 1999, the real price of crude has generally drifted upward, with a temporary fall in prices after the terrorist attacks on the United States on September 11, 2001. The

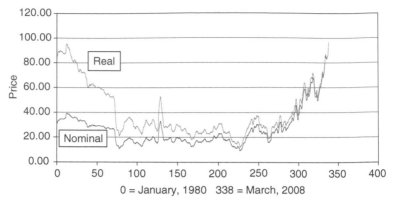

Figure 5.7. The real and nominal price for crude oil ($/bbl). Data from the Energy Information Agency.

U.S. invasion of Iraq in 2003 likely has contributed to the continued rise in the price of crude oil. On April 9, 2008, the real price for crude oil reached a record high of $112.21 per barrel. On April 23, the spot price finished at $118.30 per barrel. Since January 1999, the price path for crude has exhibited Hotelling-like increases as shown in Figure 5.7.

5.5 EXTRACTION AND PRICE PATHS UNDER MONOPOLY

As with our analysis of the competitive mining industry, we will assume that there is no variable cost to extraction. (Reserve-dependent costs will be examined in the next section.) We assume that the monopolist seeks to maximize the present value of revenues and knows the form of the inverse demand curve. If the monopolist faced a linear inverse demand curve, revenue in period t would given by $\pi_t = p_t q_t = a q_t - b q_t^2$. Hotelling simply argued that the monopolist, as a price maker, would schedule extraction so as to *equate discounted marginal revenue*. If this were not the case, extraction could be shifted from a period with lower discounted marginal revenue to a period where discounted marginal revenue were higher, and overall present value would be increased.

If the monopolist schedules extraction to equate discounted marginal revenue, then marginal revenue, given by $MR_t = a - 2bq_t$, must be rising at the rate of discount. This implies that $MR_t = (1 + \delta)^t MR_0$. For the linear inverse demand curve, marginal revenue will equal price when extraction drops to zero; that is, $MR_T = a = p_T$ when $q_T = 0$, where $t = T$ is the monopolist's (unknown) date of exhaustion, which may differ from the date of exhaustion in the competitive industry. Knowing the rate of increase in marginal revenue and its value at $t = T$, one can solve for $MR_0 = a(1 + \delta)^{-T}$, and the second expression for marginal revenue becomes $MR_t = a(1 + \delta)^{t-T}$. Equating this expression to $MR_t = a - 2bq_t$ and solving for q_t yields

$$q_t = [a/(2b)][1 - (1 + \delta)^{t-T}] \qquad (5.18)$$

Compare Equation (5.18) with Equation (5.13). While we don't know the monopolist's date of exhaustion, if a, b, δ, and R_0 are the same as in the competitive industry, and if the dates of exhaustion for both are reasonably far into the future, then the monopolist's initial rate of extraction will be approximately one-half that of the competitive industry, because $a/(2b)$ is one-half of a/b. If the monopolist's initial rate of extraction is less than that of the competitive industry, if exhaustion is optimal (which is the case with no reserve-dependent costs), and if R_0 is the same for competitors in aggregate as for the monopolist, then the date of exhaustion for the monopolist T_m will be greater than the date of exhaustion for the competitive industry T_c. When plotted in the same graph, the extraction path for the monopolist will intersect the competitive extraction path from below, and there will be an interval where the rate of extraction of the monopolist exceeds the rate of extraction from the competitive industry. The monopolist's date of exhaustion is the value of T which equates

$$\sum_{t=0}^{T-1} q_t = \sum_{t=0}^{T-1} [a/(2b)][1 - (1 + \delta)^{t-T}] = R_0 \qquad (5.19)$$

Applying the same algebra as was applied to Equation (5.14), you can show that the monopolist's date of exhaustion requires $G(T) = \delta T - 1 + \rho^T - 2\delta b R_0/a = 0$. For $a = 1$, $b = 0.1$, $\delta = 0.05$, and $R_0 = 75$, $T_m \approx 30 > T_c \approx 20$. The monopolist's extraction path and that for the competitive industry (from Figure 5.3) are shown in Figure 5.8.

In Figure 5.8, if R_0 is the same for both the competitive and monopolistic industries, then the area below the competitive extraction path and above the monopolist's extraction path to the left of their intersection will equal the area below the monopolist's extraction path and above the competitive extraction path to the right of their intersection.

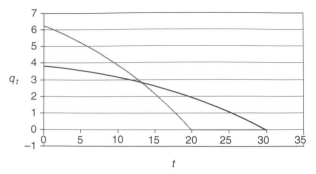

Figure 5.8. The extraction paths for the monopolistic and competitive mining industry facing a linear inverse demand curve when $a = 1$, $b = 0.1$, $\delta = 0.05$, and $R_0 = 75$.

For the linear inverse demand curve, the monopolist is able to increase the present value of its revenues by restricting extraction initially, thus raising price. Since it is optimal to exhaust initial reserves R_0, the monopolist will extend the period of positive extraction to $T_m - 1$. While the monopolist spreads extraction over a longer horizon, there is nothing socially desirable about this behavior. In fact, if $U'(q_t) = p_t$ (i.e., marginal social welfare is equal to price), then the competitive extraction path is optimal, and the monopolist's extraction path reduces the present value of social welfare. Will the monopolist's extraction always be restrictive initially?

Let's now consider the monopolist facing a constant-elasticity inverse demand curve. With the constant-elasticity inverse demand curve, revenue in period t is given by $\pi_t = aq_t^{-b}q_t = aq_t^{1-b}$, and marginal revenue would be $\text{MR}_t = (1 - b)aq_t^{-b} = (1 - b)p_t$. With marginal revenue rising at the rate of discount, we know that $\text{MR}_t = (1 + \delta)^t\text{MR}_0 = (1 + \delta)^t(1 - b)p_0$. The last two expressions imply that $p_t = (1 + \delta)^t p_0$ (i.e., that price is rising at the rate of interest), which was our result for the competitive industry. We could solve for q_t, in which case we would get the same expression as given in Equation (5.15). The conclusion: If the inverse demand curve exhibits constant elasticity, the time paths for extraction and price are the same for the competitive industry and the monopolist. The key to this unexpected result lies in the fact that the monopolist, facing a constant-elasticity inverse demand curve, cannot increase the present value of revenues by restricting the rate of extraction. In fact, points on a constant-elasticity inverse demand curve all yield the same revenue. While the monopolist is still a price maker, it is unable to shift revenue to earlier periods, as was the case with the linear inverse demand curve.

We might summarize these last two sections as follows: (1) If the mining industry is competitive with no extraction costs and complete futures markets for q_t, price will rise at the rate of discount. (2) If marginal social welfare is equal to price [i.e., $U'(q_t) = p_t$], then the competitive extraction and price paths are optimal. (3) If a monopolist can take advantage of changing elasticity of demand to increase the present value of revenues, then he or she will restrict the rate of extraction initially and spread initial reserves over a longer horizon than the competitive industry. The monopolist is not behaving out of any conservation ethic but is simply trying to maximize the present value of revenues.

5.6 RESERVE-DEPENDENT COSTS

The nonrenewable-resource models consider thus far have assumed no variable costs to extraction and that any fixed costs have been incurred (sunk). While not realistic, these assumptions kept things analytically simple and allowed us to get a feel for the dynamics of extraction and price in the competitive and monopolistic mining industry. We now consider the implications of reserve-dependent costs. Specifically, suppose that the cost of extracting q_t depends on the level of remaining reserves so that $C_t = C(q_t, R_t)$ is the cost of extracting q_t units of ore when remaining reserves are R_t. Using subscripts to denote the partial derivatives of $C(\bullet)$, it is assumed that $C_q(\bullet) > 0$, $C_{qq}(\bullet) > 0$, $C_{qR}(\bullet) = C_{Rq}(\bullet) < 0$, $C_R(\bullet) < 0$, and $C_{RR}(\bullet) > 0$. As in the fishery model of Chapter 3, higher reserves serve to lower total cost $[C_R(\bullet) < 0]$ and the marginal cost of extraction $[C_{qR}(\bullet) < 0]$.

Consider the competitive industry facing time-varying unit prices p_t for $t = 0, 1, \ldots, T$. Each competitive firm is assumed to have information on the futures prices for delivery of a unit of q_t in period t. These prices are assumed to be known through the smooth operation of futures market for q_t. These prices are not affected by the extraction decisions of an individual firm. Net revenue in period t is given by $\pi_t = p_t q_t - C(q_t, R_t)$. The representative firm will try to extract so as to

$$\text{Maximize} \sum_{t=0}^{T} \rho^t[p_t q_t - C(q_t, R_t)]$$

$$\text{Subject to } R_{t+1} - R_t = -q_t$$

$$R_0 \text{ given, } T \text{ chosen}$$

The Lagrangian for this problem may be written as

$$L = \sum_{t=0}^{T} \rho^t[p_t q_t - C(q_t, R_t) + \rho\lambda_{t+1}(-q_t + R_t - R_{t+1})] \qquad (5.20)$$

and for q_t, R_t, and λ_t positive, the first-order conditions require

$$\frac{\partial L}{\partial q_t} = \rho^t[p_t - C_q(\bullet) - \rho\lambda_{t+1}] = 0 \qquad (5.21)$$

$$\frac{\partial L}{\partial R_t} = \rho^t[-C_R(\bullet) + \rho\lambda_{t+1}] - \rho^t\lambda_t = 0 \qquad (5.22)$$

$$\frac{\partial L}{\partial(\rho\lambda_{t+1})} = \rho^t[-q_t + R_t - R_{t+1}] = 0 \qquad (5.23)$$

Dividing through by ρ^t, this system implies that $\rho\lambda_{t+1} = p_t - C_q(\bullet)$, $\lambda_t = (1 + \delta)[p_{t-1} - C_q(\bullet)]$, and $\rho\lambda_{t+1} - \lambda_t = C_R(\bullet)$. Substituting the first two expressions into the third implies that $[p_t - C_q(\bullet)] - (1 + \delta)[p_{t-1} - C_q(\bullet)] = C_R(\bullet)$. This last expression can be further manipulated to imply that

$$\frac{[p_t - C_q(\bullet)] - [p_{t-1} - C_q(\bullet)]}{p_{t-1} - C_q(\bullet)} = \delta + \frac{C_R(\bullet)}{p_{t-1} - C_q(\bullet)} \qquad (5.24)$$

In this expression, the term $p_t - C_q(\bullet)$ can be defined as the *rent* on the marginal unit extracted in period t, whereas $p_{t-1} - C_q(\bullet)$ is the *rent* on the marginal unit extracted in period $t-1$. Knowing that $C_R(\bullet) < 0$, Equation (5.24) has the following Hotelling-type interpretation: *In the competitive industry, with reserve-dependent costs, rent rises at less than the rate of discount.*

How long will the competitive industry operate? The answer will depend on initial reserves, the inverse demand curve, and the cost function. If $t = T$ is the last period for optimal positive extraction ($q_T > 0$, $q_{T+1} = 0$), then we know that any remaining reserves in period $t + 1$ must be worthless; thus $\lambda_{T+1} = 0$.

Consider the reserve-dependent cost problem with $\pi_t = pq_t - cq_t/R_t$, where $p > 0$ is the constant unit price for q_t and $c > 0$ is a cost parameter. With $t = T$ being the last period with positive extraction, the Lagrangian for the problem seeking to maximize the present value of net revenues may be written as

$$L = \sum_{t=0}^{t=T} \rho^t [pq_t - cq_t/R_t + \rho\lambda_{t+1}(R_t - q_t - R_{t+1})] \qquad (5.25)$$

On inspection, you will see that the Lagrangian is linear in q_t. Linear Lagrangians give rise to switching functions where the sign of the switching function will determine whether the optimal control (harvest or extraction) is to be set at the upper or lower bound. Suppose that $q_{max} \geq q_t \geq 0$. The switching function in this problem can be obtained from $\partial L/\partial q_t = 0$ and will imply that

$$\sigma_t \equiv p - \frac{c}{R_t} - \rho\lambda_{t+1} \qquad (5.26)$$

If $\sigma_t > 0, q_t^* = q_{max}$. If $\sigma_t \leq 0$, $q_t^* = q_{min} = 0$. With $t = T$ being the last period with positive extraction, remaining reserves must be worthless in $t = T + 1$, and $\lambda_{T+1} = 0$. With $\sigma_T = 0$, Equation (5.26) then implies that

$$R_T = \frac{c}{p} \qquad (5.27)$$

Knowing that R_T will be the level of reserves that will be abandoned, and assuming that $\sigma_t > 0$ for $R_t > R_T$, we can calculate the value of T as

$$T = \frac{R_0 - c/p}{q_{max}} - 1 \qquad (5.28)$$

Consider a simple numerical problem where $p = 1, c = 10, R_0 = 100, \delta = 0.05, q_{max} = 10$, and $q_{min} = 0$. In Spreadsheet S5.1, I specify these parameter values for $t = 0, 1, 2, \ldots, 20$. $R_T = c/p = 10, T = 9 - 1 = 8$, and $q_t^* = q_{max} = 10$ for $t = 0, 1, 2, \ldots, 8$. If you start from a nonoptimal guess for q_t^*, Solver will set $q_t^* = q_{max} = 10$ for $t = 0, 1, 2, \ldots, 8$, but it also may set $q_{19} = 10$. This does nothing to improve $\pi^* = 59.6491898$, so why bother!

By now you might be able to anticipate the analog of Equation (5.24) for the monopolist. You should be able to show that the monopolist

	A	B	C	D
1	S5.1			
2				
3	$p =$	1		
4	$c =$	10		
5	$\delta =$	0.05		
6	$\rho =$	0.952380952		
7	$R(0) =$	100		
8	$q_{MAX} =$	10		
9	$q_{MIN} =$	0	$\pi =$	59.64918978
10				
11	t	$q(t)$	$R(t)$	$(\rho^\wedge t)\pi(t)$
12	0	10	100	9.00000
13	1	10	90	8.46561
14	2	10	80	7.93651
15	3	10	70	7.40432
16	4	10	60	6.85585
17	5	10	50	6.26821
18	6	10	40	5.59662
19	7	10	30	4.73788
20	8	10	20	3.38420
21	9	0	10	0.00000
22	10	0	10	0.00000
23	11	0	10	0.00000
24	12	0	10	0.00000
25	13	0	10	0.00000
26	14	0	10	0.00000
27	15	0	10	0.00000
28	16	0	10	0.00000
29	17	0	10	0.00000
30	18	0	10	0.00000
31	19	0	10	0.00000
32	20		10	

Spreadsheet S5.1

will schedule extraction so that

$$\frac{[MR_t - C_q(\bullet)] - [MR_{t-1} - C_q(\bullet)]}{MR_{t-1} - C_q(\bullet)} = \delta + \frac{C_R(\bullet)}{MR_{t-1} - C_q(\bullet)} \quad (5.29)$$

In words, the monopolist will schedule extraction so that marginal revenue less marginal cost rises at *less* than the rate of discount, where the term $C_R(\bullet)/[MR_{t-1} - C_q(\bullet)] < 0$.

The introduction of reserve-dependent costs resulted in more realistic models for the competitive and monopolistic mining industry. The model, however, still lacks several important features, most notably the process of exploration for and acquisition of new reserves.

5.7 EXPLORATION

Geologic processes typically result in a nonuniform distribution of resources in the earth's crust. The location and size of economically recoverable reserves are uncertain. Firms and individuals typically must explore (search) for recoverable reserves, and their economic value may depend on their grade (concentration), location, technology available for extraction, future price, and cost. Exploration is a costly and risky investment. It is undertaken when a firm believes that the expected present value of discoveries will exceed the cost of prospecting, field development, and extraction. If extraction costs are reserve-dependent, a firm may have an incentive to increase exploration as its known and developed reserves decline. The prospect of future discoveries also may depend on cumulative discoveries to date. If the most obvious locations have been explored, the probability of large future discoveries may decline.

Determining the optimal rates of extraction and exploration, in the face of uncertain discovery, is a formidable problem. To keep things manageable, we will develop a two-period model, $t = 0, 1$, where $t = 0$ is the current period and $t = 1$ is the future (period). Current extraction, $q_0 \geq 0$, and exploration, $e_0 \geq 0$, are decisions that must be made in $t = 0$ based on current net revenues, exploration costs, expected discoveries, and the present value of expected future net revenues from optimal extraction in each of two possible future states $s = 0$ or $s = 1$. It will not be optimal to explore in $t = 1$ because there is no third period ($t = 2$) where discoveries could be extracted. Given the simple structure of this two-period model, the firm must optimally determine the level of four variables: $q_{1,0}$, the level of extraction in $t = 1, s = 0$; $q_{1,1}$, the level of extraction in $t = 1, s = 1$; q_0, the level of extraction in $t = 0$; and e_0, the level of exploration in $t = 0$.

Let's start by specifying the exploration/discovery process. In keeping with our theme that "simple is good," we will assume that a random process of discovery can be characterized by our binary-state variable s, where $s = 0$ will now be designated as the "no-discovery state," which will occur with probability ε. Notationally, we could write $\Pr(s = 0) = \varepsilon$. The probability of the "discovery state" $s = 1$ is then $\Pr(s = 1) = (1 - \varepsilon)$, where $1 > \varepsilon > 0$. Newly discovered reserves are available for extraction in $t = 1$, and we assume a simple discovery function that takes the form $D_s = \alpha s e_0$. This form assumes that discoveries in $s = 1$ are linear in e_0 and that no new reserves are found in $s = 0$ even if $e_0 > 0$. It is easy to modify the model to make the probability of discovery depend on e_0 (see Exercise E5.3) or to have a declining marginal product for exploratory effort, $D_s = D_s(e_0), D'_s(e_0) > 0$, and $D''_s(e_0) < 0$ (see Exercise E5.4).

The solution of this two-period, two-state problem will employ the method of *stochastic dynamic programming* (SDP), which can be employed in multiperiod, multistate problems as well. The procedure starts in the terminal period, where it is possible to determine optimal behavior, assuming remaining reserves, after extraction in $t = 0$ and the discovery state are known with certainty. Denote the unit price for production (extraction) in $t = 1$ as $p_1 > 0$, and assume that the reserve-dependent cost of extracting $q_{1,s}$ units is given by $C_{1,s} = cq_{1,s}^2/R_{1,s}$, where $c > 0$ is a cost parameter. In $s = 0$, the cost of extracting $q_{1,0}$ is $C_{1,0} = cq_{1,0}^2/(R_0 - q_0)$ because no new reserves have been discovered, and $R_{1,0} = R_0 - q_0$. In $s = 1$, the cost of extracting $q_{1,1}$ is $C_{1,1} = cq_{1,1}^2/(R_0 - q_0 + \alpha e_0)$ because remaining reserves from $t = 0$ have been augmented by αe_0 and $R_{1,1} = R_0 - q_0 + \alpha e_0$. In $t = 0$, we also will assume reserve-dependent costs, where $C_{0,q} = cq_0^2/R_0$ will be the cost of extracting q_0 from initial reserves R_0. The cost of exploratory effort will be given by the convex quadratic $C_{0,e} = we_0^2$, where $w > 0$ is a cost parameter associated with the exploration technology being employed by our hypothetical firm.

We start in $t = 1, s = 0$, where the net revenue from extracting at rate $q_{1,0}$ will be given by

$$\pi_{1,0} = p_1 q_{1,0} - cq_{1,0}^2/(R_0 - q_0) \qquad (5.30)$$

In $t = 1, s = 1$, the net revenue from $q_{1,1}$ is given by

$$\pi_{1,1} = p_1 q_{1,1} - cq_{1,1}^2/(R_0 - q_0 + \alpha e_0) \qquad (5.31)$$

$\pi_{1,0}$ can be maximized with respect to $q_{1,0}$, as can $\pi_{1,1}$ with respect to $q_{1,1}$. Setting the appropriate derivatives equal to zero, you should obtain

$$q_{1,0}^* - \frac{p_1(R_0 - q_0)}{2c} \qquad (5.32)$$

$$q_{1,1}^* = \frac{p_1(R_0 - q_0 + \alpha e_0)}{2c} \qquad (5.33)$$

Equations (5.32) and (5.33) constitute the optimal extraction policy for the future in all possible states. Note that the optimal value of $q_{1,0}$ depends on q_0 and the optimal value of $q_{1,1}$ depends on q_0 and e_0, neither of which is known at this point in the solution algorithm, but when they are known, we will know what to do in either state.

Now take the expressions for $q_{1,0}^*$ and $q_{1,1}^*$ and substitute them into Equations (5.30) and (5.31), respectively. After some algebra, you should get the following expressions for *optimized* net revenue:

$$\pi_{1,0}^* = \frac{p_1^2(R_0 - q_0)}{4c} \qquad (5.34)$$

$$\pi_{1,1}^* = \frac{p_1^2(R_0 - q_0 + \alpha e_0)}{4c} \qquad (5.35)$$

Suppose that the first-period decisions $q_0 > 0$ and $e_0 > 0$ have been made but that the size of the discovery has not been revealed. The expected value, in $t = 1$, of a (q_0, e_0) decision may be calculated as

$$E(\pi_1) = \frac{p_1^2}{4c}[\varepsilon(R_0 - q_0) + (1 - \varepsilon)(R_0 - q_0 + \alpha e_0]$$

$$= \frac{p_1^2}{4c}[R_0 - q_0 + (1 - \varepsilon)\alpha e_0] \qquad (5.36)$$

The expression for $E(\pi_1)$ depends on q_0 and e_0 and presumes optimal extraction in the future in all possible states. We can discount $E(\pi_1)$ by ρ, add it to the expression for net revenue in $t = 0$, and obtain an expression for the present value of expected net revenues that depends on q_0 and e_0. If this expression is optimized, it is called a *value function* and will depend only on R_0.

$$V(R_0) = \max_{q_0, e_0}\{p_0 q_0 - cq_0^2/R_0 - we_0^2 + \rho(p_1^2/4c)$$

$$\times [R_0 - q_0 + (1 - \varepsilon)\alpha e_0]\} \qquad (5.37)$$

$V(R_0)$ has an important interpretation. It is the expected present value of initial reserves R_0 if we behave optimally with respect to extraction and exploration in all periods and all possible states.

Setting the partial derivatives of $V(R_0)$ with respect to q_0 and e_0 equal to zero yields the following expressions for optimal first-period extraction and exploration:

$$q_0^* = \frac{R_0(4cp_0 - \rho p_1^2)}{8c^2} \tag{5.38}$$

$$e_0^* = \frac{\rho p_1^2 \alpha (1 - \varepsilon)}{8cw} \tag{5.39}$$

Assuming that the optimal levels for q_0 and e_0 are positive, one would wait until the state of the world is revealed and then use Equations (5.32) and (5.33) to determine the optimal levels for either $q_{1,0}^*$ or $q_{1,1}^*$.

There are eight parameters in this model: $R_0, p_0, p_1, c, w, \alpha, \varepsilon$, and δ. Spreadsheet S5.2 shows the optimal values for $q_0, e_0, q_{1,0}$, and $q_{1,1}$ when $R_0 = 100$, $p_0 = 1$, $p_1 = 1.1$, $c = 2$, $w = 5$, $\alpha = 250$, $\varepsilon = 0.7$,

	A	B	C	D	E
1	Optimal Extraction and Exploration in a Two-Period Model				
2					
3	R(0) =	100			
4	p(0) =	1			
5	p(1) =	1.1			
6	c =	2			
7	w =	5			
8	α =	250			
9	ε =	0.7			
10	δ =	0.05			
11	ρ =	0.952380952			
12					
13	q(0)* =	21.3988			
14	e(0)* =	1.0804			
15	q(1,0)* =	21.6153			
16	q(1,1)* =	95.8899			
17					
18	Using Solver				
19	q(0)* =	21.3988			
20	e(0)* =	1.0804			
21	V(R(0))=	29.3988			

Spreadsheet S5.2

Table 5.1. *Comparative Statics of Extraction and Exploration*

	R_0	p_0	p_1	c	w	α	ε	δ
q_0^*	+	+	−	−	0	0	0	+
e_0^*	0	0	+	−	−	+	−	−
$q_{1,0}^*$	+	−	+	−	0	0	0	−
$q_{1,1}^*$	+	−	+	−	−	+	−	−

and $\delta = 0.05$. In cell \$B\$21, I have programmed the $V(R_0) = p_0 q_0 - cq_0^2/R_0 + \rho[p_1^2/(4c)][R_0 - q_0 - (1 - \varepsilon)\alpha e_0]$, placing guesses for the optimal q_0 and e_0 in cells \$B\$19 and \$B\$20, respectively. As a check on the algebra underlying our analytic expressions for q_0^* and e_0^*, I asked Solver to maximize $V(R_0)$ by changing q_0 and e_0, and after a few iterations it converges to the values given by our analytic expressions in cells \$B\$13 and \$B\$14.

By inspection of the optimal expressions for q_0, e_0, $q_{1,0}$, and $q_{1,1}$, or through numerical analysis via Spreadsheet S5.2, one can conduct comparative statics to see how extraction and exploration change as a result of a change in one of the eight parameters. The results are summarized in Table 5.1, where a plus (+) indicates that an increase in a parameter increases the optimal value of a variable, a minus (−) indicates that an increase in a parameter will decrease the optimal value of the variable, and a zero (0) indicates no change.

The comparative statics are, for the most part, consistent with economic intuition. For example, the optimal level of extraction in the first period will (1) increase with increases in initial reserves R_0, the initial price p_0, or the discount rate δ, (2) decrease with increases in the future price p_1 or the cost of extraction c, and (3) remain unchanged for changes in the cost of exploration w, the productivity of exploration α, and the probability of no-discovery ε. The fact that the optimal level of q_0 does not depend on w, α, or ε results from the fact that $V(R_0)$ is separable in q_0 and e_0 [$\partial^2 V(R_0)/\partial q_0 \partial e_0 = 0$].

Exploratory effort is not affected by a change in R_0 or p_0, will increase with an increase in p_1 or α, and will decrease with an increase in c, w, ε, or δ. The only surprise here is that exploratory effort is not influenced by the size of initial reserves. In more complex models, it might be the case that low initial reserves would encourage greater initial exploration. The nonresponse of e_0^* to a change in p_0 makes sense because one cannot sell discoveries in the initial period.

The comparative statics of $q_{1,0}^*$ and $q_{1,1}^*$ are made complex by their dependency on q_0 and e_0, which are determined first. The logic of the comparative statics for $q_{1,0}^*$ and $q_{1,1}^*$ are more readily deduced by moving vertically down a parameter column in Table 5.1. For example, an increase in initial reserves R_0 will increase extraction in the current period and in all future states. Basically, an increase in initial reserves is optimally spread across all periods and all states. An increase in current price, because it increases the optimal q_0, will reduce the rate of extraction in either future state. An increase in p_1 will reduce extraction initially and increase it in both future states. An increase in the cost of extraction, via an increase in c, reduces all variables. An increase in the cost of exploratory effort w reduces the level of exploration and the level of extraction in future state $s = 1$ while leaving extraction in the no-discovery state ($s = 0$) unchanged. If the productivity of exploratory effort increases, the optimal level of e_0 will increase, along with the optimal rate of extraction in $s = 1$, but again, there is no change in the optimal extraction rate in $s = 0$. If the probability of no-discovery ε increases, e_0^* is reduced, as is the optimal extraction rate in $s = 1$. Finally, an increase in the discount rate increases current extraction and reduces exploration and future extraction in all states.

5.8 THE ECONOMIC MEASURE OF SCARCITY

In ourt model with reserve-dependent costs, the first-order condition for $q_t > 0$ required $p_t - C_q(\bullet) = \rho\lambda_{t+1}$ [see Equation (5.21)]. When the optimal extraction schedule has been determined, λ_{t+1} will reflect the value of the marginal unit of remaining reserves in period $t + 1$. Because λ_{t+1} is linked, via a difference equation, to all future $\lambda_{t+1+\tau}$, $\tau = 1, 2, \ldots$, it will reflect the value that the marginal unit conveys in period $t + 1$ *and* in all future periods. Recall that λ_{t+1} also was called a *shadow price* on the marginal unit of ore in the ground in period $t + 1$, presuming that remaining reserves would be optimally extracted. The equation $p_t - C_q(\bullet) = \rho\lambda_{t+1}$ simply says that the net marginal value of a unit of ore at the surface in period t [$p_t - C_q(\bullet)$] should equal the discounted marginal value if it were left in the ground and thus available in period $t + 1$ ($\rho\lambda_{t+1}$).

The economic notion of scarcity is based on net value rather than physical abundance. If we could be confident that a resource were being optimally extracted (say, by a competitive industry with adequate futures markets), then the preferred measure of resource scarcity from an economist's point of view would be $\lambda_{t+1} = (1 + \delta)[p_t - C_q(\bullet)]$. If we could observe the current spot price for q_t and estimate marginal cost $C_q(\bullet)$ and the social rate of discount δ, we could estimate the time series λ_{t+1} and observe what was happening to resource scarcity over time. This is not as easy as it sounds. Time-series data on marginal cost in extractive industries are either nonexistent or proprietary. In attempting to reconstruct the scarcity index λ_{t+1}, it may be easier to estimate the cost function $C(q_t, R_t)$ and take the partial with respect to q_t to obtain a marginal cost function that would provide an estimate of marginal cost.

The economic measure of resource scarcity can indicate a growing or declining scarcity that may be counter to a geologic (abundance-based) notion of scarcity. Note: If marginal costs increase as remaining reserves decline but market price does not increase as rapidly, then λ_{t+1} is declining, and the resource is becoming *less scarce* from an economic perspective. The fact that remaining reserves are declining would indicate geologic scarcity, but unless the market price increases at a greater rate, the resource is not becoming economically scarce.

It is also possible for a more abundant resource to become economically *more scarce*. This is what happened to crude oil in the last half of the nineteenth century. While geology and engineering led to the discovery of more oil and a reduction in the cost of extraction and refining, the demand for kerosene and other distillates increased at a greater rate, and from an economic point of view, the resource, though known reserves where more abundant, was becoming more scarce. The opposite forces were at work in the 1980s when the demand for crude oil declined as a result of improved efficiency in automobiles, appliances, and heating and air conditioning and a decline in the global economy. From 1981 through 1998, crude oil was probably less scarce, based on our economic measure of scarcity, assuming that the marginal cost of extraction was constant. Return to Figure 5.7.

Some of the first empirical studies by resource economists examined real-price trends in natural resources. Economists were interested in determining if real prices were rising over time, perhaps indicating a growing resource scarcity. Copper is a well-studied natural resource, with U.S. price data ($/pound) going back to 1870. The real price of copper has exhibited considerable volatility over the past 138 years, with some subperiods showing an upward trend in real prices and other subperiods showing a downward trend. For the period 1870–2003, economists typically estimate a declining trend or, depending on the price deflator, no trend at all. For the subperiod 1970–2003, the real price of copper did drift downward. This seemed consistent with the increased use of substitutes. Copper was once used extensively in plumbing and electrical transmission. Plastic has greatly reduced the use of copper in plumbing, as has fiber-optic cable in telecommunications. For this same subperiod (1970–2003), the known remaining reserves of copper probably declined, but the real price of copper fell because of copper substitutes. Thus, from an economic perspective, copper was likely becoming less scarce.

Beginning in 2003, the real price of copper started to increase from about $1.00/lb to about $4.00/lb in April 2008, as shown in Figure 5.9. This increase in price is thought to be the result of economic growth in China and India coupled with labor strikes by miners in Chile. Have oil (see Figure 5.7) and copper prices broken free from their flat or downward drift since 1980? Are they now signaling an era of economic scarcity, or will conservation and substitution reveal these exponential increases to be short term?

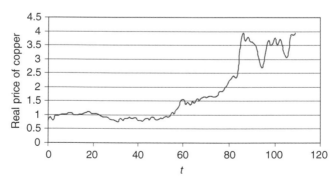

Figure 5.9. The real price of copper (CPI, March 2008 = 1.00) with March 1999 = 0 and April 2008 = 109.
Source: Comex.

The development of substitute commodities, in the case of copper, or the substitution of capital and labor, in the case of energy, can reduce economic scarcity. War, producer cartels, strikes, or a booming, resource-demanding global economy can create short-term economic scarcity, but innovators, entrepreneurs, and consumers will react to high prices by trying to provide lower-cost substitutes or by adapting their economic behavior to reduce the demand for an economically scarce commodity. These forces have been effective at ameliorating resource scarcity throughout human history. While scarcity is an ever-present economic fact of life, it is a dynamic condition, at least for the resources and commodities that flow through organized markets.

Economists are less sanguine about the private incentives to protect the quality of air and water resources, wilderness, and wildlife. The services of these resources are not bought and sold through well-developed markets. From an economic perspective, they are public goods or common property. As in our model of pure open access in Chapter 3, there may be strong private incentives to discharge waste, emit smoke, convert rainforest, or harvest wildlife for human consumption.

Changing property rights, from public to private, or sharing the revenues from tourists or trophy hunters might create incentives for firms to reduce emissions, landowners to conserve some amount of wilderness, or local villagers to refrain from harvesting wildlife. Programs that alter property rights or share the revenues generated by wilderness and wildlife have been instituted, in a limited way, in both developed and less developed countries. For example, in the United States, there is a "cap and trade program" for utilities emitting SO_2. In Africa, there are programs that funnel a portion of the fees from trophy hunting to local villagers, hoping that this might create an incentive for villagers to protect "their" wildlife. How would landless individuals on the edge of a rainforest behave if granted title to a parcel, but with continued ownership contingent *not* on complete development but on the preservation of some fraction as rainforest?

I now turn to a second article by John Tierney. This one describes a bet between the ecologist Paul Ehrlich and the economist Julian Simon. The article does a wonderful job of presenting the "opposing world views" of these two antagonists and the long history of concern about resource scarcity, population growth, and environmental quality. After you read the article, I will update the real cost of the "basket of metals" that was the basis of the bet.

Betting the Planet*

By

John Tierney

In 1980 an ecologist and an economist chose a refreshingly unacademic way to resolve their differences. They bet $1,000. Specifically, the bet was over the future price of five metals, but at stake was much more – a view of the planet's ultimate limits, a vision of humanity's destiny. It was a bet between the Cassandra and the Dr. Pangloss of our era.

They lead two intellectual schools – sometimes called the Malthusians and the Cornucopians, sometimes simply the doomsters and the boomsters – that use the latest in computer-generated graphs and foundation-generated funds to debate whether the world is getting better or going to the dogs. The argument has generally been as fruitless as it is old, since the two sides never seem to be looking at the same part of the world at the same time. Dr. Pangloss sees farm silos brimming with record harvests; Cassandra sees topsoil eroding and pesticide seeping into ground water. Dr. Pangloss sees people living longer; Cassandra sees rain forests being decimated. But in 1980 these opponents managed to agree on one way to chart and test the global future. They promised to abide by the results exactly 10 years later – in October 1990 – and to pay up out of their own pockets.

The bettors, who have never met in all the years they have been excoriating each other, are both 58-year-old professors who grew up in the Newark suburbs. The ecologist, Paul R. Ehrlich, has been one of the world's better-known scientists since publishing *The Population Bomb* in 1968. More than three million copies were sold, and he became perhaps the only author ever interviewed for an hour on *The Tonight Show*. When he is not teaching at Stanford University or

---

* Published in the *New York Times Magazine* on December 2, 1990.

studying butterflies in the Rockies, Ehrlich can generally be found on a plane on his way to give a lecture, collect an award or appear in an occasional spot on the *Today* show. This summer he won a five-year MacArthur Foundation grant for $345,000, and in September he went to Stockholm to share half of the $240,000 Cratoord Prize, the ecologist's version of the Nobel. His many personal successes haven't changed his position in the debate over humanity's fate. He is the pessimist.

The economist, Julian L. Simon of the University of Maryland, often speaks of himself as an outcast, which isn't quite true. His books carry jacket blurbs from Nobel laureate economists, and his views have helped shape policy in Washington for the past decade. But Simon has certainly never enjoyed Ehrlich's academic success or popular appeal. On the first Earth Day in 1970, while Ehrlich was in the national news helping to launch the environmental movement, Simon sat in a college auditorium listening as a zoologist, to great applause, denounced him as a reactionary whose work "lacks scholarship or substance." Simon took revenge, first by throwing a drink in his critic's face at a faculty party and then by becoming the scourge of the environmental movement. When he unveiled his happy vision of beneficent technology and human progress in *Science* magazine in 1980, it attracted one of the largest batches of angry letters in the journal's history.

In some ways, Simon goes beyond Dr. Pangloss, the tutor in *Candide* who insists that "All is for the best in this best of possible worlds." Simon believes that today's world is merely the best so far. Tomorrow's will be better still, because it will have more people producing more bright ideas. He argues that population growth constitutes not a crisis but, in the long run, a boon that will ultimately mean a cleaner environment, a healthier humanity and more abundant supplies of food and raw materials for everyone. And this progress can go on indefinitely because – "incredible as it may seem at first," he wrote in his 1980 article – the planet's resources are actually not finite. Simon also found room in the article to criticize, among others, Ehrlich, Barry Commoner, *Newsweek*, the National Wildlife Federation and the secretary general of the United Nations. It was titled "Resources, Population, Environment: An Oversupply of False Bad News."

An irate Ehrlich wondered how the article had passed peer review at America's leading scientific journal. "Could the editors have found someone to review Simon's manuscript who had to take off his shoes to count to 20?" Ehrlich asked in a rebuttal written with his wife, Anne, also an ecologist at Stanford. They provided the simple arithmetic: the planet's resources had to be divided among a population that was then growing at the unprecedented rate of 75 million people a year. The Ehrlichs called Simon the leader of a "space-age cargo cult" of economists convinced that new resources would miraculously fall from the heavens. For years the Ehrlichs had been trying to explain the ecological concept of "carrying capacity" to these economists. They had been warning that population growth was outstripping the earth's supplies of food, fresh water and minerals. But they couldn't get the economists to listen.

"To explain to one of them the inevitability of no growth in the material sector, or ... that commodities must become expensive," the Ehrlichs wrote, "would be like attempting to explain odd-day-even-day gas distribution to a cranberry."

Ehrlich decided to put his money where his mouth was by responding to an open challenge issued by Simon to all Malthusians. Simon offered to let anyone pick any natural resource – grain, oil, coal, timber, metals – and any future date. If the resource really were to become scarcer as the world's population grew, then its price should rise. Simon wanted to bet that the price would instead decline by the appointed date. Ehrlich derisively announced that he would "accept Simon's astonishing offer before other greedy people jump in." He then formed a consortium with John Harte and John P. Holdren, colleagues at the University of California at Berkeley specializing in energy and resource questions.

In October 1980 the Ehrlich group bet $1,000 on five metals – chrome, copper, nickel, tin and tungsten – in quantities that each cost $200 in the current market. A futures contract was drawn up obligating Simon to sell Ehrlich, Harte and Holdren these same quantities of the metals 10 years later, but at 1980 prices. If the 1990 combined prices turned out to be higher than $1,000, Simon would pay them the difference in cash. If prices fell, they would pay him. The contract was signed, and Ehrlich and Simon went on attacking each other throughout the 1980s. During that decade the world's population grew by more than 800 million, the greatest increase in history, and the store of metals buried in the earth's crust did not get any larger.

"Population, when unchecked, increases in a geometrical ratio. Subsistence increases only in an arithmetical ratio." – Thomas Robert Malthus, 1798. "Population Outgrows Food, Scientists Warn the World" – Front-page headline in the *New York Times*, September 15, 1948, over an article about the "dark outlook for the human race" due to "overpopulation and the dwindling of natural resources." "No Room in the Lifeboats" – Headline in the *New York Times Magazine*, April 16, 1978, over an article warning that "the cost of natural resources is going up" as increasing population ushers in the "Age of Scarcity."

"The earth has limited resources, and if we don't recycle them, we use them up." – Meredith Baxter-Birney, who played the mother on the *Family Ties* television show, in a recent Greenpeace public-service message showing the family sorting garbage in the living room.

It is such an obvious proposition in a finite world: things run out. It must have occurred to *Homo habilis* while searching for rocks to make the first tools 2.5 million years ago. Aristotle and Plato shared the same concerns as the *Family Ties* cast. The American Indians put it nicely in a proverb that has been adopted as a slogan by today's environmentalists: "We do not inherit the earth from our parents. We borrow it from our children." The idea shapes our personal actions when we bundle newspapers to avoid running out of wood for paper and land for garbage dumps. It affects our national policies when we send soldiers into the Persian Gulf to prevent Saddam Hussein from getting a "stranglehold" on the dwindling supplies of oil. It is the fear Paul Ehrlich raised in 1974: "What will we do when the pumps run dry?"

The counterargument is not nearly as intuitively convincing. It has generally consisted of a simple question: Why haven't things run out yet? The ones asking this question now tend to be economists, which is a switch, since their predecessors were the ones who initiated the modern preoccupation with resource scarcity. Economics was first called "the dismal science" in the last century because of Malthus's predictions of mass starvation. He had many successors, the most eloquent of whom perhaps was a British economist named William Stanley Jevons.

In 1865 Jevons published *The Coal Question: An Inquiry Concerning the Progress of the Nation, and the Probable Exhaustion of Our Coal Mines.* In most ways, it was quite similar to the books that appeared during the energy crisis of the 1970s. There were graphs showing parabolic curves of population and coal consumption shooting upwards, and charts showing estimates of woefully inadequate coal reserves. "The conclusion is inevitable," Jevons wrote, "that our present happy progressive condition is a thing of limited duration." Unlike the prophets a century later, though, Jevons was not sure that the answer was mandatory conservation. At first glance, he wrote, there seemed to be a clear case for the Government's limiting industry's profligate energy use. "To disperse so lavishly the cream of our mineral wealth is to be spendthrifts of our capital – to part with that which will never come back." He warned that this might lead to the sudden collapse of British civilization. Yet he noted that much of that civilization, such as "our rich literature and philosophy," might never have existed without "the lavish expenditure of our material energy" that "redeemed us from dullness and degradation a century ago." To reduce coal consumption might only bring back stagnation, he cautioned, and he ended his book with a sentence in italics: "We have to make the momentous choice between brief greatness and longer continued mediocrity."

There were many other sightings of the end of the lode. An energy crisis arose in the middle of the 19th century, when the dwindling supply of whales drove up the cost of lighting homes with oil lamps and tallow candles. In 1905 President Theodore Roosevelt warned of an American "timber famine," a concern that prompted a proposal to ban Christmas trees. In 1926 the Federal Oil Conservation Board announced that the United States had a seven-year supply of petroleum left.

Naturalists gradually replaced economists as the chief doomsayers. They dominated the conservation movement early this century, and in 1948 two of them – Fairfield Osborn, the president of the New York Zoological Society, and an ornithologist named William Vogt – started a national debate by publishing popular books: *Our Plundered Planet* and *Road to Survival*, respectively. Both men warned of overpopulation, dwindling resources and future famines. Vogt's book lamented the loss of "such irreplaceable capital goods as soils and minerals." Vogt was especially worried about one of the metals that turned up decades later in the Ehrlich-Simon bet, warning that "we might go to war to ensure access to tin sources." The world's supply of agricultural land, he wrote, was "shrinking fast" and "every year producing less food." America's recent bumper crops were "accidents of favorable weather." Since the United States was already overpopulated, "a fall in living standards is unavoidable." And if humanity did not follow Vogt's *Road to Survival* – conservation and population control – there was the alternate route presented in the book's last sentence: "Like Gadarene swine, we shall rush down a war-torn slope to a barbarian existence in the blackened rubble."

Both books made an impression on the teen-age Paul Ehrlich. He was already a naturalist himself, thanks to a mentor at the American Museum of Natural History in New York who encouraged him to study butterflies and publish papers while he was still a high-school student in New Jersey. Ehrlich went on to study zoology at the University of Pennsylvania. He married Anne in 1954 while in graduate school at the University of Kansas, and they put their Malthusian principles into practice by limiting themselves to one child. Ehrlich had a vasectomy in 1963, shortly after getting tenure at Stanford.

In the mid-60s, Ehrlich started giving public lectures about the population problem. One caught the attention of David Brower, then executive director of the Sierra Club, who led him to Ballantine Books. Rushing to publish his message in time for the 1968

Presidential election, Ehrlich produced what may be the all-time ecological best seller, *The Population Bomb.*

It was *The Tonight Show* that made him and his book famous. As Ehrlich remembers it, Joan Rivers went on first, telling jokes about her honeymoon night ("I said, 'Turn off the lights ... turn off the lights ... shut the car door.'"). Then there was a starlet whose one-word answers made things so awkward that Ehrlich was rushed on early to rescue Johnny Carson.

"I went on and did basically a monologue," Ehrlich recalls. "I'd talk until the commercial, and during the break I'd feed Johnny a question, and then I'd answer it until the next commercial. I got the highest compliment after the show, when I was walking behind Johnny and Ed McMahon up the stairs, and I heard Johnny say, 'Boy, Paul really saved the show.'"

The Tonight Show got more than 5,000 letters about Ehrlich's appearance, the first of many on the program. Ehrlich has been deluged ever since with requests for lectures, interviews and opinions. He is a rare hybrid: the academic who keeps his professional reputation intact while pleasing the masses. Scientists praise his papers on butterflies and textbooks on ecology; talk-show hosts tout his popular books and love his affably blunt style. He has never been one to mince words or hedge predictions.

The Population Bomb began: "The battle to feed all of humanity is over. In the 1970s the world will undergo famines – hundreds of millions of people are going to starve to death." Ehrlich wrote that "nothing can prevent a substantial increase in the world death rate" and that America's "vast agricultural surpluses are gone."

Six years later, in a book he wrote with his wife, *The End of Affluence,* he raised the death toll. The book told of a "nutritional disaster that seems likely to overtake humanity in the 1970s (or, at the latest, the 1980s). Due to a combination of ignorance, greed and callousness, a situation has been created that could lead to a billion or more people starving to death." The book predicted that "before 1985 mankind will enter a genuine age of scarcity" in which "the accessible supplies of many key minerals will be nearing depletion." Shortages would be felt in America as well as the rest of the world. "One general prediction can be made with confidence: the cost of feeding yourself and your family will continue to increase. There may be minor fluctuations in food prices, but the overall trend will be up."

Ehrlich was right about one thing: the world's population did grow. It is now 5.3 billion, 1.8 billion larger than when he published *The Population Bomb*. Yet somehow the average person is healthier, wealthier and better fed than in 1968. The predicted rise in the world death rate has yet to materialize – infant mortality has declined and life expectancy has increased, most dramatically in the third world. There have been famines in countries afflicted by war, drought and disastrous agricultural policies, but the number of people affected by famines has been declining steadily during the past three decades. In fact, the number is much lower than it was during the same decades of the last century, even though the world's population is much larger. Experts argue about how much hunger remains in the world, but they generally agree that the average person in the third world is better nourished today than in 1968. Food production has increased faster than population since the publication of *The Population Bomb,* just as it has since the books of Vogt, Osborn and Malthus.

The best way to see what has happened to food prices – and to get a glimpse of the Malthusian mind-set – is to consider a graph from Lester R. Brown, another widely quoted doomster. Brown has long been the chief source for Ehrlich and other ecologists on trends in agriculture – "the best person in the country on the subject" in Ehrlich's words. Brown is the president of the Worldwatch Institute in Washington, which makes news each year with what it calls the world's most widely used public-policy document, its "State of the World" report. This year's report includes a graph, below, of grain prices that is interesting for a couple of reasons.

Consider, first of all, how it compares with Brown's predictions of a decade ago. He was pessimistic then for the same reasons that Ehrlich, Vogt and Osborn had been: rising population, vanishing topsoil, the growing dependence on "nonsustainable" uses of irrigation, fertilizer, pesticides. "The period of global food

Dollars
Per Metric
Ton

World Wheat and Rice Prices, 1950–89

security is over," Brown wrote in 1981. "As the demand for food continues to press against the supply, inevitably real food prices will rise. The question no longer seems to be whether they will rise but how much." But as the graph shows, grain prices promptly fell and reached historic lows during the 1980s, continuing a long-term decline that dates back to the days of Vogt and Osborn (and Malthus, too, if you extended the graph).

Now consider how Brown analyzes this data. In a chapter titled "The Illusion of Progress" in this year's report, he focuses not on the long-term trend but on the blips in the graph in 1988 and 1989 – when prices rose because of factors like drought and a United States Government program that took farmland out of production. Looking ahead to the 1990s, Brown writes, "The first concrete economic indication of broad-based environmental deterioration now seems likely to be rising grain prices."

We are barely into the 1990s, but so far Brown's poor track record is intact. Grain prices have plummeted since he published his prediction at the start of the year. The blips in the late 1980s caused farmers to do what they always do when prices rise: plant more crops. The price of wheat has fallen by more than 40 percent in the past year, and if you plotted it on that graph, it would be at yet another all-time low. Once again Malthus's day of reckoning will have to be rescheduled.

Julian Simon remembers his first glimpse of Paul Ehrlich as being one of the more frustrating moments of his life. It was during the Earth Day furor two decades ago. Simon was sitting at home in Urbana, Ill., Ehrlich was on *The Tonight Show* and Johnny Carson was enthralled.

"Carson, the most unimpressable of people, had this look of stupefied admiration," Simon recalls. "He'd throw out a question about population growth and Ehrlich would start out by saying, 'Well, it's really very simple, Johnny.' Now the one thing I knew in those days about population was that nothing about it is simple. But what could I do? Go talk to five people? Here was a guy reaching a vast audience, leading this juggernaut of environmentalist hysteria, and I felt utterly helpless."

At this point, Simon was still in the early stages of Cornucopianism. He had started out as a Malthusian. After studying psychology at Harvard University and receiving a doctorate in business economics from the University of Chicago, he joined the faculty at the University of Illinois in 1963. He was an expert in mail-order marketing – his book on the topic sold 200,000 copies, more than any he has written since – and was looking for something else to do when he heard the grim predictions about overpopulation. In the late 1960s he began publishing papers on using marketing tools and economic incentives to persuade women to have fewer babies. But then he came across work by economists showing that countries with rapid population growth were not suffering more than other countries. In fact, many were doing better. He also came across a book, *Scarcity and Growth,* published in 1963 with the help of Resources for the Future, a conservation group dominated by economists.

The book was a revelation to him: it provided the empirical foundations of Cornucopianism. The authors, Harold J. Barnett and Chandler Morse, tracked the price of natural resources back to 1870 and found that the price of virtually everything had fallen. The average worker today could buy more coal with an hour's pay than he could when *The Coal Question* was published in the last century, just as he could buy more metals and more food. Things were actually getting less scarce as population grew.

The evidence inspired the boomster view of history, which was then refined by Simon and others, like Charles Maurice and Charles W. Smithson. These economists, then at Texas A & M University, looked back at 10,000 years of resource crises and saw a pattern: things did sometimes become scarce, but people responded with innovations. They found new supplies or practiced conservation. They managed to recycle without the benefit of government policies or moral exhortations from Greenpeace. Stone Age tribes in areas short of flint learned to resharpen their tools instead of discarding them as tribes did in flint-rich areas.

Often the temporary scarcity led to a much better substitute. The Greeks' great transition from the Bronze Age to the Iron Age 3,000 years ago, according to Maurice and Smithson, was inspired by a disruption of trade due to wars in the eastern Mediterranean. The disruption produced a shortage of the tin needed to make bronze, and the Greeks responded to the bronze crisis by starting to use iron. Similarly, timber shortages in 16th-century Britain ushered in the age of coal; the scarcity of whale oil around 1850 led to the first oil well in 1859. Temporary shortages do occur, but Cornucopians argue that as long as government doesn't interfere – by mandating conservation or setting the sort of price controls that produced America's gas lines of the 1970s – people will find alternatives that turn out to be better.

"Natural resources are not finite. Yes, you read correctly," Simon wrote in his 1981 manifesto, *The Ultimate Resource.* The title referred to human ingenuity, which Simon believed could go on indefinitely expanding the planet's carrying capacity. This idea marked the crucial difference between Simon and Ehrlich, and between economists and ecologists: the view of the world not as an closed ecosystem but as an flexible marketplace. The concept of carrying capacity might make sense in discussing Ehrlich's butterflies or Vogt's "Gadarene swine," but Simon rejected animal analogies. He liked to quote the 19th-century economist Henry George: "Both the jayhawk and the man eat chickens, but the more jayhawks, the fewer chickens, while the more men, the more chickens."

Of course, men can also produce more pollution than jayhawks, and Simon conceded that the marketplace did need some regulation. But he insisted that environmental crises were being exaggerated. He and another leading boomster, Herman Kahn, edited a book in 1984, *The Resourceful Earth,* rebutting the gloomy forecasts of the government's "Global 2000 Report" prepared under President Carter. Their book was replete with graphs showing that, by most measures, America's air and water had been getting cleaner for decades, thanks partly to greater affluence (richer societies can afford to pay for pollution controls like sewage treatment) and partly to the progress of technology (the pollution from cars today in New York City is nothing compared to the soot from coal-burning furnaces and the solid waste from horses at the turn of the century). Simon asserted that innovations would take care of new forms of pollution, and he set about disputing the various alarming estimates of tropical deforestation, species extinction, eroding topsoil, paved-over farmland and declining fisheries.

"As soon as one predicted disaster doesn't occur, the doomsayers skip to another," Simon complains. "There's nothing wrong with worrying about new problems – we need problems so we can come up with solutions that leave us better off than if they'd never come up in the first place. But why don't the doomsayers see that, in the aggregate, things are getting better? Why do they always think we're at a turning point – or at the end of the road? They deny our creative powers for solutions. It's only because we used those powers so well in the past that we can afford to worry about things like losing species and wetlands. Until we got so rich and healthy and productive at agriculture, a wetland was a swamp with malarial mosquitoes that you had to drain so you could have cropland to feed your family."

Simon's fiercest battle has been against Paul Ehrlich's idea that the world has too many people. The two have never debated directly – Ehrlich has always refused, saying that Simon is a "fringe character" – but they have lambasted each other in scholarly journal articles with titles like "An Economist in Wonderland" and "Paul Ehrlich Saying It Is So Doesn't Make It So." Simon acknowledges that rising population causes short-term problems, because it means more children to feed and raise. But he maintains that there are long-term benefits when those children become productive, resourceful adults. He has supported making abortion and family-planning services available to women to give them more freedom, but he has vehemently opposed programs that tell people how many children to have. He attacked Ehrlich for suggesting that governments should consider using coercion to limit family size and for endorsing the startling idea that the United States should consider cutting off food aid to countries that refuse to control population growth.

Among academics, Simon seems to be gaining in the debate. Many scientists are still uncomfortable with his sweeping optimism about the future – there is no guarantee, after all, that past trends will continue – and most population experts are not sure that the current rate of population growth in the third world is going to bring the long-term benefits predicted by Simon. But the consensus has been shifting against Ehrlich's idea of population growth as the great evil. Simon's work helped prompt the National Academy of Sciences to prepare a 1986 report, which noted that there was no clear evidence that population growth makes countries poorer. It concluded that slower population growth would probably benefit third world countries, but argued that other factors, like a country's economic structure and political institutions, were much more important to social well-being. The report opposed the notion of using government coercion to control family size. It noted that most experts expected the world food situation to continue improving, and it concluded that, for the foreseeable future, "the scarcity of exhaustible resources is at most a minor constraint on economic growth."

But Simon is still far behind when it comes to winning over the general public. This past Earth Day he did not fare much better than he did in 1970. Ehrlich was still the one all over national television. In the weeks leading up to Earth Day in April, Ehrlich did spots for the *Today* show and appeared on other programs promoting his new book, *The Population Explosion,* which declares that "the population bomb has detonated." At the big Earth Day rally in Washington, Ehrlich was one of the many Malthusians warning that this was humanity's last chance to save the planet. It was a scene to make Cornucopians wonder if the ancient Greeks who described Cassandra's curse – fated to be always right but never heeded – had gotten it precisely backward. The crowd of more than 200,000 applauded heartily after Ehrlich told them that population growth could produce a world in which their grandchildren would endure food riots in the streets of America.

Ehrlich did not mention Simon by name, although he did refer to him at another event that Earth Day weekend, a symposium of ecologists inside the domed auditorium of the Smithsonian's National Museum of Natural History. The symposium was devoted to the question of natural resources – "Population and Scarcity: The Forgotten Dimensions" – and Ehrlich talked about humanity squandering irreplaceable capital. He praised a colleague who had advocated the idea of governments' stopping economic growth by setting quotas on the amount of resources that could be used each year. Ehrlich criticized the shortsightedness of economists, and he got a laugh when he alluded to Simon's book: "The ultimate resource – the one thing we'll never run out of is imbeciles."

The same day Simon spoke only a block away in a small, low-ceilinged conference room at another Earth Day symposium. It was sponsored by the Competitive Enterprise Institute, a group that explores free-market solutions to environmental problems. In an intense, quiet voice, Simon declared that the Malthusians "must either turn a blind eye to the scientific evidence or be blatantly dishonest intellectually." He spoke of population growth representing "a victory over death," because it was due to the doubling of life expectancy since the Industrial Revolution. "This is an incredible gain. Human history has never shown any achievement to hold a candle to that. You'd expect lovers of human life to be jumping with joy at this incredible success. Instead, across the street we've got them lamenting that there are so many people alive."

He seemed a little disappointed that there were only 16 people in the audience to celebrate his message. "Well, there may be more of them over there," Simon said, gesturing toward the place where Ehrlich was speaking, "but we're happier."

The bet was settled this fall without ceremony. Ehrlich did not even bother to write a letter. He simply mailed Simon a sheet of calculations about metal prices – along with a check for $576.07. Simon wrote back a thank-you note, adding that he would be willing to raise the wager to as much as $20,000, pinned to any other resources and to any other year in the future.

Each of the five metals chosen by Ehrlich's group, when adjusted for inflation since 1980, had declined in price. The drop was so sharp, in fact, that Simon would have come out slightly ahead overall even without the inflation adjustment called for in the bet. Prices fell for the same Cornucopian reasons they had fallen in previous decades – entrepreneurship and continuing technological improvements. Prospectors found new lodes, such as the nickel mines around the world that ended a Canadian company's near monopoly of the market. Thanks to computers, new machines and new chemical processes, there were more efficient ways to extract and refine the ores for chrome and the other metals.

For many uses, the metals were replaced by cheaper materials, notably plastics, which became less expensive as the price of oil declined (even during this year's crisis in the Persian Gulf, the real cost of oil remained lower than in 1980). Telephone calls went through satellites and fiber-optic lines instead of copper wires. Ceramics replaced tungsten in cutting tools. Cans were made of aluminum instead of tin, and Vogt's fears about America going to war over tin remained unrealized. The most newsworthy event in the 1980s concerning that metal was the collapse of the international tin cartel, which gave up trying to set prices in 1985 when the market became inundated with excess supplies.

Is there a lesson here for the future? "Absolutely not," said Ehrlich in an interview. Nevertheless, he has no plans to take up Simon's new offer: "The bet doesn't mean anything. Julian Simon is like the guy who jumps off the Empire State Building and says how great things are going so far as he passes the 10th floor. I still think the price of those metals will go up eventually, but that's a minor point. The resource that worries me the most is the declining capacity of our planet to buffer itself against human impacts. Look at the new problems that have come up: the ozone hole, acid rain, global warming. It's true that we've kept up food production—I underestimated how badly we'd keep on depleting our topsoil and ground water—but I have no doubt that sometime in the next century food will be scarce enough that prices are really going to be high even in the United States. If we get climate change and let the ecological systems keep running downhill, we could have a gigantic population crash."

Simon was not surprised to hear about Ehrlich's reaction. "Paul Ehrlich has never been able to learn from past experience," he said, then launched into the Cornucopian line on the greenhouse crisis—how, even in the unlikely event that doomsayers are right about global warming, humanity will find some way to avert climate change or adapt, and everyone will emerge the better for it. But Simon did not get far into his argument before another cheery thought occurred to him. He stopped and smiled.

"So Ehrlich is talking about a population crash," he said. "That sounds like an even better way to make money. I'll give him heavy odds on that one."

5.9 A POSTSCRIPT TO "BETTING THE PLANET"

In Table 5.2, I recalculate the cost of the metals in "the bet" using the CPI-U index with 1984 = 100. This results in a slightly different value for the metals in 1990.

We see that in March 2008, the real cost of the basket of metals had approximately doubled. The prices of these metals are highly volatile in the short run and are strongly influenced by the rate of growth (demand) in the world economy in the long run. There is some evidence that metals prices are subject to "supercycles" and that the decade 1980–1990 was one of sluggish economic growth and declining real metal prices. Thus, Julian Simon, while being correct in his

Table 5.2. *Cost of Metals in "the Bet"*

	1980	**1990**	**March 2008**
CPI-U (1982–1984 = 100)*	77.8	127.4	213.5
Copper	$1.02/lb	$0.83/lb	1.81/lb
Chrome	$3.90/lb	$2.34/lb	$0.48/lb
Nickel	$3.06/lb	$2.95/lb	$5.86/lb
Tin	$0.87/lb	$0.24/lb	$5.22/lb
Tungsten	$14.66/lb	$6.30	$8.43
Cost of "basket"	$1,000	$618	$2,074

assessment of the economic forces that work to ameliorate resource scarcity, also probably was lucky in the timing of the bet.

Julian Simon died on February 8, 1998. John Tierney is carrying on his cornucopian world view and willingness to wager. Mr. Tierney has wagered $5,000 that the price of oil will not hit $200 per barrel in 2010. Go to *tierneylab.blogs.nytimes.com/ 2007/10/30/betting-on-cheaper-oil/*. In July 2008, the spot price for crude had risen to $147 per barrel. In December 2008, with the worldwide economy in recession, it had fallen to $46 per barrel. With the recession expected to last well into 2009, if not 2010, Mr. Tierney's bet looks good.

5.10 EXERCISES

E5.1 A frequently invoked utility function in economics takes the form

$$U(q_t) = \left[\frac{\eta}{(\eta - 1)} \right] q_t^{(\eta-1)/\eta}$$

where for this problem q_t will be the rate of extraction from a nonrenewable resource and $\eta > 0$ is a parameter. Consider the optimal depletion problem

$$\underset{\{q_t\}_{t=0}^{\infty}}{\text{Maximize}} \quad U = \sum_{t=0}^{\infty} \rho^t U(q_t)$$
$$\text{Subject to} \quad R_{t+1} = R_t - q_t$$
$$R_0 > 0 \quad \text{given}$$

where $\rho = 1/(1 + \delta)$ is the discount factor, $\delta > 0$ is the discount rate, and $R_0 > 0$ is the level of initial reserves. For the preceding utility function, what is the analytic expression for the optimal rate of extraction q_t^*? *Hint:* It will depend on ρ, η, t, and R_0. Plot q_t^* for $R_0 = 1, \delta = 0.05$, and $\eta = 1, 2, 3$.

E5.2 You are a price-taking competitive mine owner facing a constant per-unit price of $p > 0$ for every unit of a nonrenewable resource extracted from initial reserves R_0. The rate of extraction in period t is denoted by q_t, and the cost of extraction is given by $(c/2)q_t^2$. The net revenue from a positive rate of extraction in period t is given by $\pi_t = pq_t - (c/2)q_t^2$. You wish to determine the optimal rate of extraction and the date of exhaustion T^*. The Lagrangian for this problem may be written

$$L = \sum_{t=0}^{T-1} \rho^t [pq_t - (c/2)q_t^2 + \rho\lambda_{t+1}(R_t - q_t - R_{t+1})]$$

where $\rho = 1/(1+\delta)$ is the discount factor and $\delta > 0$ is the discount rate. At the unknown date of depletion $T, R_T = q_T = 0$.

(a) What are the first-order necessary conditions for this problem?

(b) From $\partial L / \partial R_t = 0$, show that $\rho\lambda_{t+1} = \lambda_t$. What is the relationship between λ_t and λ_0?

(c) With $q_T = 0$, what is the relationship between λ_0 and p?

(d) What is the expression for q_t^*, the optimal extraction rate? *Hint:* On the left-hand side you will have q_t^*, and on the right-hand side you will have an expression depending on p, c, ρ, T, and t.

(e) Using the exhaustion condition $\sum_{t=0}^{T-1} q_t^* = R_0$, solve for the implicit expression, call it $G(T)$, where $G(T) = 0$ at $T = T^*$, the optimal date of depletion.

(f) For $p = 100, c = 45.839, \delta = 0.05$, and $R_0 = 100$, solve for $T = T^*$ and plot q_t^* and λ_t.

E5.3 Consider the following modification to our simple model of extraction and exploration. As before, there are two periods, $t = 0, 1$, and two future states: $s = 0$, a "no-discovery state," and $s = 1$, a "discovery state," either of which could occur in $t = 1$. Now, however, the probability of the no-discovery state is influenced by the level of exploration in $t = 0$. The level of exploration in $t = 0$ is now denoted by X_0, and the probability of the no-discovery state is given by $\Pr(s = 0) = e^{-\beta X_0}$, where e is the base of the system of natural logarithms, $\beta > 0$, and $\Pr(s = 1) = (1 - e^{-\beta X_0})$. The amount discovered in each of the two future states is given by $D_s = s\alpha \ln(1 + X_0)$, where $\alpha > 0$ and $\ln(\bullet)$ is the natural log operator. The remaining model structure is the same as in Section 5.7, but now the cost of exploration is wX_0^2. The preceding changes affect the probabilities of the no-discovery and discovery states and remaining reserves.

(a) What are the *explicit expressions* for $q_{1,0}^*$, $q_{1,1}^*$, and q_0^*?

(b) What is the *implicit expression* $G(X_0) = 0$ that could be used to solve numerically for X_0^*?

(c) Suppose that $R_0 = 100, p_0 = 1, p_{1,1} = 1.1, c = 2, w = 5, \alpha = 250, \beta = 0.75$, and $\delta = 0.05$. What are the numerical values for $X_0^*, q_0^*, q_{1,0}^*, q_{1,1}^*, \Pr(s = 0), \Pr(s = 1)$, and $V(R_0)$, the expected present value of net revenues from optimal extraction and exploration?

E5.4 Consider one more variation on the problem of optimal extraction and risky exploration in the two-period $(t = 0, 1)$, two-state $(s = 0, 1)$ model. The amount of additional reserves available in state s is now given by $D_s = s\alpha e_0^\beta$, where $\alpha > 0$ and $1 > \beta > 0$. Recall that $s = 0$ is the "no-discovery state" and $s = 1$ is the "discovery state." We return to the subjective probabilities in Section 5.7, where $\Pr(s = 0) = \varepsilon$ and $\Pr(s = 1) = (1 - \varepsilon)$. The other modification to the problem is that now the cost of exploration is linear in e_0 and given by the term we_0, where $w > 0$ is now the unit cost of exploratory effort.

(a) Use stochastic dynamic programming to solve for the analytic expressions for $q_{1,0}^*$, $\pi_{1,0}^*$, $q_{1,1}^*$, $\pi_{1,1}^*$, q_0^*, and e_0^*.

(b) Solve for the numerical values of $q_0^*, e_0^*, q_{1,0}^*, q_{1,1}^*$, and $V(R_0)$, where $V(R_0)$ is the present value of expected net revenue from optimal extraction/exploration policies when $R_0 = 100$, $p_0 = 1, p_1 = 1.2, c = 2, w = 5, \alpha = 250, \beta = 0.5, \varepsilon = 0.7$, and $\delta = 0.05$.

E5.5 The constant-elasticity inverse demand curve took the form $p_t = aq_t^{-b}$, where $a > 0\ b > 0$ are parameters, and the elasticity of demand is given by $\eta_t = |1/{-}b|$. The benefit associated with $q_t > 0$ may be approximated by the area under the inverse demand curve, from zero to q_t, which is given by $B_t = \int_0^{q_t} as^{-b}ds = [a/(1-b)]q_t^{(1-b)}$. Suppose that the cost of extraction is reserve-dependent and given by the function $C_t = cq_t/R_t$, where $c > 0$ is a cost parameter. Then the net benefit in period t becomes $\pi_t = [a/(1-b)]q_t^{(1-b)} - cq_t/R_t$. Consider a finite-horizon problem with the Lagrangian

$$L = \sum_{t=0}^{T-1} \rho^t \{ [a/(1-b)]q_t^{(1-b)} - cq_t/R_t + \rho\lambda_{t+1}(R_t - q_t - R_{t+1}) \}$$

where $q_T = \lambda_T = 0$ and $R_T \geq 0$. Set up a spreadsheet and use Solver to find $(q_t^*)_{t=0}^{t=T-1}$ when $T = 100$, $a = 1$, $b = 0.5$, $c = 5$, $\delta = 0.05$, and $R_0 = 100$. As your initial guess, set $q_t = 1$ for $t = 0, 1, \ldots, 99$. Specify the constraints $q_t \geq 0.00001$ and $R_{100} \geq 0$ in order to keep Solver from crashing. What is the optimized value $\pi^* = \sum_{t=0}^{99} \rho^t \pi_t$? From the first-order conditions you can show that $\lambda_{t+1} = (1+\delta)(aq_t^{-b} - c/R_t)$. Does Solver's solution result in $\lambda_T \approx 0$?

6

Stock Pollutants

6.0 INTRODUCTION AND OVERVIEW

This chapter is concerned with the wastes from production or consumption that might accumulate over time. I will refer to any accumulated waste as a *stock pollutant*. Returning to Figure 1.1, extracted ore q_t was seen to generate a waste flow αq_t that might accumulate as the stock pollutant Z_t, where $\alpha > 0$ was a coefficient (parameter) with a dimension that converted the units used to measure q_t into the units used to measure Z_t. For example, if q_t were measured in metric tons (mt) and Z_t were measured in parts per million (ppm), then α would have the dimension of ppm/mt.

For *degradable wastes*, there is often a biological or chemical process where a portion of the pollution stock is decomposed (degraded) into constituent compounds that might pose little or no threat to the environment. In Figure 1.1, the rate at which the stock pollutant degrades is γZ_t, where $1 > \gamma > 0$ is a degradation coefficient indicating the fraction of the pollution stock degraded during period t. The net effect of the rates of waste flow and degradation will determine the change in the stock pollutant as given by the difference equation

$$Z_{t+1} - Z_t = -\gamma Z_t + \alpha q_t \qquad (6.1)$$

As noted in Chapter 1, if the rate of waste flow exceeds the rate of degradation, the stock pollutant will increase, whereas if the degradation rate exceeds the flow of new waste, the stock pollutant will decrease. If the rate of waste flow precisely equals the rate of degradation, the stock pollutant will be unchanged. If such an equality can be maintained, the pollution stock would be in a steady state.

Not all stock pollutants are degradable on an economic time scale. If $\gamma = 0$, a positive waste flow can only increase the level of the stock pollutant. *Nondegradable wastes* might be subject to *diffusion*, where they are dispersed by physical or perhaps biological processes and become more evenly distributed, often at a lower concentration, within the overall environment. A dynamic model with a spatial dimension is required to model diffusion. If time and space are continuous variables, models of diffusion are often based on a partial differential equation. Discrete-time spatial models can be constructed using a system of first-order difference equations where $Z_{i,t+1} - Z_{i,t} = F_i(Z_{1,t}, Z_{2,t}, \ldots, Z_{I,t}S_{1,t}, S_{2,t}, \ldots, S_{I,t})$ is the change in the concentration of the stock pollutant at location $i = 1, 2, \ldots, I$ and $S_{i,t}$ is the emission rate (waste flow) at location i in period t. Diffusion may reduce the "local" concentration of a nondegradable stock pollutant, but the overall mass of such pollutants, in a closed environment, cannot decrease.

The rate of waste generation might be more complex than a simple coefficient of proportionality, such as $\alpha > 0$. In the next section we will introduce the *commodity-residual transformation frontier*, where an economy must implicitly allocate its productive resources to choose the rate of output for a positively valued commodity and the rate of flow for a negatively valued residual (waste). This is followed by a section that formulates a measure of welfare where the damage from a stock pollutant is subtracted from the value of commodity production that generates the residual waste flow. Such a measure is consistent with the recommendation by environmental economists that the national income accounts be adjusted to reflect both the depletion of resources and the cost of environmental damage.

Sections 6.3 through 6.5 present some simple models of degradable and nondegradable stock pollutants. The emphasis is on the optimal control of stock pollutants (their concentration in the ambient environment) by (1) the implicit allocation of resources between commodity production and waste reduction, (2) the rate and location of residual deposition, and (3) the rate of extraction of a nonrenewable resource whose "consumption" produces a waste flow. These models collectively cover many of the dynamic and spatial aspects of real-world pollutants.

In Section 6.6 we will construct a two-period, two-state model of risky climate change. The model is solved using stochastic dynamic programming. The optimal reduction in greenhouse gas (GHG) emissions today requires a knowledge of optimal remediation in both future climate states. Section 6.7 analyzes two environmental policies advocated by economists – emission taxes and marketable pollution permits. Section 6.8 ends the chapter with some exercises.

6.1 THE COMMODITY-RESIDUAL TRANSFORMATION FRONTIER

Suppose, within the context of Figure 1.1, that we defined $S_t = \alpha q_t$ to be the flow of residual waste from the extraction of q_t units of ore in period t. The presumption would be that the rate of residual waste is proportional to the rate of extraction. This is but one possible relationship. In general, let $Q_t > 0$ denote the rate of production of some positively valued commodity in period t and $S_t \geq 0$ denote the rate of flow of a jointly produced negatively valued residual. The residual is negatively valued because it might accumulate as a damage-inducing stock pollutant.

Within the economy, suppose that there is a fixed bundle of resources that can be used to produce Q_t or reduce S_t. (Since the underlying bundle of resources is fixed, they will be "invisible" or implicit in our transformation function.) Let $\phi(Q_t, S_t) = 0$ denote the *commodity-residual transformation frontier*. This implicit function indicates the minimum level of S_t for a given level of Q_t or, equivalently, the maximum level of Q_t for a given level of S_t. What would the commodity-residual transformation frontier look like in $Q_t - S_t$ space? One possible curve is shown in Figure 6.1.

In this figure, the commodity rate $Q_{\min} > 0$ represents the largest rate of output that can be achieved when $S_t = 0$. If S_t were a residual that accumulated as a highly toxic stock pollutant, then the economy may find it optimal to allocate the available resources to locate at $(Q_{\min}, 0)$. If, on the other hand, S_t and its associated stock pollutant were only mildly discomforting, the economy may opt for a larger level for Q_t. To produce $Q_t > Q_{\min}$, the economy would have to divert some

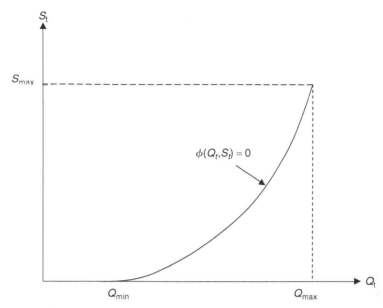

Figure 6.1. The commodity-residual transformation curve.

of the fixed resources away from residual prevention toward commodity production. This would result in a positive flow of residuals ($S_t > 0$). At the other extreme from ($Q_{min}, 0$), if all resources were devoted to production of Q_t, the economy could achieve $Q_t = Q_{max}$, but it would have to accept a flow of residuals at $S_t = S_{max}$. Points along the curve connecting ($Q_{min}, 0$) with (Q_{max}, S_{max}) define the *tradeoff menu* for Q_t and S_t, given the fixed bundle of resources. This is the commodity-residual transformation frontier implied by $\phi(Q_t, S_t) = 0$. It is a relative of the production possibility (PP) curve from introductory economics. The PP curve depicted the tradeoff between two positively valued commodities, whereas the commodity-residual transformation frontier shows the tradeoff between a commodity and its jointly produced residual.

There is a convention for the partial derivatives of $\phi(Q_t, S_t)$. The partial derivative with respect to Q_t is positive, written $\partial\phi(Q_t, S_t)/\partial Q_t = \phi_Q(\bullet) > 0$, while the partial derivative with respect to S_t is negative, written $\partial\phi(Q_t, S_t)/\partial S_t = \phi_S(\bullet) < 0$. The signs of these derivatives will come into play when we specify functional forms for $\phi(Q_t, S_t)$ and seek the optimal levels for Q_t, S_t, and Z_t.

6.2 DAMAGE FUNCTIONS AND WELFARE

In this book, a *damage function* will relate the size of the stock pollutant Z_t to the monetary damage suffered by an economy in period t. In static models of pollution, damage might depend on the level of emissions or waste flow S_t. With the pollution stock changing according to $Z_{t+1} - Z_t = -\gamma Z_t + \alpha q_t$, residual wastes emitted in period t will not become part of the pollution stock until period $t + 1$, when they will make their first "contribution" to a future flow of environmental damage.

Denoting the level of monetary damage in period t by D_t, the damage function will be written as $D_t = D(Z_t)$. The shape of the damage function will depend on the toxicity of Z_t. In a spatial model, damage might depend on location. One generally would think that larger pollution stocks would result in higher damage $D'(Z_t) > 0$ and that the damage might be "smoothly" increasing at an increasing rate $D''(Z_t) > 0$. Positive first and second derivatives would imply that the damage function is strictly convex. As it turns out, empirical studies seem to indicate that damage functions, from exposing a single individual to higher doses of some pollutant, might resemble a discontinuous step function, as shown in Figure 6.2. The step function would imply that damage is constant for a certain level (dose) of Z_t and then jumps, discontinuously, at a critical threshold. When individual step functions are aggregated across a large, diverse population, a smooth, strictly convex function might be a reasonable approximation.

The estimation of damage functions is made difficult by the need to assign dollar values to the damage to an ecosystem. This might involve estimating the value of a particular plant or animal species within that system or attempting to value human disutility, morbidity, or a shortened life. What is the monetary damage from an oil-soaked sea otter? What is the loss from a life shortened by emphysema exacerbated by air pollution? These questions pose difficult valuation problems. Damages might be imperfectly estimated by lost earnings, hospitalization costs, and the "willingness to pay" of humans to remain healthy or prevent despoilment of marine or other ecosystems. Various methods exist to estimate environmental damage (or the value of improving environmental quality). Two frequently employed methods are the *travel-cost method* and *contingent valuation*.

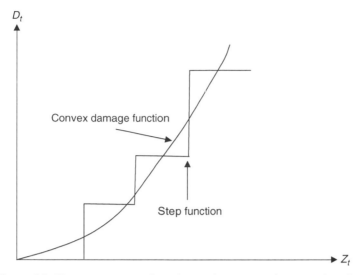

Figure 6.2. Damage as a step function and as a smooth convex function.

The travel-cost method attempts to value a favored or preferred environmental attribute by observing the additional costs that users (i.e., hikers, bikers, campers, etc.) are willing to incur to recreate in a site with preferred attributes. It is also possible to estimate the loss to users if an attribute or environmental quality is impaired. For example, clean and less congested beaches may require visitors to expend more time and money in travel and accommodations than if they visited less clean or more congested beaches closer to home. If wastes or an oil spill were to sully the more distant, pristine beach, the travel-cost premium, summed over all potential visitors, might provide an estimate of one component of the environmental damage.

Contingent valuation methods might be used to estimate other components of damage. Contingent valuation employs surveys to directly ask individuals their willingness to pay for certain attributes or the level of compensation that an individual would require to forego certain attributes. Returning to our less-than-clean, congested urban beach, a contingent valuation survey might show a visitor pictures of the beach after refuse pickup and under less congested conditions and ask the individual how much he or she would be willing to pay for a day of refuse-free, reduced-congestion beach time. Alternatively, visitors to the more distant, pristine beach might be shown pictures of washed-up

medical waste or oil-stained sand and asked what compensation payment they would require if a garbage scow or oil barge were to disgorge
its contents on the beach during the last day of their vacation.

   The preceding examples involved observing travel cost or admin-
istering surveys to visitors at a site. Such research might provide
estimates of the value of cleanup or the damage inflicted by pollution.
Contingent valuation, because it employs survey techniques, can be
used to estimate *nonuse values* as well. Most economists would agree
that individuals with a low or zero probability of visiting a pristine
environment still might be willing to pay something for its preservation or protection. Accurately measuring these values is much more
difficult because of the tendency that a respondent might have to
embed broader environmental values into a question about a particular inlet in Alaska or beach on Cape Cod. While the value that current
nonusers place on the option of future use (including the options of
unborn generations) is seen as valid, its measurement by contingent
valuation methods is imprecise and controversial. In this text, we need
not resolve these measurement issues. In the optimization problems
of this chapter, we typically will assume a convex damage function
and then solve for the optimal flow of waste at different disposal
sites. In empirical work, dynamic models might be useful in determining the environmental value implied by a certain ambient standard.
For example, if the costs of waste treatment are known, and if an
ambient standard is binding, it may be possible to estimate the smallest marginal environmental damage that would optimally justify the
ambient standard.

   Mathematically, we might hypothesize that the welfare of society
in period t depends on the flow of output Q_t and the level of the
stock pollutant Z_t, and write $W_t = W(Q_t, Z_t)$. The welfare function
might be additively separable, where $W_t = \pi(Q_t) - D(Z_t)$, with $\pi(Q_t)$
strictly concave [$\pi'(Q_t) > 0$ and $\pi''(Q_t) < 0$] and $D(Z_t)$ strictly convex
[$D'(Z_t) > 0$ and $D''(Z_t) > 0$].

   The additively separable form could reflect a national accounting
philosophy where environmental damage is deducted from the value
of newly produced goods and services. As noted earlier, such a revision
to the national income accounts has been advocated by environmental
economists for at least four decades. While such deductions from gross
domestic product are conceptually well founded, the aforementioned

difficulty of measuring environmental damage on an annual basis causes other economists to view such proposals as impractical. The dynamic models we will now consider will clarify the economic notion of damage and suggest how such damages might be measured by making use of shadow prices in a fashion similar to that proposed for measuring the scarcity of a nonrenewable resource.

6.3 A DEGRADABLE STOCK POLLUTANT

For a degradable stock pollutant with dynamics $Z_{t+1} - Z_t = -\gamma Z_t + S_t$, the degradation coefficient γ is positive. We will assume that the economy faces a commodity-residual transformation frontier implied by $\phi(Q_t, S_t) = 0$. Recall our conventions on the partial derivatives of $\phi(Q_t, S_t)$: $\phi_Q(\bullet) > 0$ and $\phi_S(\bullet) < 0$. Assume a separable welfare function, where economic well-being in period t is given by $W_t = \pi(Q_t) - D(Z_t)$, with $\pi(Q_t)$ strictly concave and $D(Z_t)$ strictly convex. The optimization problem of interest seeks to

$$\text{Maximize} \quad W = \sum_{t=0}^{\infty} \rho^t [\pi(Q_t) - D(Z_t)]$$

$$\text{Subject to} \quad Z_{t+1} - Z_t = -\gamma Z_t + S_t$$

$$\phi(Q_t, S_t) = 0$$

$$Q_{\max} \geq Q_t \geq Q_{\min}$$

$$Z_0 \text{ given}$$

If we assume that $Q_{\max} > Q_t^* > Q_{\min}$, the Lagrangian for this problem may be written as

$$L = \sum_{t=0}^{\infty} \rho^t \{\pi(Q_t) - D(Z_t) + \rho\lambda_{t+1}[(1 - \gamma)Z_t + S_t - Z_{t+1}]$$

$$-\mu_t \phi(Q_t, S_t)\}$$

Note: The commodity-residual transformation frontier is premultiplied by $-\mu_t$ and included within the expression in braces $\{\bullet\}$. By formulating the Lagrangian in this way, $\mu_t > 0$ will be interpreted as the shadow price on the implicit resources that can be used to produce Q_t or reduce S_t, and $\lambda_{t+1} < 0$ will be the shadow price on the pollution stock Z_{t+1}, which is negative because a positive stock inflicts damage.

The first-order necessary conditions require

$$\mu_t = \frac{\pi'(\bullet)}{\phi_Q(\bullet)} > 0 \tag{6.2}$$

$$\rho\lambda_{t+1} = \mu_t\phi_S(\bullet) = \frac{\pi'(\bullet)\phi_S(\bullet)}{\phi_Q(\bullet)} < 0 \tag{6.3}$$

$$(1 - \gamma)\rho\lambda_{t+1} - \lambda_t = D'(\bullet) \tag{6.4}$$

$$Z_{t+1} - Z_t = -\gamma Z_t + S_t \tag{6.5}$$

$$\phi(Q_t, S_t) = 0 \tag{6.6}$$

Equations (6.2) through (6.6) are obtained by setting the partial derivatives of the Lagrangian with respect to Q_t, S_t, Z_t, $\rho\lambda_{t+1}$, and μ_t equal to zero.

We next consider the conditions at a steady-state optimum and then the optimal approach path if $Z_0 \neq Z^*$. In steady state, $\mu = \pi'(Q)/\phi_Q(\bullet)$, and $\rho\lambda = \pi'(Q)\phi_S(\bullet)/\phi_Q(\bullet)$. Evaluating Equation (6.4) in steady state and factoring out $\rho\lambda$ implies that $\rho\lambda[(1 - \gamma) - (1 + \delta)] = D'(Z)$. Substituting in the expression for $\rho\lambda$ and simplifying implies that $-\pi'(Q)[\phi_S(\bullet)/\phi_Q(\bullet)] = D'(Z)/(\delta + \gamma)$. While this last expression may appear to be nothing more than notational gibberish, it does have a logical economic interpretation. The term $-[\phi_S(\bullet)/\phi_Q(\bullet)]$ is equal to dQ/dS and is called a *marginal rate of transformation* (MRT); in this case, it is the marginal rate at which S can be transformed into Q. In other words, if you are willing to put up with slightly higher residual emissions, how much more Q can you get? $\pi'(Q)$ is the marginal value of that additional unit of steady-state Q. Thus the left-hand side (LHS) is the marginal value of a slight increase in S that will allow a slight increase in Q. What is the cost? The cost is that a slight increase in S will lead to a slight increase in steady-state Z, which leads to an increase in marginal damage $D'(Z)$. This marginal damage is sustained over an infinite horizon and has a present value (adjusted by the degradation coefficient) of $D'(Z)/(\delta + \gamma)$. Thus this last equation says that in steady state you want to choose the mix of Q and S so that the marginal value in transformation is precisely equal to the present value of marginal damage. Makes perfect sense, right?

Equations (6.6) and (6.5) can be evaluated in steady state and imply that $\phi(Q, S) = 0$ and $Z = S/\gamma$. We will bundle these last three equation together because they can be used to solve for the steady-state levels of Q, S, and Z and simply state that

$$-\pi'(\bullet)\frac{\phi_S(\bullet)}{\phi_Q(\bullet)} = \frac{D'(\bullet)}{\delta + \gamma}$$

$$\phi(Q, S) = 0 \qquad (6.7)$$

$$Z = \frac{S}{\gamma}$$

define (Q^*, S^*, Z^*).

If $\pi(Q_t)$ and $\phi(Q_t, S_t)$ are strictly concave in Q_t, the approach from $Z_0 \neq Z^*$ will be asymptotic, with $Z_t \rightarrow Z^*$ as $t \rightarrow \infty$. If $Z_0 > Z^*$, the economy will select rates of output and residual emission where $\gamma Z_t > S_t$, and the pollution stock will decline toward Z^*. If $Z_0 < Z^*$, the economy can indulge in rates of output and residual emission in excess of those at the steady-state optimum; S_t will be greater than γZ_t, and the pollution stock will grow toward Z^*.

If the Lagrangian is linear in Q_t and S_t, the approach to Z^* may be most rapid. Recall that in Section 2.10 we analyzed a stock pollution problem where it was optimal to go from $Z_0 > Z^*$ to Z^* by imposing a moratorium on output. In that example, $Z_{t+1} - Z_t = -\gamma Z_t + \alpha Q_t$. Here we consider another example where (1) $\pi(Q_t) = pQ_t$, where $p > 0$ is the unit price for Q_t, (2) $D(Z_t) = cZ_t^2$, where $c > 0$ is a damage coefficient, and (3) the transformation frontier is given by $\phi(Q_t, S_t) = Q_t - nS_t - Q_{\min} = 0$, where $n > 0$ is a coefficient indicating the incremental increase in commodity Q_t if one is willing to put up with an incremental increase in the residual S_t. It is assumed that $Q_{\max} > Q_t^* > Q_{\min}$. The commodity-residual transformation frontier is drawn in Figure 6.3. In this case, $\phi(Q_t, S_t) = 0$ implies that $S_t = (Q_t - Q_{\min})/n$.

The optimal steady-state pollution stock Z^* is immediately implied by the first equation in the group [Equation (6.7)]. This can be shown my noting that $\phi_Q(\bullet) = 1$, $\phi_S(\bullet) = -n$, $D'(Z) = 2cZ$, and $\pi'(Q) = p$. Substituting these derivatives into $-\pi'(Q)[\phi_S(\bullet)/\phi_Q(\bullet)] = D'(Z)/(\delta + \gamma)$, one obtains $pn = 2cZ/(\delta + \gamma)$ or

$$Z^* = \frac{pn(\delta + \gamma)}{2c} \qquad (6.8)$$

Given the expression for Z^*, one can obtain expressions for S^* and Q^* by noting $S^* = \gamma Z^*$ and $Q^* = Q_{\min} + nS^*$.

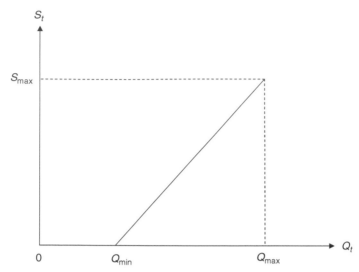

Figure 6.3. $\phi(Q_t, S_t) = Q_t - nS_t - Q_{min} = 0$ with $Q_{max} \geq Q_t \geq Q_{min}$.

Spreadsheet S6.1 shows the numerical values when $p = 2$, $n = 10$, $\delta = 0.05$, $\gamma = 0.2$, $c = 0.1$, $Q_{min} = 10$, $Q_{max} = 100$, and $Z_0 = 0$. These parameter values imply a unique steady-state optimum where $Z^* = 25$, $S^* = 5$, and $Q^* = 60$. In the body of the spreadsheet we set up a 21-period horizon ($t = 0, 1, \ldots, 20$) where we will ask Solver to determine how it wants to go from $Z_0 = 0$ to $Z^* = 25$. The choice variables will be $Q_t, t = 0, 1, \ldots, 19$, and in cell \$C\$18, we define S_t in terms of the choice for Q_t by typing $= (B18 - \$B\$9)/\$B\$4$ and fill down accordingly. In cell \$D\$19, we program the dynamics of the stock pollutant, typing $= (1 - \$B\$7) * D18 + C18$. In column E, we program the discounted net revenues. In cell \$E\$18, we type $= (\$B\$6\^{}A18) * (\$B\$3 * B18 - \$B\$8 * (D18\^{}2))$ and fill down through cell \$E\$37. The terminal function in cell \$E\$38 requires some explanation.

In this example, we are going to tell Solver that whatever it selects for Z_{20}, it has to adopt that value as a steady-state pollution stock and live with it forever. This terminal condition is identical in philosophy to the terminal condition used to approximate the infinite-horizon approach path in the bioeconomic model in Section 2.9. In particular, review the algebra underlying Equation (2.11). This approach also was employed in formulating the final function in Section 2.10, where we saw Solver

	A	B	C	D	E	F	G
1	Spreadsheet 6.1						
2							
3	$p =$	2					
4	$n =$	10			Time Paths for $Q(t)$. $S(t)$, and $Z(t)$		
5	$\delta =$	0.05					
6	$\rho =$	0.952380952					
7	$\gamma =$	0.2					
8	$c =$	0.1					
9	$Q_{min} =$	10					
10	$Q_{max} =$	100					
11	$Z(0) =$	0					
12							
13	$Z^* =$	25					
14	$S^* =$	5					
15	$Q^* =$	60		$W =$	1142.855386		
16							
17	t	$Q(t)$	$S(t)$	$Z(t)$	$(\rho^t)^*W(t)$		
18	0	100	9	0	200		
19	1	100	9	9	182.7619048		
20	2	100	9	16.2	157.6018141		
21	3	100	9	21.96	131.1096771		
22	4	100	9	26.568	106.4693313		
23	5	100	9	30.2544	84.98683304		
24	6	100	9	33.20352	66.97479138		
25	7	100	9	35.562816	52.25541165		
26	8	100	9	37.4502528	40.43970109		
27	9	100	9	38.96020224	31.07676612		
28	10	100	9	40.16816179	23.72890007		
29	11	100	9	41.13452943	18.00522726		
30	12	100	9	41.90762355	13.57297269		
31	13	100	9	42.52609884	10.15729349		
32	14	100	9	43.02087907	7.53581407		
33	15	100	9	43.41670326	5.531209761		
34	16	100	9	43.7333626	4.003573808		
35	17	100	9	43.98669008	2.843393308		
36	18	100	9	44.18935207	1.96546106		
37	19	100	9	44.35148165	1.303788068		
38	20			44.48118532	0.531522296		

Spreadsheet S6.1

adopt a most rapid approach path (MRAP) to an optimal steady-state pollution stock. Review Equation (2.13).

In the current problem, this approach implies that $S_{20} = \gamma Z_{20}$ and that $Q_{20} = Q_{min} + n\gamma Z_{20}$, which will be maintained for the rest of time as well. The final function in cell \$E\$38 is given by the expression

$$\rho^T \left[\sum_{t=T}^{\infty} \rho^{t-T}(pQ_{20} - cZ_{20}^2) \right]$$

$$= \rho^T [p(Q_{min} + n\gamma Z_{20}) - cZ_{20}^2](1 + \rho + \rho^2 + \rho^3 + \cdots)$$

$$= \rho^T [p(Q_{\min} + n\gamma Z_{20}) - cZ_{20}^2] \left(\frac{1}{1 - \rho} \right)$$

$$= \rho^T [p(Q_{\min} + n\gamma Z_{20}) - cZ_{20}^2] \frac{1 + \delta}{\delta}$$

$$= \rho^{T-1} [p(Q_{\min} + n\gamma Z_{20}) - cZ_{20}^2] / \delta$$

Thus, in cell \$E\$38, we type $=$ (\$B\$6^\$A\$37) $*$ (\$B\$3 $*$ (\$B\$9 $+$ \$B\$4 $*$ \$B\$7 $*$ \$D\$38) $-$ \$B\$8 $*$ (\$D\$38^2))/\$B\$5. This final function tells Solver that while it is free to choose values for Q_0 through Q_{19}, it must live with Z_{20} and its steady-state companions $S_{20} = \gamma Z_{20}$ and $Q_{20} = Q_{\min} + n\gamma Z_{20}$ for the rest of time. As an initial guess, we set $Q_t = Q_{\max} = 100$ for $t = 0, 1, \ldots, 19$, which results in a terminal pollution stock of $Z_{20} \approx 44.48$ and a total present value of $W \approx 1,142.86$ in cell \$E\$15. The time paths for Q_t, S_t, and Z_t are shown in the chart within Spreadsheet 6.1.

In setting up Solver, you will specify \$E\$15 as the set cell, to be maximized, and \$B\$18:\$B\$37 as the changing cells. In the constraint box, enter two constraints (the minimum and maximum levels for Q_t) by typing \$B\$18:\$B\$37<=\$B\$10 and then, as a separate constraint, \$B\$18:\$B\$37>=\$B\$9.

How does Solver change Q_t to maximize W? The results are shown in Spreadsheet S6.2. We see that Solver opts to go on a short binge, setting $Q_t = 100$ for $t = 0, 1, 2$ and $Q_3 \approx 84.29$. This is an MRAP where the value $Q_3 \approx 84.29$ avoids overshooting Z^*. This results in the pollution stock growing from $Z_0 = 0$ to $Z_4 \approx Z^* = 25$, which was calculated via Equation (6.8) *prior to* optimization. Solver more or less maintains the steady-state optimum from $t = 4$ through $t = 19$, given the incentive provided by our final function.

6.4 DIFFUSION AND A NONDEGRADABLE STOCK POLLUTANT

One of the major environmental problems in the United States is the identification, assessment, and possible remediation of sites where toxic substances had been legally or illegally dumped prior to the enactment of legislation requiring environmentally secure disposal. These sites might contain a variety of pollutants that can contaminate soils and groundwater. In the vicinity of some sites, there have been suspiciously

	A	B	C	D	E	F	G
1	Spreadsheet 6.2						
2							
3	$p =$	2					
4	$n =$	10					
5	$\delta -$	0.05					
6	$\rho =$	0.952380952					
7	$\gamma =$	0.2					
8	$c =$	0.1					
9	$Q_{min} =$	10					
10	$Q_{max} =$	100					
11	$Z(0) =$	0					
12							
13	$Z^* =$	25					
14	$S^* =$	5					
15	$Q^* =$	60		$W =$	1637.796644		
16							
17	t	$Q(t)$	$S(t)$	$Z(t)$	$(\rho^\wedge t)^*W(t)$		
18	0	100	9	0	200		
19	1	100	9	9	182.7619048		
20	2	100	9	16.2	157.6018141		
21	3	84.29402901	7.429402901	21.96	103.9748606		
22	4	60.06143494	5.006143494	24.9974029	47.41716031		
23	5	59.84361528	4.984361528	25.00406582	44.79176187		
24	6	60.2141118	5.02141118	24.98761418	43.27313335		
25	7	59.97776139	4.997776139	25.01150252	40.79168481		
26	8	59.87656589	4.987656589	25.00697816	38.72755443		
27	9	59.9706691	4.99706691	24.99323912	37.04898645		
28	10	60.06082679	5.006082679	24.9916582	35.40029825		
29	11	60.0523043	5.00523043	24.99940924	33.68194861		
30	12	59.99371008	4.999371008	25.00475782	31.99789869		
31	13	59.97126421	4.997126421	25.00317727	30.45457385		
32	14	60.00306407	5.000306407	24.99966823	29.04534024		
33	15	60.0178792	5.00178792	25.00004099	27.67558494		
34	16	59.95623081	4.995623081	25.00182071	26.29713957		
35	17	59.93340566	4.993340566	24.99707965	25.03532008		
36	18	60.1695823	5.01695823	24.99100429	24.05205371		
37	19	59.92105017	4.992105017	25.00976166	22.6728974		
38	20			24.99991435	455.0047285		

Time Paths for $Q(t)$, $S(t)$, and $Z(t)$

Spreadsheet S6.2

high rates of leukemia and other cancers. Often the firms or individuals responsible for the dump site are no longer in existence or financially incapable of paying for damages and remediation. The U.S. government has established a fund (called the *Superfund*) under the control of the Environmental Protection Agency (EPA) to cleanup such sites, but the sheer number of sites and the cost of remediation have resulted in what many regard as unacceptably slow progress. How should the EPA prioritize the known Superfund sites? Given the limited funds for cleanup, what is the optimal schedule for remediation?

Let $Z_i > 0$ denote the stock (mass) of a pollutant at site i, $i = 1, 2, \ldots, I$. We will assume that over time these initial pollution stocks will spread into surrounding soils or groundwater. The initial *volume of contamination* is assumed to be given and is denoted by $V_{i,0}$. Over time, the volume of contamination is assumed to grow according to the equation $V_{i,t+1} = (1 + \alpha_i)V_{i,t}$, where $1 > \alpha_i > 0$ is the rate at which the volume of contamination grows.

Within a volume of contaminated soil or water, the concentration of the pollutant typically will vary. The actual dynamics of a pollutant moving through nonuniform soil or an underground aquifer can be quite complex. We will simplify things by defining average concentration in period t as $C_{i,t} = Z_i/V_{i,t}$ and assume that the damage at site i in period t is a function of both the volume contaminated and the average concentration, and we will define $D_{i,t} = D_i(V_{i,t}C_{i,t})$ as the damage at site i in period t if nothing is done and the volume of contamination grows unchecked. Intuitively, one would think that an increase in the volume of contaminated soil or water would increase damage. If no additional wastes are deposited at the ith site, the growth in the volume of contamination will reduce average concentration, and the dynamics of damage at a particular site will depend on the weights assigned to $V_{i,t}$ and $C_{i,t}$ within $D_i(V_{i,t}C_{i,t})$.

Let $X_{i,t}$ be a binary-choice variable, where $X_{i,t} = 1$ indicates that the ith site has been cleaned up during or before period t, and $X_{i,t} = 0$ indicates that the ith site has *not* been cleaned up during or before period t. If $X_{i,t} = 1$, then $X_{i,\tau} = 1$ for all $\tau > t$; that is, we assume that once a site is cleaned, it stays clean.

We assume that damage occurs while a site is being cleaned, but then all future damage goes to zero so that $D_{i,t} = (1 - X_{i,t-1})D_i(V_{i,t}, C_{i,t})$, for $t = 1, 2, \ldots, T$. Finally, let K_i denote the cost of cleanup at the ith site and K the total (present value) of funds available for remediation.

In our allocation problem, we will assume that funds not spent in period t may be placed in an interest-bearing account, where they will increase by the factor $(1 + \delta)$ per period, where $\delta > 0$ is the rate of interest (discount). This introduces a scheduling dimension to our problem, where initial remediation at some sites might be optimal, while waiting for unspent funds to compound to the point where other sites can be cleaned up at a later date. Alternatively, the EPA can contract with a remediation firm for cleanup of a particular site at a future date and make a reduced present-value payment today. For example, if the EPA wanted site 5 cleaned up in $t = 9$, it would pay

$\rho^9 K_5$ today, in $t = 0$, or place $\rho^9 K_5$ dollars in an interest-bearing account until $t = 9$.

The optimal schedule of remediation becomes a *binary dynamic optimization problem* that seeks to

$$
\begin{array}{cl}
\underset{X_{i,t}=\{0,1\}_{t=0}^{T-1}}{\text{Minimize}} & \sum_{i=1}^{I} [X_{i,0}K_i + D(V_{i,0},\ C_{i,0})] + \sum_{t=1}^{T} \rho^t \\
& \times \left\{ \sum_{i=1}^{I} [(X_{i,t} - X_{i,t-1})K_i + (1 - X_{i,t-1})D_i(V_{i,t},\ C_{i,t})] \right\} \\
\text{Subject to} & \sum_{i=1}^{I} X_{i,0}K_i + \sum_{t=1}^{T} \rho^t \left\{ \sum_{i=1}^{I} [(X_{i,t} - X_{i,t-1})K_i] \right\} \leq K
\end{array}
$$

In words, the optimal cleanup schedule seeks to minimize the discounted sum of remediation costs and environmental damage. In determining the optimal schedule, the first time that $X_{i,t} = 1$, the EPA commits to make a payment of K_i dollars in period t or a present-value payment of $\rho^t K_i$. If and when $X_{i,t} = 1$, $X_{i,\tau} = 1$ for $\tau > t$, and the future coefficients on K_i are zero, thus ensuring only a onetime payment for remediation at any site. Because this is a finite-horizon problem, and damage is reduced to zero in periods *after* the period of remediation, it will never be optimal to initiate remediation in the last period, $t = T$.

Insight into the optimal scheduling of remediation might be enhanced through a numerical example. Consider the problem with five toxic sites ($I = 5$) over a 21-year horizon ($T = 20$). For the damage function with no remediation, let $D_{i,t} = \beta_i C_{i,t} V_{i,t}^2$, where $\beta_i > 0$ is a coefficient indicating the relative financial damage from pollutants at the ith site. With $C_{i,t} = Z_i/V_{i,t}$, the damage function becomes $D_{i,t} = \beta_i Z_i V_{i,t}$. The initial conditions and parameters are $V_{i,0}$, Z_i, K_i, α_i, β_i, K, and δ. Their numerical values are summarized at the top of Spreadsheet S6.3. Note that site 1 is relatively small in terms of the mass of toxics ($Z_1 = 5$) and the initial volume of contamination ($V_{1,0} = 10$). Site 1 has a relatively slow rate of rate of growth in the volume of contaminated soil or water ($\alpha_1 = 0.01$), but it is relatively damaging ($\beta_1 = 1$). Site 1 is the least costly to clean up ($K_1 = 50$).

Site 2 is the largest site in terms of the mass of pollutants ($Z_2 = 50$), volume already contaminated ($V_{2,0} = 500$), and the most rapid spread ($\alpha_2 = 0.1$). Site 2 is the most costly to clean up ($K_2 = 500$) but relatively low in damage ($\beta_2 = 0.01$). Sites 3, 4, and 5 fall between sites 1 and 2

	A	B	C	D	E	F	G	H	I	J	K
1	Optimal Sequential Clean Up of Toxic Sites										
2											
3	Parameters	Site $i=1$	Site $i=2$	Site $i=3$	Site $i=4$	Site $i=5$					
4	$Z_i =$	5	50	20	10	30					
5	$V_{i,0} =$	10	500	100	10	50					
6	$\alpha_i =$	0.01	0.1	0.02	0.02	0.04					
7	$K_i =$	50	500	200	100	300					
8	$\beta_i =$	1	0.01	0.4	0.5	0.2					
9											
10	$K =$	500		PVD =	28726.87922						
11	$\delta =$	0.05		PV$\Sigma K_i =$	0						
12	$\rho =$	0.952380952		PV(D+K) =	28726.87922						
13											
14	t	$X_{1,t}$	$X_{2,t}$	$X_{3,t}$	$X_{4,t}$	$X_{5,t}$	$(\rho^t)*K_1$	$(\rho^t)*K_2$	$(\rho^t)*K_3$	$(\rho^t)*K_4$	$(\rho^t)*K_5$
15	0	0	0	0	0	0	0	0	0	0	0
16	1	0	0	0	0	0	0	0	0	0	0
17	2	0	0	0	0	0	0	0	0	0	0
18	3	0	0	0	0	0	0	0	0	0	0
19	4	0	0	0	0	0	0	0	0	0	0
20	5	0	0	0	0	0	0	0	0	0	0
21	6	0	0	0	0	0	0	0	0	0	0
22	7	0	0	0	0	0	0	0	0	0	0
23	8	0	0	0	0	0	0	0	0	0	0
24	9	0	0	0	0	0	0	0	0	0	0
25	10	0	0	0	0	0	0	0	0	0	0
26	11	0	0	0	0	0	0	0	0	0	0
27	12	0	0	0	0	0	0	0	0	0	0
28	13	0	0	0	0	0	0	0	0	0	0
29	14	0	0	0	0	0	0	0	0	0	0
30	15	0	0	0	0	0	0	0	0	0	0
31	16	0	0	0	0	0	0	0	0	0	0

Spreadsheet S6.3

	t	$(\rho^{\wedge}t)^*D_1(\bullet)$	$(\rho^{\wedge}t)^*D_2(\bullet)$	$(\rho^{\wedge}t)^*D_3(\bullet)$	$(\rho^{\wedge}t)^*D_4(\bullet)$	$(\rho^{\wedge}t)^*D_5(\bullet)$	$(B/C)_{1,t}$	$(B/C)_{2,t}$	$(B/C)_{3,t}$	$(B/C)_{4,t}$	$(B/C)_{5,t}$
32		0	0	0	0	0	0	0	0	0	0
33		0	0	0	0	0	0	0	0	0	0
34		0	0	0	0	0	0	0	0	0	0
35		0	0	0	0	0	0	0	0	0	0
36											
37	t										
38	0	50	250	800	50	300	13.63811097	16.89076375	59.83483939	7.479354924	18.1156281
39	1	48.0952381	261.9047619	777.1428571	48.57142857	297.1428571	13.31001652	17.18530193	58.74658136	7.34332267	17.9814095
40	2	46.26303855	274.3764172	754.9387755	47.18367347	294.3129252	12.95541735	17.43956703	57.52231043	7.190288804	17.79887998
41	3	44.50063708	287.44119609	733.3690962	45.83556851	291.5099449	12.57288721	17.64604538	56.15359395	7.019199244	17.56395998
42	4	42.80537472	301.1296733	712.4156935	44.52598084	288.7336597	12.16092757	17.79629765	54.63154501	6.828943126	17.27229942
43	5	41.17469377	315.4691816	692.0609594	43.25380996	285.9838154	11.71796389	17.88085753	52.94679905	6.618349881	16.91926148
44	6	39.60613401	330.4915236	672.2877891	42.01798682	283.26016	11.24234194	17.88911991	51.08948932	6.386186165	16.49990554
45	7	38.09732891	346.2292152	653.0795665	40.81747291	280.5624442	10.73232368	17.80921736	49.04922112	6.13115264	16.0896904
46	8	36.64600209	362.7163207	634.4201504	39.6512594	277.8904209	10.18608316	17.62788382	46.81504465	5.851880581	15.44084844
47	9	35.24996392	379.9885264	616.2938604	38.51836627	275.2438455	9.601702046	17.33030416	44.37542661	5.546928326	14.78957905
48	10	33.90710815	398.0832181	598.6854642	37.41784152	272.6224755	8.977165023	16.89994814	41.7182026	5.214777532	14.04881372
49	11	32.61540879	417.0395619	581.580165	36.34876034	270.026071	8.310354928	16.3183872	38.83063404	4.853829255	13.21180035
50	12	31.37291703	436.8985886	564.963589	35.31022433	267.4543941	7.599047644	15.56509237	35.69919856	4.46239982	12.27135814
51	13	30.17775828	457.7032833	548.8217724	34.30136077	264.9072094	6.840906746	14.61721138	32.30973197	4.038716496	11.21985254
52	14	29.0281294	479.4986777	533.1411503	33.32132189	262.3842836	6.03347787	13.44932278	28.64730351	3.580912939	10.04916872
53	15	27.92229589	502.3319481	517.908546	32.36928413	259.8853857	5.174182808	12.03316483	24.69619533	3.087024417	8.750683655
54	16	26.8585938	526.2525171	503.111159	31.4444744	257.4102867	4.260313303	10.33733658	20.43986228	2.554982785	7.315236592
55	17	25.83540503	551.3121607	488.7365544	30.54603465	254.9587602	3.289024537	8.326968269	15.86088972	1.982611215	5.733097926
56	18	24.85119912	577.5651208	474.7726629	29.67329081	252.5305815	2.257328288	5.963358026	10.94094921	1.367618652	3.993936306
57	19	23.90448677	605.0682218	461.2077199	28.8254825	250.1255284	1.162085752	3.203571404	5.660751985	0.707593998	2.086783946
58	20	22.99383966	633.8809942	448.0302565	28.00189728	247.7433805					
59											
60	$\Sigma(\rho^{\wedge}t)^*D_i(\bullet)$	731.9055486	8695.381873	12766.96788	797.9354924	5734.688429					
61	$(\rho^{\wedge}t)^*K_i$	0	0	0	0	0					
62	$PV(D_i)+K_i=$	731.9055486	8695.381873	12766.96788	797.9354924	5734.688429					

Spreadsheet S6.3 (*continued*)

in these attributes. The overall (present value) budget for remediation is $K = \$500$ million, and the discount rate is $\delta = 0.05$.

In cells B15 through F35, we set $X_{i,t} = 0$ for $i = 1, 2, 3, 4, 5$ and $t = 0, 1, \ldots, 20$, indicating that no sites have been cleaned. We do this in order to see what will happen to the present value of damages at each site if nothing is done. In row 38, we program $D_{i,0} = \beta_i Z_i V_{i,0}$, or the initial damage in $t = 0$ for the five sites. In cell B39, we have programmed $= (\$B\$12^{\wedge}A39) * ((1 - B15) * \$B\$8 * \$B\$4 * ((1 + \$B\$6)^{\wedge}A39) * \$B\$5)$, which gives us the discounted damage at site 1 in $t = 1$, which depends on remediation in $t = 0, X_{1,0} = \{0, 1\}$. *Note*: If site 1 was not cleaned up in $t = 0$, the damage in $t = 1$ has grown according to $(1 + \alpha_1)$. We can fill down through cell B58 to get discounted damage through $t = 20$. For site 1, the sum of discounted damage is \$731.90 million. Similar programming for site 2 will yield a sum of discounted damage of \$8,695.38 million.

In cell G15, we have programmed $= \$B\$15 * \$B\$7$. In cell G16, we have typed $= (\$B\$12^{\wedge}A16) * (B16 - B15) * \$B\$7$, and we fill down through G35. This gives us a column indicating if and when remediation takes place at site 1 and its discounted cost. Similar programming for site 2 through site 5 has been done in columns H through K. In row 61, we sum the values in columns G, H, I, J, and K. For example, in cell B61, we type $= \text{SUM}(\$G\$15:\$G\$35)$. Thus row 60 gives the present value of damage, and row 61 gives the present value of remediation for sites $i = 1, 2, 3, 4, 5$.

In cell E10, we sum the present value of damage over all sites by typing $= \text{SUM}(\$B\$60:\$F\$60)$. In cell E11, we sum the present value of remediation cost by typing $= \text{SUM}(\$B\$61:\$F\$61)$. Finally, in cell E12, we calculate the present value of damage and remediation costs over all sites by typing $= \text{SUM}(\$B\$62:\$F\$62)$. For Spreadsheet S6.3, where initially $X_{i,t} = 0$ for $i = 1, 2, 3, 4, 5$ and $t = 0, 1, \ldots, 20$, the present value of remediation costs are zero, but the present value of damage is \$28,726.8792 million. Can we find the location and timing of remediation that will minimize the present value of damage and remediation cost subject to the constraint that the discounted sum of remediation costs be less than or equal to $K = 500$ (in cell B10)?

In Spreadsheet S6.3 we want to minimize the value in cell $\$E\$12$ by changing the values in cells $\$B\$15:\$F\$35$ subject to $\$B\$15:\$F\$35$

$=$ binary. The requirement that if $X_{i,t} = 1$, $X_{i,\tau} = 1$, for $\tau > t$, can be specified in Excel by adding the constraints \$B\$16:\$B\$35>= \$B\$15:\$B\$34, \$C\$16:\$C\$35 >= \$C\$15:\$C\$34, \$D\$16:\$D\$35 >= \$D\$15:\$D\$34, \$E\$16:\$E\$35 >= \$E\$15:\$E\$34, and \$F\$16:\$F\$35 >= \$F\$15:\$F\$34 in the Solver "Parameter" box. Finally, the budget constraint requires \$E\$11<=\$B\$10.

This is a computationally hard problem that grows exponentially in the number of sites and length of horizon. In fact, depending on your version of Excel, Solver might indicate that this problem is already too large to solve. Fortunately, because the problem is linear in $X_{i,t}$ and the benefits and costs of remediation are separable across the five sites, we can use economic intuition to find a solution without having to use Solver!

Our economic intuition leads us to a heuristic based on what might be called the *site-period benefit-cost ratio*. This heuristic will allow us to find the optimal solution because of the linearity and separability in this example. The site-period benefit-cost ratio is defined as $(B/C)_{i,t} = \sum_{\tau=t+1}^{T} \rho^\tau D_i(V_{i,\tau}C_{i,\tau})/\rho^t K_i$, for $i = 1, 2, 3, 4, 5$ and $t = 0, 1, \ldots, 19$. If a site is cleaned up in period t, the benefit is the sum of the damages that are avoided over the horizon $\tau = t + 1, t + 2, \ldots, T$. The present value of the cleanup cost is $\rho^t K_i$. There are a total of $I \times T = 100$ site-period benefit-cost ratios that must be computed for this problem. These appear in cells G38:F57. The heuristic is as follows: Find the cell with the largest $(B/C)_{i,t}$, and if the available funds allow you to cleanup that site in that period, do so. Then find the next largest $(B/C)_{i,t}$ that you can afford with the funds remaining. Proceed in this fashion until you have exhausted the budget, or any remaining funds are insufficient to clean up any remaining sites in periods $t = 0, 1, 2, \ldots, T - 1$.

In Spreadsheet S6.3, the highest site-period benefit-cost ratio is $(B/C)_{3,0} = 59.83$ found in cell I38. After cleaning up site 3, for a cost of $K_3 = 200$, you have \$300 million left, which is precisely the cost of cleaning up site 5 in $t = 0$ because it has the highest remaining site-period benefit-cost ratio of $(B/C)_{5,0} = 18.12$ in cell K38. This is the optimal solution when $K = \$500$ million.

What would the solution be if $K = \$400$ million? With this reduced budget, you still would cleanup site 3 immediately, but this would leave you with only $K = \$200$ million, not enough to undertake the immediate cleanup of site 5. The first period in which you could afford to cleanup site 5 is $t = 9$, when $\rho^9 300 = 193.38$ with a site-period cost-benefit ratio of $(B/C)_{5,9} = 14.79$. The question becomes, "Is there another site and period that would have a higher site-period, benefit-cost ratio, which we could afford with the funds remaining?" It turns out that the answer is "No." The site-period benefit-cost ratio of $(B/C)_{5,9} = 14.79$ dominates all the site-period benefit-cost ratios for sites 1 and 4. The only other contender is site 2, but with $K_2 = \$500$ million, we can only afford to cleanup site 2 in $t = 19$ at a discounted cost of $\rho^{19} K_2 = \$197.87$ million. Cleaning up site 2 in $t = 19$ has a site-period benefit-cost ratio of only $(B/C)_{2,19} = 3.20$. By waiting to clean up site 5 in $t = 9$, we will have spent \$393.38 million, and the present value of remaining damages and cleanup costs at sites 3 and 5 would be \$14,293.25. This figure is less than the present value of remaining damaged and cleanup costs if we had opted for cleaning up site 2 in $t = 19$. While that is a feasible solution, with present-value costs of \$397.87 million, the present value of remaining damages and cleanup costs would be \$16,523.90 million. Thus, when $K = \$400$, the optimal sequence is to immediately cleanup site 2 and then cleanup Site #5 when you can afford to in $t = 9$.

6.5 OPTIMAL EXTRACTION WITH A NONDEGRADABLE WASTE

Suppose that the extraction of a nonrenewable resource generates a nondegradable waste. In particular, suppose that remaining reserves change according to $R_{t+1} = R_t - q_t$, while the stock pollutant accumulates according to $Z_{t+1} = Z_t + \alpha q_t$. The welfare of the economy in period t is given by $W_t = pq_t - cZ_t^2$, where $p > 0$ is the per-unit price for q_t and $c > 0$ is a damage parameter. (This might be the case for a region or small country extracting q_t for export at a world price of p while having to contend with the local environmental damage caused by Z_t.) Finally, assume that the rate of extraction is subject to a capacity constraint so that $q_{max} \geq q_t \geq 0$.

Given the structure of this problem, there will be only two possible outcomes. Either initial reserves R_0 will be completely exhausted by some period $t = T$, in which case the nondegradable pollution stock in period $t = T$ will be $Z_T = \alpha R_0$ (which will continue to impose damage over the remaining infinite horizon) or the economy will stop extraction before exhaustion in order to keep the pollution stock from exceeding its "optimal" level. In the first case, $\alpha R_0 \leq Z^*$, whereas in the second case, $\alpha R_0 > Z^*$, where Z^* is the optimal pollution stock. In either case, if $Z_0 < Z^*$, the approach to Z^* is most rapid and will involve some initial periods where $q_t = q_{max}$.

The Lagrangian expression for this problem may be written as

$$L = \sum_{t=0}^{T-1} \rho^t [pq_t - cZ_t^2 + \rho\lambda_{t+1}(R_t - q_t - R_{t+1})$$

$$+ \rho\mu_{t+1}(Z_t + \alpha q_t - Z_{t+1})] - \rho^{T-1}cZ_T^2/\delta$$

where the last term represents the present value of damage from a pollution stock of size Z_T that will never degrade. We are again making use of a final function that reflects the present value of damage from Z_T for $t = T, T+1, T+2, \ldots$. It is derived in the same manner as the final function in cell \$E\$38 of Spreadsheet S6.1, only in this case q_t drops to zero when reserves are exhausted *or* the optimal pollution stock is reached.

Suppose that the relevant solution is one where we stop extracting to prevent the pollution stock from exceeding its optimal value $Z^* > 0$. In this case, we know that a steady state has been reached where $q^* = 0$, $R^* > 0$, and $\lambda^* = 0$ because remaining reserves are worthless. Take the partial of L with respect to q_t. Suppose that $t = T - 1$ is the last period where extraction is positive. Then $\partial L/\partial q_{T-1} = 0$ would imply that $p - \rho\lambda_T + \rho\mu_T\alpha = 0$. However, $\lambda_T = \lambda^* = 0$, implying that $\mu_T = \mu^* = -(1 + \delta)p/\alpha < 0$. Now take the partial of L with respect to Z_t and set it equal to zero. It will imply that $-2cZ_t + \rho\mu_{t+1} - \mu_t = 0$. In steady state, this implies that $Z^* = -\delta\mu/[2c(1 + \delta)] = \delta p/(2\alpha c)$ is the expression for the optimal pollution stock. The optimal extraction path in this case will have $q_t = q_{max}$ for $t = 0, 1, \ldots, T - 2$ and $0 < q_{T-1} \leq q_{max}$ with $Z_T = Z^* = \delta p/(2\alpha c)$.

In Spreadsheet S6.4, I show a numerical example of the case where depletion is not optimal because of damage from the stock pollutant. The parameter values are $\alpha = 0.1$, $p = 100$, $c = 0.5$, and $\delta = 0.05$, with initial conditions $R_0 = 1,000$ and $Z_0 = 0$. These parameter values imply that $Z^* = 50$. In this initial spreadsheet we specify $q_t = q_{max} = 100$ for $t = 0, 1, \ldots, 9$, which causes depletion in

	A	B	C	D	E
1	S6.4 Optimal Extraction with a Nondegradable Waste				
2					
3	$\alpha =$	0.1			
4	$p =$	100			
5	$c =$	0.5			
6	$\delta =$	0.05			
7	$\rho =$	0.952380952			
8	$R(0) =$	1000			
9	$Z(0) =$	0			
10	$Q_{max} =$	100			
11					
12	$Z^* =$	50		$W =$	6501.094542
13					
14	t	q_t	R_t	Z_t	$(\rho^\wedge t)W_t$
15	0	100	1000	0	10000
16	1	100	900	10	9476.190476
17	2	100	800	20	8888.888889
18	3	100	700	30	8249.649066
19	4	100	600	40	7568.862768
20	5	100	500	50	6855.853957
21	6	100	400	60	6118.966252
22	7	100	300	70	5365.644042
23	8	100	200	80	4602.507662
24	9	100	100	90	3835.423051
25	10		0	100	−64460.8916

Spreadsheet S6.4

period $t = 10$ ($R_{10} = 0$) and the pollution stock to reach $Z_{10} = 100 >$ $Z^* = 50$. In cell E15, we type $= (\$B\$7^\wedge A15) * (\$B\$4 * B15 - \$B\$5 * (D15^\wedge 2))$ and fill down through E24. In cell E25, we type $= (\$B\$7^\wedge A24) * (-\$B\$5 * (\$D\$25^\wedge 2)/\$B\$6)$, which is the present value of damage from Z_{10}. In cell E12, we type $= $ SUM($\$E\$15:\$E\$25$) to calculate the present value of welfare for this initial depletion schedule. This yields the value $W = 6,501.09454$.

Can Solver increase the present value of welfare by changing q_t? We tell Solver to maximize $\$E\$12$ by changing cells $\$B\$15:\$B\$24$ subject to $\$B\$15:\$B\$24<=100$ and $\$B\$15:\$B\$24>=0$. As we would predict, Solver recognizes that Z_t should not exceed $Z^* = 50$, and in Spreadsheet S6.5 it sets $q_5 = q_6 = \cdots = q_9 = 0$, yielding a present value for welfare of $W = 23,616.0293$.

	A	B	C	D	E
1	S6.5 Optimal Extraction with a Nondegradable Waste				
2					
3	$\alpha =$	0.1			
4	$\mu -$	100			
5	$c =$	0.5			
6	$\delta =$	0.05			
7	$\rho =$	0.952380952			
8	$R(0) =$	1000			
9	$Z(0) =$	0			
10	$Q_{max} =$	100			
11					
12	$Z^* =$	50		$W =$	23616.02933
13					
14	t	q_t	R_t	Z_t	$(\rho^t)W_t$
15	0	100	1000	0	10000
16	1	100	900	10	9476.190476
17	2	100	800	20	8888.888889
18	3	100	700	30	8249.649066
19	4	100	600	40	7568.862768
20	5	0	500	50	-979.407708
21	6	0	500	50	-932.769246
22	7	0	500	50	-888.351663
23	8	0	500	50	-846.049203
24	9	0	500	50	-805.761145
25	10		500	50	-16115.2229

Spreadsheet S6.5

6.6 CLIMATE CHANGE

In its recent report, the Intergovernmental Panel on Climate Change (IPCC, 2007) has raised the probability to 0.9 that human-generated emissions of greenhouse gases are the main cause of global warming since 1950. The report indicates that a doubling of the preindustrial atmospheric concentration of carbon dioxide is likely to increase average global temperature by 3.5 to 8.0°F and that there is a 0.1 probability of higher temperatures. A doubling of the carbon dioxide concentration above preindustrial levels also will raise sea levels, modify patterns of precipitation, change agricultural practices, and alter ecosystems at an unprecedented rate. Given the inability to forge a comprehensive international agreement on an appropriate and equitable way to reduce global emissions, many economists believe that a doubling of the carbon dioxide concentration is unavoidable and that research should shift to finding the best ways to adapt to or mitigate the effects of climate change.

In this section I present a simple two-period, two-state model to show how optimal state-dependent mitigation and reduced emissions can be determined using dynamic programming. Such a model obviously cannot capture the reality of global warming and climate change that confronts (and confounds) the IPCC, but it can identify the type of information needed to formulate the rational relationship between state-dependent mitigation in the future and reduced emissions today. The use of tractable but plausible functional forms allows the derivation of analytic expressions for optimal state-dependent mitigation and carbon emissions in the current period. These analytic expressions make the relationship between mitigation, emissions reduction, and the model's parameters completely transparent.

As in our previous two-period, two-state models, the two time periods are $t = 0$, denoting the current or present period, and $t = 1$, denoting the future. The future is uncertain from the perspective of $t = 0$ because there are two possible states reflecting different climatic conditions. The two states will be indicated by $s = 1$ and $s = 2$. The relevant policy implications would be unchanged within a multiperiod, multistate model. Let

$\overline{C} = 1$ denote the normalized level of emissions under "business as usual"

C_0 denote the chosen level of emissions in $t = 0$, where $1 \geq (\overline{C} - C_0) \geq 0$

$\alpha_0(\overline{C} - C_0)^2$ denote the cost of reducing emissions in $t = 0$, $\alpha_0 > 0$

$\dfrac{\gamma_s e^{-\beta_s M_{1,s}}}{1 + (\overline{C} - C_0)}$ denote the unmitigated damage in future state s, $\gamma_s > 0, \beta_s > 0$

$\alpha_s M_{1,s}$ denote the cost of damage mitigation in future state s, $\alpha_s > 0$, $M_{1,s} \geq 0$

$\Pr(s = 1) = \pi$ denote the probability that the future climatic state will be $s = 1$

$\Pr(s = 2) = (1 - \pi)$ denote the probability that the future climatic state will be $s = 2$

Under a policy of "business as usual," there would be no attempt to reduce emissions, and $\overline{C} = C_0 = 1$. A decision to reduce emissions in $t = 0$ would result in $1 > C_0 \geq 0$ at a cost of $\alpha_0(\overline{C} - C_0)^2$. The climate-change damage in future state s depends on the level of emissions in $t = 0$ and the level of mitigation in state s, $M_{1,s}$. With no reduction in emissions today and no mitigation in state s, that is, $M_{1,s} = 0$, the damage from climate change would be $\gamma_s > 0$. The marginal cost of mitigation in state s is assumed constant at $\alpha_s > 0$.

In the context of the preceding model, dynamic programming presumes that the optimal level of emissions today will depend on optimal state-dependent mitigation in the future. The optimal level of mitigation in state s can be easily determined by finding the level of $M_{1,s}$ that minimizes $\{\alpha_s M_{1,s} + [\gamma_s e^{-\beta_s M_{1,s}}/1 + (\overline{C} - C_0)]\}$. Taking a derivative of the expression in the braces, setting it to zero (assuming $M_{1,s} > 0$), and solving for $M_{1,s}$ yields

$$M_{1,s}^* = \frac{1}{\beta_s} \ln \left\{ \frac{\beta_s \gamma_s}{\alpha_s[1 + (\overline{C} - C_0)]} \right\} \tag{6.9}$$

Substituting the expression for $M_{1,s}^*$ back into the expression in the braces, one obtains the minimized sum of mitigation costs and unmitigated damage in climate state s. Denoting this minimized sum as $D_{1,s}^*$, some algebra will show that

$$D_{1,s}^* = \frac{\alpha_s}{\beta_s} \left(1 + \ln \left\{ \frac{\beta_s \gamma_s}{\alpha_s[1 + (\overline{C} - C_0)]} \right\} \right) \tag{6.10}$$

Note that the minimizes sum of mitigation costs and unmitigated damages depends on C_0.

We can now determine the optimal level of reduced emissions by seeking the level of C_0 that minimizes

$$D = \alpha_0(\overline{C} - C_0)^2 + \rho[\pi D_{1,1}^* + (1 - \pi)D_{1,2}^*] \tag{6.11}$$

where $\rho = 1/(1 + \delta)$ is a discount factor and $\delta > 0$ is the appropriate discount rate.

Substituting in the appropriate expressions for $D_{1,1}^*$ and $D_{1,2}^*$, taking a derivative with respect to $(\overline{C} - C_0)$, setting the derivative to zero (thus assuming $1 > C_0 > 0$), and wading through some messy algebra, it can be shown that the optimal level for C_0 is the negative root of a quadratic given by

$$C_0^* = \frac{2\overline{C} + 1}{2} - \sqrt{\frac{1}{4} + \frac{\pi(\alpha_1/\beta_1) + (1 - \pi)(\alpha_2/\beta_2)}{2\alpha_0(1 + \delta)}} \qquad (6.12)$$

For the assumed functional forms, C_0^* does not depend on γ_s, the maximum damage under business as usual with no mitigation. This might have been expected because in an economic model, the incentive to reduce emissions or to mitigate damage comes at the *margin*. The parameters influencing the marginal cost of reduced emissions, the marginal cost of mitigation, and the marginal effectiveness of mitigation are α_0, α_s, and β_s, respectively. The discount rate influences the marginal willingness to trade off the incremental cost of reducing emissions today with the expected incremental costs of mitigation and unmitigated damages in the future. Note also that the state-dependent ratios of marginal cost to marginal effectiveness for mitigation (α_s/β_s) are weighted by their appropriate subjective probabilities [π premultiplies (α_1/β_1), whereas ($1 - \pi$) premultiplies (α_2/β_2)]. A better understanding of how different parameters affect the optimal level of reduced emissions and the optimal level of state-dependent mitigation might be obtained via sensitivity analysis for a numerical example.

The numerical value of each parameter and their interpretation within the model are given below:

$\overline{C} = 1$ is the normalized level for emissions under business as usual.
$\Pr(s = 1) = \pi = 0.3$ is the probability of the low-damage state.
$\alpha_0 = 144$ is the marginal cost parameter for reducing emissions in $t = 0$.
$\alpha_1 = 1$ is the marginal cost of mitigation in future climate state $s = 1$.
$\alpha_2 = 2$ is the marginal cost of mitigation in future climate state $s = 2$.
$\beta_1 = 0.07$ is the efficiency parameter for mitigation in $s = 1$.
$\beta_2 = 0.05$ is the efficiency parameter of mitigation in $s = 2$.
$\gamma_1 = 25$ is the damage in $s = 1$ when $C_0 = 1$ and $M_{1,1} = 0$.
$\gamma_2 = 100$ is the damage in $s = 2$ when $C_0 = 1$ and $M_{1,2} = 0$.
$\delta = 0.02$ is the social rate of discount.

Collectively, these parameter values are referred to as the *base-case parameter set*. Table 6.1 provides the numerical values for the optimal

Table 6.1. *Numerical Results for the Base-Case Parameter Set and Selected Increases in a Single Parameter*

Variable	Base Case	$\pi = 0.6$	$\alpha_0 = 288$	$\alpha_1 = 1.5$	$\alpha_2 = 4$	$\beta_1 = 0.14$	$\beta_2 = 0.06$	$\gamma_1 = 50$	$\gamma_2 = 200$	$\delta = 0.04$
C_0^*	0.9001	0.9224	0.9478	0.8940	0.8253	0.9062	0.9135	0.9001	0.9001	0.9018
$M_{1,1}^*$	6.6340	6.9266	7.2673	0.7633	5.6943	8.3078	6.8089	16.5361	6.6340	6.6569
$M_{1,2}^*$	16.4210	16.8307	17.3077	16.3114	1.2426	16.5325	16.9270	16.4210	30.2840	16.4531
D^*	57.5803	42.2322	58.3312	58.0954	68.5844	55.9542	53.3915	60.4926	76.6078	56.5001

level of emissions C_0^*, state-dependent mitigation $M_{1,1}^*$ and $M_{1,2}^*$, and
the minimized value of D^* for the base case and a change in a single
parameter to the value indicated at the top of each column. Table 6.2
provides a summary of the comparative statics for this model. For the
base-case parameter set, Figure 6.4 shows a graph of D as a function of C_0 that verifies that D is convex in C_0, reaching a minimum at
$C_0^* = 0.9001$.

For the base-case parameter set, emissions are optimally reduced
from $\overline{C} = 1$ to $C_0^* = 0.9001$. This level of reduction assumes that if
state $s = 1$ is realized, a mitigation effort of $M_{1,1}^* = 6.6340$ will be
undertaken, and if the more damaging climatic state, $s = 2$, is realized,
the mitigation effort will be $M_{1,2}^* = 16.4210$. This results in a minimized

Table 6.2. *Comparative Statics*

Variable	π	α_0	α_1	α_2	β_1	β_2	γ_1	γ_2	δ
C_0^*	+	+	−	−	+	+	0	0	+
$M_{1,1}^*$	+	+	−	−	+	+	+	0	+
$M_{1,2}^*$	+	+	−	−	+	+	0	+	+
D^*	−	+	+	+	−	−	+	+	−

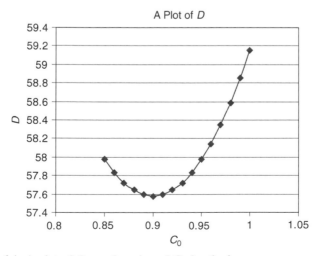

Figure 6.4. A plot of D as a function of C_0 for the base-case parameter set.

discounted expected loss of $D^* = 57.5803$. This total can be broken down into the following five components:

1. Cost of reduced emissions: $\alpha_0(\overline{C} - C_0^*)^2 = 1.4377$.
2. Discounted expected cost of $s = 1$ mitigation: $\rho\pi\alpha_1 M_{1,1}^* = 1.9512$.
3. Discounted expected cost of $s = 2$ mitigation: $\rho(1 - \pi)\alpha_2 M_{1,2}^* = 22.5387$.
4. Discounted expected unmitigated damage in $s = 1$: $\dfrac{\rho\pi\gamma_1 e^{-\beta_1 M_{1,1}^*}}{1 + (\overline{C} - C_0^*)} = 4.2017$.
5. Discounted expected unmitigated damage in $s = 2$:
$$\frac{\rho(1 - \pi)\gamma_2 e^{-\beta_2 M_{1,2}^*}}{1 + (\overline{C} - C_0^*)} = 27.4510.$$
Total $(D^*) = 57.5803$.

From Table 6.2, we see that an increase in π, α_0, β_1, β_2, or δ will result in an *increase* in optimal emissions C_0^*, whereas an increase in α_1 or α_2 will cause a *decrease* in C_0^*. As noted earlier, C_0^* does not depend on γ_1 or γ_2. Mitigation effort in state $s = 1$ depends only on γ_1, not on γ_2, and vice versa. An increase in γ_s will increase $M_{1,s}^*$.

An increase in π, β_1, β_2, or δ will *decrease* D^*, whereas increases in α_0, α_1, α_2, γ_1, or γ_2 will *increase* D^*. Recall that π is the subjective probability of the low-damage climate state, so an increase in π lowers D^*.

The overriding take-home message from these comparative static results is that mitigation is a substitute, or offset, for emissions reduction. C_0^*, $M_{1,1}^*$, and $M_{1,2}^*$ change in the same direction for all parameters, with the exception of γ_1 and γ_2. If it is optimal to increase emissions, then it is also optimal to increase state-dependent mitigation, and if it is optimal to reduce emissions, it is optimal to reduce state-dependent mitigation.

6.7 EMISSION TAXES AND MARKETABLE POLLUTION PERMITS

Environmental policy constitutes an attempt by government to correct for economic behavior that generates unacceptable environmental damage. Deterioration of air and water quality in the United States in the 1950s and 1960s led to the passage of laws by state and federal governments that established a system of standards and permits that sought to control the amount and type of wastes disposed via smokestack and outfall. The federal government also subsidized the construction of primary and secondary municipal waste water treatment plants. While progress has been made in improving the quality of many lakes and rivers, improving the quality of air in the major metropolitan areas of the United States has proven to be a more difficult problem. A combination of pollutants from point sources (i.e., factories and utilities) and mobile sources (i.e., cars, trucks, and buses) makes the formulation of effective air quality policies more difficult than in the case of waste water treatment. Economists have long advocated the use of *emission taxes* or *marketable pollution permits*, the later policy now referred to as *cap and trade*. This section will focus on these two policies.

I begin with the emission tax. Consider an industry comprised of many identical firms, each employing a technology characterized by a commodity-residual transformation function $\phi(Q_t, S_t) = 0$, as described in Section 6.1. We assume that $Q_{max} \geq Q_t \geq Q_{min}$, where $\partial\phi(\bullet)/\partial Q_t = \phi_Q > 0$, $\partial\phi(\bullet)/\partial S_t = \phi_S < 0$, $\phi(Q_{min}, 0) = 0$, and $\phi(Q_{max}, S_{max}) = 0$, as in Figure 6.1. Suppose that no firm is concerned with the dynamics of the stock pollutant, and each is exclusively interested in maximizing after-tax revenue in each period. Each firm is a price-taker, receiving $p > 0$ for each unit of Q_t. Each firm faces a tax rate of $\tau_t > 0$ for each unit of S_t emitted. This tax rate might change over time, hence the subscript. In each period, each firm faces a static optimization problem associated with the Lagrangian

$$L_t = pQ_t - \tau_t S_t - \mu_t \phi(Q_t, S_t) \tag{6.13}$$

with first-order conditions, when $Q_{max} > Q_t > Q_{min}$, that require

$$\frac{\partial L_t}{\partial Q_t} = p - \mu_t \phi_Q = 0 \tag{6.14}$$

$$\frac{\partial L_t}{\partial S_t} = -\tau_t - \mu_t \phi_S = 0 \tag{6.15}$$

$$\frac{\partial L_t}{\partial \mu_t} = -\phi(Q_t, S_t) = 0 \tag{6.16}$$

Equations (6.14) and (6.15) imply that $p/\tau_t = -\phi_Q/\phi_S$, which along with $\phi(Q_t, S_t) = 0$ provides the representative firm with two equations to solve for the levels of Q_t and S_t that maximize after-tax revenue. For example, suppose that

$$\phi(Q_t, S_t) = (Q_t - m)^2 - nS_t = 0 \qquad (6.17)$$

where $Q_{\min} = m$ and n are positive parameters. The partials of this function are $\phi_Q = 2(Q_t - m) \geq 0$ and $\phi_S = -n < 0$, and $p/\tau_t = 2(Q_t - m)/n$ implies that

$$Q_t = \frac{np}{2\tau_t} + m \qquad (6.18)$$

which on substitution into Equation (6.17) implies that

$$S_t = \frac{n}{4}\left(\frac{p}{\tau_t}\right)^2 \qquad (6.19)$$

Note that as $\tau_t \to \infty$, $Q_t \to m = Q_{\min}$, and $S_t \to 0$. As $\tau_t \to 0$, $Q_t \to Q_{\max}$ and $S_t \to S_{\max}$. In fact, τ_t must be greater than $np/[2(Q_{\max} - m)]$ before each competitive firm would choose $Q_t < Q_{\max}$ and $S_t < S_{\max}$.

To summarize, given the form of the commodity-residual transformation function in Equation (6.17), after-tax revenue maximization by each firm will imply that each will operate so as to produce Q_t and S_t as given by Equations (6.18) and (6.19), subject to $Q_{\max} \geq Q_t \geq m$ and $S_{\max} \geq S_t \geq 0$.

What is the optimal tax τ_t? Let's suppose that the environmental regulator has studied the industry and knows the form of $\phi(Q_t, S_t) = 0$. Suppose that aggregate emissions contribute to the accumulation of stock pollutant Z_t and that there are $N > 0$ firms in the industry. The regulator wants to set τ_t so as to cause each firm to adopt the levels for Q_t and S_t that will

$$\text{Maximize} \quad \sum_{t=0}^{\infty} \rho^t(pNQ_t - cZ_t^2)$$

$$\text{Subject to} \quad Z_{t+1} - Z_t = -\gamma Z_t + NS_t$$

$$\phi(Q_t, S_t) = 0$$

$$Q_{\max} \geq Q_t \geq Q_{\min}$$

$$Z_0 \text{ given}$$

Note that pNQ_t is the value of aggregate output in period t and that NS_t is the aggregate waste loading from our N identical firms. We are also assuming that damage is quadratic in the pollution stock with $c > 0$. The Lagrangian for the regulator may be written

$$L = \sum_{t=0}^{\infty} \rho^t \{pNQ_t - cZ_t^2 + \rho\lambda_{t+1}[(1-\gamma)Z_t + NS_t - Z_{t+1}]$$

$$- \mu_t\phi(Q_t, S_t)\}$$

The first-order necessary conditions for $Q_{\max} > Q_t > m$, $S_t > 0$, and $Z_t > 0$ require

$$\frac{\partial L}{\partial Q_t} = \rho^t(pN - \mu_t\phi_Q) = 0 \qquad (6.20)$$

$$\frac{\partial L}{\partial S_t} = \rho^t(N\rho\lambda_{t+1} - \mu_t\phi_S) = 0 \qquad (6.21)$$

$$\frac{\partial L}{\partial Z_t} = \rho^t[-2cZ_t + \rho\lambda_{t+1}(1-\gamma)] - \rho^t\lambda_t = 0 \qquad (6.22)$$

Equation (6.20) implies that $\mu_t = Np/\phi_Q$ and on substitution into Equation (6.21) gives $\rho\lambda_{t+1} = p\phi_S/\phi_Q$. Equation (6.22) implies $\rho\lambda_{t+1}(1-\gamma) - \lambda_t = 2cZ_t$. We will evaluate these last three expressions in steady state to determine expressions for the optimal pollution stock, rate of output, and rate of residual emissions. Knowing the optimal steady-state rate of output Q^* for the representative firm, the regulator can calculate the steady-state optimal emissions tax according to $\tau^* = np/[2(Q^* - m)]$. The expression for the optimal tax comes from solving Equation (6.18) for τ_t and presumes that all firms maximize after-tax revenue.

In steady state, we have $\mu = Np/\phi_Q$, $\rho\lambda = p\phi_S/\phi_Q$, and $-\rho\lambda(\delta + \gamma) = 2cZ$. Substituting $\rho\lambda$ into the last expression yields $-p(\phi_S/\phi_Q)(\delta + \gamma) = 2cZ$. To make things concrete, assume that the commodity-residual transformation frontier is again given by Equation (6.17) with $\phi_Q = 2(Q_t - m)$ and $\phi_S = -n$. Substituting these partials into the last steady-state equation implies that

$$Z^* = \frac{np(\delta + \gamma)}{4c(Q^* - m)} \qquad (6.23)$$

which is the analog to Equation (6.8), but for the quadratic commodity-residual transformation frontier in Equation (6.17). In steady state, we also know that $S^* = (Q^* - m)^2/n$ and that $NS^* = \gamma Z^*$. These

Table 6.3. *Steady-State Optimum with an Emissions Tax*

Variable	Base Case	$n = 20$	$p = 400$	$\delta = 0.1$	$\gamma = 0.4$	$c = 0.04$
Q^*	15	17.94	16.30	15.31	17.66	13.97
τ^*	200	251.98	317.48	188.21	130.50	251.98
S^*	2.5	3.15	3.97	2.82	5.87	1.57
Z^*	1,250	1,574.90	1,984.25	1,411.55	1,468.08	787.45

last two expressions combine with Equation (6.23) to imply $[N(Q^* - m)^2]/(\gamma n) = Z^* = [np(\delta + \gamma)]/[4c(Q^* - m)]$,which can be solved for Q^*, yielding

$$Q^* = \sqrt[3]{\frac{n^2 p(\delta + \gamma)\gamma}{4cN}} + m \qquad (6.24)$$

Knowing Q^*, the environmental regulator can set $\tau^* = np/[2(Q^* - m)]$, which will induce all firms to operate at (Q^*, S^*), where $NS^* = \gamma Z^*$. Because the commodity-residual transformation frontier is nonlinear, the optimal approach from $Z_0 < Z^*$ would require the environmental regulator to solve in advance for Q_t^* and then calculate and announce τ_t^*. From $Z_0 < Z^*$ the optimal emission tax will rise asymptotically to τ^*.

Table 6.3 reports on the comparative statics of the steady-state optimum to changes in various parameters. The base-case parameters are $n = 10, p = 200, \delta = 0.05, \gamma = 0.2, c = 0.02, N = 100$, and $Q_{min} = m = 10$. Columns 3 through 7 give the new values for Q^*, τ^*, S^*, and Z^* for a change in a single parameter to the value reported at the top of that column.

For example, when n is increased from 10 to 20, the optimal level of output for the representative firm increases from 15 to 17.94. The optimal tax increases from 200 to 251.98. Each firm now emits 3.15 units of waste in each period, and the optimal pollution stock increases from 1,250 to 1,574.90. Note that increases in p, δ, and γ increase the optimal pollution stock. Increases in n, p, and c raise the optimal emission tax τ^*, whereas increases in δ and γ lower it. The level of emissions from the representative firm increases with increases in n, p, δ, and γ and declines with an increase in c.

Another way of showing numerical comparative statics is to construct a table showing the percentage change in a variable divided by

Table 6.4. *Elasticities for Steady-State Variables in*
the Emissions Tax Model

Variable	n	p	δ	γ	c	N
Q^*	0.20	0.09	0.02	0.18	−0.07	−0.07
τ^*	0.26	0.59	−0.06	−0.35	0.26	0.26
S^*	0.26	0.59	0.13	1.35	−0.37	−0.37
Z^*	0.26	0.59	0.13	0.17	−0.37	0.25

the percentage change in the parameter. Such ratios may be interpreted as *elasticities*. The absolute changes in Table 6.3 are converted to elasticities in Table 6.4. Such a table has the advantage of conveying both the direction and the relative size of the change. The calculations in Table 6.4 are made easier by the fact that in Table 6.3 all parameters were increased by 100%. Table 6.4 also contains the elasticities of the steady-state variables for changes in N.

All the elasticities in Table 6.4 are less than 1, with the exception of the response of S^* to a change in γ. An increase in γ from 0.2 to 0.4 causes an 18% increase in Q^*, a 35% decrease in τ^*, a 135% increase in S^*, and a 17% increase in Z^*.

The second environmental policy, advocated by economists, is marketable pollution permits. Pollution permits are the key component in a cap and trade program. In such programs, the environmental regulator specifies a target quantity for total emissions of a particular pollutant in a certain year. This quantity is called the *cap* because it is supposed to set an upper limit on total emissions of that pollutant in that year. The cap then is divided into some number of permits, where each permit entitles a firm holding that permit to emit a specified amount of the pollutant in that year. For example, if the cap is 150,000 tons of SO_2, and if each permit entitles the holder to emit 1 ton of SO_2, then there would be a total of 150,000 permits that might be sold at auction and then traded among firms wishing to emit SO_2. Depending on the market price for a permit, the firm might find it less costly to not generate that ton of SO_2 or to remove it by installing pollution abatement equipment. The firm might switch to burning higher-priced but lower-sulfur coal, or it could install scrubbers to remove SO_2 from its stack gases. Firms that don't reduce or otherwise remove SO_2 will have to buy permits at auction or in the ongoing permit market. Individuals or conservation organizations are also allowed to buy permits at auction and not use them! (Many instructors in college environmental economics courses have their class buy and retire an SO_2 permit.) This would have the effect of reducing the de facto cap. If the regulator also reduces the cap (the supply of permits) over time, one would expect the pollution permit price to rise, making emission reduction and/or treatment more attractive and ultimately improving ambient environmental quality.

Such permits are, in fact, being used to reduce SO_2 emissions in the United States and will be used to reduce carbon emissions in Europe. The Chicago Board of Trade (CBOT) currently administers the auction for both spot (current year) and futures markets for SO_2 allowances. In Spreadsheet S6.6, I show the average allowance (permit) price from the March EPA spot auction for the years 1993 through 2008. These are the prices for a permit that entitles the holder to emit a ton of SO_2 in that calendar year. The price is the weighted average of winning bids for the available cap (supply) in that year and has the dimension $/ton.

With a slight modification, we can make use of the emission tax model to examine firm behavior under a cap and trade program. Let $\phi_i(Q_{i,t}, S_{i,t}) = 0$ denote the commodity-residual transformation frontier for the ith firm in a competitive industry. We will assume that the

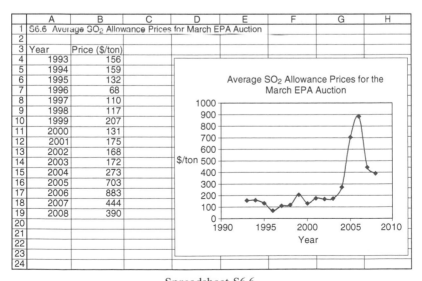

	A	B	C	D	E	F	G	H
1	S6.6 Average SO_2 Allowance Prices for March EPA Auction							
2								
3	Year	Price ($/ton)						
4	1993	156						
5	1994	159						
6	1995	132						
7	1996	68						
8	1997	110						
9	1998	117						
10	1999	207						
11	2000	131						
12	2001	175						
13	2002	168						
14	2003	172						
15	2004	273						
16	2005	703						
17	2006	883						
18	2007	444						
19	2008	390						
20								
21								
22								
23								
24								

Spreadsheet S6.6

*i*th firm has been endowed with $M_{i,t}$ permits in period t. Each permit entitles the firm to emit 1 ton of some pollutant or to sell that right to another firm, with the permit price being determined through a competitive permit market.

Each firm, though technologically different, wishes to maximize net revenue in each period. If the firm chooses to emit residuals beyond $M_{i,t}$, it must purchase permits at the market-clearing price denoted $p_{m,t} > 0$. If the firm chooses to emit at a rate less than $M_{i,t}$, it can sell the unused permits and augment its revenue. This market structure leads to the Lagrangian

$$L_{i,t} = pQ_{i,t} - p_{m,t}(S_{i,t} - M_{i,t}) - \mu_{i,t}\phi_i(Q_{i,t}, S_{i,t}) \qquad (6.25)$$

where for $Q_{i,\max} > Q_{i,t} > Q_{i,\min}$ the first-order conditions require

$$\frac{\partial L_{i,t}}{\partial Q_{i,t}} = p - \mu_{i,t}\phi_{i,Q} = 0 \qquad (6.26)$$

$$\frac{\partial L_{i,t}}{\partial S_{i,t}} = -p_{m,t} - \mu_{i,t}\phi_{i,S} = 0 \qquad (6.27)$$

$$\frac{\partial L_{i,t}}{\partial \mu_{i,t}} = -\phi_i(Q_{i,t}, S_{i,t}) = 0 \qquad (6.28)$$

Equations (6.26) and (6.27) imply that $p/p_{m,t} = -\phi_{i,Q}/\phi_{i,S}$. Recall in the emission tax model that our representative firm sought to equate the ratio of price to emission tax to the same marginal rate of transformation (i.e., $p/\tau_t = -\phi_Q/\phi_S$). Thus we can see that the clearing price for a marketable pollution permit $p_{m,t}$ is playing a role similar to that of the emission tax τ_t. Given $M_{i,t}$, the equations $p/p_{m,t} = -\phi_{i,Q}/\phi_{i,S}$ and $\phi_i(Q_{i,t}, S_{i,t}) = 0$ will permit each firm to determine its optimal levels for $Q_{i,t}$ and $S_{i,t}$ and to determine whether it will be a buyer or seller in the market for pollution permits. With a given price p for $Q_{i,t}$ (faced by all our heterogeneous but competitive firms), there will exist a demand function $S_i(p_{m,i})$, and the price that clears the pollution permit market must satisfy the following:

$$\sum_{i=1}^{I} [S_i(p_{m,t}) - M_{i,t}] = 0 \qquad (6.29)$$

where the excess demand $S_i(p_{m,i}) - M_{i,t}$ for the *i*th firm may be positive, zero, or negative, and $I > 0$ is the number of firms in the industry.

If we adopt the commodity-residual transformation frontier specified in Equation (6.17), the ith firm's rate of output and residual emissions will be determined by

$$O_{i,t} = \frac{n_i p}{2 p_{m,t}} + m_i \tag{6.30}$$

$$S_{i,t} = \frac{n_i}{4} \left(\frac{p}{p_{m,t}} \right)^2 \tag{6.31}$$

Note the similarity between Equations (6.18) and (6.19) and Equations (6.30) and (6.31). With a heterogeneous industry, we have firm-specific transformation parameters n_i and m_i, and again note the similar roles played by the emission tax and the price in the permit market.

There is a difference between these two sets of equations. In Equations (6.18) and (6.19), the firm would wait for the environmental regulator to announce this period's emission tax τ_t. In the model with marketable pollution permits, each firm will have received its allotment $M_{i,t} \geq 0$ and presumably knows p, n_i, and m_i. It then will participate in an auction or ongoing market where it will offer to buy or sell, based on the candidate marketing-clearing price, which the auctioneer announces and then modifies until there is no further desire to trade between the I firms in the industry.

Mathematically, we are able to solve for the market-clearing price $p_{m,t}$ and don't need an auctioneer. Return to Equation (6.29) and assume that we are dealing with an emission demand function given by Equation (6.31). Substituting Equation (6.31) into Equation (6.29) implies that

$$\sum_{i=1}^{I} \frac{n_i}{4} \left(\frac{p}{p_{m,t}} \right)^2 = M_t = \sum_{i=1}^{I} M_{i,t} \tag{6.32}$$

where M_t is the known total of permits that have been issued by the environmental regulator. While still unknown, the market-clearing price in the permit market will be a constant. Some algebra will reveal

$$p_{m,t} = \frac{0.5 p}{\sqrt{\dfrac{M_t}{\displaystyle\sum_{i=1}^{I} n_i}}} \tag{6.33}$$

While the environmental regulator would be able to tell the auctioneer M_t and possibly p, it is probably a stretch for him or her to know all the n_i. Thus the auctioneer, even in this model, might have to stick around to help find $p_{m,t}$. Once found, however, it will be consistent with the emission decisions by the I firms and the total number of permits available.

6.8 EXERCISES

E6.1 Consider the social net-benefit function $W_t = aq_t - (b/2)q_t^2 - (c/2)Z_t^2$, where q_t is the output of a commodity that generates a waste flow that might accumulate as a stock pollutant Z_t according to $Z_{t+1} = (1 - \gamma)Z_t + \alpha q_t$, and where $a > 0, b > 0, c > 0$, $1 > \gamma > 0$, and $1 > \alpha > 0$ are parameters. The optimization problem, seeking to maximize the present value of net benefits, has an associated Lagrangian given by

$$L = \sum_{t=0}^{\infty} \rho^t \{ aq_t - (b/2)q_t^2 - (c/2)Z_t^2$$

$$+ \rho\lambda_{t+1}[(1 - \gamma)Z_t + \alpha q_t - Z_{t+1}] \}$$

(a) What are the first-order necessary conditions for this problem?

(b) Evaluate the first-order conditions in steady state, and show that they imply an optimal steady-state pollution stock given by

$$Z^* = \frac{a\alpha(\delta + \gamma)}{(b\gamma^2 + b\gamma\delta + c\alpha^2)}$$

(c) Approximate the optimal approach to Z^* from $Z_0 = 0$ for $t = 0, 1, \ldots, 20$ when $\alpha = 0.4$, $\gamma = 0.255$, $\delta = 0.05$, $a = 4$, $b = 0.1$, $c = 3$, and $q_{max} = 10 \geq q_t \geq 0$. *Note:* Solver gets to choose q_t for $t = 0, 1, \ldots, 19$ and then must maintain Z_{20} for the rest of time by setting $q_t = (\gamma/\alpha)Z_{20}$ for $t = 20, 21, \ldots, \infty$.

E6.2 It is thought that the size of the stock pollutant Z_t may, in some instances, reduce the rate of degradation. Consider the stock pollutant with dynamics given by $Z_{t+1} = (1 - \gamma e^{-\beta Z_t})Z_t + \alpha Q_t$, where $1 > \gamma > 0, 1 > \beta > 0$, and $1 > \alpha > 0$ are parameters, and Q_t is the level of output that in turn produces a waste flow αQ_t. Suppose that a small country produces Q_t for the export market, where it obtains a per-unit price of $p > 0$. The residents of the small country bear the damage from the stock pollutant, and this gives rise to the net-benefit function $W_t = pQ_t - (c/2)Z_t^2$, where $c > 0$ is a damage coefficient. The Lagrangian for the problem of maximizing the present value of net benefits takes the form

$$L = \sum_{t=0}^{\infty} \rho^t \{ pQ_t - (c/2)Z_t^2 + \rho\lambda_{t+1}[(1 - \gamma e^{-\beta Z_t})Z_t$$

$$+ \alpha Q_t - Z_{t+1}]\}$$

(a) What are the first-order necessary conditions for this problem?

(b) Evaluate the first-order conditions in steady state, and show that they imply an *implicit equation* $G(Z) \equiv \gamma e^{-\beta Z}(1 - \beta Z) - (\alpha c/p)Z + \delta$, where $G(Z) = 0$ at $Z = Z^*$. What is the *analytical expression* for Z^* when $\beta = 0$?

(c) For $\alpha = 0.5$, $\beta = 0.1$, $\gamma = 0.2$, $\delta = 0.05$, $c = 1$, and $p = 2$, what is the numerical value for Z^*? What is the numerical value for Z^* when $\beta = 0$ and all other parameters are unchanged?

E6.3 Suppose that the net-benefit function is $W_t = a\ln(Q_t) - (c/2)Z_t^2$, where $a > 0$, and $c > 0$ are parameters, and $\ln(\bullet)$ is the natural log operator. The stock pollutant evolves according to $Z_{t+1} = (1 - \gamma)Z_t + \alpha Q_t$, where $1 > \gamma > 0$ and $1 > \alpha > 0$ are also parameters. Maximization of the present value of net benefits gives rise to the Lagrangian

$$L = \sum_{t=0}^{\infty} \rho^t \{ a\ln(Q_t) - (c/2)Z_t^2$$

$$+ \rho\lambda_{t+1}[(1 - \gamma)Z_t + \alpha Q_t - Z_{t+1}]\}$$

(a) What are the first-order necessary conditions?
(b) Evaluate the first-order conditions in steady state, and show that they imply

$$Z^* = \sqrt{\frac{a(\delta + \gamma)}{\gamma c}}$$

(c) Set up a spreadsheet to approximate the optimal path from $Z_0 = 4$ to Z^* when $a = 4$, $\gamma = 0.1$, $c = 1.4$, $\alpha = 0.5$, and $\delta = 0.04$ for the horizon $t = 0, 1, \ldots, 50$. In your initial spreadsheet, set $Q_t = 0.4$ for $t = 0, 1, \ldots, 49$. *Note:* Solver gets to choose Q_t for $t = 0, 1, \ldots, 49$ and then must maintain Z_{50} for the rest of time by setting $Q_t = (\gamma/\alpha)Z_{50}$ for $t = 50, 51, \ldots, \infty$.

E6.4 Nitrogen fertilizer is used to grow a crop. The output of the crop in period t is given by the production function $Q_t = F(N_t)$, where Q_t is the amount of the crop harvested at the end of the season in period t, N_t is the amount of nitrogen fertilizer applied during period t, and $F(N_t)$ is a strictly concave production function with $F'(N_t) > 0$ and $F''(N_t) < 0$. The fertilizer contributes to the stock of nitrogen in the underlying aquifer according to $Z_{t+1} = (1 - \gamma)Z_t + \alpha N_t$, where $1 > \gamma > 0$ is the rate of degradation in period t and $1 > \alpha > 0$ is the fraction of fertilizer applied to the crop that leaches to the aquifer. Damage from the stock pollutant is given by $(c/2)Z_t^2$, where $c > 0$ is a damage parameter. The unit cost of N_t is $\eta > 0$, and each unit of Q_t sells for $p > 0$.

(a) What is the Lagrangian for the problem that seeks to maximize the present value of *net revenue* less the damage from the stock pollutant over an infinite horizon? What are the first-order necessary conditions?
(b) Evaluate the first-order conditions in steady state, and solve for the *implicit expression* $G(Z) = 0$ that may be used to solve for the optimal steady-state stock pollutant Z^*. *Hint:* In steady state, $F'(N) = F'[(\gamma/\alpha)Z]$.
(c) Suppose that $F(N_t) = 2N_t^{0.5}$. What is the specific form for $G(Z) = 0$?
(d) Suppose that $\alpha = 0.5$, $\gamma = 0.1$, $c = 10$, $\eta = 0.692$, $p = 100$, and $\delta = 0.08$. What are the values for Z^* and N^*?

(e) Approximate the optimal approach to Z^* from $Z_0 = 0$ for the horizon $t = 0, 1, \ldots, 50$, where Solver gets to choose N_t for $t = 0, 1, \ldots, 49$ and then must maintain Z_{50} for the rest of time by setting $N_t = (\gamma/\alpha)Z_{50}$ for $t = 50, 51, \ldots, \infty$.

E6.5 In this problem, a stock pollutant adversely affects the growth rate of a renewable resource. Let Q_t denote the level of output with an associated waste flow contributing to the accumulation of a stock pollutant according to $Z_{t+1} = (1 - \gamma)Z_t + \alpha Q_t$, where $1 > \gamma > 0$ and $1 > \alpha > 0$ are again parameters. Let Y_t be the level of harvest from the renewable resource with dynamics $X_{t+1} = X_t + rX_t(1 - X_t/K)/(1 + \beta Z_t) - Y_t$, where $r > 0$ is the intrinsic growth rate, $K > 0$ is the environmental carrying capacity, and $\beta > 0$ is a parameter reflecting the toxicity of the stock pollutant to the renewable resource. ($Z_t > 0$ has the effect of reducing the de facto intrinsic growth rate.) The net-benefit function for society is given by $W_t = \varepsilon \ln(Q_t) + (1-\varepsilon) \ln(Y_t)$, where $1 > \varepsilon > 0$, and $\ln(\bullet)$ is the natural log operator. Maximizing the present value of net benefits leads to the Lagrangian

$$L = \sum_{t=0}^{\infty} \rho^t \{\varepsilon \ln(Q_t) + (1 - \varepsilon) \ln(Y_t)$$

$$+ \rho\lambda_{t+1}[(1 - \gamma)Z_t + \alpha Q_t - Z_{t+1}]$$

$$+ \rho\mu_{t+1}[X_t + rX_t(1 - X_t/K)/(1 + \beta Z_t) - Y_t - X_{t+1}]\}$$

(a) What are the first-order necessary conditions? *Hint:* You will need to take partials of L with respect to $Q_t, Y_t, Z_t, X_t, \rho\lambda_{t+1}$, and $\rho\mu_{t+1}$.

(b) Evaluate the first-order conditions in steady state, and show that they will imply

$$Z^* = \frac{\varepsilon(\delta + \gamma)}{[(1 - \varepsilon)\gamma - \varepsilon(\delta + \gamma)]\beta}$$

$$X^* = K[r - \delta(1 + \beta Z^*)]/(2r)$$

$$Y^* = \frac{rX^*(1 - X^*/K)}{(1 + \beta Z^*)}$$

and $Q^* = (\gamma/\alpha)Z^*$. What are the values for Z^*, X^*, Y^*, and Q^* when $\alpha = 0.2$, $\beta = 1$, $\delta = 0.1$, $\gamma = 0.2$, $\varepsilon = 0.25$, $r = 1$, and $K = 1$?

7

Maximin Utility with Renewable and Nonrenewable Resources

7.0 INTRODUCTION AND OVERVIEW

In the preceding chapters I have presented economic models for the management of fisheries, forests, nonrenewable resources, and stock pollutants. For renewable resources and stock pollutants, the possibility of achieving and maintaining a steady state might correspond to the now ubiquitous term *sustainability*. The term *sustainable development* became prominent in the lexicon of resource and development agencies following the Earth Summit in Rio de Janeiro in 1992. The United Nation's World Commission on Environment and Development defined *sustainable development* as "development that meets the needs of the present without compromising the ability of future generations to meet their own needs.... At a minimum, sustainable development must not endanger the natural systems that support life on Earth."

Since 1992, sustainability has been broadly adopted as a goal by individuals and governments. Making the concept operational and implementing policies that would lead to sustainable lifestyles for individuals and sustainable production and consumption in the global economy have proved difficult. If the global economy critically depends on nonrenewable resources, long-term sustainability may be open to question. Interestingly, the notion of sustainability in a macroeconomic model with a nonrenewable resource was examined by several economists in the early 1970s. Perhaps the most famous article was by Robert M. Solow, entitled, "Intergenerational Equity and Exhaustible Resources," which appeared in a special symposium issue of the *Review*

242

of Economic Studies in 1974. (In 1987, Solow was awarded the Nobel Prize in Economics for his work on macroeconomic growth models.)

Solow's 1974 article was an attempt to examine the *maximin criterion* in the context of economic growth. The maximin criterion had been discussed previously by John Rawls in his 1971 book, *A Theory of Justice*. Rawls had asked what *social contract* one would want in place if

... no one knows his place in society, his class position or social status, nor does anyone know his fortune in the distribution of natural assets and abilities, his intelligence, strength, and the like.... The principles of justice are chosen behind a veil of ignorance. (Rawls, 1971, p. 11)

To Rawls, the rational individual, not knowing his or her lot in life, would want rules in place that would maximize the utility of the least-well-off individual.

Rawls' book had a profound impact on the fields of political philosophy, ethics, and economics. Interestingly, Rawls was reluctant to extend the maximin criterion to the problem of intergenerational equity:

I believe that it is not possible, at present anyway, to define precise limits on what the rate of savings should be. How the burden of capital accumulation and raising the standard of civilization is to be shared between generations seems to admit of no definite answer. (Rawls, 1971, pp. 252–253)

As was evident in John Tierney's article, "Betting the Planet," in Chapter 5 and in the ongoing debate on energy and climate-change policy, the intertwined concepts of sustainability and intergenerational equity likely will be with us for the rest of our tenure on earth. So let's take some of the models developed in previous chapters, introduce them into a Solow-type macroeconomic growth model, and numerically examine the implications of the maximin criterion.

This is not an easy task. If we restrict ourselves to the discrete-time models used in earlier chapters, we lose the advantage of being able to take time derivatives. Much of the sustainability literature in economics is based on continuous-time models. The advantage of discrete-time models, as hopefully demonstrated in the preceding chapters, is that they allow one to quickly construct simple numerical problems on spreadsheets to see the concepts in action.

The remainder of this chapter is organized as follows: In the next section I discuss the maximin criterion in a discrete-time, nonoverlapping-generations model. This is followed by a discussion of the Gini coefficient, a commonly used index of equity. In Section 7.3 I present the nonoverlapping-generations growth model. This model will contain three state variables: the stock of manufactured capital K_t, the stock of a renewable resource X_t, and remaining reserves of a nonrenewable resource R_t. I will set the model up in a spreadsheet and determine the social contract that maximizes the minimum generational utility. The social contract will be defined as a vector of four rates: $[\alpha, \beta, \gamma_F, \gamma_U]$. α is the rate of consumption of newly produced capital goods, β is the rate of harvest from the renewable resource, γ_F is the rate of extraction from the nonrenewable resource that is devoted to the production of capital goods, and γ_U is the rate of extraction from the nonrenewable resource that is consumed directly by the current generation. If you wish, you can think of the nonrenewable resource as an energy resource so that if R_t are the remaining reserves of oil, $\gamma_F R_t$ then will be the oil extracted in period t that is used in producing the capital good, whereas $\gamma_U R_t$ will be the oil extracted in period t that is used directly by consumers to heat their homes or fuel their cars. These subtleties and distinctions will be more apparent in Section 7.3.

In Section 7.4 I extend the model to overlapping generations. In this model, a generation is born in period t and lives through the end of period $t + 1$. It is referred to as the "younger generation" in period t and the "elder generation" in period $t + 1$. In period $t + 1$, it overlaps with the younger generation born in period $t + 1$.

Section 7.5 discusses "real world" complications in the use of resources over time, the accumulation of manufactured capital and intergenerational equity. Section 7.6 contains just one numerical problem, an extension of the spreadsheets from Section 7.3. In that exercise, you are asked to find the social contract that maximizes the sum of discounted utility and compare it with the maximin social contract.

7.1 THE MAXIMIN CRITERION

In our discrete-time, finite-horizon model, where generations do not overlap, we will be concerned with a vector of generational utilities $\{U_0, U_1, \ldots, U_T\}$, where U_t is the utility of the tth generation. In the model in Section 7.3, this utility will depend on the consumption of newly produced capital goods, harvest from a renewable resource, and extraction (for direct consumption) from a nonrenewable resource. In this section we won't need to get into the details of what affects utility; we will just assume that $\{U_0, U_1, \ldots, U_T\}$ is a vector of nonnegative real numbers that might be influenced by rates of production, consumption, and resource use.

Solow (1974) asked us to consider a welfare function taking the following form

$$W(p) = \left(\sum_{t=0}^{T} \rho^t U_t^p\right)^{1/p} \tag{7.1}$$

where $\rho = 1/(1+\delta)$ is our discount factor, and $\delta \geq 0$ is society's rate of time preference. The welfare function $W(p)$ maps the vector of generational utilities onto the real line, yielding a number that can be maximized. This index of intergenerational welfare depends on the parameter p. Solow noted that as $p \to -\infty$, $W(p) \to \min\{U_0, U_1, \ldots, U_T\}$. In words, as p goes to negative infinity, the welfare function in Equation (7.1) becomes the *minimum function* and maximizing social welfare amounts to maximizing the smallest U_t. The proof of this result is shown below.

We can rewrite Equation (7.1) as

$$W(p) = (U_0^p + \rho U_1^p + \rho^2 U_2^p + \cdots + \rho^T U_T^p)^{1/p} \tag{7.2}$$

Define $U_{\min} \equiv \min\{U_0, U_1, \ldots, U_T\}$. Then $U_{\min}/U_t \leq 1$, and we can rewrite $W(p)$ yet again as

$$W(p) = U_{\min}[(U_{\min}/U_0)^{-p} + \rho(U_{\min}/U_1)^{-p}$$
$$+ \cdots + \rho^T(U_{\min}/U_T)^{-p}]^{1/p} \tag{7.3}$$

Then, with $\delta \geq 0$, $\rho^t \leq 1$ for $t = 0, 1, 2, \ldots, T$. As $p \to -\infty$, $(U_{\min}/U_t)^{-p}$ goes to zero if $U_{\min} < U_t$ or it goes to one if $U_{\min} = U_t$ and

$$\lim_{p \to -\infty} [(U_{\min}/U_0)^{-p} + \rho(U_{\min}/U_1)^{-p} + \cdots + \rho^T(U_{\min}/U_T)^{-p}]^{1/p} = 1 \tag{7.4}$$

Thus $\lim_{p \to -\infty} W(p) = U_{\min}$.

The welfare function in Equation (7.1) is a constant-elasticity welfare function, and Solow's parameter p is often replaced by $p = (\sigma - 1)/\sigma$, where $\sigma > 0$ is called the *intertemporal elasticity of substitution* (see d'Autume and Schubert, 2008, Appendix A). For the purpose of this chapter, we have shown that the maximin criterion can arise as a special case when the welfare function is a constant-elasticity function. Solow, being more Rawlsian than Rawls, might argue that the maximin criterion is ethically defensible in an intergenerational context.

7.2 THE GINI COEFFICIENT

The *Gini coefficient* is a statistical measure of dispersion commonly used to measure income inequality within a country. Consider the 45-degree line and the *Lorenz curve $L(X)$* as drawn in Figure 7.1.

On the horizontal axis, moving from left to right, the population of a country is ordered from lowest income to highest income. Thus the poorest 10% of the population would be the first 10% when moving from left to right. On the vertical axis we measure the cumulative share of income earned by the population. The Lorenz curve plots the cumulative share of total income earned by the poorest $X\%$ of the population. If earned income were equally distributed, the Lorenz curve would be the 45-degree line. If the poorest $X\%$ of the population earned $Y\%$ of the income, where $Y < X$, for $X < 1 = 100\%$, then the Lorenz curve is convex and lies below the 45-degree line. The area *below* the 45-degree line and *above* the Lorenz curve is the

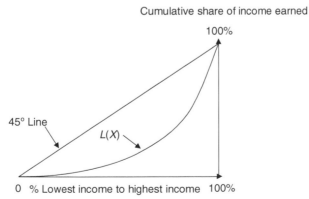

Figure 7.1. A graphic representation of the Gini coefficient.

Gini coefficient divided by two ($G/2$). If one person earned all the income, the Lorenz curve would become the X and Y axes, the area between is one-half, and $G = 1$. Mathematically, we can define the Gini coefficient as

$$G = 1 - 2 \int_0^1 L(X)\, dX \tag{7.5}$$

The United Nations has calculated the Gini coefficient for various countries. In the year 2004, the Gini coefficient for Mexico was 0.481. In the United States in 2007, the Gini coefficient was estimated to be 0.408. The country with the lowest estimated Gini coefficient was Sweden, with a $G = 0.25$, in the year 2000.

We will use the Gini coefficient to measure the equity of the intergenerational utility vector $\{U_0, U_1, \ldots, U_T\}$ for different social contracts $[\alpha, \beta, \gamma_F, \gamma_U]$. To do this, we will use the discrete-observation analogue to Equation (7.5) given by

$$G = (1/T) \left\{ T + 2 \left[1 - \frac{\sum_{t=0}^{T} (T + 2 - \operatorname{Rank} U_t) U_t}{\sum_{t=0}^{T} U_t} \right] \right\} \tag{7.6}$$

In Equation (7.6), $\operatorname{Rank} U_t$ is the rank of utility level U_t where the Excel rank function can be used to rank utility levels from the lowest, a rank of one, to the highest, a rank of $T + 1$. In Spreadsheet S7.1, I calculate the Gini coefficient for $\{U_0, U_1, U_2, \ldots, U_{10}\} = \{10, 9, 8, \ldots, 0\}$. These utilities are summed in cell B16.

In cell C4, we have typed $=$ RANK(B4, \$B\$4:\$B\$14,1), which returns the rank of the number in cell B4 compared with the numbers in cells \$B\$4:\$B\$14. Since $U_0 = 10$ is the highest utility level in the intergenerational vector, the rank function returns a value of 11. We then fill down through cell C14.

In cell D4, we have typed $=$ (\$A\$14 + 2 - C4) * B4 and fill down through cell D14. The Excel equivalent of Equation (7.6) is in cell D16, where we have typed $=$ (1/\$A\$14) * (\$A\$14 + 2 * (1 - SUM(\$D\$4:\$D\$14)/\$B\$16)). This yields a value for the Gini coefficient of $G = 0.4$.

The Excel Rank function will assign an equal rank to utility levels that have the same value, which in Spreadsheet S7.1 leads to an

	A	B	C	D
1	The Gini Coefficient and Intergenerational Welfare			
2				
3	t	U_t	Rank U_t	$(T+2\text{-Rank}U_t)U_t$
4	0	10	11	10
5	1	9	10	18
6	2	8	9	24
7	3	7	8	28
8	4	6	7	30
9	5	5	6	30
10	6	4	5	28
11	7	3	4	24
12	8	2	3	18
13	9	1	2	10
14	10	0	1	0
15				
16	$\Sigma U_t =$		55	G =	0.4

Spreadsheet S7.1 Calculating the Gini coefficient.

*in*correct calculation for the Gini coefficient. For example, in Spreadsheet S7.1, if we set $U_t = 10$ for $t = 0,1,2,\ldots,10$, we get $G = -1$ instead of the correct value of $G = 0$. In our Solow-style growth model in the next section, it is unlikely that we will have identical intergenerational utilities for a particular social contract $[\alpha, \beta, \gamma_F, \gamma_U]$, so this method for computing the Gini coefficient should not pose a problem. You should be aware, however, that equal utilities, if assigned a common rank, will not yield the correct value for G in Equation (7.6).

7.3 GROWTH WITH RESOURCES, INTERGENERATIONAL UTILITY, AND THE MAXIMIN CRITERION

The intergenerational problem is complex because the utility of a generation may depend on the consumption of capital goods, the harvest of renewable resources, and the rate of extraction from nonrenewable resources. Consider a model where

$Y_t = F(K_t, Q_{F,t})$ denotes the output of capital goods by the tth generation, where $F(K_t, Q_{F,t})$ is a production function with arguments K_t, the capital stock, and $Q_{F,t}$, the extraction from the nonrenewable resource devoted to production.

$C_t = \alpha F(K_t, Q_{F,t})$ denotes the consumption of capital goods, $1 > \alpha > 0$.

$H_t = \beta X_t$ denotes the harvest from a renewable resource of size X_t, $1 > \beta > 0$.

$U_t = U(C_t, H_t, Q_{U,t})$ denotes the utility of the tth generation, which depends on consumption of capital goods, harvest from the renewable resource, and $Q_{U,t}$, extraction from the nonrenewable resource consumed directly by the tth generation.

$Q_{F,t} = \gamma_F R_t$ and $Q_{U,t} = \gamma_U R_t$ denote the rates of extraction for production of the capital good and for direct consumption from R_t, the remaining reserves of the nonrenewable resource, $1 > \gamma_F > 0, 1 > \gamma_U > 0, 1 > (\gamma_F + \gamma_U) > 0$.

$R_{t+1} = [1 - (\gamma_F + \gamma_U)]R_t$ describes the dynamics of remaining reserves.

$K_{t+1} = K_t + (1 - \alpha)F(K_t, Q_{F,t})$ describes the dynamics of the capital stock.

$X_{t+1} = [1 - \beta + r(1 - X_t/X_c)]X_t$ describes the dynamics of the renewable resource, where $2 > r > 0$ is the intrinsic growth rate and $X_c > 0$ is the environmental carrying capacity for the renewable resource when $\beta = 0$.

$t = 0, 1, 2, \ldots, T$ are the number of generations under consideration, where $t = 0$ is the current generation and T is the terminal generation.

$[\alpha, \beta, \gamma_F, \gamma_U]$ denotes a "social contract," invariant across the generations.

The optimization problem of interest seeks to find the social contract that will

$$\underset{[\alpha, \beta, \gamma_F, \gamma_U]}{\text{Maximize}} \quad \text{Min}[U(C_0, H_0, Q_{U,0}), U(C_1, H_1, Q_{U,1}), \ldots,$$

$$U(C_T, H_T, Q_{U,T})]$$

$$\text{Subject to} \quad C_t = \alpha F(K_t, Q_{F,t})$$
$$H_t = \beta X_t$$
$$Q_{F,t} = \gamma_F R_t$$
$$Q_{U,t} = \gamma_U R_t$$
$$R_{t+1} = [1 - (\gamma_F + \gamma_U)]R_t$$
$$K_{t+1} = K_t + (1 - \alpha)F(K_t, Q_{F,t})$$
$$X_{t+1} = [1 - \beta + r(1 - X_t/X_c)]X_t$$
$$K_0 > 0, \quad X_0 > 0, \quad R_0 > 0, \quad T > 0 \quad \text{given}$$

Numerical analysis will require specification of the production function $F(K_t, Q_{F,t})$, the utility function $U(C_t, H_t, Q_{U,t})$, any parameters to those functions, the parameter values for r and X_c, and the initial conditions K_0, X_0, R_0, and T. In the numerical analysis of this Solow-type model, we will assume Cobb-Douglas forms for both the production function and the utility function; specifically, $Y_t = F(K_t, Q_{F,t}) = K_t^\omega Q_{F,t}^\eta$ and $U_t = U(C_t, H_t, Q_{U,t}) = C_t^\varepsilon H_t^\nu Q_{U,t}^\phi$, where $1 > \omega > \eta > 0$, $1 > \omega + \eta$, $1 > \varepsilon > 0$, $1 > \nu > 0$, $1 > \phi > 0$, and $1 > (\varepsilon + \nu + \phi)$. $F(K_t, Q_{F,t})$ and $U(C_t, H_t, Q_{U,t})$ exhibit declining marginal product or utility, respectively, and both functions are homogeneous of degree less than 1. These functions both have unitary elasticity of substitution between inputs, in the case of $F(K_t, Q_{F,t})$, or commodities, in the case of $U(C_t, H_t, Q_{U,t})$. This will allow capital to substitute for extraction of the nonrenewable resource in production and for consumption to substitute for extraction from the nonrenewable resource in utility. For the social contract, $[\alpha, \beta, \gamma_F, \gamma_U]$, a positive, steady-state level for X_t will be achieved at $X^* = X_c(r - \beta)/r$ provided that $2 > (r - \beta) > 0$.

Consider the maximin problem when $\omega = 0.6$, $\eta = 0.3$, $\varepsilon = 0.5$, $\nu = 0.2$, $\phi = 0.25$, $r = 1$, $X_c = 100$, $K_0 = 1$, $R_0 = 100$, and $X_0 = 100$. The initial spreadsheet is shown in Spreadsheet S7.2.

For an initial social contract, $[\alpha, \beta, \gamma_F, \gamma_U] = [0.9, 0.2, 0.05, 0.05]$, we see that the renewable resource is harvested down from $X_0 = 100$ to $X^* = X_c(r - \beta)/r = 80$, where it remains for $t = 1, 2, \ldots, 10$. The levels of extraction for production $Q_{F,t} = \gamma_F R_t$ and for consumption $Q_{U,t} = \gamma_U R_t$ are the same in each period because $\gamma_F = \gamma_U = 0.05$, causing remaining reserves to decline from $R_0 = 100$ to $R_{10} = 34.867844$. Utility declines from a maximum of $U_0 = 3.2878768$ to a minimum of $U_{10} = 2.86017475$. The Gini coefficient, computed according to Equation (7.6), is $G = 0.023572241$.

Can Solver find a better social contract, one that maximizes the minimum utility? The answer is "Yes," and as we will see, the maximin social contract will increase the utility of every generation!

The maximin social contract is shown in Spreadsheet S7.3. When Solver is asked to maximize the value in cell \$I\$28 by changing the values in cells \$I\$8:\$I\$11, it sets $\alpha = 0.63359$, $\beta = 0.49845$, $\gamma_F = 0.08162$, and $\gamma_U = 0.08663$. The maximized minimum utility is $U_2 = 3.87147761$. A *Pareto improvement* would result if a change in the social contract could increase the utility of one generation without

	A	B	C	D	E	F	G	H	I	J	K
1	Maximin Utility with Fractional Consumption, Extraction, and Harvest Rates										
2											
3	$\omega =$	0.6									
4	$\eta =$	0.3									
5	$\varepsilon =$	0.5									
6	$\nu =$	0.2									
7	$\phi =$	0.25									
8	$r =$	1						$\alpha =$	0.90000		
9	$X_c =$	100						$\beta =$	0.20000		
10								$\gamma_f =$	0.05000		
11	$K(0) =$	1						$\gamma_u =$	0.05000		
12	$R(0) =$	100									
13	$X(0) =$	100									
14											
15	t	C_t	H_t	X_t	Q_{ut}	Q_{ft}	K_t	R_t	U_t	RankU_t	$(T+2-$Rank$U_t)U_t$
16	0	1.458590937	20	100	5	5	1	100	3.287874679	11	3.287874679
17	1	1.546481269	16	80	4.5	4.5	1.16206566	90	3.153548082	10	6.307096163
18	2	1.627617597	16	80	4.05	4.05	1.333896912	81	3.151112733	9	9.4533382
19	3	1.701982912	16	80	3.645	3.645	1.514743311	72.9	3.138527782	8	12.5541113
20	4	1.769635098	16	80	3.2805	3.2805	1.703852524	65.61	3.117100958	7	15.58550479
21	5	1.830691105	16	90	2.95245	2.95245	1.900478646	59.049	3.087999136	6	18.52799481
22	6	1.885314001	16	90	2.657205	2.657205	2.103888769	53.1441	3.052264097	5	21.36584868
23	7	1.933702356	16	30	2.3914845	2.3914845	2.313368102	47.82969	3.010826309	4	24.08661047
24	8	1.976081512	16	30	2.15233605	2.15233605	2.528223919	43.046721	2.964516992	3	26.68065293
25	9	2.012696402	16	80	1.937102445	1.937102445	2.747788532	38.7420489	2.914078716	2	29.14078716
26	10	2.043805638	16	80	1.743392201	1.743392201	2.971421465	34.86784401	2.860174746	1	31.4619222

Spreadsheet S7.2 The initial maximin spreadsheet.

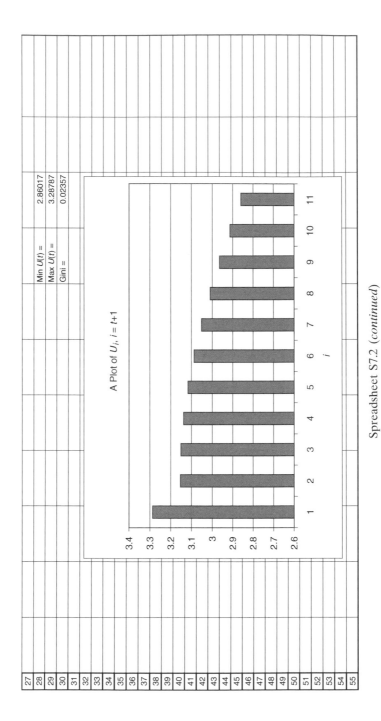

Spreadsheet S7.2 (*continued*)

252

	A	B	C	D	E	F	G	H	I	J	K
1	Maximin Utility with Fractional Consumption, Extraction, and Harvest Rates										
2											
3	$\omega =$	0.6									
4	$\eta =$	0.3									
5	$\varepsilon =$	0.5									
6	$\nu =$	0.2									
7	$\phi =$	0.25									
8	$r =$	1									
9	$X_c =$	100									
10								$\alpha =$	0.63359		
11	$K(0) =$	1						$\beta =$	0.49845		
12	$R(0) =$	100						$\gamma_l =$	0.08162		
13	$X(0) =$	100						$\gamma_u =$	0.08663		
14											
15	t	C_t	H_t	X_t	Q_{ut}	Q_{lt}	K_t	R_t	U_t	RankU_t	$(T+2-\text{Rank}U_t)U_t$
16	0	1.189439937	49.84480221	100	8.663232069	8.161692297	1	100	4.088982207	5	28.62287545
17	1	1.54078697	24.99975914	50.15519779	7.205649826	6.788493741	1.687861728	83.17507563	3.871477607	1	42.58625368
18	2	1.880183121	24.99975914	50.15519779	5.993304692	5.646334803	2.578909988	69.18093207	4.08417017	4	32.67336136
19	3	2.197194349	24.99975914	50.15519779	4.984935711	4.696343243	3.6662335	57.54129257	4.21634648	8	16.86538592
20	4	2.485457084	24.99975914	50.15519779	4.116224048	3.906187045	4.9368869	47.86001362	4.28256034	10	8.5651268
21	5	2.741508288	24.99975914	50.15519779	3.448624988	3.248974029	6.374244728	39.80760253	4.295299378	11	4.295299378
22	6	2.963927736	24.99975914	50.15519779	2.868396442	2.702336606	7.95967882	33.11000351	4.265115182	9	12.79534555
23	7	3.15271624	24.99975914	50.15519779	2.38579091	2.247670516	9.673739689	27.53927046	4.2008551	7	21.0042755
24	8	3.308845084	24.99975914	50.15519779	1.984383394	1.869501652	11.49697832	22.90580904	4.109904951	6	24.65942971
25	9	3.433928865	24.99975914	50.15519779	1.650512389	1.554959413	13.41050739	19.05192399	3.998411696	3	35.98570526
26	10	3.529987679	24.99975914	50.15519779	1.372814928	1.293338668	15.39637331	15.84645219	3.871477663	2	38.71477663
27											

Spreadsheet S7.3 The maximin social contract.

253

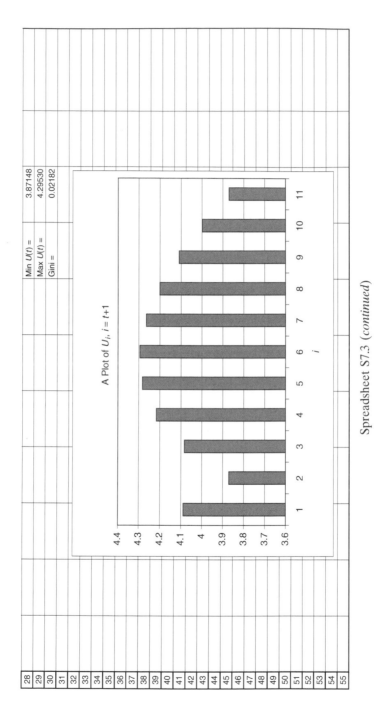

Min $U(t) =$	3.87148
Max $U(t) =$	4.29530
Gini $=$	0.02182

A Plot of U_i, $i = t+1$

Spreadsheet S7.3 (*continued*)

254

reducing the utility of any other generation. In moving from the initial social contract to the maximin contract, *all* utility levels have been increased. The stock of the renewable resource is maintained at a lower level than in the initial social contract, $X^* = 50.1551978 < 80$, and the nonrenewable resource has been depleted to a lower level, $R_{10} = 15.8464522 < 34.867844$. The terminal capital stock is higher under the maximin social contract, $K_{10} = 15.3963733 > 2.97142147$. Finally, the Gini coefficient is slightly lower under the maximin contract ($0.02181658 < 0.023572241$), indicating a more equitable use of resources and capital accumulation.

One might wonder why, in a finite-generational model, it is not optimal to completely exhaust the nonrenewable resource ($R_{10} \approx 0$). As R_t is reduced, so too are the extraction levels $Q_{F,t} = \gamma_F R_t$ and $Q_{U,t} = \gamma_U R_t$, leading lower levels for $Q_{U,t}$ and thus U_t. Remaining reserves can only be depleted so much before the utility of later generations is reduced below the maximin utility.

7.4 OVERLAPPING GENERATIONS

The simplest overlapping-generations model has a generation born in period t living through period $t+1$. In period t, the newborn generation might be referred to as the "younger generation," and in period $t + 1$, they become the "elder generation." In any period, there will be two generations present, the elder generation, born in the previous period, and the younger generation, born in the current period. We will assume that the utility of the generation born in period t, denoted $U_{t,t+1}$, will depend on consumption of the capital good, harvest from the renewable resource, and extraction from the nonrenewable resource in both periods t and $t + 1$. Consider the utility function taking the form

$$U_{t,t+1} = C_{Y,t}^{\varepsilon_Y} H_{Y,t}^{\nu_Y} Q_{Y,t}^{\phi_Y} (1 + \rho C_{E,t+1}^{\varepsilon_E} H_{E,t+1}^{\nu_E} Q_{E,t+1}^{\phi_E}) \qquad (7.7)$$

where the subscript Y refers to a consumption, harvest, or extraction flow going to the younger generation born in period t, and the subscript E refers to those flows going to the generation born in period t when it has become the elder generation in period $t + 1$. The parameter $\rho > 0$ might be regarded as a discount factor or a scaling parameter. Note that if the term $C_{Y,t}^{\varepsilon_Y} H_{Y,t}^{\nu_Y} Q_{Y,t}^{\phi_Y} \geq 0$ is regarded as the utility of the younger generation born in period t, and $C_{E,t+1}^{\varepsilon_E} H_{E,t+1}^{\nu_E} Q_{E,t+1}^{\phi_E} \geq 0$ is the utility of the elder generation in period $t + 1$, then the utility of the younger generation must be positive for $U_{t,t+1} > 0$. We will assume that the utility exponents of consumption, harvest, and nonrenewable resource flows are positive, less than one, and that $1 > (\varepsilon_Y + \nu_Y + \phi_Y) > 0$ and $1 > (\varepsilon_E + \nu_E + \phi_E) > 0$.

The social contract, with overlapping generations, is the vector of rates $[\alpha_Y, \alpha_E, \beta_Y, \beta_E, \gamma_F, \gamma_Y, \gamma_E]$ and we seek the social contract that will

$$\underset{[\alpha_Y,\alpha_E,\beta_Y,\beta_E,\gamma_F,\gamma_Y,\gamma_E]}{\text{Maximize}} \quad \text{Min}\{U_{0,1}, U_{1,2}, \ldots, U_{T-1,T}\}$$

Subject to
$$C_{Y,t} = \alpha_Y F(K_t, Q_{F,t})$$
$$C_{E,t} = \alpha_E F(K_t, Q_{F,t})$$
$$H_{Y,t} = \beta_Y X_t$$
$$H_{E,t} = \beta_E X_t$$
$$Q_{F,t} = \gamma_F R_t$$
$$Q_{Y,t} = \gamma_Y R_t$$
$$Q_{E,t} = \gamma_E R_t$$
$$R_{t+1} = [1 - (\gamma_F + \gamma_Y + \gamma_E)]R_t$$
$$K_{t+1} = K_t + [1 - (\alpha_Y + \alpha_E)]F(K_t, Q_{F,t})$$
$$X_{t+1} = [1 - (\beta_Y + \beta_E) + r(1 - X_t/X_c)]X_t$$
$$K_0 > 0, \quad X_0 > 0, \quad R_0 > 0, \quad T > 0 \quad \text{given}$$

where $U_{t,t+1}$ takes the form given in Equation (7.7) and $F(K_t, Q_{F,t}) = K_t^\omega Q_{F,t}^\eta$. We also assume that the maximin social contract will be such that $1 > (\gamma_F + \gamma_Y + \gamma_E) > 0$, $1 \geq (\alpha_Y + \alpha_E) > 0$, and $2 > r - (\beta_Y + \beta_E) > 0$.

Spreadsheet S7.4 shows the results for the initial social contract $[\alpha_Y, \alpha_E, \beta_Y, \beta_E, \gamma_F, \gamma_Y, \gamma_E] = [0.45, 0.45, 0.25, 0.25, 0.05, 0.05, 0.05]$. In Spreadsheet S7.4 we assume that $\varepsilon_Y = \varepsilon_E = \varepsilon = 0.5$, $\nu_Y = \nu_E = \nu = 0.2$, $\phi_Y = \phi_E = \phi = 0.25$, and $\rho = 0.9$. All other parameters and initial conditions are the same as in Spreadsheet S7.2 for nonoverlapping generations. Note that we need separate columns for consumption, harvest, and extraction flows for younger and elder generations and that there are no entries for the elder generation in $t = 0$ and no entries for the younger generation in $t = T = 10$. For this initial social contract we again see utility $U_{t,t+1}$ monotonically decline from $U_{0,1} = 6.96975099$ to $U_{9,10} = 3.70059491$. Can Solver find the maximin social contract, and will it constitute a Pareto improvement?

Maximin with Overlapping Generations

Parameter	Value
$\omega =$	0.6
$\eta =$	0.3
$\varepsilon =$	0.5
$\nu =$	0.2
$\phi =$	0.25
$r =$	1
$X_c =$	100
	0.9
$K(0) =$	1
$R(0) =$	100
$X(0) =$	100

Parameter	Value
$\alpha_y =$	0.45000
$\alpha_e =$	0.45000
$\beta_y =$	0.25000
$\beta_e =$	0.25000
$\gamma_y =$	0.05000
$\gamma_y =$	0.05000
$\gamma_e =$	0.05000

t	C_{yt}	C_{et}	H_{yt}	H_{et}	X_t	Q_{ft}	Q_{yt}	Q_{et}	K_t	R_t	$U(t,t+1)$	$\mathrm{Rank}\,U_t$	$(T+2-\mathrm{Rank}\,U_t)U_t$
0	0.729295469	0.760094506	12.5	25	100	5	5	5	1	100	6.969750986	10	6.969750986
1	0.760094506	0.785338551	12.5	12.5	50	4.25	4.25	4.25	1.16206566	85	5.854725807	9	11.70945161
2	0.785338551	0.805356518	12.5	12.5	50	3.6125	3.6125	3.6125	1.33097555	72.25	5.612173526	8	16.83652058
3	0.805356518	0.820508651	12.5	12.5	50	3.070625	3.070625	3.070625	1.505495228	61.4125	5.349443318	7	21.39777327
4	0.820508651	0.831171003	12.5	12.5	50	2.61003125	2.61003125	2.61003125	1.684463343	52.200625	5.074466338	6	25.37233169
5	0.831171003	0.837723906	12.5	12.5	50	2.218526563	2.218526563	2.218526563	1.866798599	44.37053125	4.793702586	5	28.76221551
6	0.837723906	0.840543511	12.5	12.5	50	1.885747578	1.885747578	1.885747578	2.051503266	37.71495156	4.512324799	4	31.58627359
7	0.840543511	0.839995667	12.5	12.5	50	1.602885441	1.602885441	1.602885441	2.237664134	32.05770883	4.234397296	3	33.87517837
8	0.839995667	0.83643162	12.5	12.5	50	1.362452625	1.362452625	1.362452625	2.424451581	27.2490525	3.963042967	2	35.6673867
9	0.83643162	0.830185094	12.5	12.5	50	1.158084731	1.158084731	1.158084731	2.611117285	23.16169463	3.700594907	1	37.00594907
10	0.830185094		12.5	12.5	50	0.984372022	0.984372022	0.984372022	2.796990978	19.68744043			

Spreadsheet S7.4 Overlapping generations, initial social contract.

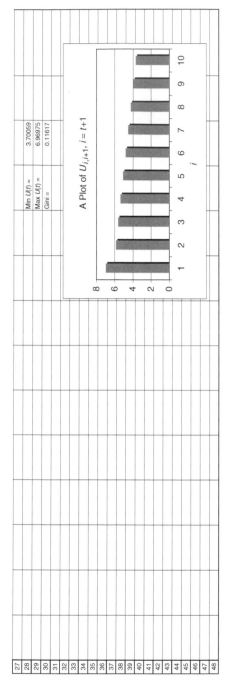

Min $U(t)$ =	3.70059	
Max $U(t)$ =	6.96975	
Gini =	0.11617	

A Plot of $U_{i,i+1}$, $i = t+1$

i

Spreadsheet S7.4 (*continued*)

Maximin with Overlapping Generations

$\omega =$	0.6		
$\eta =$	0.3		
$\varepsilon =$	0.5	$\alpha_y =$	0.39081
$\nu =$	0.2	$\alpha_\theta =$	0.22720
$\phi =$	0.25	$\beta_y =$	0.31603
$r =$	1	$\beta_\theta =$	0.18411
$X_c =$	100	$\gamma_y =$	0.08461
$\rho =$	0.9	$\gamma_y =$	0.05522
$K(0) =$	1	$\gamma_\theta =$	0.03219
$R(0) =$	100		
$X(0) =$	100		

t	C_{yt}	C_{et}	H_{yt}	H_{et}	X_t	Q_{ft}	Q_{yt}	Q_{et}	K_t	R_t	$U(t,t+1)$	$\text{Rank}U'_t$	$(T+2-\text{Rank}U)U_t$
0	0.741625547	0.565049363	31.60338417	9.202923809	100	8.460642126	5.521551036		1	100	6.182336754	3	49.45869403
1	0.971964348	0.694742551	15.79707406	9.202923809	49.98538755	7.005287329	4.571763104	2.66551371	1.724903387	82.79853024	6.071802336	1	60.71802336
2	1.195054866	0.815919752	15.79707406	9.202923809	49.98538755	5.800274947	3.785352656	2.207006175	2.674951899	68.55596609	6.549718228	5	39.29830937
3	1.403496689	0.925968149	15.79707406	9.202923809	49.98538755	4.802542406	3.134216364	1.827368675	3.843060688	56.76333231	6.836147769	8	20.50844331
4	1.592795402	1.023474109	15.79707406	9.202923809	49.98538755	3.976434526	2.595085083	1.513034405	5.214911357	46.99920487	6.958873037	10	6.958873037
5	1.760519363	1.107863738	15.79707406	9.202923809	49.98538755	3.292429343	2.148692307	1.252770249	6.771792435	38.91465085	6.947257603	9	13.89451521
6	1.90568139	1.179143236	15.79707406	9.202923809	49.98538755	2.726083105	1.77908665	1.037275354	8.492615637	32.22075895	6.829290773	7	27.31716309
7	2.028292148	1.2377711696	15.79707406	9.202923809	49.98538755	2.257156744	1.47305677	0.858848747	10.35532776	26.67831485	6.63013491	6	33.15067455
8	2.129038133	1.284225963	15.79707406	9.202923809	49.98538755	1.868892609	1.219669355	0.71111414	12.33788601	22.08925258	6.371547841	4	44.60083489
9	2.209049212	1.319503018	15.79707406	9.202923809	49.98538755	1.547415612	1.0098683	0.588792056	14.41891862	18.28957648	6.071804352	2	54.64623917
10			15.79707406	9.202923809	49.98538755	1.281237384		0.487511169	16.57815823	15.14350051			

Spreadsheet S7.5. Overlapping generations, the maximin social contract.

259

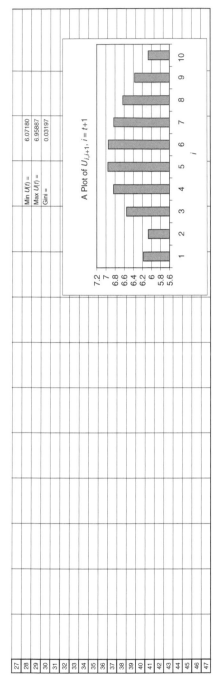

Spreadsheet S7.5 (*continued*)

260

The maximin social contract is shown in Spreadsheet S7.5. We see that Solver has opted for $[\alpha_Y, \alpha_E, \beta_Y, \beta_E, \gamma_F, \gamma_Y, \gamma_E] = [0.39081, 0.22720, 0.31603, 0.18411, 0.08461, 0.05522, 0.03219]$. The minimum utility is $U_{1,2} = 6.07180234$, which is an improvement over the minimum utility in Spreadsheet S7.4, where $U_{9,10} = 3.70059491$. In this particular overlapping-generations problem, the maximin social contract is not *Pareto superior* to the initial contract in Spreadsheet S7.4. Why?

7.5 COMPLICATIONS

Much of the economic literature on growth and sustainability with a nonrenewable resource is infinite-horizon and continuous-time. The early models assumed that utility only depended on consumption of manufactured capital. The maximin solution to these models, if one exists, was to find the largest sustainable and constant level for consumption for all generations. This, in turn, implied a constant level for utility across all generations. In Solow (1974), and in subsequent papers, variations to the basic model allowed for population growth and technological progress. Population growth, when utility was based on per-capita consumption and when the marginal productivity of labor declined, made sustainability more difficult. Technological progress made sustainability more feasible. In many models, sustainability required that the imputed value of extraction, referred to a *resource rent*, be invested in increasing the capital stock. The became known as *Hartwick's rule* (Hartwick, 1977).

Even if the current generation or generations feel altruistic toward future generations, uncertainty about future technology and preferences makes intergenerational sustainability exceedingly difficult. Specifically, current generations do not know the form and efficiency of future technologies that might generate electricity or transport people. Not knowing the technical options and efficiency of renewable energy in the future makes the optimal use of nonrenewable resources today problematic. Similarly, we can't expect future generations to have the same utility functions (preferences) as the current generation. Stocks of capital, information, infrastructure, and renewable and nonrenewable resources presumably will be useful to future generations, but we do not know what stocks they will value most. One might think that burning fossil fuels should be greatly curtailed if their continued use will result in future climate change that threatens critical life-support systems. But what if future generations figure out how to capture and sequester atmospheric carbon or reduce solar radiation? These actions are referred to as *geoengineering*. If such options become feasible, at low cost, and with no side effects, how should current generations use the remaining stocks of nonrenewable resources?

It is probably not appropriate to adopt the cavalier attitude that ingenious *Homo economicus* will come to the rescue with "just-in-time, side-effect-free" technologies to avoid climate-change tipping points, but at the same time, should we completely discount the ability of future generations to take actions to mitigate the effects of climate change at lower cost? (Remember our two-period, two-state climate-change model from Section 6.6.) It would seem that we are faced with a very difficult stochastic optimization problem with unknown tipping points (irreversibilities) and unknown future options to adapt. We have no choice but to proceed incrementally, hoping to feel the edge of the precipice before stepping off. Investing in a diverse portfolio of energy alternatives and mitigation strategies would seem only prudent.

7.6 AN EXERCISE

Construct your own version of Spreadsheet S7.2 with the initial social contract $[\alpha, \beta, \gamma_F, \gamma_U] = [0.9, 0.2, 0.05, 0.05]$. Now, with $\delta = 0.05$ and $\rho = 1/(1 + \delta)$, find the social contract that maximizes $U = \sum_{t=0}^{10} \rho^t U(C_t, H_t, Q_{U,t})$.

Answer: $[\alpha, \ \beta, \ \gamma_F, \ \gamma_U] = [0.63214, \ 0.53265, \ 0.09767, \ 0.10290]$.

Annotated Bibliography

Texts

Clark, C. W. 1985. *Bioeconomic Modelling and Fisheries Management.* John Wiley & Sons, New York.

In this text, Clark takes a more detailed look into models of fishing, including search and capture, processing and marketing, age-structured models, regulation, taxes and quotas, multispecies fisheries, fluctuations, and management under uncertainty. As always, Clark combines mathematical rigor with clear and insightful exposition.

Clark, C. W. 1990. *Mathematical Bioeconomics: The Optimal Management of Renewable Resources* (Second Edition). Wiley-Interscience, New York.

This is a frequently-cited classic text for graduate students with a background in calculus and differential equations. The second edition focuses exclusively on renewable resources. It contains chapters on optimal control theory and dynamical systems.

Conrad, J. M., and C. W. Clark. 1987. *Natural Resource Economics: Notes and Problems.* Cambridge University Press, New York.

This is a graduate-level text with a similar pedagogic philosophy to Resource Economics. *The first chapter covers the method of Lagrange multipliers, dynamic programming, the maximum principle, some numerical methods, and graphical techniques. This chapter is followed by chapters on renewable and nonrenewable resources, environmental management, and stochastic resource models.*

Hanley, N., J. F. Shogren, and B. White. 1997. *Environmental Economics in Theory and Practice.* Oxford University Press, New York.

This is a text for advanced undergraduates or graduate students with two or more semesters of calculus and intermediate or graduate microeconomics. Contrary to its title, it is a comprehensive text covering both environmental and resource economics. The text also contains two chapters (12 and 13) on the theory of nonmarket valuation and methods for estimating environmental costs and benefits (such as contingent valuation, travel cost, and hedonic pricing).

Hartwick, J. M., and N. D. Olewiler. 1998. *The Economics of Natural Resource Use* (Second Edition). Addison-Wesley, Reading, MA.

An intermediate text using graphical analysis and differential calculus. Part I of this text provides two introductory chapters. Part II contains five chapters using static (equilibrium) models to examine the allocation of land, water, and fish; the generation of pollution; and the economics of environmental policy. Part III contains five chapters developing intertemporal (dynamic) models of nonrenewable and renewable resources.

Léonard, D., and N. V. Long. 1992. *Optimal Control Theory and Static Optimization in Economics.* Cambridge University Press, New York.

This is a graduate-level text on static and dynamic optimization. Chapter 1 covers static optimization and the method of Lagrange multipliers. Section 4.2 provides a discrete-time derivation of the maximum principle.

Miranda, M. J., and P. L. Fackler. 2002. *Applied Computational Economics and Finance.* MIT Press, Cambridge, MA.

This is an advanced text with an emphasis on the numerical methods to solve dynamic optimization problems. The authors have developed a set of MATLAB functions, collectively called the CompEcon Toolbox, *that can be used to solve both deterministic and stochastic optimization problems. The CompEcon Toolbox is freely available at* http://www4.ncsu.edu/ ~pfackler/compecon/toolbox.html. *The book contains many numerical examples from resource economics, finance, macroeconomics, and agricultural economics.*

Tietenberg, T., and L. Lewis. 2009. *Environmental and Natural Resource Economics* (Eighth Edition). Addison-Wesley, Reading, MA.

A comprehensive introductory text covering both natural resource and environmental economics. The text is aimed at undergraduates with or without introductory economics. Calculus is not required.

Weitzman, M. L. 2003. *Income, Wealth, and the Maximum Principle.* Harvard University Press, Cambridge, MA.

This is an advanced text showing the relationship between the value function from dynamic programming and the maximized Hamiltonian from the maximum principle. Optimized value is wealth, and the optimized Hamiltonian is "properly accounted income." In the first part of the text, Weitzman poses 10 problems, many from the fields of resource and environmental economics, and shows how they can be transformed into a prototype problem and solved using the maximum principle. The second part of the book deals with multisector growth, dynamic-competitive equilibrium, complete national accounting, and the stochastic version of wealth, income, and the maximum principle. Clear exposition allows the reader to come away with a depth of understanding on the role optimization plays in the economic concepts of wealth and income.

Basic Concepts: Four Classic Articles

Baumol, W. J. 1968. "On the Social Rate of Discount," *American Economic Review* 57:788–802.
Baumol discusses the social rate of time preference and the effects of inflationary expectations, taxes, and risk on market rates of return.

Boulding, K. E. 1966. "The Economics of the Coming Spaceship Earth," in H. Jarrett (ed.), *Environmental Quality in a Growing Economy.* Johns Hopkins University Press, Baltimore, MD.
Boulding examines the implications of the first and second laws of thermodynamics for an economic system, along with the notion that welfare in a closed economy (spaceship) should be concerned with stock maintenance, as opposed to maximizing throughput (GDP). This article is reprinted in Markandya, A., and J. Richardson. 1992. Environmental Economics: A Reader. *St. Martins Press, New York.*

Krutilla, J. V. 1967. "Conservation Revisited," *American Economic Review* 57:777–786.
This article is concerned with the ability of markets to (1) efficiently allocate natural resources over time, (2) signal resource scarcity, and (3) account for option demand. This article is also reprinted in Markandya and Richardson (1992).

Weisbrod, B. A. 1964. "Collective Consumption Services of Individual Consumption Goods," *Quarterly Journal of Economics* 78:471–477.
This article introduced the concept of option value for a hospital or park based on the potential (uncertain) future demand by individuals.

Optimization and Economic Theory

Dorfman, R. 1969. "An Economic Interpretation of Optimal Control Theory," *American Economic Review* 59:817–831.
In the 1960s, optimal control theory and the maximum principle provided a powerful new way to pose and solve dynamic optimization problems, such as the problem of optimal saving and investment.

Spence, A. M., and D. A. Starrett. 1975. "Most Rapid Approach Paths in Accumulation Problems," *International Economic Review* 16:388–403.
This article lays out sufficient conditions for the most rapid approach path (MRAP) to be optimal in both discrete- and continuous-time models.

The Economics of Fisheries

Bjørndal, T., and J. M. Conrad. 1987. "The Dynamics of an Open Access Fishery," *Canadian Journal of Economics* 20:74–85.

This article offers an empirical analysis of the open-access forces leading to the decline and ultimately a moratorium in the North Sea herring fishery.

Brown, G. B., Jr. 1974. "An Optimal Program for Managing Common Property Resources with Congestion Externalities," *Journal of Political Economy* 82:163–174.

Brown examines how a landings tax and a tax on effort might be used to reflect user cost and (static) congestion externalities. Perhaps as a result of this article, the fishing industry successfully lobbied for a prohibition on the use of landings taxes in the Fishery Management and Conservation Act of 1976.

Brown, G. M. 2000. "Renewable Resource Management and Use without Markets," *Journal of Economic Literature* 38:875–914.

Brown surveys the interplay of poorly defined property rights and the externalities that arise in the exploitation and management of renewable resources.

Burt, O. R., and R. G. Cummings. 1970. "Production and Investment in Natural Resource Industries," *American Economic Review* 60:576–590.

This article presents a discrete-time, finite-horizon model of harvest and investment in a natural resource industry.

Clark, C. W. 1973. "The Economics of Overexploitation," *Science* 181:630–634.

This article examines the conditions that would induce the commercial extinction of a plant or animal.

Clark, C. W. 2006. *The Worldwide Crisis in Fisheries: Economic Models and Human Behavior.* Cambridge University Press, New York.

Clark brings his background in math and economics to help us understand the failure of traditional management policies that has led to the current worldwide crisis in fisheries. Clark shows how management policies that fail to take into account the economic behavior of harvesters are unlikely to promote efficiency and may not prevent overfishing. This is Clark at his best!

Clark, C. W., and G. P. Kirkwood. 1986. "On Uncertain Renewable Resource Stocks: Optimal Harvest Policies and the Value of Stock Surveys," *Journal of Environmental Economics and Management* 13:235–244.

Building on Reed (1979), Clark and Kirkwood make current-period stock unknown subject to a distribution conditional on previous-period escapement. In contrast to Reed, they find that the optimal escapement policy is not a constant escapement policy.

Conrad, J. M. 1999. "The Bioeconomics of Marine Sanctuaries," *Journal of Bioeconomics* 1:205–217.

Marine reserves may reduce the variance in the population of fish on adjacent grounds.

Egan, T. 1991. "Halibut Derby Brings Frenzy of Blood (Fish and Human)," *The New York Times,* Wednesday, May 8, p. A21.

Gordon, H. S. 1954. "The Economic Theory of a Common Property Resource: The Fishery," *Journal of Political Economy* 62:124–142.

In this article, Gordon presents the static model of open access as a way of explaining why so many fisheries end up with too many (aging and decaying) vessels chasing too few fish.

Grafton, R. Q. 1996. "Individual Transferable Quotas: Theory and Practice," *Reviews in Fish Biology and Fisheries* 6:5–20.

This is a well-written article for a general audience. Grafton first discusses the theory of ITQs and then describes the experience to date with ITQ programs in Canada, Iceland, Australia, and New Zealand. He attempts to determine the effect that ITQs have had on (1) economic efficiency, (2) employment and harvest shares, (3) compliance with management regulations, and (4) cost recovery, management costs, and the distribution of resource rents between fishers and the government. The article contains a glossary of terms used by fisheries economists when discussing ITQs.

Homans, F. R., and J. E. Wilen. 1997. "A Model of Regulated Open Access Resource Use," *Journal of Environmental Economics and Management* 32:1–21.

This article presents a more plausible model of regulation, where management authorities set a TAC according to a linear adaptive policy and fishers make decisions on fishing effort that determine season length. The TAC leads to a race for the fish and large expenditures of effort during a compressed (shortened) season. This article is summarized in Section 3.6.

Lauck, T., C. W. Clark, M. Mangel, and G. M. Munro. 1998. "Implementing the Precautionary Principle in Fisheries Management through Marine Reserves," *Ecological Applications* 8:S72–S78.

If some unknowns are unknowable (irreducible), marine reserves or no-fishing zones may be appropriate.

Nøstbakken, L. 2006. "Regime Switching in a Fishery with Stochastic Stock and Price," *Journal of Environmental Economics and Management* 51:231–241.

This article shows how stochastic stock and price can lead to threshold decisions on when to fish and when to stay in port.

Pindyck, R. S. 1984. "Uncertainty in the Theory of Renewable Resource Markets," *Review of Economic Studies* 51:289–303.

Introduced a continuous-time stochastic process (an Itô process) to describe the growth of a renewable resource. In three examples, Pindyck shows how to derive optimal feedback harvest policies.

Plourde, C. G. 1970. "A Simple Model of Replenishable Natural Resource Exploitation," *American Economic Review* 60:518–522.

A short, compact article using the maximum principle to solve for the rate of
harvest that maximizes discounted utility when (1) utility only depends on
harvest and (2) growth is logistic.

Reed, W. J. 1979. "Optimal Escapement Levels in Stochastic and Deterministic Harvesting Models," *Journal of Environmental Economics and*
Management 6:350–363.

This article presents the conditions under which constant escapement policies are
optimal. Stock is assumed to be observable in the current period. It intro-
duced a basic discrete-time model allowing subsequent authors to consider
additional sources of uncertainty in models of fishery management.

Scott, A. D. 1955. "The Fishery: The Objective of Sole Ownership," *Journal*
of Political Economy 63:116–124.

If open access results in excessive effort (E_∞) and a reduction in social welfare,
perhaps the optimal level of effort would be E_0, the level adopted by a
sole owner with exclusive harvesting rights. The sole owner would set effort
so as to maximize static rent, shown as the vertical difference between the
revenue function and cost ray in Figure 3.7. If fishery managers could limit
the number of vessels and hours fished, they might be able to restrict effort
in an open access fishery to E_0. Subsequent analysis in the 1960s and 1970s
showed that if the management objective was present-value maximization,
E_0 when $\delta > 0$ would not be optimal.

Sethi, G., C. Costello, A. Fisher, M. Hanemann, and L. Karp. 2005. "Fishery Management under Multiple Uncertainty," *Journal of Environmental*
Economics and Management 50:300–318.

This article introduces three sources of uncertainty when managing a fishery:
growth uncertainty, measurement error, and implementation error. The
authors find that measurement error may be the most important. Optimal
escapement policies are not constant.

Smith, V. L. 1968. "Economics of Production from Natural Resources,"
American Economic Review 58:409–431.

Vernon Smith, a Nobel laureate in economics, wrote two articles in the late
1960s that were the first to model the dynamics of a resource and the capital
stock of the exploiting industry as a system. Different models (or cases)
were developed to consider renewable or nonrenewable resources with or
without stock or crowding externalities. This article provided the theoretical
basis for dynamic open-access models.

Smith, V. L. 1969. "On Models of Commercial Fishing," *Journal of Political*
Economy 77:191–198.

In this article, Smith examines how three externalities – stock, mesh, and crowd-
ing – might be modeled as a result of the common-property status of most
commercial fisheries.

Smith, M. D., and J. E. Wilen. 2003. "Economic Impact of Marine Reserves:
The Importance of Spatial Behavior," *Journal of Environmental Eco-*
nomics and Management 46:182–206.

Spatial rent seeking by competitive harvesters may reduce the benefits of marine reserves below what biologists might expect initially.

Valderrama, D., and J. L. Anderson. 2007. "Improving Utilization of the Atlantic Sea Scallop Resource: An Analysis of Rotational Management of Fishing Grounds," *Land Economics* 83:86–103.

This article shows how partitioning a fishing ground into areas that are opened and closed on a rotational basis may increase yield and net revenue.

Wilen, J. 1976. "Common Property Resources and the Dynamics of Over-exploitation: The Case of the North Pacific Fur Seal," Department of Economics, Programme in Natural Resource Economics, Paper No. 3, The University of British Columbia, Vancouver, British Columbia.

This is perhaps the first empirical study of a dynamic open-access model based on the earlier work by Vernon Smith. The history of exploitation of the northern fur seal makes for fascinating reading. The seals winter along the California coast and then migrate almost 6,000 miles to breeding grounds on the Pribilof Islands. With the Alaska Purchase in 1867, the United States acquired the Pribilofs and granted exclusive harvest rights, for a 20-year period, to the Alaska Commercial Company. When the seals were migrating between breading and wintering grounds, they were subject to open access, and pressure was put on U.S. officials by the Alaska Commercial Company to prevent Canadian vessels from taking seals in the Bering Sea. Gunboat diplomacy by the United States and British intervention on behalf of Canada ultimately led to international arbitration. Wilen estimates a dynamic open-access model for different historical periods, checks for stability of the open-access equilibrium, and for the period 1882–1900, plots the likely values for the seal population and vessel numbers in "phase space."

The Economics of Forestry

Amacher, G., M. Ollikainen, and E. Koskela. 2009. *Economics of Forest Resources.* MIT Press, Cambridge, MA.

This is a comprehensive and well-written text covering the classic literature on forest economics as well as the more recent approach that views the decision on the optimal time to cut a stand of trees as an optimal stopping problem in a stochastic environment.

Binkley, C. S. 1987. "When Is the Optimal Economic Rotation Longer than the Rotation of Maximum Sustained Yield," *Journal of Environmental Economics and Management* 14:152–158.

This article establishes the conditions under which the Faustmann rotation may be longer than the rotation that maximizes mean annual increment.

Conrad, J, M., and D. Ludwig. 1994. "Forest Land Policy: The Optimal Stock of Old-Growth Forest," *Natural Resource Modeling* 8:27–45.

This article presents a continuous-time version of the old-growth forest model of Section 4.6.

Deacon, R. T. 1985. "The Simple Analytics of Forest Economics," in R. T. Deacon and M. B. Johnson (eds.), *Forestlands Public and Private.* Ballinger, San Francisco.

A clear exposition of the Faustmann rotation, pitched at the intermediate level. This article emphasizes the marginal value of waiting and the marginal cost of waiting and discusses the short- and long-run comparative statics of timber supply.

Hartman, R. 1976. "The Harvesting Decision When a Standing Forest has Value," *Economic Inquiry* 14:52–58.

From the same issue of Economic Inquiry *that contains the Samuelson classic, Hartman extends the Faustmann model so that a stand of trees provides a continuous flow of amenity value that increases with the age of the stand. He derives a first-order condition that can be used to calculate the amenity-inclusive optimal rotation.*

Hyde, W. F. 1980. *Timber Supply, Land Allocation, and Economic Efficiency.* Johns Hopkins University Press, Baltimore, MD.

This text was written at a time when there was a concern about the adequacy of private and public lands to supply sufficient timber to the U.S. economy. At the time, forest plans by the U.S. Forest Service were calling for management to meet "multiple objectives," including recreation, wildlife habitat, and watershed protection. In addition, wilderness groups were calling for an expansion of the system of national parks (such as the creation of the North Cascades National Park), where the harvest of timber would be prohibited. The forest industry and some members of the U.S. Congress were concerned that the multiple-use management doctrines and the expansion of the national park system would severely limit the land available for timber harvest and rotational forestry. Would a "timber famine" ensue? Hyde concludes that the efficient management of private and public lands currently devoted to rotational forestry should provide an adequate supply of timber in the future. In fact, more intensive silvicultural practices may lead to greater timber output from fewer hectares, further reducing the "perceived" conflict between timber supply, on the one hand, and multiple use or additions to the inventory of wilderness, on the other.

Johansson, P.-O., and K.-G. Löfgren. 1985. *The Economics of Forestry and Natural Resources.* Basil Blackwell, Oxford, England.

While the emphasis of this book is on the economics of forestry, it contains chapters on the theory of investment, benefit-cost rules for natural resources, and the economics of nonrenewable and renewable resources. The effects of different forest taxes, improved biotechnology, perfect and imperfect markets, and risk are examined in terms of the change in rotation length and other forest practices. There is an econometric analysis of the demand and supply of wood in Sweden.

Provencher, B. 1995. "Structural Estimation of the Stochastic Dynamic Decision Problems of Resource Users: An Application to the Timber Harvest Decision," *Journal of Environmental Economics and Management* 29:321–338.

In this article, Provencher presents a method for nesting a stochastic dynamic programming algorithm within a maximum-likelihood routine in order to estimate the real discount rates and parameters of the stochastic process underlying the observed behavior of resource decision makers.

Samuelson, P. A. 1976. "Economics of Forestry in an Evolving Society," *Economic Inquiry* 14:466–492.

This is a classic. The Nobel laureate and a founding father of modern (mathematical) economics surveys 125 years of writings by foresters and economists, warts (mistakes) and all. After posing and solving the infinite-rotation problem and noting the potentially strong private incentive to invest the net revenue from timber in other higher-yield investments, Samuelson considers the potential externalities and public services that forests might provide in a democratic developed country. The article was presented originally at a conference in 1974, which makes Professor Samuelson perceptive if not a prophet when he notes, "Ecologists know that soil erosion and atmospheric quality at one spot on the globe may be importantly affected by whether or not trees are being grown at places some distance away. To the degree this is so, the simple Faustmann calculus and the bouncings of futures contracts for plywood on the organized exchanges need to be altered in the interests of the public. . .."

Sohngen, B., and R. Mendelsohn. 1998. "Valuing the Impact of Large-Scale Ecological Change in a Market: The Effect of Climate Change on U.S. Timber," *American Economic Review* 88:686–710.

Sohngen and Mendelsohn build a dynamic model to examine the likely response of US timber producers and timber markets to climate change. If the climate-induced changes in forest ecosystems are adaptively responded to by forest firms and markets, the present value of the industry might increase in the range of $1 billion to $33 billion.

The Economics of Nonrenewable Resources

Arrow, K. J., and S. Chang. 1982. "Optimal Pricing, Use, and Exploration of Uncertain Natural Resource Stocks," *Journal of Environmental Economics and Management* 9:1–10.

A model of depletion and exploration is developed where the probability of discovering a field (mine) over a small increment of time depends on the size of the area explored. With constant exploration costs (per unit area explored), the model results in optimal exploration being zero or at its maximum depending on whether the sum of the unit cost of exploration plus user cost is greater than or less than the expected marginal increase in current value from exploration. This article uses dynamic programming and a first-order Taylor approximation to the Bellman equation.

Barnett, H. J., and C. Morse. 1963. *Scarcity and Growth: The Economics of Natural Resource Availability.* Johns Hopkins University Press, Baltimore, MD.

An influential study into the adequacy of natural resources and the prospects for continued economic growth in the post-World War II era. Barnett and Morse first consider whether physical measures (abundance), prices, or extraction costs might serve as an index of impending resource scarcity. They reject abundance measures as lacking an appropriate economic dimension and instead assemble relative price and unit cost indices for minerals, fossil fuels, and timber for the period 1870–1957. With the exception of timber, they did not observe any significant increase in real prices or average extraction costs. They conclude that while resource scarcity is ever-present, it is a dynamic and "kaleidoscopic" condition, with markets, human ingenuity, and commodity substitution working to mitigate the scarcity of a particular resource.

Brown, G. M., and B. C. Field. 1978. "Implications of Alternative Measures of Natural Resource Scarcity," *Journal of Political Economy* 88:229–243.

Brown and Field review various measures of resource scarcity and find commonly used measures, such as market price and average extraction cost, to be deficient. They propose resource rent as a preferred measure but note the difficulty in obtaining the time-series data to accurately estimate rent. Marginal discovery costs are suggested as a useful proxy.

Cairns, R. D. 1990. "The Economics of Exploration for Nonrenewable Resources," *Journal of Economic Surveys* 4:361–395.

This article provides a detailed survey of the economic literature on the exploration for nonrenewable resources.

Chakravorty, U., M. Moreaux, and M. Tidball. 2008. "Ordering the Extraction of Polluting Nonrenewable Resources," *American Economic Review* 98:1128–1144.

Examines the optimal depletion of two nonrenewable resources (say, coal, and natural gas) when they differentially contribute to a degradable stock pollutant (say, atmospheric carbon) that is constrained to be less than or equal to an upper bound ($Z \le \overline{Z}$).

Dasgupta, P. S., and G. M. Heal. 1979. *Economic Theory and Exhaustible Resources.* James Nisbet & Co., Ltd., and Cambridge University Press, England.

This is a graduate-level text that is broader in scope than the title might suggest. There are chapters on static allocation, externalities, intertemporal equilibrium, and renewable resources. These are followed by 10 chapters covering optimal depletion, production with a nonrenewable resource as an input, depletion and capital accumulation, intergenerational welfare, imperfect competition, taxation, uncertainty and information, and price dynamics. This is an extremely thorough and rigorous text.

Devarajan, S., and A. C. Fisher. 1981. "Hotelling's 'Economics of Exhaustible Resources': Fifty Years Later," *Journal of Economic Literature* 19:65–73.

This is a retrospective on Hotelling's 1931 article (which was rediscovered by resource economists in the 1970s). A considerable literature developed seeking to extend Hotelling's analysis to answer theoretical and policy questions raised by the energy "crisis" of the early and mid-1970s.

Devarajan, S., and A. C. Fisher. 1982. "Exploration and Scarcity," *Journal of Political Economy* 90:1279–1290.

Resource rent (price less marginal extraction cost) was argued by Brown and Field to be the preferred measure of resource scarcity, with marginal discovery cost as an empirically more tractable alternative. In a two-period model, Devarajan and Fisher show that resource rent will be equal to marginal exploration costs when optimizing firms face a deterministic discovery process and may bound resource rent when discovery is uncertain.

Farzin, Y. H. 1984. "The Effect of the Discount Rate on Depletion of Exhaustible Resources," *Journal of Political Economy* 92:841–851.

Farzin shows that if the production cost of a substitute (backstop) depends on the cost of capital (thus on the rate of discount), a decrease (increase) in the discount rate might cause the nonrenewable resource to be extracted more (less) rapidly. If a decrease in the discount rate lowers the "choke-off" price, this will lower the initial price of the nonrenewable resource and may lead to more rapid depletion. If an increase in the discount rate raises the choke-off price, the initial price of the nonrenewable resource increases and will result in less rapid depletion. This result is opposite to the "standard" result, where the choke-off price was regarded as a constant.

Farzin, Y. H. 1995. "Technological Change and the Dynamics of Resource Scarcity Measures," *Journal of Environmental Economics and Management* 29:105–120.

This article examines the effect that technological change has on measures of resource scarcity (cost, price, and rent). Depending on the form of technological change, the three measures may move together, or they may move inconsistently. The article provides a theoretical basis for why the different measures may diverge empirically. Rent remains the preferred measure.

Fischer, C., and R. Laxminarayan. 2005. "Sequential Development and Exploitation of an Exhaustible Resource: Do Monopoly Rights Promote Conservation," *Journal of Environmental Economics and Management* 49:500–515.

With multiple resource deposits (pools) and significant setup costs, rates of extraction by a monopolist may be slower or faster than a social planner.

Fisher, A. C. 1981. *Resource and Environmental Economics.* Cambridge University Press, Cambridge, England.

This text is accessible to students with intermediate microeconomics and calculus. Chapters 2 and 4 are excellent introductions to models of optimal depletion, monopoly, uncertainty, exploration, and measures of resource scarcity.

Gaudet, G., M. Moreaux, and S. W. Salant. 2001. "Intertemporal Depletion of Sites by Spatially Distributed Users," *American Economic Review* 91:1149–1159.

This article develops optimality conditions for the use of multiple sites by multiple users and the timing and subsequent reallocation of sites and users when a new site is developed (made available).

Gray, L. C. 1914. "Rent under the Assumption of Exhaustibility," *Quarterly Journal of Economics* 28:466–489.

Perhaps the first article to recognize an additional (user) cost to marginal extraction today. In the context of a simple arithmetic example, Gray shows that the present value of marginal net revenue (rent) must be the same in all periods with positive extraction.

Halvorsen, R., and T. R. Smith. 1984. "On Measuring Natural Resource Scarcity," *Journal of Political Economy* 92:954–964.

Halvorsen and Smith note that many resource industries are vertically integrated and that this can further exacerbate the problem of measuring scarcity using rent at the time of extraction. With duality theory, they show how to econometrically estimate the shadow price on a nonrenewable resource. An empirical study of Canadian mining shows that the shadow price for ore declined significantly from 1956 through 1974.

Hotelling, H. 1931. "The Economics of Exhaustible Resources," *Journal of Political Economy* 39:137–175.

This is the classic article on nonrenewable resources. Hotelling examines price paths and extraction under competition, monopoly, and welfare maximization. Hotelling's use of the calculus of variations probably made this article inaccessible to most of the economics profession at the time it was published. Hotelling illustrates the theory and mathematics with numerical examples and graphical analysis. In addition to the core sections on competition, monopoly, and welfare maximization, Hotelling considers discontinuous solutions, valuation of the mine under monopoly, the effects of cumulative production, severance taxes, and duopoly. This article, along with his work on the economics of depreciation, duopoly, stability analysis, and the travel-cost method for estimating recreational demand, made Hotelling not only the father of resource economics but also one of the brightest minds in economics in the early twentieth century.

Krautkraemer, J. 1998. "Nonrenewable Resource Scarcity," *Journal of Economic Literature* 36:2065–2107.

A fine review by the late Professor Krautkraemer.

Livernois, J. 1992. "A Note on the Effect of Tax Brackets on Nonrenewable Resource Extraction," *Journal of Environmental Economics and Management* 22:272–280.

This article shows how progressive tax rates for a severance tax or a profits tax, when imposed on a firm extracting a nonrenewable resource, might lead to constant extraction rates over some interval of time.

Olson, L. J., and K. C. Knapp. 1997. "Exhaustible Resource Allocation in an Overlapping Generations Economy," *Journal of Environmental Economics and Management* 32:277–292.

This article reveals that overlapping generations (OLG) models can result in atypical behavior. In a finite-horizon model, the rate of extraction may increase and price may decrease over the entire horizon. In an infinite-horizon model, cycles in extraction and prices may occur.

Pindyck, R. A. 1978. "The Optimal Exploration and Production of Nonrenewable Resources," *Journal of Political Economy* 86:841–861.

This article develops a deterministic model with two state variables ("proved" reserves and cumulative discoveries) where competitive producers (or a monopolist) must simultaneously determine the level of extraction and exploration. One possible outcome is a pattern of extraction and discovery that gives rise to a U-shaped price path. The appendix contains a neat numerical example where a model is estimated and solved for extraction (10^6 barrels) and exploration (wells drilled) for the Permian region of Texas.

Pindyck, R. S. 1980. "Uncertainty and Natural Resource Markets," *Journal of Political Economy* 88:1203–1225.

In this article, Professor Pindyck considers a model with continuous price and reserve uncertainty. With nonlinear reserve-dependent extraction costs $C(R)$, with $C'(R)<0$ and $C''(R)>0$, fluctuations in reserves will raise expected (future) costs, and there is an incentive to speed up the rate of production. Price would begin lower and rise more rapidly. The model is extended to include exploration that might be undertaken to (1) reduce uncertainty about the size of future reserves and/or (2) improve the allocation of future exploratory effort. The article employs dynamic programming and Itô's lemma.

Review of Economic Studies. 1974. "Symposium on the Economics of Exhaustible Resources." Volume 41.

This was a special issue containing papers by Robert Solow, Joseph Stiglitz, Milton Weinstein and Richard Zeckhauser, Claude Henry, and Partha Dasgupta and Geoffrey Heal.

Smith, V. K. 1980. "The Evaluation of Natural Resource Adequacy: Elusive Quest or Frontier of Economic Analysis?" *Land Economics* 56: 257–298.

Smith provides a nice review of Barnett and Morse and the economic research, based on more sophisticated theory and econometrics, that sought to reassess the adequacy of natural resources in the 1970s. While reexamination provided continued support for Barnett and Morse's optimistic assessment, Smith notes some important caveats and inherent limitations in empirical economic analysis and calls for continued economic research.

Solow, R. M. 1974. "The Economics of Resources or the Resources of Economics," *American Economic Review* 64(Proceedings):1–14.

This article is based on the Richard T. Ely Lecture given by Professor Solow at the American Economic Association meetings in December 1973. It is an erudite exposition on the role of nonrenewable resources in an economy and the role that markets might play in their optimal depletion, conservation, and exploration.

Stiglitz, J. E. 1976. "Monopoly and the Rate of Extraction of Exhaustible Resources," *American Economic Review* 66:655–661.

Stiglitz examines when a monopolist might be able to restrict the initial rate of extraction.

Swierzbinski, J. E., and R. Mendelsohn. 1989. "Information and Exhaustible Resources: A Bayesian Analysis," *Journal of Environmental Economics and Management* 16:193–208.

In a continuous-time model, where information gathering allows a mine owner to update his or her estimate of the size of remaining reserves, Swierzbinski and Mendelsohn show that observed resource prices will be a random variable, even though the expected rate of change in price is consistent with the Hotelling rule.

Vincent, J. R., T. Panayotou, and J. M. Hartwick. 1997, "Resource Depletion and Sustainability in Small Open Economies," *Journal of Environmental Economics and Management* 33:274–286.

A small (price-taking) country extracting and exporting a nonrenewable resource may need to invest resource rents in other forms of capital to sustain domestic consumption.

Stock Pollutants

The early literature on stock pollutants was an extension of the theory of optimal capital accumulation and economic growth. Now, however, production and/or consumption might result in a waste flow that could accumulate as a stock pollutant. The earliest of these articles appeared in the early 1970s.

Conrad, J. M., and L. J. Olson. 1992. "The Economics of a Stock Pollutant: Aldicarb on Long Island," *Environmental and Resource Economics* 2:245–258.

This article looks at an incident of groundwater contamination by the pesticide aldicarb, the likely time path for concentration following a moratorium on its use in 1979, and whether, given the New York State health standard, it would ever be optimal to use aldicarb again once the standard was reestablished.

Cropper, M. 1976. "Regulating Activities with Catastrophic Environmental Effects," *Journal of Environmental Economics and Management* 3:1–15.

D'Arge, R. C., and K. C. Kogiku. 1973. "Economic Growth and the Environment," *Review of Economic Studies* 40:61–77.

Falk, I., and R. Mendelsohn. 1993. "The Economics of Controlling Stock Pollutants: An Efficient Strategy for Greenhouse Gases," *Journal of Environmental Economics and Management* 25:76–88.

This article presents a model to control a stock pollutant where increasing marginal damage from an increasing pollution stock leads to higher abatement over time. An example of global warming is presented.

Forster, B. 1972. "A Note on the Optimal Control of Pollution," *Journal of Economic Theory* 5:537–539

Forster, B. 1972. "Optimal Consumption Planning in a Polluted Environment," *Swedish Journal of Economics* 74:281–285.

Forster, B. A. 1977. "On a One-State Variable Optimal Control Problem," in J. D. Pitchford and S. J. Turnovsky (eds.), *Applications of Control Theory to Economic Analysis.* North Holland, Amsterdam, pp. 35–56.

Goeschl, T., and G. Perino. 2007. "Innovation without Magic Bullets: Stock Pollution and R&D Sequences," *Journal of Environmental Economics and Management* 54:146–161.

New technologies and products are never perfectly clean. If each new product creates its own stock pollutant, and if damage is additive across pollutants, there will be a tight link between damage control and the sequence of R&D and new products. New products may allow for replacement of higher-polluting products and a diversification of the "pollution portfolio."

Gonzalez, F. 2008. "Precautionary Principle and Robustness for a Stock Pollutant with Multiplicative Risk," *Environmental and Resource Economics* 41:25–46.

The precautionary principle, through robust control, leads to higher steady-state pollution taxes when there is uncertainty about the future damage of a pollution stock.

Harford, J. 1997. "Stock Pollution, Child-Bearing Externalities, and the Social Discount Rate," *Journal of Environmental Economics and Management* 33:94–105.

A stock pollutant results from the production of a good used for consumption, child-bearing, and capital bequests. Optimality in this model requires a pollution tax and a tax per child equal to the discounted present value of all the pollution taxes that the child and its descendants would pay.

Harford, J. 1998. "The Ultimate Externality," *American Economic Review* 88:260–265.

Harford derives similar conclusions in a two-period (two-generation) model as in his multigeneration model (JEEM, 1997). The math and exposition in this article are clearer and cleaner.

Hoel, M., and L. Karp. 2002. "Taxes versus Quotas for a Stock Pollutant," *Resource and Energy Economics* 24:367–384.

The authors examine the relative merit of taxes or quotas in a world where the regulator and the polluter have asymmetric information about abatement costs and environmental damage depends on a pollution stock.

Karp, L., and J. Livernois. 1994. "Using Automatic Tax Changes to Control Pollution Emissions," *Journal of Environmental Economics and Management* 27:38–48.

Suppose that a regulator, not knowing the cost of pollution abatement, imposes an emission tax on polluting firms, with the tax rate increasing if emissions continue to exceed a target. This article looks at the welfare implications of such a tax, depending on whether firms behave strategically.

Keeler, E., A. M. Spence, and R. Zeckhauser. 1972. "The Optimal Control of Pollution," *Journal of Economic Theory* 4:19–34.

Kennedy, J. O. S. 1995. "Changes in Optimal Pollution Taxes as Population Increases," *Journal of Environmental Economics and Management* 28: 19–33.

In a two-period model, Kennedy examines the types of taxes that may be needed to compensate for immigration when pollution is "depletable" and when it is "undepletable."

Lieb, C. M. 2004. "The Environmental Kuznets Curve and Flow versus Stock Pollution: The Neglect of Future Damages," *Environmental and Resource Economics* 29:483–506.

The author offers an explanation for the inverted-U Kuznets curve for a flow pollutant (the flow pollutant increases initially as GDP increases, reaches a peak, and then declines as more prosperous citizens demand greater pollution control), whereas the stock-pollutant-income relationship may increase monotonically.

Plourde, C. G. 1972. "A Model of Waste Accumulation and Disposal," *Canadian Journal of Economics* 5:119–125.

Smith, V. L. 1972. "Dynamics of Waste Accumulation: Disposal Versus Recycling," *Quarterly Journal of Economics* 86:600–616.

Tahvonen, O. 1996. "Trade with Polluting Nonrenewable Resources," *Journal of Environmental Economics and Management* 30:1–17.

This article considers the rate of extraction and an excise tax on the consumption of a nonrenewable resource that generates waste flows that might accumulate as a stock pollutant. Extraction costs may depend on the rate of extraction and remaining reserves. The resource sector might be competitive or a price-making monopoly (cartel). The latter case results in a differential game. Time paths are derived for a numerical example.

Tahvonen, O., and J. Kuuluvainen. 1993. "Economic Growth, Pollution, and Renewable Resources," *Journal of Environmental Economics and Management* 24:101–118.

I his articel contains models where a stock pollutant reduces human welfare directly and where the stock pollutant also might adversely affect the growth of a renewable resource, which is a factor of production.

Tahvonen, O., and S. Seppo. 1996. "Nonconvexities in Optimal Pollution Accumulation," *Journal of Environmental Economics and Management* 31:160–177.

This article shows how bounded damage or a nonmonotonic pollution decay function may result in multiple steady-state optima, thus changing the economic properties of pollution control.

Wirl, F. 1994. "Pigouvian Taxation of Energy for Flow and Stock Externalities and Strategic, Noncompetitive Energy Pricing," *Journal of Environmental Economics and Management* 26:1–18.

Suppose that energy is produced and marketed by a price-making cartel that is subject to taxation by a consumer-oriented government. Further, suppose that the consumption of energy results in a flow externality (acid rain) and a stock externality (global warming). This article explores the time paths for price and the energy tax that result from a differential game between the taxing government and the price-making cartel.

Xepapadeas, A. P. 1992. "Environmental Policy Design and Dynamic Nonpoint-Source Pollution," *Journal of Environmental Economics and Management* 23:22–39.

This article looks at the role of dynamic taxes (charges) to keep observed concentrations of a pollutant close to desired levels. This is an advanced article, employing both deterministic and stochastic models.

Maximin

Alvarez-Cuadrado, F., and N. Van Long. 2009. "A Mixed Bentham-Rawls Criterion for Intergenerational Equity," *Journal of Environmental Economics and Management* 58:154–168.

This article examines the properties of maximizing a welfare function that weights the discounted sum of intergeneration utilities (a Bentham criterion) with the minimum utility in an infinite sequence of utilities (the Rawls or, more accurately, Solow criterion). This weighted function has some nice properties, including nondictatorship by the present generation and nondictatorship by a future generation.

Asheim, G. B. 1988. "Rawlsian Intergenerational Justice as a Markov-Perfect Equilibrium in a Resource Technology," *Review of Economic Studies* 55:469–484.

Asheim examines a model where the welfare of the generation in period t *takes the recursive form* $W(t) = U(t) + \beta W(t+1)$, *where* U(t) *is the felicity of generation* t *and* β *is the weight that generation* t *attaches to the self-determined welfare of generation* t + 1, *given by* W(t + 1). *The best, time-consistent program of consumption and resource use is shown to be a subgame – perfect Nash equilibrium.*

d'Autume, A., and K. Schubert. 2008. "Hartwick's Rule and Maximin Paths when the Exhaustible Resource has Amenity Value," *Journal of Environmental Economics and Management* 56:260–274.

The authors consider the case where utility depends on consumption and the stock of the nonrenewable resource. They use Hartwick's rule to find the highest sustainable level for utility.

Hartwick, J. M. 1977. "Intergenerational Equity and the Investing of Rents from Exhaustible Resources," *American Economic Review* 66:972–974.

With a Cobb-Douglas production function requiring inputs of manufactured capital and a nonrenewable resource, Hartwick shows that by investing resource "rent" (the discounted shadow price in our models) to build up the capital stock, an economy can sustain constant consumption per capita. When utility only depends on consumption, this would imply constant utility across generations.

Howarth, R. B. 1995. "Sustainability under Uncertainty: A Deontological Approach," *Land Economics* 71:417–427.

A deontologic or "Kantian" approach to intergenerational welfare is taken where each successive generation has the duty to ensure that the expected welfare of its offspring is no less that its own perceived welfare. In a world of uncertainty, this moral rule may preclude actions that increase the welfare of the current generation while reducing the options of future generations to respond to new information.

Rawls, J. 1971. *A Theory of Justice*, Harvard University Press, Cambridge, MA.

Argues that a social contract that would maximize the welfare of the least fortunate individual is likely to be collectively chosen by individuals if they did not know their lot in life. Maximin is a compelling criterion if the principles of justice are chosen behind a "veil of ignorance."

Solow, R. M. 1974. "Intergenerational Equity and Exhaustible Resources," *Review of Economic Studies, Symposium on the Economics of Exhaustible Resources* 29–45.

Examines the role and limits that a nonrenewable resource might place on the utility of future generations within a macroeconomic growth model. Solow argues that the maximin criterion may be appropriate when considering intergenerational equity.

Withagen, C., and G. B. Asheim. 1998. "Characterizing Sustainability: The Converse of Hartwick's Rule," *Journal of Economic Dynamics and Control* 23:159–165.

The authors show that Hartwick's rule is necessary for constant consumption and utility in Solow's 1974 model.

Index

1838483R00160

Made in the USA
San Bernardino, CA
07 February 2013